T0271118

Nichols and May: Interviews

Conversations with Filmmakers Series
Gerald Peary, General Editor

NICHOLS AND MAY

I N T E R V I E W S

Edited by Robert E. Kapsis

University Press of Mississippi / Jackson

For Cora, Sadie, and Virginia

Publication of this work was made possible in part by a generous grant from Queens College, City University of New York.

The University Press of Mississippi is the scholarly publishing agency of the Mississippi Institutions of Higher Learning: Alcorn State University, Delta State University, Jackson State University, Mississippi State University, Mississippi University for Women, Mississippi Valley State University, University of Mississippi, and University of Southern Mississippi.

www.upress.state.ms.us

The University Press of Mississippi is a member of the Association of University Presses.

First printing 2020
∞

Library of Congress Cataloging-in-Publication Data

Names: Kapsis, Robert E., editor.
Title: Nichols and May : interviews / edited by Robert E. Kapsis.
Other titles: Conversations with filmmakers series.
Description: Jackson : University Press of Mississippi, 2020. | Series:
   Conversations with filmmakers series | Includes bibliographical
   references and index.
Identifiers: LCCN 2020028765 (print) | LCCN 2020028766 (ebook) | ISBN
   9781496828330 (hardback) | ISBN 9781496831040 (trade paperback) | ISBN
   9781496831064 (epub) | ISBN 9781496831057 (epub) | ISBN 9781496831071
   (pdf) | ISBN 9781496831088 (pdf)
Subjects: LCSH: Nichols, Mike—Interviews. | May, Elaine,
   1932-—Interviews. | Motion picture producers and directors—Interviews.
   | Screenwriters—Interviews. | Theatrical producers and
   directors—Interviews. | Comedians—United States—Interviews. | LCGFT:
   Interviews.
Classification: LCC PN1998.2.N53 A5 2020 (print) | LCC PN1998.2.N53
   (ebook) | DDC 791.4302/330922 [B]—dc23
LC record available at https://lccn.loc.gov/2020028765
LC ebook record available at https://lccn.loc.gov/2020028766

British Library Cataloging-in-Publication Data available

Contents

Introduction

Elaine May: Do bad reviews bother you?

Mike Nichols: My doctor has told me that a bad review of any kind would be actively dangerous for me. I can only hope that simple humanity will prevent anyone from, in effect, making an attempt on my life. (May, "Still in Fine Feather," *Los Angeles Times*, March 3, 1996, https://www.latimes.com/archives/la-xpm-1996-03-03-ca-42630-story.html)

This collection of interviews and profiles focuses on the often-intertwined careers of Mike Nichols (1931–2014) and Elaine May (b. 1932). These interviews serve as a vehicle for exploring their trajectory, from their early meteoric success as a sketch comedy duo in the late fifties and early sixties, through their breakup and subsequent immersion in other creative and artistic pursuits, to their sporadic reunions late in their respective careers. After they went their separate ways, Nichols became an enormously successful A-list stage and film director, while May, less prolific, engaged in a broader range of artistic endeavors: film directing, screenwriting and script doctoring, playwriting, stage and screen acting, and occasional newspaper pieces. It can be argued that in recent years, Nichols's work has been unfairly devalued, especially his career as a prestige Hollywood filmmaker. Meanwhile, May is the one who has proved to be the more successful in establishing and maintaining a reputation as one of the unique artistic geniuses of our time.

Unlike the once standard art-history view that artistic reputations are based on works, the reputational approach applied here "expects change in an artist's reputation also to reflect changes in the aesthetic judgments and standards of critics, aestheticians, and other key art-world members rather than simply changes emanating from the works themselves" (Robert E. Kapsis, *Hitchcock: The Making of a Reputation*, 1992, 7). Moreover, this approach assumes that an artistic text, e.g., a film or screenplay, is complex and multifaceted, "engag[ing] with a particular set of audience needs and expectations and chang[ing] as these needs and expectations change" (Robin Bates in *Cinema Journal*, Winter 1987).

Consider, for example, the current cultural environment where gender inequality concerns often shape how a film is interpreted or evaluated. Today, we might expect the four feature films May directed in the 1970s and 1980s (*A New Leaf*, 1971; *The Heartbreak Kid*, 1972; *Mikey and Nicky*, 1976; and *Ishtar*, 1987) to be viewed more favorably or, at the least, noticeably differently now than when these films were first released. In fact, several of the interviews in this volume confirm this—even for *Ishtar*, formerly recalled chiefly as one of the great Hollywood disasters (see Brody 2013).[1]

Many entries in the present volume show the efforts of influential journalists (e.g., Joyce Haber of the *Los Angeles Times*) and film and theater critics (e.g., Vincent Canby and Frank Rich of the *New York Times*) to elevate May's and Nichols's reputations. Through the decades, both the *New York Times* and the *Los Angeles Times* have been especially keen to keep their readers informed about the latest Nichols and/or May events, which accounts for the inclusion here of a relatively high number of pieces from these two publications. These interviews also display the important role of self-promotion in establishing or elevating a reputation. In this regard, the contrast between Nichols and May could not be greater. Nichols agreed to literally hundreds of interviews. May was the opposite, unwavering in her resolve to avoid live interviews and similar self-promotion events. Instead, Nichols often effectively became her voice and spokesperson in dealings with the media, and "May," the celebrity, by default, became largely indistinguishable from "May according to Mike Nichols."

Most of the Nichols interviews selected for this volume focus on his career as a film director, while some touch also on his accomplishments as a stage director and producer and as the sketch comedian he was at the beginning of his career, as half of the legendary comedy duo of Nichols and May. They range over more than five decades and enable the reader to examine Nichols's own assessment of his artistry at different points in his career. Especially revealing are late-career interviews where we witness Nichols showing his frustration about how the critical film establishment regarded his work—often unfavorably, in comparison to other directors, particularly directors of his generation such as Robert Altman (see, e.g., Biskind 1994 and Brody 2016).

Still, few would dispute the claim that Nichols became one of the most honored film and theater directors of our time. In 1968 he won the Academy Award for Best Director for *The Graduate*. Other noteworthy films include *Who's Afraid of Virginia Woolf?*, *Catch-22*, *Carnal Knowledge*, *Silkwood*, *Working Girl*, *The Birdcage*, *Primary Colors*, and the TV dramatic adaptations *Wit* and *Angels in America*. In the theater, he staged the original Broadway productions of Neil Simon's *Barefoot in the Park*, *The Odd Couple*, *Plaza Suite*, and *The Prisoner of Second Avenue*, as well as Murray Schisgals's *Luv* and Tom Stoppard's *The Real Thing*, and won Tony Awards for each. Late in his career he took home two more Tonys for directing the Monty Python

---

1. Note: Citations in the form (Author surname date) are for interviews and profiles included in this volume.

musical *Spamalot* and a revival of Arthur Miller's *Death of a Salesman*. Overall, Nichols won seven Tonys as Best Director of a play or musical—the most in this category for anyone in history—and two more as producer of a Best Play or Best Musical. In television, as director and producer of *Wit* and *Angels in America*, he also owns four Emmys. Since he shared with May a 1961 Grammy for their album *An Evening with Mike Nichols and Elaine May*, with the Emmy wins he became one of just fifteen people to date to have claimed all four of the major American performance art awards.

And yet, despite all the accolades bestowed on him by his peers, Nichols has not been a topic of particular interest among film and media scholars—something that Kyle Stevens addressed in his 2015 book-length study, *Mike Nichols: Sex, Language, and the Reinvention of Psychological Realism*. Moreover, many influential journalistic film critics, such as Andrew Sarris and Richard Brody, have often been dismissive of the view of Nichols as a filmmaker of artistic stature. At the same time, prominent theater critics, including Walter Kerr and Frank Rich, have been quite demonstrative and consistent over the years in their praise of Nichols as an extraordinary stage director.

This book's other major concern is shedding light on Elaine May and her reputational history. Many critics have come to regard her career as singularly brilliant, a pronouncement that on occasion has been made at Nichols's expense (see, for example, Haber 1968 and Brody 2016). The interviews presented here show how her work has been assessed by critics in the film, theater, and comedy art worlds, especially in recent years with regard to gender inequality issues. For two further examples, see the recent appreciation of May by feminist commentator Mac Pogue posted on bitchmedia.org, and the program notes for "The Comic Vision of Elaine May," a three-day event presented by the Harvard Film Archive in November of 2010.

Here is Pogue commenting on May's historical importance as a woman comedian: "May's appearance in comedy seemed like a fluke in the male-dominated world of comedy in the sixties. Not until the 1968 appearance of *The Carol Burnett Show* was there a more established female voice in comedy" (bitchmedia.org, December 26, 2011, https://www.bitchmedia.org/post/adventures-in-feministory-elaine-may-feminist-film-history). As for her role as a film director, the Harvard program notes summarize her career: "One of the only women filmmakers active in postwar Hollywood since Ida Lupino—and, like Lupino, also an accomplished actress—May had to fight at almost every step against an increasingly obstructionist studio establishment in order to direct the four remarkable features that have cemented her reputation as a willful iconoclast, unyielding perfectionist, and brilliantly original artist," adding that the last of May's quartet of films, *Ishtar* (1987), was an "infamous box office failure [which] seems to have forced an effective and woefully premature end to May's filmmaking career to date" (see https://harvardfilmarchive.org/programs/the-comic-vision-of-elaine-may).

The frequent charge from cultural critics that May's career suffered from gender discrimination is an issue that May herself has brought up in recent public appearances. As she confessed during a 2006 interview, May wanted to appear "nice" and "pleasant" to studio personnel even though she was, in her own words, "just as rotten as any guy." And that toughness, to "fight just as hard [as men] to get your way" would often get her in trouble with the studio brass. So, she advises, "I think the real trick is, for women, [to] start out tough. They don't start out tough. They start by saying, 'Don't be afraid of me. I'm only a woman.' And they're not *only* women, they're just as tough as guys. In that way, I think I did have trouble. But only because I seemed so pleasant" (Nichols 2006).

Nichols and May: From Chicago Improv Clubs to Broadway, 1957–1961

> **Nichols:** [Elaine May and I] met at the University of Chicago. My first impression of her was of a beautiful and dangerous girl that interested me enormously, scared me. [. . .] I said, "May I sit down?" and she said, "Eeef you wish," and just like that we were in an improvisa-tion—we did a whole long spy mystery improvisation for the benefit of the other people on the bench. That's how we met. And then we were friends. (Smith 1999)

A *New Yorker* profile of Nichols and May opens this volume and describes how they came together in the Chicago of the mid-1950s to form the comedy duo "Nichols and May," and how they quickly achieved success and critical acclaim when they took their act to New York to perform in venues such as the Blue Angel nightclub. It also touches on their early television work, as guest stars on variety shows and specials and as voice performers in animated beer commercials. Their hit Broadway show, *An Evening with Mike Nichols and Elaine May*, is discussed in depth, especially May's dazzling contribution:

> Miss May is the team's virtuoso actor. She is a short, buxom young woman, as uncom-promisingly brunette as Mike Nichols is blond, with an enormous amount of crazy hair and crazy energy. She can arrange her features and tune her voice in so many different ways that it is impossible to say what she really looks or sounds like. As a movie starlet [. . .] she is clearly one of the most alluring women in America. [. . .] Her portrayal of a solemn, inarticulate little girl is one of the most meticulously observed, most heartfelt, and funniest characterizations on Broadway. [. . .] The theater was evidently her destiny. (Rice 1961)

The show ran for over a year, and in fact, it was the experience of appearing night after night in it that led Nichols and May, at the height of their fame, to retire their comedy act (see Sweet 1978 and Kashner 2013).

Mike Nichols: The Making of an A-List Director, 1962–1972

Soon after splitting up with May, Nichols turned to stage directing with Neil Simon's *Barefoot in the Park*. "On the first day of rehearsal," he would later say, "I thought, 'Well, look at this. Here is what I was meant to do.' I knew instantly that I was home" (quoted by Peter Marks in the *Washington Post*, December 7, 2003). By the mid-1960s, Nichols had amassed an unbroken string of Broadway hits with *Barefoot in the Park*, *The Odd Couple*, *Luv*, and *The Apple Tree*. In 1966, with all four running simultaneously on Broadway, he made his Hollywood debut directing *Who's Afraid of Virginia Woolf?*, adapted from Edward Albee's play. It went on to be nominated for thirteen Academy Awards, including one for Best Director. Nichols was always very animated when discussing his first film, as interviews from the period attest (see Canby 1966), as well as later interviews when he is looking back at what he considered a high-water mark of his career (see Biskind 1994, Smith 1999, and Brody 2016).

Nichols's second film, *The Graduate*, was released in 1967 and quickly became a box office phenomenon. Seven months after its release, studio executive Joseph E. Levine gushed, "It's absolutely incredible. There's no way to describe it. It's like an explosion, a dam bursting. The business just grows and grows and grows" (quoted by Jacob R. Brackman in the *New Yorker*, July 27, 1968). Although reviews were mixed—the major critics seemed to either love it or hate it—the film won Nichols a Best Director Oscar (his only Academy Award), as well as directing awards from the Golden Globes, the Directors Guild of America, the New York Film Critics Circle, and BAFTA. Like its predecessor, *The Graduate* is a film that Nichols often spoke of fondly (see, for instance, Day 1968 and Smith 1999).

By the late sixties, Nichols was America's highest-paid and most sought-after director of both mainstream Broadway plays and classy, challenging Hollywood films. Profiles and interviews of Nichols from this period (see Canby 1966, Haber 1967, and Ephron 1969) characteristically portrayed Nichols as relatively easy-going, and always a scintillating and charming conversationalist and raconteur who seemed refreshingly modest about his fame and great wealth.

This benign view of Nichols is encapsulated in "And Not a Sign of Mike Fright," Charles Champlin's breezy piece in the *Los Angeles Times* (July 28, 1965), based on observing the director at work with Elizabeth Taylor and Richard Burton on the *Who's Afraid of Virginia Woolf?* shoot. Champlin reports, "You look in vain for any sign of nervousness." As Nichols expressed it, working on this film was "the happiest I've ever been," and how could it be otherwise? "I'm in love with the Burtons. [. . .]

This is the first time I've worked with stars of this magnitude. [. . .] What astonishes me, it stuns me, is that they're immensely more cooperative and flexible than anyone I've ever worked with. I've had more trouble with minor players on Broadway." But we now have corroboration from multiple sources, including testimony from an older and chastened Nichols, that directing *Virginia Woolf* was, in fact, a harrowing experience (see, e.g., a later Champlin profile from 1986, in this volume).

Vincent Canby's refreshingly nuanced, openly cynical article on Nichols from 1966 (included in this volume) stands in sharp contrast to Champlin's puff piece—its darker hues effectively captured in its title, "The Cold Loneliness of It All." Canby's stated original objective in interviewing Nichols was to "to study the effect of the Hollywood environment on irreverent genius. [. . .] To see [for example] if he still had his sense of humor." Disappointingly, Canby found Nichols's rose-colored descriptions of working in Hollywood largely humorless and devoid of the irony he expected from the man who once mocked Hollywood stereotypes. Contrary to what Canby might have already known, or at least suspected, Nichols claimed that he had no problems working with Taylor and Burton on *Virginia Woolf*—surprising, considering that he was a first-time film director. Canby's ambiguity about interviewing Nichols is of interest considering that a few years after this article appeared, Canby becomes the chief film critic of the *New York Times* and a powerful advocate of the careers of both Nichols and May—warts and all.

Catch-22 (1970) was Nichols's next film after *The Graduate* and the first Nichols film Canby reviewed as head film critic of the *Times*. But his rave ("It's the best American film I've seen this year") was a minority position, as this screen adaptation of Joseph Heller's novel opened to mostly negative reviews and audience indifference. Even during the filming, Nichols had conceded to on-location observers that he feared he might be about to experience his first major flop (see Ephron 1969). He felt blindsided when, shortly before the film opened, he attended a screening of a similarly themed new movie and realized his own shortcomings. "We were waylaid by *M*A*S*H*, which was fresher and more alive, improvisational, and funnier than *Catch-22*," Nichols admitted. "It just cut us off at the knees" (quoted in Peter Biskind, *Easy Riders, Raging Bulls*, 1998, 81). In a remarkably honest self-evaluation of his career, Nichols would confess, "Robert Altman is doing what I would have expected me to be doing. When it works for him, it's better than anything. When it doesn't work, as with all of us, it's not. Every time I decide that I'm going to go in that direction, something pulls me into a style that is much more spare and not so free. [. . .] I can be very excited by the kind of richness of texture of, say, *McCabe and Mrs. Miller* [. . .] but I'm just drawn in another direction [. . .] [and] don't seem to have any control over it" (Sweet 1978).

But Nora Ephron, who had picked up on Nichols's unease during the shoot, also noted one of the major reasons for his overall success as a director: "What matters [to actors] is that the film is a chance to work with Nichols, who, at thirty-seven, is the most successful director in America and probably the most popular actor's director in the world. Says Orson Welles, 'Nobody's in his league with actors'" (Ephron 1969).

Elaine May: Portrait of an Artist, 1962–1972

If you should ask "Where is Mike Nichols?" the answer would come easily. He is in his triplex tower apartment high over Central Park West with all New York glowing at his feet. Jacqueline Kennedy and Leonard Bernstein come there to dine. Producers send scripts and contracts and large weekly checks there. [. . .] But if the question is "Whatever became of Elaine May?" then it takes more time to tell. (Thompson 1967)

What is striking about May's career during much of the sixties is how amorphous and disappointing it must have seemed to her contemporary admirers. Between 1962 and 1966 May was involved in several writing projects that failed to get off the ground. Two were for the theater: a one-act play called *Not Enough Rope* that opened Off Broadway in March 1962 and flopped, and a full-length drama, *A Matter of Position*, starring Mike Nichols as a man who "decides to go to bed and not get up" (Shepard 1962). Scheduled to open on Broadway in the fall of 1962, *A Matter of Position* never made it beyond a trial run in Philadelphia. "We broke up over Elaine's play," said Nichols. "She wrote a play for me, as it were. It was also *about* me, which made part of the problem" (Sweet 1978).

During rehearsals, Nichols and the director, Fred Coe, demanded changes and cuts, which May refused to make. In retaliation, May took out an injunction to prevent them from altering her script (see Janet Coleman, *The Compass*, 1990, 271). "Cuts and revisions were made up to the point where they would change the nature of the material and emasculate the play," she explained to the *New York Times* (October 10, 1962) shortly before the play's premature closing. After this debacle, Nichols and May felt betrayed, each by the other, and stopped speaking. Their estrangement would last through much of the 1960s. And May's setbacks as a writer continued when her screenplay adaptation of Evelyn Waugh's comic novel *The Loved One*, which some who read it considered brilliant, was rejected by the film's director, who replaced it with Terry Southern's and Christopher Isherwood's version.

Luckless in her writing career, May accepted acting roles in two 1967 Hollywood comedies, *Enter Laughing* (Carl Reiner) and *Luv* (Clive Donner). *Enter Laughing* was based on an autobiographical novel by its director, while *Luv* was adapted from Murray Schisgal's Broadway comedy that Mike Nichols had directed but declined to expand into a film. One of *Luv*'s stars was Jack Lemmon, who enthusiastically endorsed casting May to costar: "My God, she's perfect! Can we get her?" That she didn't disappoint him is clear from Lemmon's remarks after working with her:

> "She's the finest actress I've ever worked with. [. . .] Elaine is touched with genius, like Judy Holliday. She approaches a scene like a director and a writer, not like an actor, and she can go so deep so fast on a scene, and her mind works at such a great speed, that it's difficult for her to communicate with other actors. [. . .] Some of our finest footage is where she's not saying a word but just reacting." (quoted in Thompson 1967)

May's Relationship with the Press, 1962–1967: Throughout May's long career there have been periods where she seemed to disappear from the spotlight altogether. 1962–1967 was such a period. When she did grant a rare interview, she favored a prestigious publication like the *New York Times* or the *Los Angeles Times*, but from the evidence in these pieces, it is extremely difficult to gauge how she felt about this downturn phase of her career. Instead, she repeatedly used the interview setting as an occasion for improvisation—as an opportunity for a provocative, informal performance piece involving not only herself but, through playful cajoling, also the bemused interviewer. We see her operating in this manner in her hilarious Q & A for the *New York Times* (Shepard 1962) that took place during a break from a rehearsal of *A Matter of Position*.

> Q: What is the play about? [. . .]
>
> A: It's about a man who decides to go to bed and not get up.
>
> Q: Why?
>
> A: Because he doesn't like being up anymore.
>
> Q: Is it symbolic?
>
> A: What?
>
> Q: Does it have an inner meaning?
>
> A: What do you mean?
>
> Q: How should I know what I mean? I'm only asking the question. What I mean, could it go Off Broadway as well?
>
> A: Not likely. [. . .]
>
> Q: Have you had any quibbles with the director or the cast on their approach to your play?
>
> A: No.
>
> Q: Has this led to bloodshed?
>
> A: Occasionally.

The interviewer's non-sequitur question about whether "bloodshed" had erupted during rehearsals would suggest he had prior knowledge about some of the "quibbles" plaguing the project.

Not until five years later, in 1967, would another May interview appear in the *New York Times*. And this one was an all-out fabrication, penned by May under the pseudonym "Kevin M. Johnson" ("Elaine May: 'Do You Mind Interviewing Me in the Kitchen?'" *New York Times*, January 8, 1967, https://timesmachine.nytimes.com/timesmachine/1967/01/08/83571386.html?pageNumber=103). The occasion was to publicize May's appearances in the movie versions of *Luv* and *Enter Laughing*. The first part of the article deals with May's genuine anxiety about being interviewed. The ersatz interviewer "Johnson" asks the faux May "whether she was always this nervous [. . .] and she protested loudly that she was not nervous, that she loved being interviewed and that if [he] wrote she was nervous she would send a public denial to the *New York Times*."

Then "Johnson" asks "May" about her role in *Luv*.

"What approach are you going to use to make the part as hilarious in the movie as
     Miss [Anne] Jackson did on the stage?"
"I'm going to copy her."
"You are going to copy her entire performance?"
"Well, as much as I can. I won't be able to copy it entirely because in some places the
     movie is different from the play. I won't be as hilarious in those places."
"Don't you have any ideas of your own about the part?"
"*That's* my own idea."

After more in a similar vein, the interviewer asks whether she was being serious (in an aside acknowledging that he is "aware that Miss May had previously been a comedienne"). "'Look, don't start,' she said, instantly wary. 'I don't want this interview to sound like I'm kidding. That's all in the past.'"

Out of the Doldrums: After her brief stint in Hollywood, May returned to New York with no shortage of projects to keep her busy, including revising her play *A Matter of Position*. A production of the revised version opened in Stockbridge, Massachusetts, in July 1968, with Arthur Penn directing and May costarring, and received a number of favorable notices from critics such as Kevin Kelly in the *Boston Globe*, who called it "a first-rate piece of work" and "utterly irresistible" (July 21, 1968).

During that summer, May was also at work on *Adaptation*, a one-act play that opened Off Broadway in early 1969 as part of a double bill with Terrence McNally's one-acter, *Next*. May directed both plays, which received enthusiastic reviews and garnered for May two Outer Critics Circle Awards, for Best Director and Best New

Playwright. In the *New York Times*, Walter Kerr explained why May's play was superior to a play currently on Broadway, *Play It Again, Sam*, by another former nightclub comic, Woody Allen. "[May's] comedy climbs through time and change to explode in our faces because we have been following two faces that have themselves been changing. You can't do the joke as a stand-up gag, as a one-liner told in the third person [as Allen does with the jokes in his play]. Not and get all of it. It's got to be moved through" (February 23, 1969).

Elaine May: Master Film Director: In spring 1968, it was announced that May had written a screenplay titled *A New Leaf*, and that she would direct and also star in the film. Stories reporting this news tended to stress her versatility. "The busy Miss May," as A. H. Weiler called her in the *New York Times* (May 12, 1968), "who has done just about everything there is to do in the world of nightclubs, theater, TV, and film, has just been engaged to direct a movie and costar in it." Joyce Haber in the *Los Angeles Times* (May 16, 1968) reflected on the old Nichols and May partnership from the perspective of gender inequality, pointing out that after their breakup, Nichols quickly made his mark as a theater and film director, while May "stayed home, for the most part, like a good little third-time housewife." Once, people had wondered "Who *really* has the brains?" in the Nichols-May duo, "as though they were a couple of kids competing for grades and one had to be sneaking a look over the other's shoulder." But now that she is directing a movie, "it will be hard to prove she's looking over anybody's shoulder because she will also write the screenplay and star in it." Case closed.

Over the course of *A New Leaf*'s production history, spanning nearly two years, May had little to say publicly about the film. A *New York Times* reporter, on location early in the filming, found in May a difficult and elusive interview subject. Her most revealing answer came when the probing journalist asked her what made her decide to direct her own first screenplay—fear of studio interference. "You may never see [your script] again as you wrote it. That's the traditional Hollywood way [. . .]. So I'm directing this because I wondered if it could be kept unchanged" (Howard Thompson in the *New York Times*, August 26, 1969).

May was similarly reticent during a second *Times* attempt to interview her about *A New Leaf*, which by that time (January 1970) "had gone through about seven producers and was something like $1.5 million over its budget." We learn very little about the troubled production from this interview, which in places reads almost like one of those bogus interviews May penned herself—except for this candid utterance: "I really didn't know anything, but when I told them that, they thought that was my technique," she said. "People would ask me where to put the camera and I'd say, 'I don't know'" (Lemon 1970).

To actually learn about the inside doings of May's production, we quote her blunt costar, Walter Matthau, from the earlier *Times* interview. "She's a tough little lady, that one. You suggest one thing, OK. Then a minute later, if you deviate from one single comma, you find out who's in supreme authority."

The real bombshell came three months before the film's release in 1971, when it was reported that May had filed a suit to enjoin Paramount Pictures from releasing *A New Leaf*, and "to stop them from using her name crediting her as the writer-director of the film," as May's attorney said, "since the product as it stands now is not hers" (*New York Times*, January 19, 1971). The studio had taken over the final editing from May and dramatically reduced the film's length, eliminating two murder sequences. "I wanted to get away with murder," May quipped following a 2013 Austin Film Festival screening of the film. She had wanted to see "if she could craft a romantic comedy where the audience would stick with her lead even after doing the deed." "It was a love story," May explained, "but what was interesting was that he murdered a guy. And [the studio] took the murder out and we went to court [. . .] and the judge saw the movie and he said, 'It's such a nice movie, why do you want to sue?'" (Stephen Saito, *The Moveable Fest* (blog), January 1, 2014, http://moveablefest.com/elaine-may-new-leaf/). May lost the suit, and her first picture was shown in theaters with her three credits—writer, director, actor—intact. Though hardly a director's cut, *A New Leaf* was praised by most critics and made Gene Siskel's list of the best movies of 1971, though it was only modestly successful at the box office.

Critical Reassessments of Nichols and May, 1971–1992

After completing his fourth feature film, the critically beloved *Carnal Knowledge* (1971), Nichols returned triumphantly to Broadway to direct Neil Simon's new play, *The Prisoner of Second Avenue* (1972), as well as a revival of Anton Chekhov's *Uncle Vanya* (1973). But after the poor showings of his next two films, *The Day of the Dolphin* (1974) and *The Fortune* (1975), Nichols turned his back on Hollywood and retreated to Broadway again. Only in 1982 did he return to filmmaking with *Silkwood*, but its popular and critical success proved to be an anomaly. With few exceptions, notably *Working Girl* (1988), Nichols's subsequent films from the 1980s and early nineties failed to ignite much enthusiasm from either critics or audiences. Nichols would look back at much of this period with real angst.

In her 1984 profile (included in this volume), Barbara Gelb describes how, after his early successes, Nichols hit a creative lull in 1973.

> "People said I was afraid of failure," Nichols says. "I really just felt dead mentally, jaded. I'd always *loved* rehearsing, but I could barely arouse my own interest. I must have been depressed without knowing it." [. . .] He concedes that at this time he was at one of the "low points" of his life. [. . .] He was sleepwalking through his work. Not until the making of *Silkwood* did he regain his creative enthusiasm. [. . .] Nichols says [. . .] "I was interested

in the theme of being asleep and waking up. It was, in fact, the situation in which I found *myself* at the time." (Gelb 1984)

After *Silkwood*, Nichols experienced another high directing the 1984 Broadway production of Tom Stoppard's *The Real Thing*. He told Gelb, "Tom and I had nothing but laughs and joy" working on the play, which won them both Tonys (two for Nichols, who coproduced).

But ten years later, Nichols confessed to Peter Biskind that in the late eighties, he had experienced another crisis—"a *crise de conscience*, triggered, he says, by a severe depression brought on by Halcion, a sleeping pill":

> [Nichols] would begin to feel he was subject to some vague retribution "for having escaped, for no particular reason, the Holocaust. That my whole life is on borrowed time. [. . .] It never occurred to me, you know, it's fifty-odd years that I've felt this guilt. I was once very close to doing *Sophie's Choice*. I tried to picture myself on the crane saying 'OK, all you Jews: Camera left. SS guards on the right.' And I knew I couldn't do it. I don't think I can deal with the Holocaust. [. . .] I don't think I can." (Biskind 1994)

As for May, with the considerable success of *A New Leaf*, she was once again a hot property. At the end of 1971, her next film project was announced, *The Heartbreak Kid*, which "will revolve around a man who ditches his bride on their honeymoon when he spies an irresistible cutie" (as a *New York Times* reporter put it). This time May was to direct a Neil Simon screenplay based on a short story by Bruce Jay Friedman. News was also circulating about *Mikey and Nicky*, a second film May was planning to direct in 1972 based on her own screenplay. The *Times* reporter asked May whether *Mikey and Nicky* was a comedy. "I certainly hope so," she replied. "It's the story of a very loose Italian and a very uptight Jewish guy who grow up together and work their way into the numbers racket" (*New York Times*, November 21, 1971).

May received a significant boost to her directorial career with the 1972 release of *The Heartbreak Kid*, a huge commercial and critical success. Vincent Canby hailed May's second film as "a first-class American comedy, as startling in its way as was *The Graduate*. It's a movie that manages the marvelous and very peculiar trick of blending the mechanisms and the cruelties of Neil Simon's comedy with the sense and sensibility of F. Scott Fitzgerald." Canby noted that the "laughs without shame" that characterized Simon's comedy were here softened and humanized by "a real understanding of character—which is something that I suspect, can be attributed to Miss May" (*New York Times*, September 18, 1972). Other critics expressed similar views, siding with Canby's conclusion that May was the film's real auteur.

After the success of *The Heartbreak Kid*, many felt let down by May's eagerly awaited follow-up, *Mikey and Nicky*. It was perhaps a comedy, as May had earlier characterized it, but a very black one, or rather a gritty existential crime drama about the betrayal of a male friendship. It opened in 1976 in a limited release, after litigation between May and Paramount once again led to the studio taking control of the film. Reviews were mostly negative. Among the critics turned off was Canby, who wrote: "It's a [story] told in such insistently claustrophobic detail that to watch it is to risk an artificially induced anxiety attack. It's nearly two hours of being locked in a telephone booth with a couple of Method actors [John Cassavetes and Peter Falk] who won't stop talking, though they have nothing of interest to say. [. . .] Miss May is a witty, gifted, very intelligent director. It took guts for her to attempt a film like this, but she failed" (*New York Times*, December 22, 1976). But aside from the reviews, what proved to be most damaging to May's directorial reputation was the controversy surrounding the three-and-a-half-year process of making *Mikey and Nicky*—where May's insistence on delivering *her* film, cut *her* way, again got her into serious trouble with the studio brass (see Tobias 1976).

Forced to retreat from film directing, May adapted, establishing a formidable new career as a screenwriter, and particularly as a script doctor. Her most visible achievement was a screenplay credit and Oscar nomination for *Heaven Can Wait* (1978), which she shared with the film's director Warren Beatty. The rest of her writing assignments over the next several years involved uncredited rewrites on important film such as *Reds* (1981), *Tootsie* (1982), and *Labyrinth* (1986). She also worked on several of Mike Nichols's films during the period. "On *Wolf* [1994]," says Nichols, "Elaine saved my ass, it's as simple as that. She came and did a fantastic rewrite job. But she very rarely takes credit on movies" (May, *The Birdcage: The Shooting Script*, 1997, xv). May explained, "You can make a deal if you're going to do the original writing. But if you're going to do the original rewriting, you can't" (Kashner 2013).

May's fourth film, *Ishtar*, came out in 1987. Reviews were generally poor, but it was the "extravagant rumormongering" (Janet Maslin in the *New York Times*, May 15, 1987) surrounding its production that destroyed her career as a film director (see Blum 1987 and VanAirsdale 2011).

A partial explanation came in 2006, when the Film Society of Lincoln Center sponsored a special screening of *Ishtar*, following which May took to the stage to be interviewed by Nichols (Nichols 2006). The worst problem plaguing *Ishtar*, according to May, was that the studio, Columbia Pictures, changed regimes midway in the shoot, and the new president was David Puttnam, who held a major grudge against Warren Beatty, *Ishtar*'s producer and costar. This resulted in Puttnam's bad-mouthing his own studio's film—"studio suicide," as Nichols characterized it.

Ishtar "had three great previews," said May. But then, Nichols noted, "stories began to appear [. . .] about what a problem it was." "And many of the details were not true," according to May. "The film was political and it was a satire [. . .]. When these articles started coming out, I [initially] thought [. . .] it's the CIA. [. . .] It was sort of glorious to think that I was going to be taken down by the CIA, and then it turned out to be David Puttnam."

Curiously, despite the *Ishtar* disaster, much suggests that May's reputation among major film critics actually improved during this period. *A New Leaf* and *The Heartbreak Kid* began to be viewed as exemplary screwball comedies, and some even wrote favorably of the much-maligned *Ishtar*. But more than any of her other films, *Mikey and Nicky* came to be seen as a major work, resembling a theater-of-the-absurd play, influenced positively by the bleak improvisatory cinema of John Cassavetes. *Mikey and Nicky* received many critical accolades when it was reissued in May's approved cut in 1985, bolstered by an earlier endorsement from one of America's most respected critics, Stanley Kauffmann, in the *New Republic* (January 1 and 8, 1977). He would later rate it among the top ten American films of the 1970s (James Monaco, *American Film Now*, 1979, 418), and would dub it "unique, unremitting, important" upon its re-release (*New Republic*, May 20, 1985).

Nichols and May Reunited, 1996–1998

Occasionally, over the years, Nichols and May appeared at a political or charity event where they might reenact a short sketch from their old act. And in 1980, for a six-week run, they starred in a revival of *Who's Afraid of Virginia Woolf?* The event was supposed to be off-limits to critics, but Frank Rich, chief drama critic for the *New York Times*, covered it for the paper at the urging of Arthur Gelb, the *Times'* cultural editor. Initially skeptical, at the end of the performance Rich had high praise for the entire cast: "We arrive expecting to watch two rusty stand-up comics do a novelty act. We leave having seen four thinking actors shed startling new light on one of the great dark plays of our time" (*New York Times*, May 4, 1980; see also Rich, *Hot Seat*, 1998, 13). In 1992 they were together once again, this time for a tribute by the Museum of Television and Radio in New York City honoring their work in television, after which they responded to questions from the press (Hall 1992).

But not until 1996 would May and Nichols again establish a more formal working relationship, when Nichols directed *The Birdcage* and May, credited this time, provided the screenplay adaptation of the French film *La Cage aux folles*. Nichols contributed a foreword to the published script, praising May's work and expressing his joy at working with her again:

She's been the most trusted friend, she's been a part of whatever I did and I, to some extent, of what she did. [. . .] It's been a great joy being reunited with Elaine and redis-covering the whole mood of our partnership, a partnership in which if I don't think of something she thinks of it, and vice versa. And we're somehow better working with each other than with other people. I can't completely explain why it took us so long to really work together again. It seems to me life is a series of realizations of something very, very obvious that took you thirty or forty years to get to. (May, *The Birdcage: The Shooting Script*, 1997, xvi)

Two years later they teamed up again on another film project, *Primary Colors* (1998), the film version of Joe Klein's political novel inspired by the first Bill Clinton presidential campaign. May's screenplay was nominated for an Oscar and a Writers Guild Award. In a revealing *Los Angeles Times* profile, Patrick Goldstein got Nichols to talk about the symbiotic nature of their working relationship, and supplied further insights from actors who had observed them on the set. Emma Thompson, who costarred as a Hillary Clinton–inspired character, told Goldstein she had seen Nichols weeping uncontrollably on the set, and had "come to the conclusion that men are more sentimental than women—especially when the woman in question is Elaine May. 'We'd been doing a particularly emotional scene,' Thompson recalls. 'And Mike would be standing behind the video monitor, these huge tears rolling down his cheeks. And Elaine would be right behind him, staring balefully at the monitor. And when the scene was over, Mike would be wiping his eyes and Elaine would say, quite impassively, 'For the next take, I think [the actors] should move slightly to the left'" (Goldstein 1998).

How Nichols and May Outdid Themselves, 2003–2013

Nichols's directorial accomplishments during this ten-year period were formidable. They included: (1) his Emmy Award–winning adaptation of Tony Kushner's *Angels in America* as a miniseries for HBO in 2003 (see Ansen and Peyser 2003); (2) his Tony Award–winning direction of the Monty Python musical *Spamalot* in 2005, and (3) his Tony Award–winning direction in 2012 of a new Broadway production of Arthur Miller's *Death of a Salesman*. During this period, both Nichols and May were recipients of numerous awards and tributes (see Smith 1999 and Nichols 2006). There were even occasions honoring May's work that included her participating in Q & A's (see VanAirsdale 2011). And in 2010, May was one of many guest speakers at an American Film Institute gala honoring Nichols, but it was her brilliantly written and hilariously delivered spiel about Mike and his cousin Albert Einstein that stole the show (May 2010).

Nichols's Death and May's Rebirth, 2014–present

Mike Nichols died on November 19, 2014, and many of the testimonials and tributes that followed are deeply moving. The most ambitious and insightful of all, however, is a 2016 tribute by Elaine May in the *American Masters* PBS series—May's first foray into film directing since 1987. Appropriately, our final entry is Richard Brody's *New Yorker* essay on May's documentary—an ingenious double-profile that happens also to be the closest thing we can offer of May seriously engaged in conversation with Nichols. Brody titled it "A Lovingly Obsessive Tribute to Mike Nichols, by Elaine May."

An issue May dared raise in her documentary, which Brody elaborates on, is the question of authorship and Nichols's deteriorating filmmaking reputation late in his career:

> May caps the tribute with a clip of Nichols sharing his assessment of cinema history—an assessment that's laced with resentment at his unbeloved place in it, his ranking among the unoriginal entertainers of the time rather than alongside May as one of its prime cinematic artists. It's in this editorial touch—the placement, at the film's apex, as its climactic moment, of Nichols's lacerating allegations of critical misjudgments—that May tips her directorial hand. His culminating spew of bile wrenches the show out of the merely anecdotal, out of autohagiography, and into the twisted guts of an unquiet soul who went to the grave resentfully despite the worldly rewards ("we're famous, we have money") that he earlier thought would be enough. [. . .] And, of course, the rebuke to critics ["The people who describe all our work to us often don't know what they're talking about"], though coming from Nichols's mouth, is all the more pertinent under May's editorial touch, given that her career, not his, was buried by critical incomprehension, indifference, and derision. (Brody 2016)

Interest in May's career has continued unabated among the public as well as critics and cultural gatekeepers, as special showings and retrospectives of her films, new productions of her plays, and reassessments of her body of work call attention to her importance as a groundbreaking female artist and creative genius. The most recent showcase of her talents came in the fall of 2018, when May, at age eighty-six, starred in an acclaimed Broadway revival of Kenneth Lonergan's *The Waverly Gallery*. *New York Times* chief theater critic Ben Brantley's ecstatic review was headlined, "Elaine May might break your heart in *The Waverly Gallery*," and @nytimesarts called it "A performance for the ages." In June 2019, May was awarded the Tony Award for Best Leading Actress in a Play for her work. Her witty, self-deprecating acceptance speech ended with the quip that the actor who played her grandson described her offstage death so movingly onstage that May, watching from the wings, thought, "I'm gonna win this guy's Tony."

Shortly before the limited run ended, Manohla Dargis, *Times* film critic, was advising readers to "clear your calendar" for a retrospective of "Elaine May's filmmaking brilliance" at New York's Film Forum, featuring her work as director, screenwriter and actor. "She remains a criminally underappreciated moviemaker," said Dargis (*New York Times*, January 22, 2019).

Not unexpectedly, there were no new interviews with May from around this time. As has been the case throughout her career, May deemed that the less said publicly the better, especially as she has excelled in nurturing and channeling her genius in unexpected ways that critics are able to discover afresh.

In November 2019, it was reported that May was planning to direct her first narrative film since *Ishtar*, to be titled *Crackpot*.

How better to conclude than to quote May's final line in her *Playbill* biography for *The Waverly Gallery*? With a change of pronoun, it applies to Mike Nichols also: "She has done more, but this is enough."

As with all the books in the *Conversations with Filmmakers* series, the interviews are reproduced as they originally appeared and have not been edited in any significant way. Indeed many of the repetitions that will be found here are integral to the story that is being told. I would like to express my gratitude to all those who granted their permission to make this material available. I would like to add thanks to Craig Gill of the University Press of Mississippi for his guidance and support, and to Valerie Jones of the Press, who has always been a joy to work with. I owe particular appreciation to Andy Beveridge and Elizabeth Hendrey of Queens College for their aid in securing much-needed financial support, especially for covering permissions fees that, in a number of cases, became almost prohibitively expensive. Finally, special thanks must go to Kathie Coblentz, who provided invaluable assistance.

REK

Mike Nichols: Chronology

1931   Mikhail (Michael) Igor Peschkowsky is born on November 6 to Pavel
        (Paul) Nikolayevich (also spelled Nikolaevich or Nicholaiyevitch) Pesch-
        kowsky (1900–1944) and Brigitte Landauer Peschkowsky (1906–1985) in
        Berlin, Germany. His father, a physician, is from a wealthy Russian Jewish
        family that fled Russia after the 1917 Revolution. His mother's family are
        upper-middle-class German Jewish intellectuals. His maternal grandpar-
        ents are the anarchist author and activist Gustav Landauer and the poet
        Hedwig Lachmann, and a distant cousin on his mother's side is Albert
        Einstein (a fact May would riff on in a 2010 tribute to Nichols).

1938–43 With Nazi persecutions of Jews accelerating, Paul Peschkowsky departs
        for the United States in August 1938, sending for his family soon after-
        ward. His wife is too ill to travel, so seven-year-old Michael and his three-
        year-old brother make the journey alone, in April 1939; their mother
        joins them in early 1940. They settle in New York City, on Manhattan's
        West Side. Paul Peschkowsky changes the family name to Nichols, an An-
        glicization of his patronymic, and sets up a successful medical practice.

1939–44 Nichols attends public and private schools in New York (P.S. 87 and the
        Dalton School) and Cherry Lawn School in Darien, Connecticut. At Dal-
        ton one of his classmates is his future collaborator Buck Henry. Henry
        recalls him as "Igor Peschkowsky," who spoke no English.

1943   In December, Nichols's father becomes a naturalized citizen of the
        United States. He dies the following June of leukemia, leaving his family
        with little money.

1945–49 Nichols attends the Walden School, a private progressive school in New
        York, on a scholarship. After graduating, he briefly attends New York
        University, but drops out.

1947   Nichols and his brother acquire US citizenship when Nichols's mother
        becomes a naturalized citizen. Nichols sees the second performance
        of Tennessee Williams's *A Streetcar Named Desire* on Broadway and is
        transfixed, calling it a life-altering experience.

1950–53 Enrolls in a premed program at the University of Chicago and works
        odd jobs to pay his way. Acts and directs in Paul Sills's company Tonight

at 8:30. Onstage in Strindberg's *Miss Julie*, and knowing he was bad in the role, he sees Elaine May for the first time, glaring at him hostilely from the front row. "My first impression of her was of a beautiful and dangerous girl that interested me enormously, scared me," he would tell an interviewer years later. A few weeks afterwards, they meet by chance in a railway station and improvise a comedy sketch for an audience of commuters, after which they become friends.

1953   Joins the staff of classical music station WFMT as an announcer. Creates a folk music program on Saturday nights, *The Midnight Special*. He hosts the show for over a year (it continues on the station to this day).

1954–55   Drops out of college and returns to New York to study Method acting under Lee Strasberg.

1955–58   Returns to Chicago to join Paul Sills's and David Shepherd's Compass Players, considered to be the first improvisational theater company in the US (its successor is the still-active Second City). Its members include May, Shelley Berman, Barbara Harris, and Del Close. Starts improvising satirical comedy sketches with May, leading to the formation of the comedy duo "Nichols and May."

1957   Marries Patricia Scott, a singer. They divorce in 1960.

1958–62   Nichols and May take their act to New York. With Jack Rollins as their manager, they become an overnight sensation, performing in nightclubs (the Village Vanguard, the Blue Angel), on the radio (brief spots for the NBC program *Monitor*), and on television variety shows (an appearance on *Omnibus* made them nationally famous); they also provide the voices for a series of animated beer commercials. They eventually release three best-selling record albums of their routines, and tour the country, appearing in nightclubs and casinos.

1960–61   They star in a Broadway show, *An Evening with Mike Nichols and Elaine May*, directed by Arthur Penn. It runs for over a year. Their album of the same title wins the 1961 Grammy Award for Best Comedy Performance. After the show closes, Nichols and May retire their comedy act and embark on separate careers.

1962   Nichols stars in May's play *A Matter of Position*, which closes after a brief tryout in Philadelphia; its scheduled Broadway opening is canceled. Nichols will later blame the duo's breakup on this episode, not the closing of their Broadway show.

1963   Nichols directs his first Broadway production, Neil Simon's *Barefoot in the Park*, and wins a Tony Award for Best Direction of a Play. Marries Margot Callas, who had been the aging poet Robert Graves's muse or "White Goddess" earlier in the decade. They have a daughter, Daisy, and divorce in 1974.

1964	Directs an Off-Broadway production of Ann Jellicoe's *The Knack*. The *New York Times* predicts that he "is going to be our most gifted director of comedy if he isn't careful."
1964–65	Directs two more Broadway productions, Murray Schisgal's *Luv* (1964) and Simon's *The Odd Couple* (1965), and receives a 1965 Tony Award for Best Direction of a Play for both.
1965	Directs his first musical, *The Apple Tree*, by Jerry Bock and Sheldon Harnick (Harnick had been briefly married to May), and is nominated for a Tony Award for Best Direction of a Musical.
1966	Travels to Los Angeles to direct his first film, *Who's Afraid of Virginia Woolf?*, adapted from Edward Albee's corrosive Broadway hit and starring Elizabeth Taylor and Richard Burton. It opens to rave reviews and strong box office. Nominated for thirteen Academy Awards, it receives five (Nichols is nominated but fails to win as Best Director).
1967	Directs his second film, *The Graduate*, which quickly becomes a box office phenomenon and is nominated for seven Academy Awards, winning Nichols his only Oscar, as Best Director. Buck Henry, Nichols's old schoolmate, cowrites the script and will work on several other Nichols films.
1968–71	Directs two more Neil Simon Broadway hits, *Plaza Suite* (1968) and *The Prisoner of Second Avenue* (1971), and wins two more Tony Awards for Best Direction of a Play.
1970	Directs the film version of *Catch-22*, after Joseph Heller's satirical novel. It opens to mostly negative reviews and general audience indifference; Nichols concedes that Robert Altman's similarly themed *M*A*S*H* (1970) is a superior film.
1971	Directs and produces *Carnal Knowledge* from a Jules Feiffer script; Feiffer had intended it as a play, but Nichols thought it required the intimate concentration on facial expressions only possible on film. The critics approve. Nichols later calls it "the darkest movie I ever made."
1973–81	Directs *The Day of the Dolphin* (1973), a thriller featuring talking dolphins; directs and produces *The Fortune* (1975), an acerbic period comedy. Both movies are box office failures; the critics and Nichols himself agree, and he takes a hiatus from filmmaking that lasts nearly a decade. In this period he returns to theatrical direction, with varying success; he will later describe himself as often grappling with depression.
1973	Directs a Broadway revival of Chekhov's *Uncle Vanya* from a new version he cotranslated. Is nominated for a Tony for Best Direction of a Play, but does not win.
1975	Marries Anglo-Irish novelist Annabel Davis-Goff. The couple have a son, Max, and a daughter, Jenny. They divorce in 1986.

1976   Directs David Rabe's *Streamers* Off Broadway. Directs the American premiere of Trevor Griffiths's *Comedians* on Broadway; is nominated for a Tony for Best Direction of a Play.

1977   Coproduces the Broadway hit musical *Annie* (Charles Strouse; Martin Charnin; Thomas Meehan), winning a share in the Tony for Best Musical. Directs and coproduces D. L. Coburn's *The Gin Game* on Broadway with Hume Cronyn and Jessica Tandy. Is nominated for a Tony for Best Direction of a Play; the play is nominated for Best Play.

1980   Stars with May in a New Haven revival of Edward Albee's *Who's Afraid of Virginia Woolf?* Critics are not invited, but the *New York Times'* Frank Rich goes anyway and is favorably impressed.

1980–81 On Broadway, directs comedies by Jean Kerr and Neil Simon (*Lunch Hour* and *Fools*). Both are panned by critics and have abbreviated runs.

1983   Returning to film, he directs and produces *Silkwood*, inspired by the life of nuclear whistleblower Karen Silkwood. Nichols finds an analogy in Silkwood's story to his own "awakening" from career and personal doldrums. The critical and box office reception are favorable, and the film is nominated for five Academy Awards, including Best Director.

1984   Directs and produces David Rabe's *Hurlyburly* Off Broadway; it later transfers to Broadway. On Broadway, directs and produces the American premiere of Tom Stoppard's *The Real Thing*. Wins a Tony for Best Direction of a Play and another as producer of the Best Play.

1986   Directs *Heartburn*, the film adaptation of Nora Ephron's novel, a fictionalized account of her marriage to Carl Bernstein. Ephron also wrote the screenplay; May serves as script doctor, uncredited. It is a critical and commercial disappointment. Directs Andrew Bergman's comedy *Social Security* on Broadway, his last Broadway credit for six years.

1988   Directs the film adaptation of Neil Simon's semi-autobiographical *Biloxi Blues*. Directs *Working Girl*, a romantic comedy about a young woman determined to rise in the business world. A commercial and critical success, it is nominated for five Academy Awards, including Best Director. Directs Steve Martin and Robin Williams in an Off-Broadway revival of Beckett's *Waiting for Godot*. Marries television journalist Diane Sawyer. The marriage lasts until his death in 2014.

1990   Directs and produces *Postcards from the Edge*. Carrie Fisher adapted the screenplay from her novel about a drug-addicted actress's difficult relationship with her mother. The film scores well with critics and at the box office.

1991   Directs and produces *Regarding Henry*, a film about a brain-injured shooting survivor. The critical reception is generally negative.

1992   Directs the American premiere of Ariel Dorfman's *Death and the Maiden* on Broadway, followed by another long hiatus in Broadway productions until 2003. Nichols and May are honored for their work in television in a tribute by the Museum of Television and Radio in New York City.

1993   Produces *The Remains of the Day*, directed by James Ivory. It is nominated for eight Academy Awards, including Best Picture

1994   Directs the werewolf movie *Wolf* with Jack Nicholson as the title character. May helps with screenplay rewrites, uncredited. Reviews are mixed, but the box office is solid.

1996   Directs and produces *The Birdcage* from a script by May, after the French film *La Cage aux folles*. It is the first major Nichols–May collaboration in thirty-four years, and a commercial and critical hit.

1997   Produces and costars in the film version of Wallace Shawn's play *The Designated Mourner* (David Hare directed). He had also costarred in the play's original London production.

1998   Directs and produces *Primary Colors*, a film based on Joe Klein's satirical novel about a Clintonesque political couple. May again provides the screenplay. The film is critically acclaimed, with two Academy Award nominations, but does poorly commercially.

1999   Is honored in the Film Society of Lincoln Center's annual Gala Tribute.

2000   Directs and produces *What Planet Are You From?*, a science fiction comedy film that receives poor reviews and bombs at the box office.

2001   Directs the TV movie *Wit*, starring Emma Thompson in an adaptation of Margaret Edson's Pulitzer Prize–winning drama about an English professor facing death. Nichols is also executive producer and cowrote the teleplay with Thompson. Nominated for seven Primetime Emmy Awards, it wins three, including awards for Nichols as director and as producer of the Outstanding Made for Television Movie; he and Thompson are also nominated for the teleplay. Is awarded the National Medal of the Arts by President George W. Bush "for his brilliant and creative contributions to comedy, theater and movie direction and production."

2003   Directs *Angels in America* as a TV miniseries, adapted from Tony Kushner's acclaimed Pulitzer Prize–winning drama about the national resonance of the AIDS crisis. It is nominated for twenty-one Primetime Emmy Awards and wins eleven (a record at the time); Nichols again receives two, as director and as executive producer of the Outstanding Miniseries. An honoree at the annual Kennedy Center Honors.

2003–04 Produces two Broadway shows, *The Play What I Wrote* (Hamish McColl, Sean Foley, and Eddie Braben, 2003) and a Whoopi Goldberg solo show,

Whoopi (2004); both are nominated for a Tony as "Best Special Theatrical Event."

2004   Directs and produces *Closer*, the film adaptation of a play by Patrick Marber about complicated relationships among four people, filmed on location in London. It is moderately successful with critics and at the US box office and greatly successful internationally.

2005   Directs the Monty Python Broadway musical *Spamalot*. Wins his only Tony in the category Best Direction of a Musical.

2007   Directs his last film, *Charlie Wilson's War*, based on the true story of a congressman who became involved in a CIA covert operation to support the Afghan side in the Soviet–Afghan War. It is generally a hit with critics and audiences.

2010   Receives the American Film Institute Lifetime Achievement Award. Elaine May is among those offering testimonials.

2012   Directs a Broadway revival of Arthur Miller's *Death of a Salesman*. Wins a Tony for Best Direction of a Play, his seventh in the Best Direction category.

2013   Directs a Broadway revival of Harold Pinter's *Betrayal*, his last credit as director.

2014   Nichols last appears before an audience, and before a camera, in interview sessions with theater director Jack O'Brien for *Becoming Mike Nichols*, a documentary by Douglas McGrath (shown on HBO in 2016). November 19: Mike Nichols dies in New York City. He has just turned eighty-three.

2016   Elaine May directs an *American Masters* series tribute to Nichols, featuring extensive interview footage with Nichols and his collaborators.

Elaine May: Chronology

1932   Elaine Iva Berlin is born on April 21 in Philadelphia, Pennsylvania, to Yiddish theater impresario and actor Jack Berlin and actress Ida Berlin.

1933–44 As a child, Elaine Berlin performs with her father in the family troupe, mostly playing roles as little boys, and tours extensively around the country. She is eleven when her father dies, and soon after she and her mother move to Los Angeles.

1945–47 Attends Hollywood High School but drops out.

1948–49 Marries Marvin May, an engineer and toy inventor; they have a child, Jeannie, who will become an actress, appearing in her mother's film *The Heartbreak Kid*. The marriage breaks up after a year; May's mother mostly raises Jeannie, who takes the name Jeannie Berlin. Studies acting with a former Moscow Art Theatre coach and Stanislavski disciple, Maria Ouspenskaya.

1950–54 Moves to Chicago after learning that the University of Chicago was one of only a handful of colleges that would accept a high school dropout. Audits classes but never formally enrolls. Is introduced to Mike Nichols after seeing him onstage in Strindberg's *Miss Julie*; "I loathed him on sight." A few weeks later, after a chance meeting during which they improvised a comedy sketch for an audience of railway commuters, they begin spending time together as "dead-broke theater junkies." Acts in and directs plays as a member of David Shepherd's and Paul Sills's repertory theater company, the Playwrights Theatre Club.

1955–58 May is a charter member of the Compass Players, the successor to Playwrights Theatre Club. It is considered to be the first improvisational theater company in the US. She quickly becomes its most prominent and charismatic member. Nichols joins the troupe later in 1955; May resumes her friendship with him and they start developing improvised satirical comedy sketches together, leading to the formation of "Nichols and May."

1958–61 Nichols and May take their act to New York and quickly become a sensation, appearing in nightclubs and on television and radio. Their success cumulates in a Broadway show that runs more than a year, after which they stop performing as a team. For details, see the Nichols chronology.

1962   Marries lyricist Sheldon Harnick; they divorce the next year. Is commissioned to write a screenplay adaptation of Evelyn Waugh's comic novel *The Loved One*, but the resulting script, although reputed to be brilliant, is rejected by the film's director, who has a different concept. Writes a three-act play, *A Matter of Position*. A production starring Mike Nichols is scheduled to open on Broadway in fall 1962, but folds after a tryout in Philadelphia, in part because May refuses to allow script changes. According to Nichols, "We didn't break up when we closed [our comedy act] [...]. We broke up over Elaine's play."

1963–66   Undertakes several writing projects, but most do not come to fruition.

1963   Her one-act play *Not Enough Rope* has a short run Off Broadway, together with one-acters by Arnold Weinstein and Kenneth Koch, under the title *3 x 3*. Marries her psychoanalyst, David Rubinfine; the marriage lasts until his death in 1982.

1964   Stages an improvisational revue, *The Third Ear*, Off Broadway.

1966   Agrees to star in *The Office*, a Broadway play by the avant-garde playwright María Irene Fornés, but it closes in previews.

1967   Appears in two film comedies, *Enter Laughing* (Carl Reiner) and *Luv* (Clive Donner; adapted from Murray Schisgal's Broadway hit, which Nichols had directed). They fail to create much of a stir, but several reviewers praise May's acting.

1968   Costars in a new production of her play *A Matter of Position* in Stockbridge, Massachusetts, under Arthur Penn's direction, and receives several favorable notices.

1969–70   Her one-act play *Adaptation* runs Off Broadway as part of a double bill with Terrence McNally's one-acter, *Next*. May directs both plays, which receive enthusiastic reviews and garner for May two Outer Critics Circle Awards, Best Director and Best New Playwright.

1971   Writes, directs, and costars with Walter Matthau in the film *A New Leaf*, a screwball comedy. Angered by studio-imposed alterations, May tries to take her name off the film and unsuccessfully sues to keep it from being released. Nevertheless, it opens to mostly rave reviews and is nominated for a Best Picture Golden Globe; May is nominated for a Golden Globe as an actress and a Writers Guild of America award as a screenwriter. Writes the screenplay for Otto Preminger's *Such Good Friends*, from a novel by Lois Gold. Since other writers had worked with Preminger before she was brought in, she insists on being credited under a pseudonym, Esther Dale.

1972   Directs *The Heartbreak Kid* from a screenplay by Neil Simon. It is a commercial and critical hit and receives Oscar nominations for supporting actors Eddie Albert and Jeannie Berlin. It also makes several end-of-the-year best-film lists in publications including *Time, Newsweek*, the *New Yorker*, and the *New York Times*.

1976   More than three years after filming began, *Mikey and Nicky*, a gritty crime drama May wrote and directed, receives a limited release after litigation between May and Paramount leads to the studio taking control of the film. Reviews are mostly negative (Stanley Kauffmann in the *New Republic* is a notable exception). More damaging to May's directorial reputation is the controversy surrounding the making of the film—her insistence on delivering exactly the film she intended to make. In trouble again with the studio heads, she is forced to retreat from film directing.

1978–86   Establishes a formidable career in screenwriting and script doctoring. Her most visible achievement is a screenwriting credit and Oscar nomination for her work on *Heaven Can Wait*, which she shares with director Warren Beatty. Engages in a number of uncredited script doctoring assignments for several important films, including *Reds* (Beatty, 1981), *Tootsie* (Sydney Pollack, 1982), and *Labyrinth* (Jim Henson, 1986).

1978   Costars with Walter Matthau in the screen version of Neil Simon's *California Suite* (Herbert Ross).

1980   Stars with Nichols in a New Haven revival of Edward Albee's *Who's Afraid of Virginia Woolf?* Critics are not invited, but the *New York Times'* Frank Rich goes anyway and is favorably impressed.

1985   *Mikey and Nicky* is re-released in a newly edited version approved by May, to a generally warmer reception than it received on its original release.

1986   Tribute to May at New York's Museum of Modern Art, which screens May's approved version of *Mikey and Nicky* as part of its ongoing fiftieth anniversary tribute to the Directors Guild of America. May participates in a Q & A afterwards.

1987   Writes and directs *Ishtar*, a satirical comedy starring Warren Beatty and Dustin Hoffman. After an onslaught of negative prerelease publicity, it receives mixed reviews, but its high production costs are not justified by its poor box office, and its failure puts an effective end to May's career as a film director.

1990   Acts in the film *In the Spirit* (Sandra Seacat), coscripted by and starring Jeannie Berlin.

1991   Her comedy *Mr. Gogol and Mr. Preen* opens Off Broadway.

1992   May and Nichols are honored for their work in television in a tribute by the Museum of Television and Radio in New York City.

1994   Receives the American Comedy Awards' Lifetime Achievement Award in Comedy. Uncredited script doctor for Nichols's *Wolf*.

1995   Her one-act play *Hotline* opens Off Broadway as part of the anthology play *Death Defying Acts*, together with one-acters by David Mamet and Woody Allen. It is included in the collection *The Best American Short Plays 1994–1995*, in which her biographical note states, "She is currently working on her apartment."

1996   May and Nichols collaborate on *The Birdcage*, which May adapted from the French film *La Cage aux folles* and Nichols directed.

1998   May partners again with Nichols on *Primary Colors*, a film based on Joe Klein's political novel; May adapted it for the screen and Nichols directed. She is nominated for an Oscar and wins a British Academy of Film and Television Arts (BAFTA) award. *Power Plays* opens Off Broadway: two one-act plays by May and one by Alan Arkin, directed by Arkin and starring them both (the two other actors are Arkin's son Antony and May's daughter Jeannie Berlin).

1999   Begins a relationship with director Stanley Donen, which lasts until his death in 2019.

2000   A new version of her play *A Matter of Position* titled *Taller Than a Dwarf* opens on Broadway under Alan Arkin's direction. It flops. Acts in Woody Allen's *Small Time Crooks* and receives a Best Supporting Actress award from the National Society of Film Critics. Shares the US Comedy Arts Festival's Career Tribute award with Mike Nichols.

2002   Stanley Donen directs May's musical play *Adult Entertainment* in an Off-Broadway production starring her daughter Jeannie Berlin and Danny Aiello.

2005   Her play *After the Night and the Music*, officially "three new plays in two acts," opens on Broadway for a brief run; the cast includes Jeannie Berlin.

2006   The Film Society of Lincoln Center sponsors a special screening of *Ishtar*, which is beginning to achieve cult status among film aficionados. Afterwards, May is interviewed onstage by Nichols.

2010   "The Comic Vision of Elaine May," a three-day event presented by the Harvard Film Archive with screenings of her four films as director; May appears in person at two.

2011–12   Her one-act play *George Is Dead* is performed on Broadway as part of the anthology play *Relatively Speaking*, with one-acters by Ethan Coen and Woody Allen; directed by John Turturro.

2011   May's own director's cut of *Ishtar* is screened at New York's 92nd Street Y.

2013   Is awarded the National Medal of Arts by President Obama for her life-time contributions.

2016   Directs an *American Masters* series tribute to Nichols—her first directorial assignment since 1987. Receives a Writers Guild of America West Laurel Award for Screenwriting Achievement to honor her career and body of work.

2017   Stars in Woody Allen's television series *Crisis in Six Acts*, produced by Amazon.

2018–19   Stars on Broadway in a revival of *The Waverly Gallery*, Kenneth Lonergan's Pulitzer Prize–nominated drama. She receives ecstatic notices—"A performance for the ages," tweeted @nytimesarts.

2019   New York's Film Forum offers a seven-film retrospective of May's films, showcasing her work as director, screenwriter, and actor. It plays to packed houses. In the opinion of Manohla Dargis, film critic of the *New York Times*: "She remains a criminally underappreciated moviemaker."

2019   May wins the Tony Award for Best Performance by a Leading Actress in a Play for her role in *The Waverly Gallery*. At year's end, it is reported that May is to direct her first feature film since 1987, titled *Crackpot*.

2020   The Los Angeles Film Critics Association honors May with its Career Achievement Award.

Mike Nichols: Filmography

As Director

WHO'S AFRAID OF VIRGINIA WOOLF? (1966)
Warner Bros.
Producer: Ernest Lehman (uncredited)
Director: **Mike Nichols**
Screenplay: Ernest Lehman, after the play by Edward Albee
Cinematography: Haskell Wexler (black and white)
Editing: Sam O'Steen
Production Design: Richard Sylbert
Music: Alex North
Cast: Elizabeth Taylor (Martha), Richard Burton (George), George Segal (Nick), Sandy Dennis (Honey)
131 minutes
Academy Awards: Best Actress in a Leading Role, Elizabeth Taylor; Best Actress in a Supporting Role, Sandy Dennis; Best Cinematography, Black-and-White, Haskell Wexler; Best Art Direction–Set Decoration, Black-and-White, Richard Sylbert, George James Hopkins; Best Costume Design, Black-and-White, Irene Sharaff
Academy Award Nominations: Best Picture, Ernest Lehman; Best Actor in a Leading Role, Richard Burton; Best Actor in a Supporting Role, George Segal; Best Director, **Mike Nichols**; Best Writing, Screenplay Based on Material from Another Medium, Ernest Lehman; Best Sound, George Groves; Best Film Editing, Sam O'Steen; Best Music, Original Music Score, Alex North

THE GRADUATE (1967)
Embassy Pictures
Producer: Lawrence Turman
Executive Producer: Joseph E. Levine (uncredited)
Director: **Mike Nichols**
Screenplay: Calder Willingham, Buck Henry; based on the novel by Charles Webb
Cinematography: Robert Surtees (Technicolor)

Editing: Sam O'Steen
Production Design: Richard Sylbert
Music: Simon and Garfunkel; additional music by Dave Grusin
Cast: Anne Bancroft (Mrs. Robinson), Dustin Hoffman (Ben Braddock), Katharine Ross (Elaine Robinson), William Daniels (Mr. Braddock), Murray Hamilton (Mr. Robinson), Elizabeth Wilson (Mrs. Braddock)
106 minutes
Academy Award: Best Director, **Mike Nichols**
Academy Award Nominations: Best Picture, Lawrence Turman; Best Actor in a Leading Role, Dustin Hoffman; Best Actress in a Leading Role, Anne Bancroft; Best Actress in a Supporting Role, Katharine Ross; Best Writing, Screenplay Based on Material from Another Medium, Calder Willingham, Buck Henry; Best Cinematography, Robert Surtees

CATCH-22 (1970)
Filmways Productions / Paramount Pictures
Producers: John Calley, Martin Ransohoff
Associate Producer: Clive Reed
Director: **Mike Nichols**
Screenplay: Buck Henry; based on the novel by Joseph Heller
Cinematography: David Watkin (Technicolor, Panavision)
Editing: Sam O'Steen
Production Design: Richard Sylbert
Music: Richard Strauss (from *Also Sprach Zarathustra*)
Cast: Alan Arkin (Capt. John Yossarian), Martin Balsam (Col. Cathcart), Richard Benjamin (Maj. Danby), Art Garfunkel (Capt. Nately), Bob Newhart (Maj. Major Major), Anthony Perkins (Chaplain Capt. A. T. Tappman), Paula Prentiss (Nurse Duckett), Orson Welles (Brig. Gen. Dreedle)
122 minutes

CARNAL KNOWLEDGE (1971)
Embassy Pictures
Producer: **Mike Nichols**
Executive Producer: Joseph E. Levine
Associate Producer: Clive Reed
Director: **Mike Nichols**
Screenplay: Jules Feiffer
Cinematography: Giuseppe Rotunno (Technicolor, Panavision)
Editing: Sam O'Steen
Production Design: Richard Sylbert

Cast: Jack Nicholson (Jonathan), Ann-Margret (Bobbie), Art Garfunkel (Sandy), Candice Bergen (Susan), Rita Moreno (Louise), Cynthia O'Neal (Cindy), Carol Kane (Jennifer),
98 minutes
Academy Award Nomination: Best Actress in a Supporting Role, Ann-Margret

THE DAY OF THE DOLPHIN (1973)
Embassy Pictures
Producer: Robert E. Relyea
Executive Producer: Joseph E. Levine
Associate Producer: Dick Birkmayer
Director: **Mike Nichols**
Screenplay: Buck Henry, after the novel by Robert Merle
Cinematography: William A. Fraker (Technicolor, Panavision)
Editing: Sam O'Steen
Production Design: Richard Sylbert
Music: Georges Delerue
Cast: George C. Scott (Jake Terrell), Trish Van Devere (Maggie Terrell), Paul Sorvino (Curtis Mahoney), John Dehner (Wallingford), Severn Darden (Schwinn)
104 minutes
Academy Award Nominations: Best Sound, Richard Portman, Larry Jost; Best Music, Original Dramatic Score, Georges Delerue

THE FORTUNE (1975)
Columbia Pictures Corporation
Producers: Don Devlin, **Mike Nichols**
Executive Producer: Hank Moonjean
Associate Producer: Robert E. Schultz
Director: **Mike Nichols**
Screenplay: Carole Eastman (as Adrien Joyce)
Cinematography: John A. Alonzo (Technicolor, Panavision)
Editing: Stu Linder
Production Design: Richard Sylbert
Music: David Shire (uncredited)
Cast: Stockard Channing (Freddie), Jack Nicholson (Oscar), Warren Beatty (Nicky Stumpo), Ian Wolfe (Justice of Peace)
88 minutes

GILDA LIVE (DOCUMENTARY) (1980)
Broadway Productions / Warner Bros.

Producers: Ron Delsener, Lorne Michaels
Associate Producers: Barbara Burns, Burtt Harris
Director: **Mike Nichols**
Screenplay: Anne Beatts, Lorne Michaels, Marilyn Suzanne Miller, Don Novello, Michael O'Donoghue, Gilda Radner, Paul Shaffer, Rosie Shuster, Alan Zweibel
Cinematography: Ted Churchill (Technicolor)
Editing: Ellen Hovde, Lynzee Klingman, Muffie Meyer
Production Design: Eugene Lee, Franne Lee
Music: Paul Shaffer, Michael O'Donoghue, Cheryl Hardwick, Marvin Hamilsch
Cast: Gilda Radner (Herself / Various Characters), Don Novello (Father Guido Sarducci), Paul Shaffer (Don Kirshner / The Candy Slice Group), Howard Shore (The Candy Slice Group)
96 minutes

SILKWOOD (1983)
ABC Motion Pictures / Twentieth Century Fox
Producers: Michael Hausman, **Mike Nichols**
Executive Producers: Larry Cano, Buzz Hirsch
Associate Producers: Tom Stovall, Joel Tuber
Director: **Mike Nichols**
Screenplay: Nora Ephron, Alice Arlen
Cinematography: Miroslav Ondrícek (Technicolor)
Editing: Sam O'Steen
Production Design: Patrizia von Brandenstein
Music: Georges Delerue
Cast: Meryl Streep (Karen Silkwood), Kurt Russell (Drew Stephens), Cher (Dolly Pelliker), Craig T. Nelson (Winston), Diana Scarwid (Angela)
131 minutes
Academy Award Nominations: Best Actress in a Leading Role, Meryl Streep; Best Actress in a Supporting Role, Cher; Best Director, **Mike Nichols**; Best Writing, Screenplay Written Directly for the Screen, Nora Ephron, Alice Arlen; Best Film Editing, Sam O'Steen

HEARTBURN (1986)
Paramount Pictures
Producers: Robert Greenhut, **Mike Nichols**
Associate Producer: Joel Tuber
Director: **Mike Nichols**
Screenplay: Nora Ephron, based on her novel
Cinematography: Néstor Almendros (Technicolor)

Editing: Sam O'Steen
Production Design: Tony Walton
Music: Carly Simon
Cast: Meryl Streep (Rachel), Jack Nicholson (Mark), Jeff Daniels (Richard), Maureen Stapleton (Vera), Stockard Channing (Julie)
108 minutes

BILOXI BLUES (1988)
Rastar Pictures / Universal Pictures
Producer: Ray Stark
Executive Producers: Joseph M. Caracciolo, Marykay Powell
Director: **Mike Nichols**
Screenplay: Neil Simon, based on his play
Cinematography: Bill Butler (color, widescreen)
Editing: Sam O'Steen
Production Design: Paul Sylbert
Music: Georges Delerue
Cast: Matthew Broderick (Eugene Morris Jerome), Christopher Walken (Sgt. Toomey), Matt Mulhern (Joseph Wykowski), Corey Parker (Arnold B. Epstein), Markus Flanagan (Roy Selridge)
106 minutes

WORKING GIRL (1988)
Twentieth Century Fox
Producer: Douglas Wick
Executive Producers: Robert Greenhut, Laurence Mark
Director: **Mike Nichols**
Screenplay: Kevin Wade
Cinematography: Michael Ballhaus (DeLuxe)
Editing: Sam O'Steen
Production Design: Patrizia von Brandenstein
Music: Carly Simon, Rob Mounsey
Cast: Harrison Ford (Jack Trainer), Sigourney Weaver (Katharine Parker), Melanie Griffith (Tess McGill), Alec Baldwin (Mick Dugan), Joan Cusack (Cyn)
113 minutes
Academy Award: Best Music, Original Song, Carly Simon
Academy Award Nominations: Best Picture, Douglas Wick; Best Actress in a Leading Role, Melanie Griffith; Best Actress in a Supporting Role, Joan Cusack; Best Actress in a Supporting Role, Sigourney Weaver; Best Director, **Mike Nichols**

POSTCARDS FROM THE EDGE (1990)
Columbia Pictures Corporation
Producers: John Calley, **Mike Nichols**
Executive Producers: Robert Greenhut, Neil Machlis
Associate Producer: Sue McNair
Director: **Mike Nichols**
Screenplay: Carrie Fisher, based on her novel
Cinematography: Michael Ballhaus (Technicolor)
Editing: Sam O'Steen
Production Design: Patrizia von Brandenstein
Music: Carly Simon
Cast: Meryl Streep (Suzanne Vale), Shirley MacLaine (Doris Mann), Dennis Quaid (Jack Faulkner), Gene Hackman (Lowell Kolchek), Richard Dreyfuss (Doctor Frankenthal)
101 minutes
Academy Award Nominations: Best Actress in a Leading Role, Meryl Streep; Best Music, Original Song, Shel Silverstein

REGARDING HENRY (1991)
Paramount Pictures
Producers: **Mike Nichols**, Scott Rudin
Executive Producer: Robert Greenhut
Associate Producer: Susan MacNair
Coproducer: J. J. Abrams
Director: **Mike Nichols**
Screenplay: J. J. Abrams
Cinematography: Giuseppe Rotunno (Technicolor)
Editing: Sam O'Steen
Production Design: Tony Walton
Music: Hans Zimmer
Cast: Harrison Ford (Henry Turner), Annette Bening (Sarah Turner), Rebecca Miller (Linda), Bruce Altman (Bruce, Henry's Partner), Elizabeth Wilson (Jessica, Henry's Secretary)
108 minutes

WOLF (1994)
Columbia Pictures Corporation
Producer: Douglas Wick
Executive Producers: Robert Greenhut, Neil Machlis

Associate Producers: Jim Harrison, Michele Imperato
Director: **Mike Nichols**
Screenplay: Jim Harrison, Wesley Strick
Cinematography: Giuseppe Rotunno (Technicolor)
Editing: Sam O'Steen
Production Design: Jim Dultz, Bo Welch
Music: Ennio Morricone
Cast: Jack Nicholson (Will Randall), Michelle Pfeiffer (Laura Alden), James Spader (Stewart Swinton), Kate Nelligan (Charlotte Randall), Richard Jenkins (Detective Bridger), Christopher Plummer (Raymond Alden)
125 minutes

THE BIRDCAGE (1996)
United Artists
Producer: **Mike Nichols**
Executive Producers: Marcello Danon, Neil Machlis
Associate Producer: Michele Imperato
Director: **Mike Nichols**
Screenplay: **Elaine May**, based on a screenplay by Francis Veber, Édouard Molinaro, Marcello Danon, and Jean Poiret, and a play by Jean Poiret
Cinematography: Emmanuel Lubezki (color)
Editing: Arthur Schmidt
Production Design: Bo Welch
Music Supervisor: Steven Goldstein
Cast: Robin Williams (Armand Goldman), Gene Hackman (Sen. Kevin Keeley), Nathan Lane (Albert Goldman), Dianne Wiest (Louise Keeley), Dan Futterman (Val Goldman), Calista Flockhart (Barbara Keeley), Hank Azaria (Agador)
117 minutes
Academy Award Nomination: Best Art Direction–Set Decoration, Bo Welch, Cheryl Carasik

PRIMARY COLORS (1998)
Award Entertainment, Icarus Productions / Universal Pictures
Producer: **Mike Nichols**
Executive Producers: Jonathan D. Krane, Neil Machlis
Associate Producer: Michael Haley
Coproducer: Michele Imperato
Director: **Mike Nichols**
Screenplay: **Elaine May**, based on a novel by Joe Klein
Cinematography: Michael Ballhaus (DeLuxe, widescreen)

Editing: Arthur Schmidt
Production Design: Bo Welch
Music: Ry Cooder
Cast: John Travolta (Governor Jack Stanton), Emma Thompson (Susan Stanton), Billy Bob Thornton (Richard Jemmons), Kathy Bates (Libby Holden), Adrian Lester (Henry Burton)
143 minutes
Academy Award Nominations: Best Actress in a Supporting Role, Kathy Bates; Best Writing, Screenplay Based on Material Previously Produced or Published, **Elaine May**

WHAT PLANET ARE YOU FROM? (2000)
Brillstein-Grey Entertainment, Columbia Pictures Corporation / Columbia Pictures Corporation
Producers: Neil Machlis, **Mike Nichols**, Garry Shandling
Executive Producers: Bernie Brillstein, Brad Grey
Associate Producer: Michael Haley
Coproducer: Michele Imperato-Stabile
Director: **Mike Nichols**
Screenplay: Garry Shandling, Michael Leeson, Ed Solomon, Peter Tolan, based on a story by Garry Shandling and Michael Leeson
Cinematography: Michael Ballhaus (DeLuxe)
Editing: Richard Marks
Production Design: Bo Welch
Music: Carter Burwell
Cast: Garry Shandling (Harold Anderson), Annette Bening (Susan), John Goodman (Roland Jones), Greg Kinnear (Perry Gordon), Ben Kingsley (Graydon), Judy Greer (Rebecca), Linda Fiorentino (Helen Gordon)
105 minutes

WIT (TV MOVIE) (2001)
HBO Films, Avenue Pictures / HBO
Producer: Simon Bosanquet
Executive Producers: Cary Brokaw, **Mike Nichols**
Associate Producer: Paul A. Levin
Coproducers: Mike Haley, Julie Lynn, Charles F. Ryan
Director: **Mike Nichols**
Teleplay: Emma Thompson, **Mike Nichols**, based on the play by Margaret Edson
Cinematography: Seamus McGarvey (color)
Editing: John Bloom
Production Design: Stuart Wurtzel

Music: Henryk Mikolaj Górecki
Cast: Emma Thompson (Vivian Bearing), Christopher Lloyd (Dr. Harvey Kelekian), Eileen Atkins (Evelyn "E.M." Ashford), Audra McDonald (Susie Monahan), Jonathan M. Woodward (Dr. Jason Posner), Harold Pinter (Mr. Bearing, Vivian's Father)
99 minutes
Primetime Emmy Awards: Outstanding Made for Television Movie, Simon Bosanquet, Cary Brokaw, **Mike Nichols**; For a Miniseries, Movie or a Special: Outstanding Directing, **Mike Nichols**; Outstanding Single Camera Picture Editing, John Bloom
Primetime Emmy Award Nominations: In a Miniseries or a Movie: Outstanding Lead Actress, Emma Thompson; Outstanding Supporting Actress, Audra McDonald; Outstanding Writing for a Miniseries or a Movie, Emma Thompson, **Mike Nichols**; Outstanding Casting for a Miniseries, Movie or a Special

ANGELS IN AMERICA (TV MINISERIES) (2003)
Avenue Pictures, HBO Films, Panorama Films
Producer: Celia D. Costas
Executive Producers: Cary Brokaw, **Mike Nichols**
Co-Executive Producer: Michael Haley
Associate Producer: Paul A. Levin
Director: **Mike Nichols**
Teleplay: Tony Kushner, based on his play
Cinematography: Stephen Goldblatt (color)
Editing: John Bloom, Antonia Van Drimmelen
Production Design: Stuart Wurtzel
Music: Thomas Newman
Cast: Mary-Louise Parker (Harper Pitt), Jeffrey Wright (Belize, Mr. Lies, Continental Principality), Justin Kirk (Prior Walter, Man in Park), Ben Shenkman (Louis Ironson, Continental Principality), Meryl Streep (Hannah Pitt, The Rabbi, Ethel Rosenberg, Continental Principality), Patrick Wilson (Joe Pitt), Emma Thompson (Nurse Emily, Homeless Woman, the Angel)
352 minutes (6 parts)
Primetime Emmy Awards: Outstanding Miniseries or Movie, Cary Brokaw, **Mike Nichols**, Michael Haley, Celia D. Costas; In a Miniseries or a Movie: Outstanding Lead Actress, Meryl Streep; Outstanding Lead Actor, Al Pacino; Outstanding Supporting Actress, Mary-Louise Parker; Outstanding Supporting Actor, Jeffrey Wright; Outstanding Writing for a Miniseries, Movie or a Dramatic Special, Tony Kushner; Outstanding Directing for a Miniseries, Movie or a Dramatic Special, **Mike Nichols**; Outstanding Art Direction for a Miniseries or a Movie, Stuart Wurtzel, John Kasarda, George DeTitta Jr.; Outstanding Sound Mixing for a Miniseries or a Movie; For a Miniseries, Movie or a Special: Outstanding Casting; Outstanding Makeup

Primetime Emmy Award Nominations: In a Miniseries or a Movie: Outstanding Lead Actress, Emma Thompson; Outstanding Supporting Actor, Patrick Wilson, Justin Kirk, Ben Shenkman; Outstanding Cinematography for a Miniseries or Movie, Stephen Goldblatt; For a Miniseries or a Movie: Outstanding Single Camera Picture Editing, John Bloom, Antonia Van Drimmelen; Outstanding Hairstyling; For a Miniseries, Movie or a Special: Outstanding Costumes; Outstanding Special Visual Effects; Outstanding Main Title Design

CLOSER (2004)
Columbia Pictures Corporation, Inside Track 2, Avenue Pictures / Columbia Pictures Corporation
Producers: Cary Brokaw, John Calley, **Mike Nichols**
Coproducer: Michael Haley
Executive Producers: Celia D. Costas, Robert Fox, Scott Rudin
Co–Executive Producers: James Clayton, Duncan Reid, Paula Jalfon
Associate Producers: Mary Bailey, Paul A. Levin
Director: **Mike Nichols**
Screenplay: Patrick Marber, based on his play
Cinematography: Stephen Goldblatt (DeLuxe)
Editing: John Bloom, Antonia Van Drimmelen
Production Design: Tim Hatley
Music: W. A. Mozart (from *Così fan tutte*), Gioachino Rossini (from *La Cenerentola*), Damien Rice, and others
Cast: Julia Roberts (Anna), Jude Law (Dan), Natalie Portman (Alice), Clive Owen (Larry)
104 minutes
Academy Award Nominations: Best Performance by an Actor in a Supporting Role, Clive Owen; Best Performance by an Actress in a Supporting Role, Natalie Portman

CHARLIE WILSON'S WAR (2007)
Relativity Media, Participant Productions, Playtone / Universal Pictures
Producers: Gary Goetzman, Tom Hanks
Coproducer: Mike Haley
Executive Producers: Celia Costas, Ryan Kavanaugh, Jeff Skoll
Associate Producers: Mary Bailey, Edward Hunt, Paul A. Levin
Director: **Mike Nichols**
Screenplay: Aaron Sorkin, based on the book by George Crile
Cinematography: Stephen Goldblatt (DeLuxe)
Editing: John Bloom, Antonia Van Drimmelen
Production Design: Victor Kempster

Music: James Newton Howard
Cast: Tom Hanks (Charlie Wilson), Amy Adams (Bonnie Bach), Julia Roberts (Joanne Herring), Philip Seymour Hoffman (Gust Avrakotos)
102 minutes
Academy Award Nomination: Best Performance by an Actor in a Supporting Role, Philip Seymour Hoffman

As Producer, Directed by Others

THE ANNIE CHRISTMAS SHOW (TV SPECIAL) (1977)
Martin Charmin Productions / NBC Universal Network
Producer: Martin Charnin
Executive Producer: **Mike Nichols**
Director: Martin Charnin
Teleplay: Thomas Meehan
Music: Charles Strouse (from the musical *Annie*)
Choreographer: Peter Gennaro
Cast: Andrea McArdle (Little Orphan Annie), Reid Shelton (Oliver Warbucks), Dorothy Loudon (Miss Hannigan)

THE LONGSHOT (1986)
Orion Pictures
Producer: Lang Elliott
Executive Producer: **Mike Nichols**
Associate Producer: Tom Egan
Director: Paul Bartel
Screenplay: Tim Conway
Cinematography: Robby Müller (DeLuxe)
Editing: Alan Toomayan
Production Design: Joseph M. Altadonna
Music: Charles Fox
Cast: Tim Conway (Dooley), Jack Weston (Elton), Harvey Korman (Lou), Ted Wass (Stump)
89 minutes

THE REMAINS OF THE DAY (1993)
Merchant Ivory Productions / Columbia Pictures Corporation
Producers: John Calley, Ismail Merchant, **Mike Nichols**
Executive Producer: Paul Bradley
Associate Producer: Donald Rosenfeld

Director: James Ivory
Screenplay: Ruth Prawer Jhabvala, based on the novel by Kazuo Ishiguro
Cinematography: Tony Pierce-Roberts (Technicolor, Panavision)
Editing: Andrew Marcus
Production Design: Luciana Arrighi
Music: Richard Robbins
Cast: Christopher Reeve (Lewis), Anthony Hopkins (Stevens), Emma Thompson (Miss Kenton), James Fox (Lord Darlington), Peter Vaughan (Father)
134 minutes
Academy Award Nominations: Best Picture, **Mike Nichols**, John Calley, Ismail Merchant; Best Actor in a Leading Role, Anthony Hopkins; Best Actress in a Leading Role, Emma Thompson; Best Director, James Ivory; Best Writing, Screenplay Based on Material Previously Produced or Published, Ruth Prawer Jhabvala; Best Art Direction–Set Decoration, Luciana Arrighi, Ian Whittaker; Best Costume Design, Jenny Beavan, John Bright; Best Music, Original Score, Richard Robbins

THE DESIGNATED MOURNER (1997)
British Broadcasting Corporation (BBC), Greenpoint Films / First Look International
Producers: Donna Grey, David Hare, **Mike Nichols**
Executive Producers: Simon Curtis, Mark Shivas
Director: David Hare
Screenplay: Wallace Shawn (play)
Cinematography: Oliver Stapleton (color)
Editing: George Akers
Production Design: Bob Crowley
Music: Richard Hartley
Cast: **Mike Nichols** (Jack), Miranda Richardson (Judy), David De Keyser (Howard)
94 minutes

FRIENDS WITH KIDS (2012)
Red Granite Pictures, Points West Pictures, Locomotive / Columbia Pictures Corporation
Producers: Joshua Astrachan, Riza Aziz, Jon Hamm, Jake Kasdan, Joey McFarland, Jennifer Westfeldt
Coproducer: Kathryn Dean
Executive Producers: Lucy Barzun Donnelly, Joe Gatta, Christian Mercuri, **Mike Nichols**, John Sloss
Associate Producers: Christine Kim, Missy Yager
Director: Jennifer Westfeldt
Screenplay: Jennifer Westfeldt

Cinematography: William Rexer II (color)
Editing: Tara Timpone
Production Design: Ray Kluga
Music: The 88, Marcelo Zarvos
Cast: Adam Scott (Jason Fryman), Jennifer Westfeldt (Julie Keller), Maya Rudolph (Leslie), Chris O'Dowd (Alex), Kristen Wiig (Missy), Jon Hamm (Ben)
107 minutes

CRESCENDO: THE POWER OF MUSIC (DOCUMENTARY) (2014)
Producers: Jamie Bernstein, Elizabeth Kling
Executive Producers: Anthony Drazan, Geralyn White Dreyfous, **Mike Nichols**, Rick Rosenthal, Nancy Stephens
Associate Producers: Malika Jamison, Hugo Kenzo, Sara Zandieh
Directors: Jamie Bernstein, Elizabeth Kling
Cinematography: Ben Bloodwell, Claudia Raschke (color)
Editing: Jonathan Oppenheim
85 minutes

Mike Nichols is also credited as executive producer on the TV series *Family* (1976–1980).

As Writer and Performer

BACH TO BACH (SHORT) (1967)
Short Ends / Pathé Contemporary Films
Producer: Paul Leaf
Director: Paul Leaf
Written by: **Mike Nichols**, **Elaine May**
Cinematography: Victor Lukens (Eastmancolor)
Editing: Ralph Rosenblum
Art Direction: Paul Leaf
Music: Martin Rubinstein
Cast: **Mike Nichols** (voice of Man), **Elaine May** (voice of Woman) (from the Nichols and May comedy album *Improvisations to Music*)
6 minutes

As Actor Only

THE RED MILL (TELEVISION SERIES THE DUPONT SHOW OF THE MONTH)
(1958)
Talent Associates / CBS
Producer: Fred Coe
Director: Delbert Mann
Written by: Robert Alan Aurthur, adapted from the musical comedy book by Henry
Blossom
Art Direction: Robert Tyler Lee
Music: Victor Herbert
Cast: Shirley Jones (Gretchen Van Damm), Harpo Marx (Narrator), **Elaine May**
(Candy Carter), **Mike Nichols** (Rod Carter), Donald O'Connor (Johnny Shaw),
Elaine Strich (Aunt Bertha)
90 minutes

JOURNEY TO THE DAY (TELEVISION SERIES PLAYHOUSE 90) (1960)
CBS Television Network
Producer: Fred Coe
Director: John Frankenheimer
Written by: Roger O. Hirson, based on the book by John Bartlow Martin
Music: Jerry Goldsmith
Cast: Mary Astor (Helen May Whitfield), James Dunn (Melvin Cooper), James Greg-
ory (Dr. Endicott), Steven Hill (Dr. Edward Gutera), **Mike Nichols** (Arthur Millman)
90 minutes

Theatrical Credits (Broadway and Off Broadway)

Broadway

As Writer and Performer
An Evening with Mike Nichols and Elaine May, 1960 (with Elaine May)

As Director
Barefoot in the Park, by Neil Simon, 1963; *Luv*, by Murray Schisgal, 1964; *The Odd
Couple*, by Neil Simon, 1965; *The Apple Tree*, by Jerry Bock and Sheldon Harnick
(musical), 1966; *The Little Foxes*, by Lillian Hellman (revival), 1967; *Plaza Suite*, by
Neil Simon, 1968; *The Prisoner of Second Avenue*, by Neil Simon, 1971; *Uncle Vanya*,
by Anton Chekhov (revival) (also cotranslator), 1973; *Comedians*, by Trevor Griffiths
(US premiere), 1976; *Streamers*, by David Rabe, 1976; *The Gin Game*, by D. L. Coburn

(also producer), 1977; *Lunch Hour*, by Jean Kerr, 1980; *Fools*, by Neil Simon, 1981; *Hurlyburly*, by David Rabe (also producer), 1984; *The Real Thing*, by Tom Stoppard (US premiere) (also producer), 1984; *Social Security*, by Andrew Bergman, 1986; *Death and the Maiden*, by Ariel Dorfman (US premiere), 1992; *Spamalot*, by Monty Python (musical), 2005; *The Country Girl*, by Clifford Odets (revival), 2008; *Death of a Salesman*, by Arthur Miller (revival), 2012; *Betrayal*, by Harold Pinter (revival), 2013

As Producer, Directed by Others

Annie, by Charles Strouse (music), Martin Charnin (book), Thomas Meehan (lyrics) (musical), 1977; *Billy Bishop Goes to War*, by John Gray (play with music) (US premiere), 1980 (transferred to Off Broadway, 1980); *Grown Ups*, by Jules Feiffer, 1981; *Whoopi Goldberg*, by Whoopi Goldberg (solo show), 1984; *The Play What I Wrote*, by Hamish McColl, Sean Foley, and Eddie Braben (US premiere), 2003; *Whoopi*, by Whoopi Goldberg (solo show), 2004

Off Broadway

As Director

The Knack, by Ann Jellicoe (US premiere), 1964; *Streamers*, by David Rabe, 1976; *Drinks before Dinner*, by E. L. Doctorow, 1978; *Hurlyburly*, by David Rabe, 1984 (transferred to Broadway, 1984); *Standup Shakespeare*, "Material By" William Shakespeare (cabaret), 1987; *Waiting for Godot*, by Samuel Beckett (revival), 1988; *Elliot Loves*, by Jules Feiffer, 1990; *James Naughton: Street of Dreams*, by James Naughton (solo show) (also producer), 1999; *The Seagull*, by Anton Chekhov (revival), 2001

As Producer, Directed by Others

Word of Mouth, by James Lecesne, 1995; *On the Line*, by Joe Roland, 2006

Nichols won or was nominated for the following Tony Awards:
Best Director (Dramatic): *Barefoot in the Park* (won)
Best Direction of a Play: *Luv*, with *The Odd Couple, Plaza Suite, The Prisoner of Second Avenue, The Real Thing, Death of a Salesman* (won); *Uncle Vanya, Comedians, Streamers, The Gin Game* (nominated)
Best Direction of a Musical: *Spamalot* (won); *The Apple Tree* (nominated)
Best Play (as producer): *The Real Thing* (won); *The Gin Game, Hurlyburly* (nominated)
Best Musical (as producer): *Annie* (won)
Best Special Theatrical Event (as producer): *The Play What I Wrote, Whoopi* (nominated)

Elaine May: Filmography

As Director

A NEW LEAF (1971)
Aries Productions, Elkins Entertainment / Paramount Pictures
Producers: Hillard Elkins, Howard W. Koch, Joseph Manduke
Associate Producer: Florence Nerlinger
Director: **Elaine May**
Screenplay: **Elaine May**; based on the story "The Green Heart" by Jack Ritchie
Cinematography: Gayne Rescher (color)
Production Design: Warren Clymer, Richard Fried
Editing: Don Guidice, Fredric Steinkamp
Cast: Walter Matthau (Henry Graham), **Elaine May** (Henrietta Lowell), Jack Weston (Andy McPherson), George Rose (Harold), James Coco (Uncle Harry), Ida Berlin (Maid, uncredited)
102 minutes

THE HEARTBREAK KID (1972)
Palomar Pictures International / Twentieth Century Fox
Associate Producers: Michael Hausman, Erik Lee Preminger
Producer: Edgar J. Scherick
Director: **Elaine May**
Screenplay: Neil Simon, based on the story "A Change of Plan" by Bruce Jay Friedman
Cinematography: Owen Roizman (color)
Editing: John Carter
Art Direction: Richard Sylbert
Music: Garry Sherman
Cast: Charles Grodin (Lenny Cantrow), Cybill Shepherd (Kelly Corcoran), Jeannie Berlin (Lila Kolodny), Audra Lindley (Mrs. Corcoran), Eddie Albert (Mr. Corcoran)
106 minutes
Academy Award Nominations: Best Actor in a Supporting Role, Eddie Albert; Best Actress in a Supporting Role, Jeannie Berlin

MIKEY AND NICKY (1976; DIRECTOR-APPROVED CUT, 1985)
Paramount Pictures
Producer: Michael Hausman
Director: **Elaine May**
Screenplay: **Elaine May**
Cinematography: Victor J. Kemper (director of photography), Bernie Abramson, Lucien Ballard, Jack Cooperman, Jerry File (color)
Editing: John Carter, Sheldon Kahn
Production Design: Paul Sylbert
Music: John Strauss
Cast: Peter Falk (Mikey), John Cassavetes (Nicky Godalin), Ned Beatty (Kinney), Rose Arrick (Annie), Carol Grace (Nellie)
119 minutes

ISHTAR (1987)
Columbia Pictures Corporation, Delphi V Productions / Columbia Pictures Corporation
Producer: Warren Beatty
Associate Producers: David L. MacLeod, Nigel Wooll
Director: **Elaine May**
Screenplay: **Elaine May**
Cinematography: Vittorio Storaro (Technicolor)
Editing: Richard P. Cirincione, William Reynolds, Stephen A. Rotter
Production Design: Paul Sylbert
Music: Dave Grusin
Original Songs: **Elaine May**, Paul Williams
Cast: Warren Beatty (Lyle Rogers), Dustin Hoffman (Chuck Clarke), Isabelle Adjani (Shirra Assel), Charles Grodin (Jim Harrison), Jack Weston (Marty Freed)
107 minutes

MIKE NICHOLS (DOCUMENTARY; TELEVISION SERIES AMERICAN MASTERS) (2016)
Jumer Productions, Witnesses Documentary Productions, Bennington Productions, in association with Thirteen Productions for WNET / Public Broadcasting Service (PBS)
Executive Producers: Roy Furman, Michael Kantor (for *American Masters*)
Producer: Julian Schlossberg
Associate Producers: Meyer Ackerman, Jim Fantaci
Director: **Elaine May**
Cinematography: Michael Claeys (color)
Editing: Michael Claeys

With: **Mike Nichols**, Julian Schlossberg (interviewer, off camera)
53 minutes

As Writer and Performer

BACH TO BACH (SHORT) (1967)
Short Ends / Pathé Contemporary Films
Producer: Paul Leaf
Director: Paul Leaf
Written by: **Mike Nichols, Elaine May**
Cinematography: Victor Lukens (Eastmancolor)
Editing: Ralph Rosenblum
Art Direction: Paul Leaf
Music: Martin Rubinstein
Cast: **Mike Nichols** (voice of Man), **Elaine May** (voice of Woman) (from the Nichols and May comedy album *Improvisations to Music*)
6 minutes

As Writer, Directed by Others (Credited Work Only)

SUCH GOOD FRIENDS (1971)
Sigma Productions, Inc. / Paramount Pictures
Producer: Otto Preminger
Associate Producers: Erik Lee Preminger, Nat Rudich
Director: Otto Preminger
Screenplay: **Elaine May** (as Esther Dale), based on the novel by Lois Gould; adaptation: David Shaber
Cinematography: Gayne Rescher (Movielab)
Editing: Moe Howard (as Harry Howard)
Production Design: Rouben Ter-Arutunian
Music: Thomas Z. Shepard
Cast: Dyan Cannon (Julie), James Coco (Timmy), Jennifer O'Neill (Miranda), Ken Howard (Cal), Nina Foch (Julie's Mother)
101 minutes

HEAVEN CAN WAIT (1978)
Paramount Pictures
Producer: Warren Beatty
Executive Producers: Howard W. Koch Jr., Charles H. Maguire
Directors: Warren Beatty, Buck Henry

Screenplay: **Elaine May**, Warren Beatty; based on a play by Harry Segall
Cinematography: William A. Fraker (color)
Editing: Robert C. Jones, Don Zimmerman
Production Design: Paul Sylbert
Art Direction: Edwin O'Donovan
Music: Dave Grusin
Cast: Warren Beatty (Joe Pendleton), Julie Christie (Betty Logan), James Mason (Mr. Jordan), Jack Warden (Max Corkle)
101 minutes
Academy Award: Best Art Direction–Set Decoration, Paul Sylbert, Edwin O'Donovan, George Gaines
Academy Award Nominations: Best Picture, Warren Beatty; Best Actor in a Leading Role, Warren Beatty; Best Actor in a Supporting Role, Jack Warden; Best Actress in a Supporting Role, Dyan Cannon; Best Director, Warren Beatty, Buck Henry; Best Writing, Screenplay Based on Material from Another Medium, **Elaine May**, Warren Beatty; Best Cinematography, William A. Fraker; Best Music, Original Score, Dave Grusin

THE BIRDCAGE (1996)
Director: **Mike Nichols**
Screenplay: **Elaine May**
See the Nichols Filmography

PRIMARY COLORS (1998)
Director: **Mike Nichols**
Screenplay: **Elaine May** (Academy Award Nomination, Best Writing, Screenplay Based on Material Previously Produced or Published)
See the Nichols Filmography

As Actor Only

THE RED MILL (TELEVISION SERIES THE DUPONT SHOW OF THE MONTH) (1958)
Cast: Shirley Jones (Gretchen Van Damm), Harpo Marx (Narrator), **Elaine May** (Candy Carter), **Mike Nichols** (Rod Carter), Donald O'Connor (Johnny Shaw), Elaine Strich (Aunt Bertha)
See the Nichols Filmography

ENTER LAUGHING (1967)
Acre Enterprises, Sajo / Columbia Pictures Corporation
Producers: Carl Reiner, Joseph Stein
Associate Producer: Kurt Neumann
Director: Carl Reiner
Screenplay: Joseph Stein, Carl Reiner, based on the play by Joseph Stein, adapted from a novel by Carl Reiner
Cinematography: Joseph Biroc (Pathécolor)
Editing: Charles Nelson
Art Direction: Walter M. Simonds
Music: Quincy Jones
Cast: José Ferrer (Harrison B. Marlowe), Shelley Winters (Mrs. Emma Kolowitz), **Elaine May** (Angela Marlowe), Jack Gilford (Mr. Foreman), Janet Margolin (Wanda)
112 minutes

LUV (1967)
Jalem Productions / Columbia Pictures Corporation
Producer: Martin Manulis
Director: Clive Donner
Screenplay: Elliott Baker, after the play by Murray Schisgal
Cinematography: Ernest Laszlo (Technicolor, widescreen)
Editing: Harold F. Kress
Production Design: Albert Brenner
Music: Gerry Mulligan
Cast: Jack Lemmon (Harry Berlin), Peter Falk (Milt Manville), **Elaine May** (Ellen Manville), Nina Wayne (Linda), Eddie Mayehoff (Attorney Goodhart)
93 minutes

CALIFORNIA SUITE (1978)
Columbia Pictures Corporation, Rastar, Major Studio Partners / Columbia Pictures Corporation
Producer: Ray Stark
Associate Producer: Ronald L. Schwary
Director: Herbert Ross
Screenplay: Neil Simon, based on his play
Cinematography: David M. Walsh (color)
Editing: Michael A. Stevenson
Production Design: Albert Brenner
Music: Claude Bolling

Cast: Jane Fonda (Hannah Warren), Alan Alda (Bill Warren), Maggie Smith (Diana Barrie), Michael Caine (Sidney Cochran), Walter Matthau (Marvin Michaels), **Elaine May** (Millie Michaels), Herbert Edelman (Harry Michaels)
103 minutes
Academy Award: Best Actress in a Supporting Role, Maggie Smith
Academy Award Nominations: Best Writing, Screenplay Based on Material from Another Medium, Neil Simon; Best Art Direction–Set Decoration, Albert Brenner, Marvin March

IN THE SPIRIT (1990)
Castle Hill Productions
Producers: Beverly Irby, Julian Schlossberg
Associate Producer: Phillip Schopper
Director: Sandra Seacat
Screenplay: Jeannie Berlin, Laurie Jones
Cinematography: Richard Quinlan (color)
Editing: Brad Fuller
Production Design: Michael Smith
Art Direction: Jackie Jacobson
Music: Patrick Williams
Cast: Jeannie Berlin (Crystal), Olympia Dukakis (Sue), Peter Falk (Roger Flan), Melanie Griffith (Lureen), **Elaine May** (Marianne Flan), Marlo Thomas (Reva Prosky)
94 minutes

SMALL TOWN CROOKS (2000)
DreamWorks, Sweetland Films / DreamWorks Distribution
Executive Producer: J. E. Beaucaire
Co–Executive Producers: Letty Aronson, Charles H. Joffe, Jack Rollins
Producer: Jean Doumanian
Coproducer: Helen Robin
Director: Woody Allen
Screenplay: Woody Allen
Cinematography: Zhao Fei (Technicolor)
Editing: Alisa Lepselter
Production Design: Santo Loquasto
Art Direction: Tom Warren
Cast: Woody Allen (Ray Winkler), Tracey Ullman (Frances "Frenchy" Winkler), Hugh Grant (David Grant), **Elaine May** (May Sloan), Michael Rapaport (Denny Doyle), Tony Darrow (Tommy Beal), Jon Lovitz (Benny Borkowski), Elaine Stritch (Chi Chi Potter)
94 minutes

CRISIS IN SIX SCENES (TV SERIES, 6 EPISODES, 2016)
Amazon Studios / Amazon Instant Video
Producer: Helen Robin
Executive Producer: Erika Aronson
Director: Woody Allen
Screenplay: Woody Allen
Cinematography: Eigil Bryld (color)
Editing: Alisa Lepselter
Production Design: Carl Sprague
Cast: Woody Allen (Sidney J. Munsinger), Miley Cyrus (Lennie Dale), **Elaine May** (Kay Munsinger), Rachel Brosnahan (Ellie), John Magaro (Alan Brockman)
23 minutes/episode

Theatrical Credits (Broadway and Off Broadway)

Broadway

As Writer and Performer

An Evening with Mike Nichols and Elaine May, 1960 (with Mike Nichols)

As Playwright

A Matter of Position, 1962 (closed after a Philadelphia tryout before a scheduled Broadway opening; revived in summer stock, Stockbridge, Massachusetts, 1968, with May also as actor); *Taller Than a Dwarf*, 2000 (adapted from her 1962 play *A Matter of Position*); *After the Night and the Music*, 2005; *George Is Dead*, 2011 (one of three one-act plays under the title *Relatively Speaking*, also *Talking Cure* by Ethan Coen, *Honeymoon Motel* by Woody Allen)

As Actor Only

The Office, by María Irene Fornés, 1966 (closed after ten previews before a scheduled Broadway opening); *The Waverly Gallery*, by Kenneth Lonergan (revival), 2018

Off Broadway

As Playwright

Not Enough Rope, 1962 (one of three one-act plays under the title *3 x 3*, also *The Twenty-five Cent White Cap* by Arnold Weinstein and *George Washington Crossing the Delaware* by Kenneth Koch); *Adaptation*, 1969 (performed with *Next* by Terrence McNally under the title *Adaptation / Next*; May also directed both); *Mr. Gogol and Mr. Preen*, 1991; *Hotline*, 1995 (one of three one-act plays under the title *Death Defying*

Acts, also *An Interview* by David Mamet, *Central Park West* by Woody Allen); *The Way of All Fish* and *In and Out of the Light*, 1998 (also actor) (two one-act plays performed with *Virtual Reality* by Alan Arkin under the title *Power Plays*); *Adult Entertainment*, 2002 (also lyricist)

May won two Outer Critics Circle Awards for *Adaptation / Next*: Best Director, Best New Playwright. She also won the Tony Award for Best Performance by a Leading Actress in a Play for her role in *The Waverly Gallery*.

Nichols and May: Interviews

Profile: A Tilted Insight

Robert Rice / 1961

From the *New Yorker*, April 15, 1961, pp. 47–75.

One surprising development in the entertainment business during the last half-dozen years has been the ascent of a generation of young comedians whose public attitude is indignation and whose subject matter is man's inhumanity to man—of which, if their work is a reflection of their state of mind, they consider themselves to be outstanding victims. Gone is the time when being jocose about Bing Crosby's toupee, Jayne Mansfield's structure, or the outcome of the daily double at Hialeah was fashionable; the new comedy covers a bleak political psychological-sociological-cultural range that reaches from the way public affairs are conducted in Washington to the way private ones are conducted in Westchester. Of the members of the group of suffering entertainers—though it may be disrespectful to use the word "group" to describe people who spend much of their time being disrespectful to groups—the two who have devised the most striking way of making their pain laughable are the team of Mike Nichols and Elaine May. Nichols and May use the Stanislavski method of acting to perform comedy sketches in classic blackout form. The result is a wholly original technique that allows them, at one and the same time, to make funny faces and wear funny hats and to deal accurately and candidly with what one man who has worked with them calls "the secrets of the family"—the appalling (to them, at least) relationships that habitually exist between mothers and sons, fathers and daughters, brothers and sisters, husbands and wives, or, in short, males and females. As depicted by Nichols and May, mothers tend to whine, grown-up sons to snivel, adolescents to pant or prattle, unfaithful wives to simper, little boys to bluster, and husbands to drone. Their attitude toward the people they have invented is rigorously unsentimental but by no means unemotional; as well they might, they often seem to be enraged by the way their characters are behaving. A comment that both of them feel is a just description of what they do and how they do it was recently made by the critic Walter Kerr, who wrote, "It's a good thing Mike Nichols and Elaine May are partners. How would either of them ever find anyone else he'd distrust so much?"

One thing most Nichols and May characters are addicted to is clichés, spoken in tones of embarrassed and embarrassing sincerity. "I can't stand to see you this way," one of them, horrified by the agonies the other one is going through in an effort to give up smoking, will say, to the accompaniment of those circumstantial spasms of the larynx, the nostrils, and the jawline that are characteristic equally of a congenital clown and of a Method actor. Or "I wouldn't respect you and I wouldn't respect myself," or "Darling, I'm so ashamed." Not only is the acting of Nichols and May so substantial that they can construct believable characters out of literary rubble like that, but their literary discipline is substantial enough for them to know when a character is so solidly built that he can deliver a punch line. In view of the fact that family secrets, even when they are handled in a resolutely anti-soap-opera manner, are an inexhaustible source of best-selling copy, no one need be flabbergasted to learn that Nichols and May, neither of whom has yet reached thirty, have been deriving from their work in nightclubs, television, and radio, and on Broadway, where their show *An Evening with Mike Nichols and Elaine May* is in its seventh month, gross annual receipts of nearly half a million dollars.

Nichols is light-haired, light-eyed, and light-skinned. He is not only the male lead but the master of ceremonies, and in the latter role he is debonair and self-assured enough. Once he plunges into a scene, though, it becomes apparent that he is a doomed man. His full-lipped and rather fleshy face is peculiarly suited to expressing the nuances of frustration, from the compressed mouth and round eyes of helpless resignation, through a whole gamut of pouts, to the expanded nostrils and knitted brows of ineffectual anger. His somewhat nasal voice can ring just about all the changes on querulousness. As the doomed man, he is flimflammed by telephone operators, browbeaten by his mother, and terrified when his girlfriend submits to his amorous advances. Sometimes he tries to be satanically dominant—with his little sister, say, or with an audience of women gathered to hear him lecture on the drama—but his masterfulness and malevolence are usually feeble. Nichols's characterizations are ably conceived and executed, but there is no more doubt in his mind than in anyone else's that Miss May is the team's virtuoso actor. She is a short, buxom young woman, as uncompromisingly brunette as Nichols is blond, with an enormous amount of crazy hair and crazy energy. She can arrange her features and tune her voice in so many different ways that it is impossible to say what she really looks or sounds like. As a movie starlet with wide eyes, a dazzling smile, and a husky voice, she is clearly one of the most alluring women in America; as a mother with sagging shoulders and jowls, twitching hands, and a whine, she is one of the most repellent; as an Englishwoman with protruding teeth, a rigid spine, and clipped diction, or as a clubwoman with unmanageable eyebrows, aimless gestures, and a shrill cackle, she is one of the most absurd.

However, describing Nichols and May as solo performers is beside the point, for the essence of the act is that it is a duet. If there is a difference in kind between the contributions of the two, it is that Nichols, as the one less likely to lose himself in what he is doing, is the one more likely to know when the moment has come to change the direction of a scene or to end it. Certainly it is Nichols who has taken day-by-day command of the team's career. Alexander H. Cohen, the producer of *An Evening with Mike Nichols and Elaine May*, estimates that he has a telephone conversation about business with Miss May every ten or twelve days and that he has one with Nichols three or four times every day. "Mike's middle name is Emergency," Cohen, who has limitless affection for the eccentricities of actors in general and for those of Nichols and May in particular, said not long ago. "He may call me at home from his dressing room during intermission to tell me the theater is 'in total darkness,' and when I check with the stage manager I'll find that one bulb burned out up on the bridge and has already been replaced." The sort of thing that exasperates Miss May professionally is of a different order, which she recently summarized by imagining a situation in which the team appears on a television show with Dinah Shore. The hypothetical script calls for Miss Shore and Miss May to exchange the customary inconsequences before the team goes into its act, with Miss Shore beginning by saying, "Why, Elaine, you're wearing the same dress I am." Miss May finds it psychologically impossible to make any reply but "Certainly, didn't you see it at dress rehearsal?" and her part of the badinage is suppressed. Because Miss May's imagination teems with mortifying predicaments like that, Nichols handles most of the public chitchat for the pair.

In most respects, though, Nichols and May are a team that carries teamwork to extraordinary lengths. As trained and convinced Method actors—Nichols took lessons from Lee Strasberg, the theoretician-in-chief of the Actors Studio, and Miss May studied under the late Maria Ouspenskaya, an alumna of the Moscow Art Theatre—they both insist that establishing and maintaining a believable personal relationship onstage is the foundation of good acting, and therefore of good comedy, and that any effects, however showy, that are irrelevant to such a relationship are inartistic, and therefore unfunny. The way they compose their pieces is an even more impressive demonstration of teamwork than the way they perform them. The characters Nichols plays and the words Nichols speaks were invented by Nichols, and the characters Miss May plays and the words Miss May speaks were invented by Miss May. Everything they do started as an improvisation and was gradually hardened and polished in the course of performance without ever having been written down or even discussed much. "We've killed some promising things with too much talk, so we've learned to talk very carefully," Miss May said recently. Miss May tends to use words in a special way. There is little carefulness in the accepted sense in the way they talk to each other privately during practically every intermission. In fact, these colloquies are often conducted in such injurious terms that the team sounds much like a married couple on the way home from a particularly disorderly cocktail party; how-dare-you-treat-me-this-way is a recurrent theme. The sense in which they can be said to exercise care after the curtain comes down is that they confine themselves to discussing their general attitude toward each other while the curtain was up, and avoid all mention of details of inflection, gesture, or grimace. They cherish the spontaneous nature of their work so fiercely that they have a calculated policy of remaining as ignorant as they can of such minutiae. Their instinctive reflex when one of the scenes is analyzed in their presence is not to listen, and when one of them is written down, not to look. In order to be able to cue *Evening*'s backstage crew properly, the show's stage manager, shortly after it opened, obtained a script by the use of a tape recorder and a typist. One day, Miss May injudiciously read what she had been saying in a solo scene as a Parent-Teacher Association chairlady. She was amazed to find that, in her words, "there isn't a joke in it." The discovery made her so self-conscious that she wasn't satisfied with the way she performed the scene for a couple of weeks, which was how long it took her to stop listening to herself telling all those non-jokes and to regain her confidence that her acting was funny enough to compensate for the absence of verbal wit. Since Miss May and Nichols have more respect than any audience for their mysterious ability to mesh their separate notions into a coherent piece ad lib, it is improbable that they have ever studied the script of one of their joint numbers. They are able to account for their rapport only in the most general way. A recent manful, if not altogether lucid, attempt by Nichols to explain it was, "Neither of us is capable of having a different kind of idea from the other." As for Miss May, she defines the element that binds their work together as "a tilted insight."

Although it is clear from what Nichols and May do that their insight tilts in the direction of being aggrieved, they seldom make their grievances explicit. Their method of voicing an opinion is to embed it in an ostensibly factual report rather than to proclaim it in an editorial. They make known their suspicion of mother love, for example, by enacting a seven-and-a-half-minute telephone conversation between a young man and his mother, who has phoned him because for weeks he has neglected to phone her. The sketch, one of their most renowned, reaches its climax when Nichols says, "I feel awful," and Miss May replies, "Arthur, if I could only believe that, I'd be the happiest mother in the world." They have a forthright attitude toward adultery, which, in essence, seems to be that committing it and not committing it are equally pointless; it takes them ten and a half minutes to expound this theory by way of a series of three scenes in the lobby of a hotel. The first is between a conscience-stricken American couple. (**Nichols:** "You want to know how bad *I* feel? If I hadn't rented that room already, I'd say forget it.") The second is between a tight-lipped English couple. (**Miss May:** "I'm early." **Nichols** [*not moving*]: "Nice to have the extra time." **Miss May** [*sitting down*]: "Yes.") The third is between a preposterously exuberant French couple. (**Nichols:** "Where's George?" **Miss May:** "My husband? . . . But, darling, I don't know. Didn't *you* bring him?") In much the same deprecatory manner, they deal at length with female civic-mindedness, industrial bureaucracy, modern child-rearing, radio journalism, the cult of southern squalor, and adolescent courtship. In addition, they have made dozens of summary, but no less disenchanted, comments on subjects they evidently regard as not complicated enough to merit exhaustive treatment, like space travel, Christmas, police corruption, summer camps, the presidential election, psychiatry, and almost anyone's literary output. Their evaluation of the novels of Fyodor Dostoyevsky takes just ten seconds; Miss May laughs hilariously for nine and a half seconds, Nichols says, "Unhappy woman!" and the lights go out. The painstakingly documentary nature of almost any Nichols and May scene that runs much longer than ten seconds tends to provoke a kind of laughter that, while voluminous, is distinctly uneasy. At a midweek matinée, there is generally a tinge of hysteria in the obbligato of soprano giggles that accompanies Miss May's impersonation of the PTA chairlady, and few audiences are able to keep their mirth from sounding shrill as they watch "Teenagers," a detailed examination of what a high-school boy and a high-school girl on their first date say and do in the back seat of a parked car. Some people even find Nichols and May too precise to be funny at all, among them a number of ardent admirers who look upon the team less as entertainers than as important social critics, or even leaders of a crusade for a more decent world. One such devotee, a social critic himself, recently asserted that he remembers being moved by just three broadcasts: the radio announcement of the Japanese attack on Pearl Harbor, the radio announcement of the death of Franklin D. Roosevelt, and the first television performance of "Teenagers." Few comedians, surely, have ever received such an accolade—and still fewer, not including Nichols and May, have ever sought one.

Perhaps the most complete, and certainly the most complex, statement given by Nichols and May of their distrust of each other and everything else is an eighteen-and-a-half-minute scene they call "Pirandello." It uses that skeptical Italian playwright's system of questioning the integrity of all human relationships to demonstrate that two small children who play at being their parents and apparently become their parents really are two actors playing a scene in which children become their parents—or, rather, *really* are Mike Nichols and Elaine May playing two actors playing a scene in which children become their parents. It is a piece that gives Nichols and May a chance to be leery of each other from, so to speak, the cradle to the grave, and it provides a splendid setting for the disclosure of family secrets as well. It lets them express in detail what is conceivably a chief ingredient of their common view of life—that people, whether they are children, adults, actors, or Nichols and May, treat each other in much the same way: abominably. It lets them disparage in passing, to name just a few of the objects of their scorn, "Zorro" comic books, cocktail parties, the theatrical temperament, profane language, witty women, and skeptical Italian playwrights who question the integrity of all human relationships. It lets them display their profound sense of theater, since they have worked the material so that it yields suspense and a number of frightening climaxes as well as laughter. And it lets them act their heads off—particularly Miss May. Her portrayal of a solemn, inarticulate little girl is one of the most meticulously observed, most heartfelt, and funniest characterizations on Broadway. Nichols and May use "Pirandello" to close the first half of *Evening*, presumably so that an audience can smoke off its shock in the lobby. As a matter of fact, though "Pirandello" may be their definitive statement, it is the only thing of its kind they do. The ways they unburden themselves most naturally and most often are by turning everyday events into melodramas, by turning melodramas into everyday events, and by enacting Most Embarrassing Moments, a category of human experience they seem to be inordinately, not to say painfully, well acquainted with. The dialogue about giving up smoking and the telephone conversation between the mother and son are fair examples of the first method. Typical of the second are a pair of radio skits, one a version of *Oedipus Rex* that has Oedipus saying plaintively to Jocasta, "Look, sweetheart, you're my mother," the other a domestic contretemps that has the husband saying cheerily to his wife when she tells him she has been chosen to be the first woman into space, "I'll manage the house somehow." As for Most Embarrassing Moments, perhaps the funniest radio skit they ever did was about a psychiatrist with the hiccups, and another effective one concerned a traffic policeman trying to elicit a bribe from a woman driver too obtuse to understand his hints. They also operate quite often in the area of humor that is currently known as "sick." False teeth, falling hair, protruding ears, and gross overweight crop up a good deal in their work. "Sweetie, have you ever thought of bleaching your mustache?" is a fairly characteristic thing for Nichols to say to Miss May when they are groping for new material.

Nichols and May do a good deal of groping in the course of discovering what they want to say. Since they shoot from the hip, they necessarily score a great many partial hits and total misses. For the last year or so, they have been recording a series of one- to five-minute improvised comedy spots that are inserted, at the average rate of five times a weekend, into NBC radio's weekend program called *Monitor*. By now they must have attempted more than six hundred taped spots. Perhaps three hundred have been considered usable by the *Monitor* people, many of them after considerable cutting and splicing, and of those not more than a dozen or so represent Nichols and May at the top of their form. They have also been improvising regularly for the last year as the voices in a series of cartoon television tributes—for which they receive no billing, only a great deal of money—to Jax Beer, a New Orleans beverage that both of them now stock in their iceboxes. Their percentage of successes for Jax has been higher than for *Monitor*, but the percentage of real triumphs almost certainly much smaller. In a nightclub or a theater, they do only their high-gloss set pieces, except for one improvisation, toward the end of each show, based on a suggestion from the audience, and they themselves say that the improvisation is seldom on a par with the rest of the pieces. When it does come off, though, it shakes an audience more than any set piece ever can. It also shakes Nichols and May. Things they are quite unable to explain happen to them when they are carried away by an improvisation. Once, in a nightclub, they held a couple of hundred semi-sober delegates to a sales convention spellbound for fifteen or twenty minutes with an improvisation inspired by Plato's *Dialogues*, a work that they had no reason to believe any member of their audience except the one who suggested it was familiar with, and, moreover, one that they themselves had had no idea they felt any passion about. On another occasion, Nichols suddenly became aware, with a feeling much like terror, that he was speaking fluent Yiddish—a language he didn't know he knew.

Nichols and May began their life together with an improvisation. It was a performance designed solely for their private entertainment, though it may well have also entertained, or astounded, a number of loiterers in the waiting room of the Randolph Street station of the Illinois Central in Chicago, which is where it took place. One evening in the spring of 1954, Nichols was walking through the waiting room on his way to a train and Miss May was sitting on a bench reading a magazine. They knew each other by sight, both having for a time hung around the University of Chicago and been associated with various little-theater groups that originated on or around its campus. As Nichols remembers it, he had avoided becoming acquainted with Miss May, because he was sure she was sneering at him. He still speaks of "the look of utter contempt" that he believes was on her face as she watched him playing a part in Strindberg's *Miss Julie*—the first time he recalls seeing her. Miss May denies that she ever regarded Nichols with contempt. "I didn't regard him at all," she said recently. In any case, that day in the waiting room Nichols resolved to face up to Miss May. He sat down beside her and, talking out of the corner of his mouth, assumed the character of a secret agent making contact with a colleague. She responded in a heavy Russian accent, and they went into a long scene that Nichols recalls as "half spy, half pickup." They no longer remember just what they said, of course, but if by any chance the scene foreshadowed a spy spot they did a few months ago for *Monitor*, it may have begun something like this:

> NICHOLS: I beg your pardon. Do you have a light?
> MISS MAY: Yes, certainly.
> NICHOLS: I had a lighter, but (*pause*) *I lost it on Fifty-Seventh Street!*
> MISS MAY: Oh. Then you're Agent X-9?

They both enjoyed their performance immensely. "It took the place of a lot of chitchat and coffee cups," Miss May said not long ago. In subsequent weeks, they had further meetings and conversations, and evidently discovered how much they had in common. Both of them were, as an old Chicago acquaintance of theirs has put it, "on the lam from their childhoods," which in Nichols's case had been spent largely in New York and in Miss May's largely in Los Angeles. Both of them had found the University of Chicago campus an asylum for insurgent spirits like theirs. Both of them were fascinated by the sort of theater—Strindberg, Pirandello, Brecht—that is a good deal more likely to fascinate insurgent spirits in Chicago than commercial managers in New York or Los Angeles. Both of them had sharp tongues. And both of them were broke. Nichols recalls that one evening in Chicago he was so hungry, and so reluctant to cadge either another meal from friends or another package of bologna from a grocery store, that he dined on a jar of mustard, the only eatable in his room. He also recalls that when Miss May asked him to eat with her, in a cellar she was then occupying, the dish she was most likely to serve was a delight consisting of a small amount of hamburger, a small amount of cream cheese, and a large amount of ketchup. He says it was delicious. It is possible that he really thought so, since not long ago a friend who was sitting with him in the living room of his East Side penthouse watched him sup, with every evidence of pleasure, on a glass of butterscotch Metrecal and a can of corn, eaten cold out of the can.

The trail that led Nichols to the Illinois Central waiting room began in Berlin, where he was born in November 1931, to parents who qualified in almost every possible respect as objects of Nazi persecution. His father was a Russian-born Jewish doctor, Paul Peschkowsky, who, after the revolution, had settled in Germany. His mother's family was prominently identified with the German Social Democratic Party; in fact, her father was an early victim of Nazi assassins. Hitler became chancellor when Nichols was two. Nichols's chief memories of his personal life in the Germany of the thirties are of attending a segregated school for Jewish children and of being taunted and jostled sometimes on his way to and from school by boys with respectable ancestors. He was able to leave the country at an early enough age to have been spared experiences more devastating than those. In 1938, his father acquired the papers that were needed to effect his own departure from Germany and admission to the United States, and sailed for New York, with the idea of sending for his family when he had qualified to practice medicine here and was able to earn a living. Upon his arrival, he took the name of Nichols. A year later, Michael arrived, accompanied only by his younger brother—now an intern in San Francisco. Their mother was ill and had been unable to make the trip with them, as she had planned. She came in 1941,[1] only a few weeks before the United States entered the war. Dr. Nichols rapidly built up a good enough practice to maintain the family comfortably in the West Seventies, near Central Park. For the first three or four years here, Michael was bandied about from school to school; finally, he was installed, for his high-school years, in the Walden School, an institution of the kind known as progressive. It is possible that his attitude as an adolescent toward the adult world is recapitulated in the last line of a summer-camp spot that he and Miss May did for *Monitor*. The camp director says, "If I didn't hate kids so much, I'd close this camp." In 1944, Dr. Nichols was stricken with leukemia, and died. Since he had not been working long enough in this country to accumulate much of a reserve, the family had to reduce its standard of living sharply, but Michael was able to continue at Walden as a scholarship student. However, organized education was one of many things he had little use for. Once he had squeezed through Walden, with a minimum of effort, he had no idea of undertaking any further formal studies, except, perhaps, those connected with the theater, a vocation to which he felt called but for which he was certain he would never be chosen. "I knew I was bright, but I didn't think I had any talent," he said recently. "I simply couldn't imagine a part anyone would cast me for." He did make a halfhearted investigation of the Department of Dramatic Arts of New York University, but when he discovered that one thing NYU students were expected to master was the words and melody of the school anthem ("Oh grim, gray Palisades . . ."), he left indignantly and got a job as a shipping clerk in a company that made costume jewelry. After a year there, it occurred to him that if it came to choosing between rhinestones and alma-mater songs, there was probably something to be said for alma-mater songs. He therefore enrolled in an academic course at the University of Chicago, but he made a point of seldom attending classes or taking examinations. The intellectual and artistic ferment on the Chicago campus did stimulate him, though, and he began to come to grips with his destiny when he joined practically every theater group in sight. One of his first appearances was in the production of *Miss Julie* that was the occasion of Miss May's giving him the alleged fisheye. Presently, he was able to free himself partly from a mustard-eating economy by getting a job as an announcer for an FM radio station that concentrated on classical music, which he admires and knows a good deal about. He was on his way from the radio station to his lodgings, on the South Side, when he encountered Miss May in the waiting room.

Miss May arrived at Nichols by just as rocky a road. She was born in 1932 in Philadelphia, though it might as well have been any other large city in the United States, Canada, or Mexico, because her father, Jack Berlin, was the director of, the writer for, and the principal actor in a traveling Jewish theatrical company. She herself began appearing onstage at an early age, playing little boys, who, to the best of her recollection, were all named Benny. When she was ten, her father died and her mother went into partnership with one of Miss May's uncles, who operated a Chicago establishment called Fogarty's Grill. A couple of years later, the family moved to Los Angeles. Miss May's schooling was brief indeed. Because she was on the road, she didn't start it until she was eight, and because her resistance to education was monumental, even by comparison with Nichols's, she stopped it when she was fourteen. The only thing she ever liked to do in school, she has said, was diagram sentences. Mathematics she found impenetrable and history inconceivable. She has too hard a time remembering what year anything happened to *her* to be able to say what year something happened to Pepin the Short. While still in her teens, she was married to a young man named Marvin May, and something more than a year later she had a daughter, who, to show how circular life can be, is now attending the Walden School. (The Mays' marriage was ended by divorce some seven years ago.) Miss May looks back with distaste on her years in Los Angeles, a city she abhorred and abhors. "I feel in opposition to almost everything anyway, but it comes to its height in Los Angeles," she recently explained. Though she says she felt no specific urge then, and feels none now, to be an actress—or, in her words, "be anything"—the theater was evidently her destiny, just as it was Nichols's, because soon after her marriage she drifted into Mme. Ouspenskaya's acting classes. She acquired a good deal of useful training there, she thinks, though she had a difficult time at first, particularly with a standard Method exercise in which the actor is expected to portray a seed that gradually sprouts from the ground, grows into a tree, buds, and bursts into leaf. Miss May has always been strict about living the part she is playing. "They all had to wait for me. I couldn't bud to save my life. I knew I wasn't a tree," she recalled not long ago. She also drifted into association with various theater enthusiasts in Los Angeles, and when some of them moved to Chicago to pursue their work, she followed, and found herself in the circle in which Nichols had been moving.

The friendship that developed between Nichols and Miss May after the scene in the station was only a prologue to their professional association. When about six months had passed, Nichols resolved that the time had come for him to plunge, and he returned to New York to study under Strasberg. At first, he tried living in the city and paying his way by working. He got a job as a waiter in a Howard Johnson's restaurant, for example, but it ended abruptly after two weeks, when, upon being asked for the fortieth time in one day, what kind of ice cream the establishment served, he grinned maniacally—he has one of the best maniacal grins in the business—and answered, "Chicken." There were other on-the-job crises, and so he moved to Philadelphia (life is circular), where his mother, who had remarried, was living, and still lives. He got a job with a Philadelphia radio station and commuted to New York twice a week for his lessons with Strasberg. Meanwhile, back in Chicago, Miss May joined one of the theater companies that Nichols had been in. She acted in an assortment of plays that included *Peer Gynt, Red Gloves, Murder in the Cathedral,* and *A Midsummer Night's Dream,* and both she and the company scored such smashing successes that when she had been with it for only a few months her salary was raised from twelve dollars a week to twenty-five. Then, in the spring of 1955, the fire department closed the company's theater, and one of its producers, David Shepherd, who was a theater buff with a little money and a lot of admiration for what went on in European cabarets, said, as Miss May recalls it, "The hell with all the forms," and organized Compass Players—not a theater but a nightclub, in which half a dozen actors (four male and two female), using brief scenarios based on ideas they either thought up themselves or elicited from the spectators, improvised scenes. Compass, of which Miss May was a charter member, proved sufficiently attractive to the drinking public to pay its performers fifty-five dollars a week. Late in 1955, a vacancy occurred at Compass, and Nichols, in Philadelphia, was asked by Shepherd to come to Chicago and fill it. Nichols had not maintained any contact with Miss May during the time they were apart—"Neither of us ever maintains any contact with anybody," he remarked a few weeks ago—but they had no difficulty in resuming their friendship at the point where they had suspended it, and they found working with each other, and at Compass, exhilarating. Most of the major pieces they do today had their origin at Compass. (Compass cheated about improvising in one respect; if a scene worked out well, it was kept in the repertory, though it changed from one performance to the next.) As a matter of fact, one of their scenes, a series of hysterical dialogues between a man who has lost his last dime in a coin telephone and a procession of operators, was first performed by Miss May and Shelley Berman, a contemporary of theirs at Compass who has also graduated from the fifty-five-dollar-a-week class. It is the only big Nichols and May number that involves no family secret. Considerably more representative of what they used to do together was a scene, evidently containing the first inklings of "Pirandello," that covered the history, from childhood to old age, of a couple who spent their lives playing games with each other. (A Compass improvisation could go on for an hour, if that was the way the actors felt about it.) The scene started with their playing Monopoly, proceeded through gin rummy, and finally arrived at chess. Nichols always lost. At last, when they were doddering and palsied, he was able to cry "Checkmate!" Miss May dropped dead. Nichols paid her no attention. "I won! I won!" he shouted, jumping with glee. End of scene.

Nichols and Miss May spent a couple of years exchanging joyous thoughts like that with each other and with their colleagues. Then Compass suffered a complex of business ailments, and in the fall of 1957 it had to be disbanded. Shepherd reconstituted the company in St. Louis, with the idea of taking it on to New York, and a new Compass, with Nichols and May as its cadre, did enjoy a four-month run in St. Louis, in what Miss May has graphically described as "a tiny place called the Crystal Palace." The move to New York did not come about, though. The only insurance that the team had taken out against such an emergency was to get, from a friend of Nichols's, the name, address, and telephone number of Jack Rollins, a New York manager who was presumably looking for new acts to manage. Since both Nichols and May were in New York, participating in the abortive negotiations for Compass to appear here, they called on Rollins and, over lunch at the Russian Tea Room, gave him an idea of what they did. He was struck by the excerpts they offered between mouthfuls of beef Stroganoff, and asked them to return a day or two later for a more formal audition, in his office. On the basis of that performance, he undertook to represent them. They returned to St. Louis, where Compass had three or four weeks to run before making its next-to-last disappearance from any stage. (It was revived for about six months in 1958.) Meanwhile, Rollins arranged for them to have an audition at the Blue Angel when they got back to town. In discussing the audition, Rollins uses such inescapable managerial adjectives as "unique," "exciting," and, of course, "great," but for once they seem to be approximately accurate. (He has also said of the audition, "They're so un–show business they didn't know to be scared.") The audience at the Blue Angel cheered them, and the club's owner immediately offered them a booking in ten days, when he would be changing shows. He was so carried away, in fact, that when they looked forlorn at the idea of having to wait so long to work—they had just forty dollars between them at the time—he put them at once into another of his clubs, the Village Vanguard, to serve as a curtain-raiser for Mort Sahl until the vacancy at the Blue Angel occurred.

Since then, Nichols and May have coasted rapidly uphill. At the moment, any nightclub in the country would be glad to get them; the two records they have made are selling well. *Evening* does close to capacity business on West Forty-Fifth Street; *Monitor* is pleased with them; they have won a couple of scrolls for excellence in making commercials; and not long ago Rollins informed an acquaintance, in a hushed voice, that offers for television spectaculars had been coming in at such a rate that he had had to reject eight of them that very week. The abrupt transition from the obscurity and penury of Compass to the luxuries of stardom has left Nichols puzzled and Miss May rather breathless. Nichols, who, of course, spent much of his childhood in the neighborhood of Central Park West, has had no trouble adjusting to taxicabs, Brooks Brothers shirts, and a penthouse. He says, though, that success has made no inward impression on him, whatever it has done outwardly. "My ambitions are not connected with success," he told a friend not long ago. "I perceive nothing operationally different in my life." Miss May, on the other hand, speaks of having money as "an enormous kind of adventure." When she arrived in New York, she had seldom worn high heels, had sometimes worn secondhand clothes, and had had her hair set only twice. Climbing out of her black stockings and tennis shoes and making the acquaintance of Lord & Taylor saleswomen, interior decorators, and an eminent hairdresser named Mr. Kenneth has been a process that has alternately entertained and repelled her. "My dresser at the theater is a nice lady," she told a friend shortly after the show opened. "She lets me dress myself, mostly." Miss May says that while she was having a decorator do the apartment—a roomy one on Riverside Drive— where she lives with her daughter, Jeannie, she couldn't resist occasionally saying to an antique dealer who was becoming particularly rhapsodic over a cobbler's bench or a dry sink, "You mean it's secondhand?"

The way Miss May organizes her life would distress any employer less purposefully tolerant than Alexander H. Cohen. He says, "Elaine relates to things that are important, and she knows what's important. She may be late for half-hour call at the theater, or forget to comb her hair, but she never misses a dinner with Jeannie." Some months ago, he tried to reshape Miss May into the model of efficiency that he thought at first she should be, but he soon gave up. The occasion of his change of heart was a strong lecture that he delivered to her in his office one afternoon. In the course of it, he laid out a complete daily schedule for her, reproved her for neglecting a number of chores she had undertaken to do, and gave her various pieces of avuncular advice about how to live her life. She sat speechless through the whole thing, he remembers, her eyes cast down and her hands in her lap, and when he had run out of things to say, she left quietly and with every evidence of contrition. It was closing time by then, and Cohen started clearing the top of his desk—a task he faithfully performs every day, since he *is* a model of efficiency. Concealed in the mass of papers he found a page from a small memorandum pad. It was covered with Miss May's handwriting, and read:

Wake up (open eyes), get out of bed.
Get hair fixed.
Take bath (get towel, soap, washcloth; undress; fill tub).
Dry self.
Dress (put on underwear, dress and/or skirt & blouse, shoes).
Comb hair.
Do other things (as thou wouldst have them, etc.).
Correct Alex's souvenir program.
Look for hat.
Give insurance policies to Ronnie at 6:00.
BUY STAMPS.
Avoid answering phone in case it is Michael (or answer in disguise).
Avoid door in case it is neighbor (or answer in disguise).
BE AT ALEX'S AT 4:00!

Cohen never attempted to lecture Miss May again. He simply gave her the use of a limousine and chauffeur for the run of the show.

In the years since Compass expired, Nichols and May, despite their voluminous improvising, have developed few new full-scale pieces. And since by now they have exposed a good part of their repertory—a fragment at a time on television and almost *in toto* in the theater—they do not have the material to do eight spectaculars in a week, or in a year, even if Rollins wanted them to. What's more, they are not at all sure that working up a new *Evening*'s worth of numbers—presumably from those *Monitor* spots—is what they want to do. Both of them apparently have the feeling that if they aren't careful, their career as entertainers will develop a sinister force of its own that will compel them to keep on doing the same thing long after they have ceased to get any satisfaction from it. Miss May recently quoted with approval something that Nichols said to her soon after they became rich and famous: "You do your work and you have your career, and the two are diametrically opposed." On her own, she added, "The funniest thing that has happened to us is that we make our living this way—but nobody laughs." What their career is is made clear to them every day, in a seemingly endless series of interviews with newspapermen, luncheons with advertising-agency executives, conferences with Rollins, and long-distance telephone conversations with movie producers—not to mention the laughter and applause of their audiences and the pay checks that are sent to Rollins every week. They wish they could be equally clear about their work.

Miss May has written a play—a comedy about family secrets, of course—which she hopes will be produced next season. Nichols would like to write a play, too, but he hasn't yet been able to build up enough resolution to sit down to it. He has been in what he considers a state of torpor ever since *Evening* settled down to its run. "I can't think of the show as a full-time job," he said plaintively not long ago. "There are twenty-two other hours in the day." As to whether or not, separately or together, they have a message worth delivering, Miss May is a good deal more positive than Nichols, who recently said, with vehemence, "I have no sense of mission about our work. I have nothing I want to tell people." Miss May has things she wants to tell people. "Remember Swift and the Irish babies?" she asked a friend a few weeks ago. "That's the way you have to go." That's the way she does go, too. "The nice thing is to make an audience laugh and laugh and laugh, and shudder later," she says. Note the word "nice."

Note

1. Actually, in March 1940.—REK

Elaine May: Q & A about Her Play

Richard F. Shepard / 1962

Elaine May, of Nichols and May fame, is a painstaking woman when it comes to words. This despite a career devoted, with Mike Nichols, to making the word "improvisation" mean high entertainment rather than the cliché finger-in-the-dike sort of thing.

Since she realizes that the relationship of words to human events may be equated with that of sticks and stones on bones, a transcript of her comments follows in toto. The occasion was during a break from the rehearsal of *A Matter of Position*, a full-length comedy she has written in which Mr. Nichols stars under the direction of Fred Coe, who is producing it with Arthur Cantor. It will open here at the Booth on October 25, after a run in New Haven starting October 15.

Miss May's insistence on accurate, full reportage stems from a horror of the sort of thing that results in the person being interviewed emerging in print saying, "Hello, I come from Yugoslavia, but I love Florida oranges and detest green pajamas." As she notes, this sort of information is generally elicited from a number of questions, not necessarily related. She also admires, as she has demonstrated in performance, an economy of words and a compactness of thought.

So, with a deferential nod to those who digest full texts of presidential press conferences, here is the entire, unexpurgated, record.

Q: When did you begin writing your play?
A: Three years ago.

Q: When did you finish it?
A: About a year ago.

Q: What inspired you to write this play?
A: I don't know.

Q: Well, how did you come to start it?
A: Fred Coe asked me to write a *Playhouse 90* for Michael and myself. Then I did and he said it would make a good play. So I made it into a play.

Q: What changes did you make for the play?
A: I changed it for the stage.

Q: What do you mean?
A: I mean I originally wrote it for television and then rewrote it for the stage.

Q: What did you do to the play? Did you expand it or rewrite the lines?
A: Well, I expanded it and that made it necessary to rewrite the lines.

Q: How long have you been in rehearsal?
A: Two weeks.

Q: Have you been making many changes during rehearsal?
A: No.

Q: How many?
A: Three.

Q: What is the play about?
A: The whole play?

Q: Yes.
A: It's about a man who decides to go to bed and not get up.

Q: Why?
A: Because he doesn't like being up anymore.

Q: Is it symbolic?
A: What?

Q: Does it have an inner meaning?
A: What do you mean?

Q: How should I know what I mean? I'm only asking the question. What I mean, could it go Off Broadway as well?
A: Not likely.

Q: How many people are in the cast?
A: Nine.

Q: Where is the locale of the play?
A: In an apartment.

Q: Is the whole play in an apartment?
A: Yes.

Q: How many rooms?
A: Two and a half.

Q: Do you feel happier watching the rehearsal, knowing that just your lines and not your performance are in balance?
A: Much.

Q: Do you ever wish that you were onstage doing the lines?
A: No.

Q: Have you had any quibbles with the director or the cast on their approach to your play?
A: No.

Q: Has this led to bloodshed?
A: Occasionally.

Q: Have you ever written for Mike Nichols before?
A: No.

Q: Is it coming along the way you thought it would? Are there more difficulties than you had anticipated? Are the characterizations as valid as when you conceived them? Has Mr. Coe tried to monkey with your work?
A: What do you mean, monkey?

Q: I mean, changing your message for purposes of staging.
A: No.

Q: Does that cover parts 1, 2 and 3 of the previous question?
A: What was the previous question?

Q: Is it coming along the way you thought it would? Are there more difficulties than you had anticipated? Are the characterizations as valid as when you conceived them?
A: Yes.

Q: Do you have any other thoughts on the state of contemporary drama?
A: Other than what?

Q: I mean, do you think there is a crucial need for more humor in the theater today?
A: Can I come back to that?

Q: Thank you, Miss May.
A: Maybe you're welcome.

The Cold Loneliness of It All

Vincent Canby / 1966

The following is a transcript of a tape-recorded colloquy which the reporter held with himself after an interview with Mike Nichols, the thirty-five-year-old Broadway director who has just made his Hollywood debut directing Richard Burton and Elizabeth Taylor in the film version of Edward Albee's *Who's Afraid of Virginia Woolf?* The reporter, who visited Mr. Nichols during the latter's recent trip to New York from Hollywood, intended the Nichols interview as his first major effort in a new genre of newspaper journalism called "unfact reportage." Why that effort failed is explained below.

Q: Sir, what influenced you to choose Mike Nichols as the subject of your first experiment in what you call "unfact reportage?"
A: Oh, Mike wasn't my first try. I've been interviewing people for years. Bette Davis, Andrei Gromyko, Otto Preminger, President Arturo Illia of Argentina. Taking notes, notes, notes. You might call them finger exercises.

Q: Until you were ready?
A: Yes.

Q: But why Mike Nichols?
A: I'm not really sure. The choice, I suppose, is part of the creative process. Mike had always interested me, ever since I first saw him and Elaine May on that *Omnibus* TV show years ago. I followed their careers as club and television entertainers. They were truly two of the great satirists of our time. I still treasure their interviews with bogus Hollywood personalities and pompous authors. I wasn't at all surprised that, after they parted amicably, he went on to further success as a Broadway and Off-Broadway director with four hits (*Barefoot in the Park*, *Luv*, *The Odd Couple* and *The*

Knack) running simultaneously. In Mike, I suppose, I wanted to study the effect of the Hollywood environment on irreverent genius.

Q: To see if he still had his sense of humor?
A: Exactly. I always say: if Mike has to lose something, I hope it isn't his sense of humor.

Q: Has he?
A: No, thank heavens. Though it took some time to get through to it. I mean, interviewing him at his Central Park West, twenty-second floor, triplex penthouse apartment.

Q: Can you explain?
A: Well, I'm essentially a floor-through boy myself, and I'm still impressed by a duplex. So, a triplex—well—inspires a certain amount of awe. That is, until I realized—

Q: You realized—
A: That a triplex is, after all—well—it's just High Camp.

Q: Do you know Mike well? Are you close?
A: Very. I interviewed him once before for about an hour.

Q: Did you take notes this time?
A: Yes, but he talks so fast and has so many ideas. Then he has a way of suddenly stopping and looking at you, daring you, *challenging* you to ask another question immediately.

Q: Could you?
A: Usually, but often I'd start fumbling with my pad or dropping the sheet of questions I'd brought. That would bore him, and then, too, if he went on too long with an answer, or wouldn't stick to the point, *I'd* get bored—or just bemused watching those clouds go clickety-clack past the windows.

Q: Was he a difficult interview?
A: Not at all. He's not what I'd call an old shoe—that is, comfortable. But difficult? No. He's agreeable, quick, sardonic. Perhaps also a bit diffuse.

Q: Please elaborate.
A: Well, to put him at his ease and to gain his confidence, I started by asking him simple questions to which I confidently expected to receive simple answers. For

example, I asked him who was his favorite movie director—the man whose works he might have studied before tackling *Who's Afraid of Virginia Woolf?*—

Q: And—

A: Instead of one name, he rattled off about twenty, so fast I couldn't possibly take them all down. Fellini, Truffaut, Stevens, Kazan, Wilder, Lester, and some others I don't recall. His tastes are, you might say, eclectic, although he is partial to Fellini and he thinks *8 1/2* the greatest film ever made. He cries when he sees it, but not always in the same places. Before he started work on *Virginia Woolf*, Mike always cried during the harem sequence of *8 1/2*. When he started making his own movie, he cried during the scenes in *8 1/2* showing the making of the film-within-the-film. It's Mike's old Pirandello hang-up, I think.

Q: Being a first-time film director, was Mike subject to any put-downs on the part of his crew?

A: Do you mean, did they have to tell him which end of the viewfinder to look through? No. He had a simply marvelous crew, and then he feels that the basics of filmmaking really are not all that complex. He did fire one man though.

Q: Who was that?

A: An assistant director who once said: "Oh, well, it's just another film after all." Mike fired him on the spot because of his attitude. Mike was quite shaken. It was the first time in his life he had ever fired anyone.

Q: How about his relations with the Burtons?

A: Well, as you know, they are old friends. Their being old friends helped ease the tension of his making his directorial debut to the extent that he wasn't overwhelmed by their professional or private reputations.

Q: Were there any problems?

A: If you're referring to reports that the Burtons did get a bit cranky now and then, Mike didn't mention it. He did say, however, that when the picture ran over its original shooting schedule, the Burtons waived $175,000 in overtime pay out of deference to him.

Q: How much did the film cost?

A: About $6 million, give or take a few pennies.

Q: Isn't that rather a lot for what was originally a one-set play?

A: Not really when you consider that $500,000 was paid for the film rights and the

Burtons received $2 million, leaving only about $3.5 million for Mike, producer-screenwriter Ernest Lehman, all the other actors, sets, film stock, laboratory work, transportation, coffee, etc.

Q: With all that money riding on his back, wasn't Mike under tremendous pressure?
A: Not in the least. He was never bothered by the Warner Bros. front office at all. Actually, his description of Hollywood more or less destroys all the stereotypes Mike and Elaine used to find so humorous.

Q: In what way?
A: When he went out to do the film, people couldn't have been sweeter. There was none of that "so here's the smart kid from New York" stuff. Joe Mankiewicz, Otto Preminger, and William Wyler jointly took him to lunch and offered their help. Billy Wilder advised him to buy a shirt at Sears to wear on the set. Although people tend to look at Hollywood as a congealed mass, in reality it's a town where most people don't know one another. The nicest thing about it is that people there are in love with their work. As Mike said, all this sounds like something you'd say in an interview.

Q: Hollywood is also a town that loves success, and Mike went out there as a big New York success. Right?
A: Right, and he acknowledges this indirectly. He remembers his first trip to Hollywood years ago, when he and Elaine played the Mocambo. Mike was married at the time and Hollywood was hell on wives. The Mocambo had live birds in glass cages in the wall, and during every show, one or two birds would die and plummet to the floor, thump, thump. It was a ghastly experience.

Q: What is he doing now?
A: Still editing *Virginia Woolf*, which will be released in July or October.

Q: After that?
A: He is due to direct another film, *The Graduate*, in September, and he is talking to Lillian Hellman about a Broadway revival of *The Little Foxes*. He and Elaine are working on a new recording, *Men, Women, and Children*, and somewhere in the distant future, there may be a film starring Elaine, directed by Mike, with a script by the two of them.

Q: After all the time you've spent with Mike—
A: It adds up to about two hours now—

Q: What conclusion did you reach?

A: You mean on the effect of the Hollywood environment on irreverent genius? To be perfectly frank, I'm not sure. The experience is still too freshly minted. Maybe in another five years, I'll be able to be subjective, for subjectivity is the essence of unfact reportage. I'm still too objective. Maybe you should talk to the people Mike sees in New York: Jackie and Lee and Stas and Truman and Lennie and Felicia—that crowd.

Q: Can you tell me why, if the purpose of unfact reportage is to eliminate extraneous detail, you were unable to write your Nichols profile after you lost your notes?

A: I didn't *lose* them. I simply couldn't read them. My handwriting is sloppy, but I'm fastidious about my possessions. Unless I keep a record of all the facts I find superfluous, those facts might otherwise steal into my reportage and destroy the inspiration of the moment. Is it really meaningful that, at thirty-five, Mike has had two marriages that went phffft, has a small daughter, that he was born in Berlin and came to this country at eight, or that his real name is Michael Igor Peschkowsky? Earlier I told you that, sitting in Mike's triplex apartment with the five telephones and God knows how many rooms, I had become bemused by the clouds going by the windows. Well, that was unfact reportage. It was a cold winter day when I saw Mike, but the sky over New York was absolutely Bay-of-Naples blue and virginally clear, unmarred by even a jet contrail. However, if I had told you that, you wouldn't have felt the scene as I felt it, the height, the cold loneliness of it all.

Mike Nichols: Director as Star

Mel Gussow / 1966

When Mike Nichols came to America in 1939 at the age of seven, as a refugee from Nazi Germany, he could speak only two sentences in English: "I do not speak English" and "Do not kiss me." From there on, he improvised.

Today, at thirty-five, he has improvised his way into a spectacular double success, as a celebrated satiric comedian (in partnership with Elaine May) and as America's highest-paid, most sought-after director, its only star director of the moment. With four hits running simultaneously on Broadway—*Barefoot in the Park, Luv, The Odd Couple*, and his new *The Apple Tree*—as well as the movie hit of the year, *Who's Afraid of Virginia Woolf?*, Nichols has more marquees lit up than producer David Merrick. In fact, between them, they run Broadway.

In a world where a playwright's or a star's name is no assurance of commercial success, director Mike Nichols sells tickets. Before *The Apple Tree* opened on Broadway, the "new Mike Nichols show," the "first Mike Nichols musical," had a million-dollar advance, and since it opened—to mixed reviews—it has been selling out almost every performance. Partially, of course, it is a testament to the versatility and charm of Barbara Harris, but Nichols also gets star billing.

Nichols today is one of those absolute American success stories—a fellow who is recompensed enormously for being himself. He is under a retainer to CBS, at a substantial (and unquoted) figure, to do whatever, whenever, he wants on network television. Recently he was named movie director of the year by the National Association of Theatre Owners. ("I sleep a little better every night knowing that Jack Valenti is my president," he said as he accepted the award.) He can call his own shots on Broadway and in Hollywood. Says his agent, Robert Lantz: "In the beginning he was a comedian, and they said, 'Let's give him a comedy.' But now he's done a serious movie and a musical. All the barriers have fallen. He's being offered everything from the stock-exchange report to the sports pages."

Conspiracy: But Nichols's success cannot be measured in dollars and offers alone. He has brought freshness, fun, and excitement to a dreary and predictable Broadway. And ex-actor Nichols has made stars out of such new types as Alan Arkin (*Luv*) and veteran Walter Matthau (*The Odd Couple*). Critic Susan Sontag says, "To me the direction of the actors in *Virginia Woolf* is brilliant. Elizabeth Taylor gave the best performance of her life. She's a real actress. If someone has the capacity, Mike can get it out of them." "A director's chief virtue should be to persuade you through a role," says Richard Burton. "Mike's the only one I know who can do it. He conspires with you to get your best. He'd make me throw away a line where I'd have hit it hard. I've seen the film [*Virginia Woolf*] with an audience, and he was right every time. I didn't think I could learn anything about comedy—I'd done all of Shakespeare's. But from him I learned."

Playwrights also learn from him. "People who work with Mike are spoiled for all time," says Neil Simon, "because he is the best, the brightest, the strongest, and it's never as much fun with anyone else." "He's a good director," says Edward Albee with characteristic restraint. "There are very few good directors. Only about two and a half."

That makes Nichols almost half the supply of good directors and therefore he is a rich one—he received a quarter of a million dollar salary for *Virginia Woolf* and he gets a healthy cut of the take from all his shows. He lives in an elegant triplex terrace tower apartment overlooking all of New York City. In his living room are pictures by Matisse, Picasso, Rousseau, and, over the fireplace, a tiny little Vuillard, which is lit by a sound switch at a handclap. He has a butler to serve the right wine with every meal, and a chauffeur to transport him in a Lincoln Continental. Separated from his second wife, he has a beautiful two-and-a-half-year-old daughter named Daisy. He even has a horse of his own, an Arabian named Nancy. Among his close friends are the most important people in several worlds, including Jacqueline Kennedy, the André Previns, the Richard Avedons, the Leonard Bernsteins, Julie Andrews, Penelope Gilliatt, the Alan Arkins, Ulu Grosbard. Yes, but in the worlds of Passionella, the chimney sweep who becomes a movie star in *The Apple Tree*, is he "truly content"?

Ambivalence: Coming out of *The Apple Tree* after a recent performance, Nichols heard someone say, "Big deal Mike Nichols, what's so hot about him?" Feigning deafness, he walked on, and said later, "There's no way to let them know I don't think I'm a big deal. I can't turn around and say, 'I agree with you.'" Nor, for that matter, can he turn around and say, "I am *so* a big deal." Nichols is torn by a curious ambivalence, a feeling "of terrible arrogance and self-deprecation, at the same time. I'm doing it better than anyone and I can't do it at all. I'm a fraud."

Nichols has the great grace of laughter, and one of his favorite laugh-objects is himself. Sitting one evening in a Hollywood restaurant, a waitress told him: "Those people over there just have to know who you are." "Manny Gumbiner," said Nichols. "You know, *The Manny Gumbiner Show* on television." The waitress dutifully reported the information and, as Nichols watched, the people nodded happily. Often his wit is Thurberish and bizarre. Burton recalls a dinner party at Mike's house in Hollywood. "The butler offered him the avocados and said, 'These avocados, sir, was picked from your own garden.' Mike gazed at him and said, 'That is deeply moving. I must visit that tree sometime.'" And he notes with relish that there is another Mike Nichols, who costars "with Anna Brazzou in a Greek movie that keeps coming back to Forty-Second Street. I'm afraid to see it. It may be me."

One night in Sardi's, someone said to Nichols, "I understand you were born in Berlin." "Not anymore," he snapped. Actually he was born in Berlin, as Michael Igor Peschkowsky, the son of a German mother and a Russian father whose patronymic was Nicholaiyevitch, later Anglicized to Nichols. His father, a doctor and the son of a doctor (Mike's only brother is a doctor at the Mayo Clinic), fled from Russia to Germany, learned German, took his medical exam, fled from Germany to America, learned English, took his medical exam, set up practice in Manhattan, then sent for his family.

Since their mother was sick (she joined them the following year), Mike and his younger brother were shipped by themselves on a boat from Germany to America, where they were met by their father. At first the two boys were boarded with patients of his on Long Island. "They were horrible English people," remembers Mike. "My brother was three and they shook his hand goodnight."

"Another Fake": As a youngster Mike went through a series of progressive private schools—Dalton in New York, Cherry Lawn in Darien, Connecticut, and Walden in New York—with no apparent success. "I didn't enjoy school very much," he says, and then lists some of the things he didn't learn. "I never had any geography of any kind and to this day I have the handwriting of an idiot," which may be one reason he is reserved about giving autographs. "Let's see his handwriting," demanded a fan recently, looked at it, then shouted, "Another fake!"

When he was twelve, his father died, leaving his family with little money. Mike continued his education on scholarships. He was lonely, had few friends, but remembers his enemies vividly. "There was one guy at Cherry Lawn who used to hold my head under the water. He would stand on it." When he and Elaine May were appearing at the Blue Angel, this childhood bully appeared one night and said, "You don't remember me." "It was as if I had been waiting for that moment for fifteen years," says Nichols. "I said, 'Your name is so-and-so and you were a son of bitch. What are you doing now?'" "I'm selling used cars," said the former bully. "I'm so glad," said Nichols.

By fourteen he was stagestruck. "I read every word by O'Neill. At Cherry Lawn the dramatics teacher said I was intelligent and not in any way suited to the theater. I think she was right." Still, "he always said his main interest was theater," recalls Lucile Kohn, who taught him Latin at Walden, "but I thought it was just a pipe dream." Miss Kohn, now eighty-four and retired, tells of having lunch recently with another former Walden teacher. "I asked him, 'What do you think of our most famous student?' He guessed some names. Finally I said, 'Mike Nichols.' He said, 'You don't mean that was *our* Mike Nichols?'"

After graduating from Walden, "I registered at NYU, and the first day they made us sing 'Oh Grim, Gray Palisades.' I got depressed and went home. I worked a year in a stable, shoveling manure and giving riding lessons, and as a shipping clerk for Caedmon Records. I would get terrific ideas like 'Let's have Robert Frost reading his own work,' and they would say, 'Take this package to 105th Street.'"

Cadavers: Finally he went to the University of Chicago, working his way through two years as a jingle judge, a night janitor in a nursery, a classic disk jockey, and a post-office truck driver. "I never could find any address. Imagine a five-ton post-office truck stopping a little old lady and asking directions."

For a while he was a premed, until they got to cadavers. Actually he had planned to be a psychiatrist, which, he says now, "would have been some mess." Instead, he cut most of his classes and became a campus egghead and theater person in the intense intellectual atmosphere of Robert Hutchins's university. His first bit of directing was a production of Yeats's *Purgatory*.

He also acted. In *Miss Julie*, he was the "lecherous, coarse butler. I was very bad. One night in the audience a dark-haired, hostile girl was staring at me. I knew she hated it and I hated her because she was right. Then Sydney Harris wrote a rave review of the play. Holding a copy of the review, I was walking down the street and I passed a friend with this hostile girl next to him. I showed him the review and she read it over his shoulder and said, 'Ha!' and walked away. The next time I saw her she was in the Illinois Central station sitting on a bench. I went up to her and said, in a foreign accent, 'May I sit down?' She said, 'If you vish.' We played a whole spy scene together." That was of course the world's first Mike Nichols–Elaine May skit.

Lake Michigan: Both became members of the off-campus Playwrights Theatre, which later became the Compass, an improvisational theater. "I thought, I can't do this at all," he recalls, and then found suddenly that he could. "It became mostly a pleasure because of Elaine's generosity. I loved it. You could do awful scenes, good scenes, fifty scenes, and if you really screwed up you could run down to Lake Michigan and jump in, and run back and do another scene. The process was pleasurable. We made things on the spot, together, and in front of the audience."

Three years passed. Then "the group sort of fell apart." He and Elaine struck out for St. Louis for a while, then to New York. "We never had any plans to be a comedy team or be in show business or anything." But agent Jack Rollins got them an audition at the Blue Angel. They played there and at the Village Vanguard, doing mostly their best scenes from the Compass, began appearing on television, became an overnight sensation, and gave birth to a whole new kind of comedy—satiric, acerbic, situational. Spoofing anxieties and banalities in everyday life, they conjured up a hilariously diverse array of conflicting couples—first-daters tangled up in the back seat of a car, an anguished telephoner and a super-stubborn operator, a pushy mother and her put-upon scientist son. ("I feel awful," the son says after a particularly frustrating talk with his mother. "If I could only believe that," she says, "I'd be the happiest mother in the world.")

Suddenly they were rich, famous, deluged, and dazzled—and in Hollywood about to sign up for a television series. A roomful of agents watched breathlessly as Nichols picked up the first contract, began to sign, then stopped. "I don't think I will," he said, and giggled. The agents groaned, Elaine laughed, and they flew back to New York.

"Leftover Half": After their two-man show closed on Broadway, the team broke up. "Elaine no longer enjoyed it terribly," says Mike. "Mainly she wanted to write. . . . I was the leftover half of a comedy team. I really felt for a long while that what I was able to do came from my special connection with Elaine. Without her, there was not much I could do. I was in a Slough of Despond."

He did have some acting offers. "I didn't and don't think I can act and I suffer when I act other people's words. Tyrone Guthrie asked me to play Hamlet. I said it wasn't possible." The year before, Nichols had almost played Iago, Off Broadway, to Richard Burton's Othello and Julie Andrews's Desdemona. "We had our first reading. As Richard and I read together, my voice got higher and higher, and more and more midwestern. Iago became a squeaking Chicagoan. At the end, I closed the book and said, so long, everybody."

Nichols then "mooched around wondering what would happen next." What happened was an offer, for five hundred dollars, to direct the Bucks County tryout of a new comedy called *Nobody Loves Me*. When the author took the play home for repairs, Nichols hied himself off to Vancouver for the summer to direct *The Importance of Being Earnest* and to play the Dauphin opposite Susan Kohner's Saint Joan. "That terrible summer! One day I had a fit—about Canada. I said 'Blow it up! We don't need it. We can get our ginger ale somewhere else.'"

Soon he was doing *Nobody Loves Me* on Broadway, except that now it was called *Barefoot in the Park*. It was a smash hit, and Mike Nichols was a director. "Here I am," he thought, "at home, the first thing I really like. It fits." And he realized he had always been "kind of directing. I used to nag Elaine about certain things. I used to scream about the lights a lot." Wasn't it an unsettling experience? "It was a settling experience. It was a very happy time discovering directing."

"Me Too": Soon everyone was talking about the Mike Nichols touch—everyone except Mike Nichols. "The great thing about Mike is that he cuts right through the nonsense," says Buck Henry, who is collaborating with him on the screenplays of his next two movies, *The Graduate* and *Catch-22*. He once asked me to tell him what *Virginia Woolf* is about. I said, 'Well, it's about reality and illusion and the kind of games people play to fill in gaps of emptiness.' I blubbered on until I was up to my neck in theory. When I was finished he said, 'It's about a man and a woman named George and Martha who invite a young couple over for drinks after a faculty party. They drink and talk and argue for ten to twelve hours, until you get to know them.'"

Nichols explains, "There's only one question the audience asks: Why are you telling me this? There has to be a good strong reason. If it's funny, that's a reason. If it's not funny, you better have a very strong other reason. The more clearly and specifically you answer this question, the more you've done your job. Whether it's poetic theater, stylistic theater, musical theater, naturalistic theater, the aim is always, *in a way*, to imitate life believably, to make the people in the audience say, me too, I know that."

Fun: Nichols is slavish about detail. In rehearsal, his most vehement criticism is "too general!" He works over a play, line by line, gesture by gesture, always in the hope of finding one new thing. In preparing the Adam and Eve episode in *The Apple Tree*, one day he asked Alan Alda, as Adam, to be a doctor, and Barbara Harris, as Eve, to be a flamenco dancer. "We improvised," says Miss Harris, "and we had fun, and then went back to the scene. It helped free us from the importance of the scene."

The sensitive, mercurial Miss Harris appreciates the fact that Nichols lets her have "private things." On the other hand, Alan Arkin says, "When there was any hint of conflict or indecision in the air, he could smell it. He brings it out. None of this hiding in corners and saying, 'Why don't you try this? And don't tell the others.'" The truth is that Nichols improvises his method to suit the actor. "I love to talk with Alda," he says. "I love to go into corners with Barbara, and who wouldn't? I don't go home and make a chart about who likes secrets, who likes openness." During the tryout of *Barefoot*, "you couldn't see Robert Redford onstage." All you could see was his forceful costar, Elizabeth Ashley. "I told him that being onstage is like being in a battle and that the first thing you do is admit you're in a battle. That night you couldn't see Ashley. Altogether we finally balanced it out."

Does all this make Nichols kind of a psychotherapist? "It has nothing to do with their private life," he says. "It has more to do with my private life. Directing brings out the father in me—an edgy dad. Acting brings out the destructive baby in me. It's better to be worrying about other people than about myself." What this leads to is a kind of mutual trust, which is why Nichols could tell Barbara Harris one day, "That was the worst performance I have ever seen on any stage in the world," and two days later, "That was the best performance I've ever seen on any stage in the world." As Barbara says, "I knew that somewhere in the middle, I was all right."

Cucumber: Mostly Nichols is a collaborator, an audience, an appreciator, but unlike many directors he doesn't rely simply on his own judgment. Before he makes up his mind, he tries everything, listens to everybody. "I don't know what I do," he says. Alan Arkin recalls that when he first began working on *Luv*, Nichols seemed unconcerned. "I was going through the torture of the damned, and he was as calm as a cucumber." Getting madder and madder, Arkin finally stopped Nichols after the rehearsal and said, "Why are you uninvolved in this experience?" But, adds Arkin, "he *was* involved. He has a way of speaking that avoids passion but he feels very deeply." John Kenneth Galbraith recalls watching *The Odd Couple* with him. "I was enormously struck by Mike's capacity to look at a play as though it were nothing he'd had anything to do with himself, to give a cold-blooded analysis of the strengths and weaknesses of the play and its direction. I never knew anyone else in the theater who didn't try to pretend that every catastrophic weakness was in reality a strength."

Nichols's critics argue that all he has done up to now is to make the commercial more entertaining—and more commercial. Robert Brustein thinks that "Nichols is becoming famous directing precisely the kind of spineless comedies and boneless musicals that he once would have satirized." But Susan Sontag, who knew him at the University of Chicago, says the question is "How ambitious is Mike willing to be? He's one of the few people in this country who could direct Brecht properly." Nichols says he would like to try his hand at such favorites of his as Chekhov, Pinter, and Beckett, and in any case he has already proven that he is not one to be pegged by his past or by anyone's prejudgment about his future. Perhaps somewhere there is the real Mike Nichols playwright, for whom the Mike Nichols touch would be the touch of life. Or perhaps, as the brilliantly witty film sequences in *The Apple Tree* suggests, movies will turn out to be the medium that releases his best talents and energies.

In any case, the plush-lined pressures of success have left Nichols with a somewhat startled look, like a little boy suddenly transformed into a giant. But he can handle the pressure, and he loves the plush. "He says he can live on a loaf of bread," says one friend, "but he needs a staff of ten to keep the loaf of bread." He wants to be liked, and he is, by people in and out of show business. He is courted by socialites and the new class of well-heeled, well-placed, well-buffed culture buffs. His company manners are impeccable, and his style is enormous. He is close to many people, most of whom he doesn't see often. Alan Arkin calls their relationship "intimacy without proximity."

"Mike wants to make it in all kinds of worlds," says one friend. "There's a dichotomy in him about wanting to be known in Jackie Kennedy's world, and a fear that it would take his energy away from something else. The danger of being fashionable bugs him." Nichols loves his lavish apartment, but says he would not feel "too terrible" if it burned down. "If your life is ruled by things, you become a thing," he insists. "The only way to save yourself is passion. Madness, maybe." Typically he greets the morning, "Thank you, God, for Another Perfect Day," uttered in a tone of absolute despair.

Protector: All ambiguities intact, Nichols sat recently for questions. What would he like that he doesn't have? "A St. Bernard and Jane Fonda. But they're not practical in the city." Then he announced, "Movies are dreams. Plays are public events. That's a distinction, not a value judgement."

He had just seen François Truffaut's *Fahrenheit 451.* "I think it's a great picture, and it has absolutely awful things in it. After I saw it, I saw to myself, forget the movies. Some friends said, you're crazy, it's not half the picture *Virginia Woolf* is. I know they're wrong. But I'll try again. It's not modesty. I know what I've done. I think I served Edward Albee and Elizabeth Taylor and Richard Burton well, and did what I set out to do, which was to let *Virginia Woolf* take place on screen. I did not intrude myself terribly. I protected Albee's idea from misunderstanding, slurring, or twisting.

"It's very depressing to be described as a Success, a Maker of Hits. Not to mention names, but some people have worked for twenty years in the theater on the strength of one hit. Who wants to be a Success? That's an odd profession. I didn't know how great a man Fellini was until *Giulietta.* A beautiful failure!" When *Virginia Woolf* opened in Hollywood, "it got terrifying raves—'Not since *Citizen Kane.*' That panicked and depressed me. When it was brought into the realm of reality with some quibbles and cavils and strong reservations, I felt good. I could breathe again."

As for his future: "I'm forming a theater. I want to start a repertory company from the other end, not with a building, but with people." As people he would like in his theater, he lists Barbara Harris, Alan Arkin, Alan Alda, Robert Redford, Ulu Grosbard, Paul Sills, Elaine May, Maureen Stapleton, Larry Blyden, Sandy Dennis. Obviously many have commitments, but hopefully most will react as Barbara Harris does: "Yes," she says, without reservations.

Projects: Nichols himself is booked up through early 1968. From now until late spring he will be busy working on his movie of Charles Webb's novel *The Graduate,* which, he says, "will be partly improvised." In the fall he will probably revive Lillian Hellman's *The Little Foxes* on Broadway. And in January 1968, he is scheduled to begin filming Joseph Heller's comic masterpiece, *Catch-22,* with Alan Arkin playing that heroic coward Yossarian, and many of Nichols's favorite actors (Anthony Perkins, Jack Lemmon, Henry Fonda) probably playing supporting roles.

Before going to Hollywood for *The Graduate,* Nichols flew to Berlin to see the Berliner Ensemble "because I hear that it's the greatest theater in the world." It was his first trip to Germany since he had fled in 1939. He had to change planes in Frankfurt. "There was a sign for an exhibition of model airplanes. Admission, sixty pfennigs for adults, thirty pfennigs for children and cripples. I went into a coffee shop and asked for a cup of coffee and a glass of soda. The man said, 'It is forbidden to serve soda. It is strictly forbidden to serve soda without whiskey.'" In West Berlin, he visited his birthplace, but "it wasn't there. There was a small modern apartment house. Ours was an old house. It was gone."

A Beginning: Unnerved, he finally made it to East Berlin, where he saturated himself in the Berliner Ensemble. He saw *Coriolanus, Schweik in the Second World War, Arturo Ui,* marveled at the theater, the expansive stage, the realistic props, the low ticket prices, the hardworking actors. "They spend two hours a day in the gym. They perform seven nights a week." He mused over Brechtian theory, "which has nothing to do with theater as magic, rather with theater as bread. The theater is informed by one idea—from the usher to the last bow: theater is a dialogue between the playwright and the audience." His head full of Brecht, he flew back to New York, then to Jamaica, where sitting in the sun he thought about Nichols. "I feel good," he said. "I wouldn't change anything in my life. It's a beginning. Now we'll find out if I can do anything." He paused, and added in a burst of joy, "Wait! You're going to see such failures, you wouldn't believe it!"

Whatever Happened to Elaine May?

Thomas Thompson / 1967

If you should ask "Where is Mike Nichols?" the answer would come easily. He is in his triplex tower apartment high over Central Park West with all New York glowing at his feet. Jacqueline Kennedy and Leonard Bernstein come there to dine. Producers send scripts and contracts and large weekly checks there. Nichols is a director of such stature that if someone had the exclusive rights to the Second Coming, he couldn't get Nichols to commit to the project until late 1973.

But if the question is "Whatever became of Elaine May?" then it takes more time to tell. For a while recently the other half of what was once America's most brilliant satirical team was living out in Hollywood in an old and gloomy Normanesque hotel, a place favored by New York intellectuals who think that by staying there they are not "going Hollywood."

From her window Elaine could muse on a thirty-foot plastic image of a Las Vegas showgirl—in blue and red and flesh colors—revolving sensuously over the Sunset Strip. After a few weeks of tomblike solitude, Elaine felt she was beginning to like the statue and fled to a wildly modern apartment hotel on the Strip.

Here everything is like a movie set—all aluminum and orange and plastic—and here, she has discovered, is where the action is. "At night I get notes slipped under my door," Elaine has told a friend. "Notes like, 'Rhoda, come back, I love you.' And all night long I hear voices whispering, 'Bernice, is that you in there?'"

The studio car comes to fetch her early, at six-something, and she emerges blindly into a living room strewn with typing paper, as if a storm had blown in during the night. Elaine has been writing. Some of the papers bear fragments of an enchanting series of stories called *Jonathan's Foot*, extensions of bedtime stories she has invented for her own four daughters. Another work begins with a grim suicide note. Dominating everything in the room is an electric typewriter—the fountain from which all these papers have erupted.

In the studio car Elaine slumps back, her eyes half closed, hair in disarray, face blank. The limousine passes the Mocambo, once a glamorous nightclub where the big stars went, but now an open parking lot.

"Michael and I once played there," Elaine offers. "I remember one performance in which absolutely no one laughed. At the end they clapped heartily, but nobody laughed. I also remember there was a huge glass wall with tropical birds flying around inside. Every night during our performance, one of the birds would die. We would learn this because the next night the old wardrobe woman would come to me and say, 'Well, another bird died last night.'" The limousine reaches Columbia Studios. Women like Rita Hayworth and Kim Novak once swept through the gates here like empresses. Elaine is sometimes stopped and asked to show her credentials. She has worked here twice in six months, with star billing both times, but some of the telephone operators still do not know her name.

Elaine is not even sure what she is being paid. But in this, her second movie, a picture called *Luv* to be released this week, her name will get star billing with Jack Lemmon's and Peter Falk's. As a play *Luv* was directed by Mike Nichols, but he refused to expand it into a film. This worries Elaine. She wonders if Michael knows something she doesn't.

In her dressing trailer a legion of men and women descend on her—rolling, teasing, pulling, patting, padding, coloring. Their job is to make beautiful people, and Elaine is clearly annoyed by it all. She mutters as a wardrobe lady reaches routinely up her backside to straighten an errant hem. Someone compliments Elaine on how nice she looks, and indeed she does. From the earlier chaos has come a slender young woman, about thirty-four, with long brunette hair abetted by a fall, large hazel eyes, and serviceable cheekbones. "Thank you," she replies, lighting up a Dutch Schimmelpenninck cigar. "It's the makeup. Underneath all this is a truly plain person."

Everyone laughs. It is a moderately funny remark. But it is Elaine May who has uttered it in that famous voice, and so it becomes almost as funny as W. C. Fields threatening to slice Charlie McCarthy into Venetian blinds, or Jack Benny coming out onstage, folding his arms, and saying, "Well!" Some entertainers are on third base before they ever come to bat.

But there is no great warmth in the laughter. Hollywood is suspicious of smart ladies, especially smart New York ladies, and Elaine is both. Someone once asked Mike Nichols if there was any subject in which Elaine was deficient. "With the possible exception of grand opera, and I am not even positive on that," answered Nichols, "there is none." Well, Hollywood won't have that. When Marilyn Monroe revealed that she was reading *The Brothers Karamazov* and wanted to play Grushenka, the trade reaction was "What a smart press agent!" Elaine read Dostoyevsky when she was seventeen and doesn't even have a press agent, so Hollywood is very uncertain about her.

The dressing trailer next to hers belongs to Jack Lemmon. When he was casting *Luv* last year, producer Martin Manulis offered Lemmon a long list of potential leading women. One name he tossed in like a man who lights a firecracker and runs away with his fingers stuck in his ears. "What about Elaine May?" he said softly and carefully. As Manulis tells it now, "Jack went white. Absolutely ashen. He was silent for a few moments and I thought maybe I'd offended him."

Not so.

"My God," breathed Lemmon, "she's perfect! Can we get her?"

At that point, about a year ago, Elaine's telephone was not exactly as busy as Liz Taylor's. In fact, after the team of Nichols and May broke up amicably in 1961—with their smash hit *An Evening with Mike Nichols and Elaine May* still playing to full Broadway houses—she had sunk almost out of sight. Mike had risen swiftly to the top of the show-business world through his direction of an unbroken string of hits—*The Knack*, *Barefoot in the Park*, *Luv*, *The Odd Couple*, and *The Apple Tree* on and Off Broadway and *Who's Afraid of Virginia Woolf?* for films. Elaine's career since then had been mostly a disaster. But it had been Elaine who wanted to close the show. "She told me she was tired of what we had been doing for so many years. It was always a rule between us that we would respect the other's wishes," said Nichols afterward.

Acting came first in the chronology of Elaine May. Her father was a famous Jewish actor named Jack Berlin, who took his troupe all over America doing Yiddish plays. Elaine was born in Philadelphia in 1932 and—naturally—made her stage debut in her father's arms. At the age of three she was doing toddler roles. By the time she was ten she had been in more than fifty schools, some for only a few weeks at a time. "I kept learning that Mesopotamia was the first city," she says. "I also frequently learned the multiplication tables up to five."

At night she was onstage with her father, playing the part of a little boy called Bennie in an enormously tragic drama that they performed all over the US. But at the age of eleven she had to give it up. "I developed breasts, and our people do not believe in breast binding."

That same year her father died, and Mrs. Berlin took her to Los Angeles. When she was fifteen, Elaine quit school. At sixteen she married a man named Marvin May, whose occupation in life was building models of ships and airplanes. After one child—a daughter, Jeannie—the marriage broke up. There followed a few years of odd jobs—private detective (in which she sat at a bar and watched the bartender as he rang up purchases on the cash register, to see if he was honest); roofing salesman ("I don't reveal any details because the FHA may still be after me")—and studying acting and reading classical literature. She wanted to go to college, but none in California would take her without a high school diploma. Hearing that the University of Chicago did not require one, Elaine—with seven dollars—hitchhiked across the country.

At the university, Elaine drifted happily in and out of classes without ever formally enrolling, sitting at the back and leaping up occasionally to inform an instructor that he was wrong. And she went to student dramatic productions. The leading actor one night was Mike Nichols. And as he tells it now: "I sensed her out there. In a dark brown trench coat, hostile. I was terrible and she knew it. The next day we got an incredibly good review from one of the critics and I was showing it to a friend. Elaine walked by, saw the clipping and said, loudly, 'Ha!'"

They met again—accidentally—a few months later in the waiting room of the Illinois Central Railroad station. Mike, assuming the manner of a foreign spy, walked up to her and said, "May I seeet down, plis?" Elaine picked up promptly in best Marlene Dietrich: "If you weesh." And then, first to the puzzlement and then to the delight of bystanders, they proceeded to develop a lengthy, completely impromptu drama of espionage and intrigue. It later became one of their most famous routines.

"People had always told me I should meet Elaine," Mike remembers. "It was said that she and I had the cruelest tongues on the campus." Sweetly enough, however, Elaine began plying Mike with odd hamburgers of her own devising—meat, catsup, and cream cheese—and encouraging his talent for acting. "She was the only one who had any faith in me," says Mike. "I remember at the time the campus impression was that Elaine was really dangerous. She could, God knows, defend herself when attacked. But her toughness was an illusion."

They opened as a team in Chicago in 1954, improvising skits as part of a performing group known as the Compass Players. As they got more confident, they would ask the audience to tell them what to act out. (This kind of improvisation-on-demand became a Nichols-May trademark.) People found the team so hilarious that in 1957 Mike and Elaine took their act to New York.

A TV appearance on *Omnibus* shot them to national fame and made their routines part of comic folklore: the desperate man pleading with a series of telephone operators to return his last dime; the mother telephoning her rocket-scientist son and reducing him to sniveling tears ("Mama, let me tell you, I feel awful." "Oh God, Sonny, if I could only believe that, I'd be the happiest mother in the world!"); the two teenagers in the back seat of a car trying to be passionate and manage cigarettes at the same time.

They were the rarest of comedians. They had both "snob and mob appeal," as one writer put it. "Mike structured the material for the skits," says Harvey Medlinsky, an old friend and stage manager. But Elaine, friends say, came up with most of the ideas. They did not get married, in spite of the press's efforts to drum up an affair or uncover one. "One radio man was interviewing us once," recalls Elaine, "and he said to me, 'Are you and Mike married?' I said, 'No.' He wasn't paying much attention and he said to Mike, 'Fine, how long have you been married?' Mike said, 'But we're not.'

The radio man, who was fooling with his tape recorder by this time, said, 'Wonderful! How many children have you got, Elaine?' I gave up and said, 'Four!'"

But their relationship was probably closer than that of many a husband and wife. They put enormous personal trust in one another and each could see, with frightening clarity, into the other's mind—being able mutually to spot the madnesses and excesses of the world and communicate them to each other.

Audiences everywhere found them wildly funny. They often broke each other up onstage, as on the night when Elaine was improvising in the style of William Faulkner: "And there she was, feeling the armpits—glad that they were there." And if they suddenly lost a guaranteed laugh in one of their set sketches, a laugh that had been there for months, they would sit down diligently and trace back to the night they lost it, discovering eventually that a new inflection, say, or an added shrug of the shoulder had spoiled the joke.

Improvisation became an art to them, a deceptively simple one. "It's nothing more than quickly creating a situation between two people," Elaine would explain, "and throwing up some kind of problem for one of them. Take, for example, a man going to get his laundry. If he gets it right away, then the event is over. But if the laundry isn't ready, then the situation is extended. And if the man needs his laundry desperately to go on a trip, you can go on a step further."

Mike and Elaine took this art to recording studios and spent days at a time dreaming up hundreds of ten-second improvisations for use in advertisements by beer companies. Elaine was a housewife and Mike, her husband, comes home:

ELAINE: I have something to tell you, darling.
MIKE: Fine, darling, can I have a beer, please?
ELAINE: Of course, darling, here is a glass of cold, extra-dry, sparkling [Jax Beer].
MIKE: Thank you.
ELAINE: You're welcome. Phyllis shaved the dog today.

The commercials were fun, and genuine improvisations, since Mike and Elaine were allowed to say whatever came off the top of their heads. But to Elaine all of what they were doing—the commercials, their solidly booked show, the guest shots on TV, everything—left her somehow unsatisfied. "I told Mike there was no way we could top ourselves," says Elaine. Besides, she thought privately, Kennedy's election had changed the country's mood and the bland and foolish targets at which they had been slashing with such precision no longer really existed.

And so, on July 1, 1961, they closed their show and moved their separate ways.

"Elaine wanted to write," says Nichols. "My main image of her is Elaine coming into a room with papers falling out of her arms and trailing behind her." Elaine's first solo effort as a playwright was a very short one-act play called *Not Enough Rope*. Its opening Off Broadway in March 1962, on a bill with two other one-acters by new writers, brought the first-string critics downtown to see what the famous comedienne had wrought.

It turned out to be not a play at all but a fragment of a play, a typical Nichols-May skit. A girl bounces across the hall of her rooming house, greets the man who has just moved in, and says effusively, "Hi there, I'm your neighbor. I wonder if I could borrow some rope." She wants to hang herself but botches the job when all her new neighbor can offer is a length of twine. The play flopped.

It went back into Elaine's enormous storehouse of papers—unfinished plays, scenes, poems, scenarios, everything but novels—to be revised. Elaine is constantly revising her works—perhaps because she would prefer not to let them out—attacking them with a fierce black pencil until no one but she could possibly decipher them.

Out of these odds and ends came a play she had written for television and then expanded into a comedy for Broadway. The central figure in *A Matter of Position* was a young market researcher who was insanely worried that people would not like him. Elaine asked Mike Nichols to star and he agreed. The theater world could not have been more anticipatory. What followed could be called a Tragedy in Three Acts, with an Epilogue:

ACT ONE

Time: October 1962. Place: The Walnut Street Theatre in Philadelphia.

At the first reading of the play Elaine is alarmed. Director Fred Coe does not seem to know the names of some of the characters or what they do in the play. Rehearsals go badly. Elaine lurks anxiously in the darkened theater, chain-smoking, rather like a mother watching through the glass of an operating amphitheater while her child undergoes surgery. She is convinced that Coe does not understand the play. She doesn't like some of the actors' performances. She even feels Mike is playing badly. On opening night in Philadelphia the first act goes so terribly that Elaine rushes out to the lobby and overhears people saying to each other, "Who can I warn to stay away from this one?"

ACT TWO

Coe and producer Arthur Cantor demand that Elaine cut the play drastically. "It's forty minutes too long," says Coe. "You can't have people streaming out of the theater at one in the morning." Elaine begs to get up onstage during rehearsals to work with the actors. She says she can get the time down that way.

Coe agrees, though ordinarily no author ever has that privilege. After a few days it is apparent that the experiment is not working. Nightlong conferences, telephone calls. Elaine begs Mike to join her side. He is wedged between loyalty to Elaine and obedience to the director. Coe and producer Cantor, who have raised $125,000 for the play, make arbitrary cuts. Elaine blows up. The play folds after seventeen performances.

ACT III

ELAINE: I usually believe that anything can be fixed—even terminal cancer, if they try. But somewhere in Philadelphia, I realized I had absolutely nothing to say about the making of my play. They didn't even want me in the theater. Cuts and revisions were made until they changed the material and emasculated the play. A play is more than a formula of words and jokes and scenes. Somewhere it must have something to do with the realities of human behavior.

NICHOLS: It was not a pleasant experience. I behaved very badly toward Elaine.

COE: Elaine is a very talented girl. Elaine is a very difficult girl. I have found that the two are synonymous.

EPILOGUE

Elaine's second marriage, to lyricist Sheldon Harnick, breaks up the same week her play folds, having lasted only two months. "The usual thing," she says. "We couldn't get along."

Embittered and hurt, even at Mike, who she felt had not stuck by her, Elaine snatched her play from the ruins and began rewriting it.

But in the spring of 1962, a Hollywood columnist reported: "Stepping off the plane from New York this morning will be that sharp and shining comedienne Elaine May, here to write the screenplay of *The Loved One*, Evelyn Waugh's hilarious comedy about a supercemetery."

On the basis of a superb skit she and Mike had done on the high cost of dying, Elaine had been commissioned by the prospective producers of *The Loved One* to wring something filmable out of Waugh's novella. Her first move was to go to Forest Lawn cemetery, with coproducer John Calley posing as her husband who had just lost his father. "It was rather like an enormous supermarket of death," Elaine said later. "You could wander in and out of various departments. In one section they wanted to sell us a special plot—when John's mother passed away, she could be buried on top of his father, locked away for eternity."

The script Elaine turned in is still talked about in Hollywood. Elizabeth Taylor read it and told Mike Nichols, "Richard and I think it's the best script we ever saw. We want to do the picture." But Tony Richardson, who came on as director, wanted to expand the picture into a satire on Los Angeles cultism. Elaine lost interest and, by mutual consent, withdrew. Terry Southern and Christopher Isherwood wrote a new script. The Burtons lost interest. The movie was a disaster.

With her own score thus nothing-for-three, Elaine next accepted the offer of producers Fryer, Carr, and Harris, who had a novel idea. Why not a Broadway musical made up of two separate one-act musicals? The first would be based on Fellini's old film, *Nights of Cabiria*. Elaine would write an original to conclude the evening.

But it did not turn out that way. The Fellini story could not be compressed into one act and the play Elaine had written—about a family of thieves—was dropped.

During these professionally miserable years Elaine had been undergoing analysis, and in 1963 she married a New York psychiatrist who was the father of three daughters. Becoming thus an instant mother to four girls (her daughter from her first marriage was now a teenager), she withdrew almost completely from show business to play—and play well—the new role of homemaker. The family moved into an enormous five-story brownstone near the Hudson River in Manhattan. From time to time, when she felt the household was running well, Elaine would descend into the basement of the brownstone for a little creativity.

"I arranged a place there," she says. "I would usually take two weeks to make sure that all the pencils were sharpened, that the pens had the right kind of points, that I had the perfect amount of three-hole notebook paper, good erasers, plenty of hot water, apples, and coffee. Then, rather than sitting down to write, I would rearrange furniture for days. Then I would make long lists of instructions like 'Don't bother mother under the penalty of death for anything.' Then, when I couldn't find anything else to do, I would start to write and immediately I would hear the kids yelling and I would run upstairs—spared."

Last winter, with things secure at home, Elaine sallied forth once more on her own—this time as an actress. She agreed to star in a Broadway play called *The Office*, with no less a person than Jerome Robbins as director. The producer elected to preview the play in New York rather than take it out of town. Midway through the first act at the first preview, Elaine—alone on the stage—for the first time in her professional life heard boos from an audience. She wasn't sure whether they were booing her or the play, although everyone later assured her the boos were not her fault.

Producer Ivor David Balding said, "Elaine was marvelous and brilliant in the part, but the audience was not expecting a serious play with Elaine in it." That was, in fact, exactly the trouble: *The Office* could not decide whether it was a comedy or a drama. Even the few funny moments—Elaine as an incompetent secretary sitting at a typewriter, elaborately punching one key and then furiously erasing—could not save it. Toward the end she was called upon to talk and to dance with a portrait that was hanging on the wall. "I never understood why I was supposed to do this," she says. The play closed after ten previews and was never exposed to the critics.

Last spring an unlikely shepherd led Elaine out of the valley of professional darkness. Carl Reiner, the former New York comic who had migrated to Hollywood and become very big out there as a writer, actor, and producer of such TV series as *The Dick Van Dyke Show*, was then cowriting the movie version of his semiautobiographical Broadway play *Enter Laughing*. And he was stuck. A principal female role—that of a man-trap actress in a gyp-joint acting company in New York of the twenties—was not well written. "We had tried to make the dame a little more than two-dimensional, but she didn't come out that way in the script," says Reiner. "We needed an actress who was bigger than life, who could make something out of it. I just sort of thought of Elaine right away."

Elaine had been offered movie roles before, but, as she puts it, "they were all female Tony Randall parts," and she turned them all down. But whether because Reiner was an especially good salesman or because she was so depressed by her fortunes in New York, Elaine traveled west last spring. "Elaine is going to suffer in Hollywood," said Mike Nichols at the time. "She must have complete control of a given situation. Out there she will be at the mercy of many people."

"Elaine didn't know a damn thing about making movies at first," says Reiner, "but she was deathly serious about learning. She stood around the set and soaked up everything. I had a little trouble getting through to her at first, because she talks in a funny kind of shorthand. You're walking down a path with her and all of a sudden she takes a right turn."

Elaine developed instant rapport with Reiner, partly because he encouraged her to improvise, make suggestions. "I think she's either the sexiest funny woman I ever saw or the funniest sexy woman," says Reiner. "She's got a great face—like Loretta Young—and I think, if she wanted, she could be a major movie star. But not in drama. She thinks only in curves."

Because *Enter Laughing*, to be released in August, was the first totally pleasant show-business experience she had had in years, Elaine next accepted the lead role in *Luv* at the same studio. This time she faced a young British director, Clive Donner, who had made the pop-op film *What's New, Pussycat?* Hardly had the film begun before it seemed that Mike Nichols's prediction would come true. Elaine decided that she and Peter Falk had not played an important scene properly. She asked to have it reshot. The producer refused, as did Donner. Elaine insisted. Members of the production staff began going to Elaine's dressing trailer between takes to reassure her that the scene had been played well.

Elaine was not to be comforted. She offered to pay for the retake herself. One of the staff suggested that Elaine was behaving childishly. "We all go down the drain together," she retorted. "This is a great way to get a comedy—fill everyone with an enormous sense of rage." Eventually the scene was reshot, removing the small crisis, but whether this was done simply to pacify Elaine or because from an artistic viewpoint the film needed it, no one connected with the production was saying. From then on the picture went smoothly, and both leading man Lemmon and director Donner were full of praise for Elaine when it was done.

"She's the finest actress I've ever worked with," says Lemmon flatly, "and I've never expressed an opinion about a leading lady before. I've had opinions, but I've never expressed them. I think Elaine is touched with genius, like Judy Holliday. She approaches a scene like a director and a writer, not like an actor, and she can go so deep so fast on a scene, and her mind works at such great speed, that it's difficult for her to communicate with other actors."

Lemmon says that he watched with wonder as Elaine developed her character. "She put a 10 percent coating on top of her role, another level of 'comedy by attitude.' She has one of the greatest pusses of all time, and some of our finest footage is where she's not saying a word but just reacting. It was a marvelous experience to act *with* somebody and not *at* somebody. It's damn rare out here."

"The devastating thing about Elaine," says Donner, "is that she's better at everything—writing, acting, directing—than almost anyone else I know. Her range in the movies is wide. But not so wide that you could put her in, say, a western. Essentially she's a product of our urban, bright, liberal world. Within that typing, she could play anything."

Now that the film is finished, Elaine has packed up her manuscripts, her slight wardrobe, asked the producer "Can I buy my wig, at cost?" (he is considering it), and returned to New York. She feels as if she has just eaten an enormous Chinese dinner and is still hungry. "I have no earthly idea how the film will turn out," she says. "It's up to them now." She makes "them" sound like all the villains of the world. She didn't even want to talk about the film to reporters, refused interviews, and told the *New York Times* she would interview herself for publication, using a fictitious name as the inquiring reporter. (The story appeared under the byline Kevin M. Johnson in the Sunday *Times* for January 8.) To one reporter in Hollywood, she said, "Just say she's pretty in a funny, offhand sort of way and that her favorite color is puce."

It seems for Elaine a time for contemplation—whether to pursue a career in Hollywood or to return to writing, or somehow to attempt to do both, although there has never been a woman who was both a great actress and a great writer. Or could she find another Mike Nichols to relate to?

"I feel sad for Elaine," says a friend who knows her well. "She could sell out—write gag plays like Jean Kerr and make a fortune, and be on magazine covers like Mike Nichols. She could take pratfalls and be funnier than Lucille Ball. She could hole up somewhere and write tragedies blacker than Lillian Hellman's. Hell, she could teach philosophy at Radcliffe. She has so many things going for her that, in a curious sort of way, I don't think she'll ever be happy."

Elaine May Has a Thing on Not Talking to Press: Nonlinear Interview with Elaine May

Joyce Haber / 1968

From the *Los Angeles Times*, July 7, 1968.

Interviews, like almost everything else, ought to have a beginning, a middle, and end, with a line of logic running through the whole enterprise. Or so I used to believe. But then I met Elaine May.

Miss May is, among other things, a creature to delight Marshall McLuhan. Of course you know all about that sage's message. He holds that the linear, orderly progression of thought is a quaint convention of the past. After interviewing Elaine May, you are convinced that he is right. Miss May conveys a contagious impression of chaos—charming chaos, to be sure, but unsettling nevertheless.

My encounter with her occurred not long ago when she was briefly in town to discuss a forthcoming movie. To appreciate what follows you must allow me to set the scene. That morning I had risen at 6:00 a.m. Never mind the dreary domestic reasons: suffice it to say that this was about five hours earlier than I had wanted to get up.

Although Miss May has a thing about not seeing journalists (rather than grant an interview to the *New York Times*, she wrote one herself, and very well, too), she was prevailed upon to receive me. The place: producer Hillard Elkins's house in Coldwater Canyon. The time: 10:30 a.m. I arrive at the appointed hour. Miss May is still asleep. So am I, but manage to conceal the fact. After twenty minutes, Miss May wanders in, dazedly, barefoot, wearing a mustard-colored wool knit hostess gown like a hair shirt. She directs her thin, sharp features in my general direction and speaks through a yawn. "I arrived here yesterday and Mr. Elkins had arranged all my appointments," she says. "I feel like the Pope, Miss Springer."

My name is not Springer, but I let that pass for the present. She is obviously suffering from the morning light. When she learns that I got up at six, she is wholly sympathetic.

We discuss day people versus night people and determine that we are both night people married to day people. This makes us sisters under the skin—that pale, night-people skin—but she still calls me Miss Springer.

I decide I had better clear that up after all. It turns out that she is thinking about a press agent named John Springer. That is very odd, because he's not *her* press agent, nor was it even his—Springer's—Hollywood representative who helped arrange this interview. It was David Horowitz, who represents some people called Solters and Sabinson.

Horowitz is, in fact, at my side now. Miss May fixes him. "How did you get here, anyway? Or Miss Haber." (She has it right!) "You're not my press agent are you? I don't have a press agent." Horowitz mumbles that she's correct, he doesn't know why he's here, he apologizes for existing: he simply felt that we two girls should meet.

"Oh, I'm having a fine time with Miss Haber," she remarks. "Miss Haber and I are mutually unconscious and we are doing fine together."

Why doesn't she like to give interviews? "Because, if I don't like the interviewer, I become not so much hostile as sullen and childish. And if I *do* like the interviewer, I read the story and feel personally betrayed by what he's said."

Since this is a nonlinear or McLuhan interview, here is as good (or bad) a place as any to pause and bring you up to date on Elaine May's recent activities. She was, of course, until a few years ago, Mike Nichols's comedy partner, and together they constituted the most brilliant satirical team in memory. Since they broke up the act, Mike Nichols has become a showbiz magnate, while Elaine May has had (it must be faced) a string of failures. Obsessed by a desire to write, she did one play that closed out of town, and tried a couple of movie scripts that didn't work out. She also appeared in a disastrous black comedy by someone else, and was her inimitable self in two forgettable movies, Enter Laughing *and* Luv. *Altogether, not very encouraging for a girl of immense talent.*

End of background. Let us return to the conversation. The phone in the Elkins house keeps ringing, so Elaine May is off on the sins of the telephone company and public utilities in general. "I don't know about here," she says, "but something has snapped with the phone company in New York. You can call for an extension and the man comes to take out your phone. The man arrived, I said, 'I want an extension,' and he said, pointing to this paper in his hand, 'I have this order to take out your phone, lady!'

"Con Ed is impossible. The phone company at least you can argue with or make them nervous or they lose their cool or something. But Con Edison you can't get to. We had this six-floor brownstone and we moved because once you got downstairs it was like you couldn't get back up. So we moved across the street to an apartment. We hadn't lived in the brownstone for a month, but we kept getting this electric bill for seventy-five dollars. They kept saying, 'We have a yearly average.' I kept saying, 'But I've moved. There's no one there . . .'"

Where is her apartment? At Riverside Drive and Eighty-First Street in Manhattan. The household includes a dog, "a platonic mutt, the descendant of all of them who, when you go to an island like Jamaica, bark at your car. Its name is Bernice. My daughter brought it home from the street. She said it was being kicked. Now I know why. But who can throw out a dog named Bernice?"

Background time again. The daughter mentioned in the preceding passage is her daughter by her first marriage to a man named Marvin May, about whose occupation she is vague. She married him at sixteen, and it didn't last long. Afterwards Elaine worked at some odd jobs, including private eye and roofing salesman (if you believe that, you'll believe anything), then she moved on to the University of Chicago, where she met Nichols. Her second husband was Sheldon Harnick, the lyricist. At present she is married to a psychoanalyst. She says: "Why don't you just say I'm married to a doctor? It'll make my mother happy. . . . A psychiatrist is like a priest. If you mention him it will take three of his patients four years longer to get well."

What is she up to at the moment? Well, she is rewriting the play that closed out of town. It's called *A Matter of Position* and is to be done again in stock this summer. Will she bring it to Broadway? "Oh, no, not I. If it works, then someone else will bring it in, I suppose. I just want to see it—like doing it in your living room. And see if people throw things this time."

What else? "To tell you the truth, I don't know what I'm doing. Mr. Elkins became my personal manager a few hours ago."

Elkins is the producer in whose house all this is taking place, remember? He wants her to do a screenplay adaptation for Paramount of a novel that was notorious a few years ago, *The Hundred Dollar Misunderstanding*. She is a little baffled about how to do it, because "I think in the whole book there are only three pages where there is no sexual activity." She has also written a screenplay called *A New Leaf*, which she will direct and in which she will star.

ELKINS: "Basically, in feeling, it's an Italian comedy done in English style set in
America."
MAY: "Is *that* what you're telling people? It's basically this simple comedy, this teeny-
tweeny comedy."
ELKINS: "I've sold it to three studios, don't stop me."
MAY: "You didn't have to tell Miss Springer that. She's a friend."

Springer again! This time she is flustered and apologizes by claiming that she *never* gets names right. "Arthur Penn, the director, has a little girl named Molly whom I call Becky. I don't think she's even offended anymore. It's like a mark of schizophrenia . . . cortical damage . . ." The voice trails off.

In a nonlinear, nonchronological way, it seems useful at this point to bring up the fact that Miss May is the daughter of a well-known Yiddish actor, Jack Berlin, with whom she toured all over America when she was a child. Most frequently she played a little boy named Bennie, but she had to quit at eleven because as she has remarked, "Our people don't believe in breast binding." She is now thirty-six.

Old enough, Elkins obviously feels, to accept some direction. Clearly, he is trying to organize Elaine May. Should Elaine May be organized? It's a sort of existential question, like, should a writer be analyzed? Or will he lose his talent along with his neuroses? I don't think Miss May thinks she ought to be organized, and I don't think so, either. "In life, you don't decide for yourself what you'll do," she says. "It just happens. It's all Kafkaesque."

Sipping coffee desperately, she is still worried about the business of being interviewed. "Years ago in an interview this lady was having terrible trouble thinking of questions. She said, 'What is the most important thing in your life?' and I said, 'Grooming.' Can you imagine? Me? Grooming? (Wiggling her bare toes.) The poor dear lady believed it. She started taking notes like crazy. I went on for half an hour about putting lemon juice on my elbows."

The worst kind of interviews, Elaine May thinks, is a tape-recorder interview. "Sometimes they put the mike right in front of your mouth—and you lick it." Anyway, she adds, "make me sound literate and highly intelligent, with sparkle."

When I woke up later that day, at around 3:00 p.m., I reviewed our conversation and decided that part of the time, Elaine May had been putting me on, in a sleepy, half-conscious, friendly way. I also decided that with her, the line between put-on and reality is blessedly vague. Also that she is literate, highly intelligent, and full of sparkle.

She has a nonlinear kind of genius which will find its great and proper outlet some day—take it from Miss Springer.

It Depends on How You Look at It

Barry Day / 1968

From *Films and Filming* 15, no. 2 (November 1968): 4–8.

The Graduate made Mike Nichols. After only two pictures he has become the world's highest paid film director. Here he explains to Barry Day how he made *The Graduate*.

Mike Nichols: I find it very hard to divide anybody up into generations. I would say if I were part of a generation, it must have been the shortest generation in the world. I'm not able to divide things into generations. I know different kinds of *people*.

It seems to me that categorization probably starts with the press. Groups are made that never existed; the "angry young men," the "new comedians," the "new generation of directors," and it's about as artificial as "swinging London," according to *Time* magazine. If you read *Time* magazine about swinging London, you expect people to be making it in the streets, but it's good, gray London as it always was with a small number of people in mod clothes. In the same way, there are people like Renoir and various other directors that did a great many things that people are doing now that just weren't labeled.

Barry Day: A kind of media "packaging," you think?
Nichols: Well, I think it does come from magazines. They have to give names to things in order to have a hook to write about them and as soon as you've given a hook, you're missing some of the truth.

Day: Whose work do you admire?
Nichols: I admire Fellini, not only because of his craft, but because of the man he is and because of his vitality and joy in life. He and his films are exactly the same, which I think is the best thing possible for an artist and he's one of the few artists there have been in film. When I met him for the first time recently, we didn't talk about film, we talked about politics and women and various other things. He sees the world very clearly and at the end of talking about it for a while, he said: "You know, we're living

in a wonderful time." I don't know anybody else who could say that of our present world, and see it clearly and also mean it. So that interests me more than technique, because if the technique *and* the man *and* the idea are all the same, I think that's the best you can do.

Day: So technique is like learning a language and then using it to express something?
Nichols: Yes, it's like any language, it's quite simple, and I think film technique can be learned rather quickly, it's just a question of how lucidly it is used and how little it is used for its own sake. I think in any form, whether it's writing or music or film, the technique and idea should be indistinguishable from one another—if the technique expresses the moment, expresses the event, expresses what's happening and to whom it's happening—that's one of the most interesting decisions in making a movie. To whom is this particular thing happening?—If the technique expresses those things, then it serves and you should be unaware of it.

Day: But you would never consciously think, "Now that's an interesting technique; I hope I can use it sometime"?
Nichols: No, I think something somewhat different happens. For instance, there's a dazzling stroke in *Persona*. It's as arresting as when Truffaut froze the film for the first time . . . something nobody has been able to imitate because just doing it is not very interesting. But there's a stroke of that kind in *Persona* and what Bergman does is to do a scene on one person and then do it again on the other person—same words, a rather long speech. And it can't be imitated or repeated because it's what his whole film is built to . . . it's what his film is *about* and something happens at the end of it that is a result of this, but what you think—what I thought when I saw it was, "Of course, how simple . . . it's always been there. How interesting that no one has done it." But I don't think you really think: "I can use that," because it's like life. You know, you go through your life and you think "Today this happened and I learned that so I'll always know A," but it never comes up again. Next time you think, "Now I've learned B so if B ever comes up I'll know how to deal with B," and that doesn't come up again either. In my experience you usually come up against C or D the next day.

Day: How did you actually get into films?
Nichols: I started four years ago and I hadn't known that I wanted to, or was going to be a director. I was a performer with Elaine May and then when we stopped that— when that sort of ran out for us—and I directed a play, I then discovered that was what I'd been thinking about for many years . . . all the time I was studying acting and I was an unsuccessful actor and all the time Elaine and I were doing what we did, I realized with hindsight that I'd been thinking in terms of directing. Then I did some

plays and I found that I was very happy directing plays, but that movies were what I preferred to see. As with everybody my age, movies have been at least as much a part of my life as my own experience. My memories of movies are as real, as sharp, as my memories of my childhood and they're all mixed in together. So that making movies seemed to me the last magical, impossible thing to do and I let it be known that I wanted to direct. I was offered some movies that I wasn't interested in and then I found *The Graduate*. . . . Larry Turman brought me *The Graduate*. And I said yes, I wanted to do it and then *Virginia Woolf* came up, so I did that first.

Day: With *The Graduate* the "youth thing" is very evident in the United States. You're told constantly that half the population is under twenty-five . . . the "Generation Gap" . . . the pangs of growing up and so on. The subject is obviously of now and many people have already made films about it. What attracted you towards this subject?

Nichols: I had no awareness of, or concern with, any generation gap. I think what people forget when they talk about the generation gap is that everyone starts out as a baby, goes through childhood and adolescence, ends up as an adult, and dies. What interested me about *The Graduate* was an entirely different thing. I'm, to this day, startled and inarticulate when people consider it a picture about the generation gap. What interested me was the idea of people acquiring objects . . . that the objects then turn the people into objects and that's, as far as I was concerned, what was the core of *The Graduate* and that's what we thought about when we made it.

Day: Because people are so interested in this youth thing, they're reading a lot of that into it, aren't they?

Nichols: Yes, and a lot of it is there. It just seems to me that whatever is in the picture about living your life and making certain choices, applies to more than just people of a certain age. *The Graduate*, as far as I could make it, is about my own life also and I'm thirty-six. I said that to some college students when they asked, "What is *your* relationship to *The Graduate*?" and I said, "Well, you know what Flaubert said," and the student said, "About *The Graduate*?" . . . so I gave up that tack.

I don't think Benjamin is "typical"—whatever that is. You see, that's where the generation thing seems to me a useless categorization, because I'm convinced that if you take any swinging member of the "new" generation, one of "the kids," and you take them quietly aside and say, "Tell me truthfully, do you feel like one of your generation?" he'll say, "Well, don't tell anybody . . . frankly, I really don't. I dress like them, you know, and I can do the dances and I turn on, but I feel different. They don't seem to notice though, so please don't let them know." Because I don't see how anybody can feel a member of anything that generalized. And if you do think of yourself as an instance of a generality, then you're in terrible trouble.

Day: So this is a film about somebody who is finding out about himself?

Nichols: I think it's somebody who is trying to become (1) active instead of passive and (2) not to be used as an object because of being surrounded by objects and things.

Day: And by people who are objects in that sense?

Nichols: Well, and to whom he is an object. He is a thing, he's a status symbol. He's somebody who has been well brought up, done well, but *now* what's he supposed to do? It's also, I guess, about trying to do the impossible anyway. It's not unlike working for McCarthy even though people say Humphrey has all the delegates. What do you do then? Do you stay at home and say "Damn it!"? Maybe you try anyway. The picture is about trying even though it's hopeless.

Day: The scene that sticks in my mind is where, as you say, he is used as a status symbol, in the party that the parents give for him where there are a lot of people around and one guest comes up to Benjamin with the line : "I want to say one word to you . . . 'Plastics.'"

Nichols: Well, a very interesting thing happened after the picture came out. Dustin is a gentle and nice boy—very shy—and after the picture was released he became quite celebrated. I would see him on television in various immensely vulgar TV shows being interviewed and having Israeli starlets flirting with him and having moronic interviewers asking unanswerable questions and he seemed exactly like the boy in the picture. There was no way to answer anything that was said to him; there was no way for him to *behave.*

It's a reality and it is, by the way, how I feel a great deal of the time in a group when meeting people or, worst of all, in a public situation like being interviewed, God help us, or anything like that. You feel there's no way to say what you're thinking because the situation is so alien to you and you to it.

Day: It must have been difficult to find someone who was mature enough to suggest the immaturity in a controlled kind of way?

Nichols: That's exactly what the problem was. I discovered that boys who really were that age couldn't get the distance to get rid of the self-pity and that Dustin could have an *attitude* towards that point in one's life—in all our lives. I'd run again and again into kids who were that age who thought that it was the most important and the only problem in the world. Well it's not and Dustin knew that.

Day: I was conscious when I saw the film that there seemed to be a lot of images which were suggesting he was out of his depth . . . the fish in the tank . . . the people by the pool . . . Benjamin floating on the pool or skin diving. How deliberate is that?

Nichols: Very deliberate. I never cared whether it was perceptible. In fact, ideally it wouldn't be perceptible, but the image of the experience was meant to be being cut off from people by glass, being underwater.

Day: There's the phone booth and the bar where he meets Mrs. Robinson . . . the church . . .

Nichols: Mainly it came out of the experience of living in California because one of the problems we had in the picture that Dick Sylbert, the art director, and I talked about for months was this, that if we designed—I'm tempted to say a mise-en-scène, but I'll control myself—the surrounding that was accurate, what was to prevent it from looking like a Doris Day picture, because that's been seen in most Hollywood pictures for the last twenty years? So we went into what is the experience of living in Beverly Hills or a middle-class area of California and that seemed to me the main thing about it. There was glass and beyond the glass was greenery and you don't really know if it's real or not. And then that was also a metaphor for the feeling you get in a place like that; also at that point in your life when you have everything material that you want but you don't know what it's for.

Day: This comes out very clearly in the way that Anne Bancroft is going about this house . . . everything is there and she doesn't know what she wants.

Nichols: It seemed to me at the time that I knew quite a bit about the people, and had both known them and been them and she seemed to me someone who had made a poor choice knowingly. She said, "All right, screw it, I'll give up whatever that other thing is"—and whatever it is it's something between people, some personal experience of other people—in exchange for clothes, rings, and fur coats. It's the worst bargain of any bargain you can make. To exchange *seeming* something to other people for being it. That seems to me the great American danger we're all in, that we'll bargain away the experience of being alive for the appearance of it. California is like America in italics, like a parody of everything that's most dangerous to us.

Day: Everything could be made of plastic?

Nichols: Yes, but also that since appearances have become, or are so terribly important, the danger is that we'll say, "Well, maybe we're not enjoying it very much but to the neighbors it looks terrific."

Day: Coincidentally, Dick Lester has also dealt with this to an extent in *Petulia*, hasn't he?

Nichols: What I liked so much about *Petulia* was that it seemed to me it was about suffering in a time and place where there was no expression allowed for it. It seems to me a very Chekhovian picture. I kept thinking of Chekhov—that there are immense feelings under the words that are never expressed *in* the words and the environment doesn't permit an expression of the feelings. I think my favorite thing in *Petulia* is that scene where she's back with her husband and family in that horrifying bedroom, and she's practically like one of the dolls in the room. So that it is a great deal like Chekhov, that the contrast between the rigor, the stricture of the place and the feelings of the people in it is what causes the suffering. That's partly what we were concerned with in *The Graduate* and I think that's what's moving in *Petulia*.

Day: And the Christie part is also rather like Anne Bancroft. She is going to sell out for something—she's had her little fling and she's going to settle for what she had to begin with.
Nichols: Yes. Well, it's again that Chekhovian thing of—"Was the other thing real to begin with? What was it really . . . did they make *that* up?" It's what you feel after a passionate affair really is over . . . there's a moment where you feel, "How did I do all the things . . . what was I sitting by that phone for three hours for . . . who was that doing it?" When it's gone, it's gone.

Day: Getting back to *The Graduate*, with the character of Mrs. Robinson I had a slight feeling that one's sympathy is almost staying with her rather than going with Ben after their break.
Nichols: I think she is the most interesting person in the picture. She is the most *considerable* person. The moment that I decided that I wanted to do *The Graduate* was in reading the novel when Benjamin asks her . . . they've just had this conversation about art which she says she doesn't know anything about . . . and it's also in the novel when he says, "What was your major subject at school?" and she won't answer and finally she answers and says, "Art." That sort of clicked for me because that was when I realized or decided that I knew Mrs. Robinson. That she had *been* Benjamin—that she had been at the same point Benjamin is in the picture—and had come to where she is presently with full knowledge. She is a very intelligent and cynical woman. She knows what's happening to her.

Day: She can see that he will go through all the same things and very likely end up where she is?
Nichols: That's my opinion. Many people have decided something else. If it's really successful, you should be able to guess about a character in a film, much as you do about people in life. We're always saying "So-and-so will never marry so-and-so," and then they get married, but we don't know what's going to happen to people we know, or ourselves, and I don't *know* what's going to happen to the people in the picture. If I knew them—if they existed—my guess would be that Benjamin will become like his parents.

Day: There seems to be a deliberate change of pace somehow in the second half. Did you deliberately change the pace and let people off the hook? Benjamin becomes less of a person towards the end. Although the fight he is going through is still real, he's a different person.

Nichols: Well, the picture is entirely from Benjamin's point of view. Nothing happens that doesn't happen to him or through his eyes. It was meant to be the following things: First, that he comes home and is almost catatonic from this bombardment of *things*. He even says to Mrs. Robinson in their first scene . . . she says: "What's bothering you?" and he says, "Oh . . . just things, things in general." He goes into a kind of trance as one does from this out of a kind of self-destructive and also horny motive.

And then that whole montage of the swimming pool and hotel and the parents was meant to be the subjective experience of screwing somebody and when you're not you're thinking about it and when you are, you're worrying about people knowing about it and you don't really know where you are, when.

And then his next experience is meant to be finding someone with whom he can be himself, building it into the high, romantic hope that that is or seems when it happens to one, and going with it. Since it's from his point of view, it's extremely romantic; California changes, the country changes, the look changes, the music changes, the rhythm of the whole thing changes.

If you're cynical about that experience, as some of us are, you see it one way. I mean, Cyril Connolly said that love was a disease and that once you'd had the first shot of it you were immune forever. Well, if you're immune, you see Elaine and the whole of the second part of the picture as a *trap*, which I think is perfectly possible to see it as. If you're not immune, you see it as a possibility in life. I think both.

Day: But did you have any theories as to how color might help to tell the story?
Nichols: The main thing I knew was that I wanted the world to change when he fell in love with Elaine. So that, before Elaine, the picture has a kind of cold, glassy, plastic look—or is meant to. The long lenses and diffused shots (which I happen to think should be put on the shelf for the next fifty years anyway) don't come in until he has certain feelings for Elaine. They're meant to be an expression of him and Elaine.

Day: Was Anne Bancroft your first choice for the part?
Nichols: Yes and no. We discussed Jeanne Moreau and I discussed it with her because I wanted very much to work with her and then I realized—first there was a schedule difficulty—but also it became apparent that Mrs. Robinson had to be American or it was all over. To bring in a French actress would be old Europe and young America again. We'd had Anne Bancroft in mind all through that and then she was able to do it and I can't think of anybody else.

Day: You've made two films which, at first glance, appear very different. In a sense, I think they're both very romantic pictures because the people that are truly in love either get or get to keep each other. Do you have a romantic view of life when the chips are down?

Nichols: No, I don't think so. I don't think people get to keep each other.

Day: With your two characters in *Virginia Woolf* their relationship is so strong that other people will batter themselves to death on them but they will themselves stay together. They may hate, but they love as well.

Nichols: Yes, they stayed together. I think one can stay together as they stayed together, which is a kind of back-to-back-against-the-world staying together. But, one is after all then back to back. I think that's possible.

Day: A needing more than a loving, then?

Nichols: Well, both. Most of all a kind of . . . what I find moving about the people in *Virginia Woolf* is that they see each other clearly and that, vicious as they can be, they want, oddly enough, the best for each other. I think that is possible . . . I think the idea that once people have found each other you can end the picture and you know what happens from then on . . . this does not coincide with my view and this is not what the end of *The Graduate* was meant to be.

If there is anything I like in *The Graduate*, it's the last three minutes of it—sitting on the bus, stunned and very well aware that it's not the end of anything. They don't know what the hell to say to each other. It seems to be perfectly possible that in two more miles Elaine may say, "Oh, my God, I have no clothes." Many things are possible—it's not an end. Benjamin has many choices open to him, but people die and people leave each other and people calcify and one or all of those will happen to him.

I think the main thing was that it was worth the attempt. I had a teacher in college who was talking about a Greek tragedy and he said that all Greek tragedy—not that I'm making comparison—but that all Greek tragedy was about the fact that it was hopeless but that you give a cry anyway. It's not a cry of complaint, or pain or rage even . . . it's just a pure cry and that it's worth making it even though nothing comes of it.

Day: Can you say anything about *Catch-22* that you are now planning?

Nichols: I can't say very much about it because we haven't started it yet and I'm still thinking about it all the time and frightened of it as I am of everything until it's done. *Catch-22* is about dying. That's really all I know right now. It presents terrific technical problems—twenty-five bombers, sixty speaking parts, and so forth, but that doesn't worry me as much as finding the proper mode—to get the metaphor—what the experience is of either knowing or not knowing you're dying.

Day: What do you think has made this book such a "cult" book? *Catch-22* is like *Catcher in the Rye*, isn't it? It means a lot to people. What do you think it means?
Nichols: It's hard to know. I think it probably is a recognizable memory of what it's like to be in the war. People are always saying about it that it's a man's book, whatever that is. Well, if it is, it must be because men read it and say, "Well, yes—that's what I felt like."

I think it's something that happens with Vietnam and probably with any war, that it becomes an abstraction—some think, "Those aren't real people getting killed."

Day: Even if they are on television in color?
Nichols: So is everybody in color on television getting killed and people can possibly no longer distinguish between the ones that will rise again for next week's segment of the television series—and the Vietnamese who will not.

You know, when you're growing up you keep thinking when you get in a fight—one blow and you're down or the other guy is down. And then slowly as you grow older you accept that kind of movie fight that goes on for fifteen minutes and the whole bar is broken, all the mirrors are smashed, the chairs . . . I never understand why they're still conscious and, in the same way, I think from seeing it so much in films and television in some less than conscious way people—since death is very hard to hold in your mind altogether—people have literally, to some extent, forgotten that when you die, you're dead. All the tragedies we've had like Dr. King and the Kennedys . . . well, after a Kennedy is assassinated, we still see him on television and I don't think it necessarily penetrates to people that it's over at that moment. It seems, in the case of public figures, people we see on film and television—they seem to go on afterwards. I think it changes somewhat the idea of death and I think the only way to live your life is to know all the time that it's going to end.

Day: Have you any ambition to do an original screenplay of your own?
Nichols: Yes, I have. I don't think it could be entirely my own, because I'm not good at sitting in a room and making anything myself. I think it will come out of, say, me and Buck Henry or someone like that. It's the next thing I want to do after *Catch-22*. I know I will try it if I'm still around.

On Location with *Catch-22*

Nora Ephron / 1969

From Nora Ephron, *Wallflower at the Orgy* (New York: Viking Press, 1970), 63–179; previously published in slightly different form in the *New York Times*, March 16, 1969, under the title "Yossarian Is Alive and Well in the Mexican Desert." Reprinted by permission.

March 1969

It is a moment of intense concentration. Mike Nichols is sitting in a blue director's chair, his face contorted, his hands clenched, his eyes squeezed shut. He finally opens his mouth to speak. "Bladder," he says. "Whimsy. Dailies. Rumble. Barren. Crystal. Pastry."

"No," says Tony Perkins, who is seated next to him. "Not pastry."

"Strudel," says Nichols triumphantly. "Strudel. Pepsi. Cancer. Stopwatch . . ."

A film is being shot here. Not at the moment, of course. At the moment, the director of the film is playing a memory game with one of the actors while the crew figures out how to work a broken water machine that is holding up the shooting. The name of the film is *Catch-22*. It is budgeted at $11 million, is on location in the Mexican desert, and is based on Joseph Heller's best-selling World War II novel. "I've tried, as they say, to preserve the integrity of the novel," says screenwriter Buck Henry. "Don't print that unless you put after it: 'He said this with a glint in his eye and a twitch in his cheek and a kick in the groin.' Because if that line so much as looks as if I said it seriously, I'll kill you." Among the graffiti scrawled on the wall of the portable men's room on the set is one that reads, HELP SAVE JOE HELLER.

A film is being shot here—between memory games, word games, repartee, kibitzing, and general good cheer. *Catch-22*, the story of Captain John Yossarian and his ultimate refusal to fly any more bombing missions. The movie of the year. A film actors signed up for before they knew what parts they were playing or how much money they would get for their work. With Alan Arkin starring as Yossarian, and Orson Welles (General Dreedle), Martin Balsam (Colonel Cathcart), Dick Benjamin (Major Danby), Norman Fell (Sergeant Towser), Jack Gilford (Doc Daneeka), Tony Perkins (Chaplain Tappman), and Paula Prentiss (Nurse Duckett). Art Garfunkel, of Simon and Garfunkel, will make his acting debut as Captain Nately, "What I feel like here," said Seth Allen, a young actor in the film, "is a near great."

Whether *Catch-22* will be a masterpiece, merely a very funny film, or the first failure for Mike Nichols after those two smash-hit movies and seven hit plays is at this point almost an irrelevant question for the actors in it. What matters is that the film is a chance to work with Nichols, who, at thirty-seven, is the most successful director in America and probably the most popular actor's director in the world.

Says Orson Welles, "Nobody's in his league with actors." What's more, he is the one of a handful of American directors since Welles made *Citizen Kane* in 1941 who have had complete creative control over the final product—including the contractual right of final cut and the option of not showing his rushes to studio executives.

Nichols is too modest and far too intelligent not to realize the absurdity of being in this position after making two films and directing for only seven years. "Every time you get too much for what you've put in," he said, "you know it's going to come out of your ass later." But, for now, he is going about his business—wandering about the set, in stylish fatigue jacket and slender corduroy pants; offering Oreos and Oh Henrys to the crew; bringing his low-key techniques to his actors' assistance; and somehow managing to keep his macroproduction company happy and on schedule. *Catch-22* is to shoot in Mexico for four months, move to Los Angeles for four weeks of airplane-interior shots, and then to Rome until mid-June. After ten months of editing, it will be ready for release in mid-1970.

It has taken eight years to bring Heller's book to the shooting stage. In the interim, the novel, after a slow beginning and mixed reviews, has become a modern classic, with a Modern Library edition and two million paperback copies in print. The film property has passed from Columbia to Paramount / Filmways, from Richard Brooks (who did little or nothing with it for four years) to Mike Nichols, from Jack Lemmon (who originally wanted to play Yossarian) to Arkin, and from one unsuccessful treatment by Richard Quine to four drafts by Henry (whose previous film credits include *The Graduate* and *Candy*). It took Nichols, producer John Calley, and designer Richard Sylbert over a year just to find the ideal spot to build the island of Pianosa and its air base—largely because the logical locations in Italy, Sicily, Sardinia, and Corsica no longer look like Italy, Sicily, Sardinia, and Corsica did in 1944.

Casting began, with Nichols selecting a group of actors, all of whom look like ordinary people, to play fighter pilots, and with Frank Tallman, the stunt pilot, rounding up a group of authentic fighter pilots, all of whom look like movie stars, to fly the planes. Tallman also set to work locating and assembling a squadron of B-25s—eighteen of them, each purchased, repaired, and made skyworthy at an average cost of ten thousand dollars. (One of the planes, a wedding present from heiress

Barbara Hutton to playboy Porfirio Rubirosa, came complete with reclining seats, bed, and leather-paneled toilet.)

Sylbert and Calley finally found the location on the northwest coast of Mexico, twenty miles from the town of Guaymas, Sonora, the home of Guaymas shrimp and little else. The location was a flawless one photographically—with ocean flanking it on one side and mountains set just two miles behind—but it was reachable only by boat. It cost $180,000 to build the five-mile-long highway to the spot, and $250,000 more for the six-thousand-foot-long runway. Both construction jobs were undertaken, ecstatically, by the mayor of Guaymas, who just happens to own a contracting company. Seventy-five *peones* working with machetes cleared the one-mile-square site of cactus, brush, and rattlesnakes, leaving only mesquite trees, which resembled the small olive trees native to Italy. And Pianosa rose from the sand, with its tents, corrugated tin huts, mess hall, control tower, lister-bag setups, and piles of bombs stacked like supermarket oranges along the runway. War-beaten stone buildings were designed with collapsible walls, in preparation for the moment in *Catch-22* when Milo Minderbinder (played by Jon Voight) leads the men in a bombing raid on their own base.

The most critical problem Nichols and Henry faced in translating the book to cinematic terms was in finding a style for Heller's macabre comedy. "The book, and, as a result, the film, have to be somewhat dreamlike, not quite real—either something remembered, or a nightmare," said Nichols. "That's very hard to do with living actors, with pores and noses, because they're so definitely there. If you're making a film in which an officer says, 'You mean the enlisted men pray to the same God that we do?' and in which the men bomb their own base, you have to find a style that makes it clear, from the beginning, that such things can happen."

The solution was to make the story arise from a fever Yossarian develops after being stabbed in the side by Nately's whore; the film leaps back and forth from vaguely-remembered-horror to farce to better-remembered-horror. "The picture will be cut as if Yossarian's delirium were cutting it," Henry explained. The style has been further carried out in the set—which has a ghostly quality—and in Nichols's decision to send home two hundred extras after the first week of shooting, leaving only Yossarian and his friends to fill out the huge air base. In addition, David Watkin, the English cinematographer who shot the Richard Lester Beatles films, has lit *Catch-22* so that all the actors are in shadow and the background is burned out; the effect is of a subliminal limbo.

Like the novel, the film hangs on the notion of Catch-22, a masterpiece of muddled military logic. "Let me get this straight," says Yossarian to Doc Daneeka in the script. "In order to be grounded I have to be crazy. And I must be crazy to keep flying. But if I ask to be grounded—that means I'm not crazy anymore and I have to keep flying."

"You got it," says Doc Daneeka. "That's Catch-22."

As a multitude of reporters and critics have observed since the book was published in October 1961, *Catch-22* has almost become a primer for the thinking that has seemed to be guiding the war in Vietnam. At the same time, the predicament of Yossarian has become more relevant in the context of the antiwar movement in this country. "The interesting thing about the book," said Buck Henry, who despite his disclaimer has been quite faithful to the novel, "is the enormous power of prophecy Heller had. He was writing about a man who had finally decided to opt out and who in the end ends up in Sweden. That was a total absurdity when he wrote it, a really far-out kind of insanity. Well, it's come true."

That *Catch-22* is being made in an atmosphere of such good feeling is as much a part of the Nichols approach as any of the directing techniques he utilizes. "If you're on the set shooting," Nichols explained, "and you say, 'Let's do it again,' and there's one guy who rolls his eyes or turns away or groans, it sours it for everybody. John and Buck and I said, 'Let's see if for once we can have nobody like that—just people who like each other.' And it worked." Many of the cast members are old friends and about half have worked with Nichols before. They have been laughing ever since a chartered jet brought them from Los Angeles to Mexico on January 2 and landed them smack in the middle of the utterly barren, desolate desert. "Look at this," Bob Newhart said, as he stepped out of the plane. Everyone looked around at what looked like the end of the world. "Ten years ago I could have bought land here," said Newhart, "and look at it now."

When the film is between takes, the cast sits around and roars with laughter as Bob Newhart spins out a routine on night life in Guaymas (there is none) or Buck Henry and Tony Perkins improvise on the subject of free falling and parachute jumping:

PERKINS: "What about all this we hear about the free-fall mass?"
HENRY: "There are two free-fall masses."
PERKINS: "The eleven o'clock and the seven o'clock?"
HENRY: "No. In the fall of 1965 a town of thirteen hundred people in Nevada went up and made a fall."
PERKINS: "I was speaking of the free-fall mass, not the mass free fall."
HENRY: "The free-fall mass is where the falling priest throws the wafer and the parishioners jump out of the plane and dive for it. It's called diving for the wafer. That's where the expression comes from. Dive for the wafer, dig for the wine."
PERKINS: "What about this lady who jumped with her cats?"
HENRY: "Well, actually, that story was not reported accurately. There was a lady, but she jumped with her lawyer, whose name was Katz."

When the film is shooting, the director and crew stand behind the camera, biting their lips and gritting their teeth to keep from exploding with laughter during the take.

Nichols's snorts of appreciation affect the actors in about the same way the bowl of food did Pavlov's dogs. "I'm so overjoyed when he laughs," said Paula Prentiss, "that I don't even care that half the time I don't know what he's laughing at."

"You never get hung up if Mike is directing you," said Miss Prentiss's husband, Dick Benjamin. "If you're doing a scene you're not comfortable with, he senses it, and before it can get to be a problem for you, he gives you two or three specific things to do—like a piece of business or a new line or something. And you think, Oh, I get to do *that*. Like a kid who's been given a birthday present. Everything else sort of falls into place and you get your little goodies. And Mike talks in terms of that. He'll say, 'I've really got a present for so-and-so when he gets to Rome.' And he means he's got some wonderful shot, something to do, some way the actor will look that is just sensational. And you really take it as a present."

Sometimes Nichols will give an actor a short suggestion or line reading that will suddenly clarify the role. To Benjamin, who was playing a scene in which he was supposed to be terrified of Orson Welles's General Dreedle, Nichols—who was himself terrified of Orson Welles—said simply, "Watch me." To Austin Pendleton, who was confused as to how to play Welles's son-in-law, Colonel Moodus, Nichols gave a line reading that, said Pendleton, "gave me the key to the whole thing. I realized he wanted me to play the kind of person who says the most insulting things as if he's being terribly friendly." To Norman Fell, Nichols suggested playing Sergeant Towser as a military mammy; as a result, Fell delivers the most blood-curdling lines with a funny little smile on his face, as if he were talking about chicken and gravy and wonderful biscuits.

Occasionally, Nichols will add an especially intimate gift to the proceedings. One morning he was shooting a close-up of Buck Henry (who also appears in the film, as Colonel Korn) and Martin Balsam (Colonel Cathcart). Henry was to lean over and whisper to Balsam, "He's talking to you." Balsam was to pop to attention and deliver an answer. Nichols shot two takes of the scene and then called Henry over for a conference. "Let's do another," he said. Henry returned to position and the scene began again. "He's talking to you!" hissed Henry, and he leaned over and goosed Balsam. Balsam jumped, his eyes bugged out of his head, and he managed to deliver his line before losing his composure. The crew broke up. "Nichols Directs," said Henry, "—a Monograph on the Unusual Techniques of a Young American Director: 'Use three fingers,' he said to me."

On another occasion, Nichols was shooting a love scene between Arkin and Miss Prentiss (Nurse Duckett). The footage—of Yossarian's hand sliding up Duckett's leg—was fine, but Nichols had not been able to get the right vocal reaction from the actress. He called a take for sound only. And as Arkin began to slip his hand up Miss Prentiss's skirt, Nichols grabbed her from behind and plunked his hands onto her breasts. "I let out this great hoot," said Miss Prentiss, "which Mike was very happy with. Then I was so overcome with emotion I had to go into a corner and be alone. Whenever someone touches me, I'm in love with him for about eight hours."

"It's perfectly possible," Nichols conceded, "that we can have this great time now, making the film, and then have it not be a good picture. The two have nothing to do with each other. But then, none of us knows whether the picture is any good even long after it's finished, so you might as well be happy while it's going on. And when the actors break up and the crew is stuffing handkerchiefs into their mouths trying not to laugh at Dick Benjamin—or whoever it is—I love it. I love it now. Afterward, it's up for grabs anyway."

For the actors, at least, making an air-force film has turned out to be very much like being in the air force. Not when they are working: when they work, making *Catch-22* is like being at a party, a festival, a love-in. But because so many of the actors have small parts, they have a great deal of time to kill in a town where there is almost nothing to do. As a result, many of them spend their empty days discussing how many days of shooting each has to go. When they tire of kicking that subject around, they move on to other tried-and-true service talk. "I'll tell you what we do around here in our free time," said Alan Arkin. "We sit in the barracks out at the set with our muddy boots on and talk about women. That's what you do in the army, isn't it? Sit around in your muddy boots and talk about women? I don't know why we do it. Almost everyone here is with his wife or his girlfriend. But that's what we do."

They complain about the food in the mess hall—that is, the mess hall on the set, which doubles as a lunch commissary complete with regulation army trays. They complain about the living accommodations at the Playa de Cortés, Guaymas's somewhat unsatisfactory attempt at a luxury hotel. They complain about their isolation from the outside world. And they complain about the incredible difficulty of obtaining newspapers and placing long-distance calls. "We make bets on who's going to go insane," says Bob Newhart, "or has already gone insane. In fact, maybe we've all gone insane and we're all together and we don't know it and we'll go home and my wife will call Paramount and say, 'Listen, my husband is insane.' We have no norm here. We have no way of judging."

That everyone in this squadron of professed lunatics is good-natured, noncompetitive, and thoroughly professional is small consolation. By February, several of the cast members had begun to complain that the company was *too* nice. "If only there were a lemon here," said Tony Perkins. "It would give us something to talk about."

Any location—outside of London, Paris, and Rome—is bound to breed complaint; but the actors, who seem to be playing a private game of Kvetch-22, have hardly been on a dull movie. Within the first two weeks of shooting, a case of hepatitis broke out, requiring that the entire company be inoculated. A B-25, caught in prop wash, nearly crashed into the control tower while shooting was going on. Susanne Benton, a starlet who plays General Dreedle's WAC, complete with seven pairs of falsies and a rubber behind by Frederick's of Hollywood, was accidentally clobbered by a camera during a take and passed out cold. Two actors, mistakenly released for a short trip to New York, were headed off on the way to the airport by a hastily dispatched helicopter, which landed, à la James Bond, ahead of them on the highway. There was even an unexpected, action-packed visit from John Wayne—though reports differ as to exactly what happened during it.

According to consensus, Wayne, on his way to make a Western in Durango, radioed the field for permission to land his plane. Permission was granted. When Wayne arrived, producer Calley met him and asked if he would like to see the shooting, which was going on in a tent some distance away. No, Wayne said, he wanted to drive to a part of the location to see some land he was thinking of buying. But some time later, he showed up at the shooting. He stood around, apparently waiting for a welcoming party; but none of the actors knew him, and Nichols and Henry did not emerge to greet him. Wayne went to the Playa de Cortés and spent the evening in the bar, drinking, smashing glassware, and complaining that he had been snubbed—possibly for political reasons. Ultimately, he fell and broke a couple of ribs.

"We didn't snub him at all," Henry said later. "We were in the tent, and for some undiscernible dumb reason, no one said, 'Come on out and meet the big guy.' We're trying to make up for it by getting a print of *The Green Berets* and showing it to the crew. In the meantime, we've just been sitting around here, watching the days go by, and waiting for him to come back and bomb us."

The arrival of Orson Welles, for two weeks of shooting in February, was just the therapy the company needed: at the very least, it gave everyone something to talk about. The situation was almost melodramatically ironic: Welles, the great American director now unable to obtain big-money backing for his films, was being directed by thirty-seven-year-old Nichols; Welles, who had tried, unsuccessfully, to buy *Catch-22* for himself in 1962, was appearing in it to pay for his new film *Dead Reckoning*. The cast spent days preparing for his arrival. *Touch of Evil* was flown in and microscopically viewed. *Citizen Kane* was discussed over dinner. Tony Perkins, who had appeared in Welles's *The Trial*, was repeatedly asked What Orson Welles Was Really Like. Bob Balaban, a young actor who plays Orr in the film, laid plans to retrieve one of Welles's cigar butts for an admiring friend. And Nichols began to combat his panic by imagining what it would be like to direct a man of Welles's stature.

"Before he came," said Nichols, "I had two fantasies. The first was that he would say his first line, and I would say, 'NO, NO, NO, Orson!'" He laughed. "Then I thought perhaps not. The second was that he would arrive on the set and I would say, 'Mr. Welles, now if you'd be so kind as to move over here . . .' And he'd look at me and raise one eyebrow and say, 'Over there?' And I'd say, 'What? Oh, uh, where do *you* think it should be?'"

Welles landed in Guaymas with an entourage that included a cook and filmmaker Peter Bogdanovich, who was interviewing him for a Truffaut-Hitchcock type memoir. For the eight days it took to shoot his two scenes, he dominated the set. He stood on the runway, his huge wet Havana cigar tilting just below his squinting eyes and sagging eye pouches, addressing Nichols and the assembled cast and crew. Day after day he told fascinating stories of dubbing in Bavaria, looping in Italy, and shooting in Yugoslavia. He also told Nichols how to direct the film, the crew how to move the camera, film editor Sam O'Steen how to cut a scene, and most of the actors how to deliver their lines. Welles even lectured Martin Balsam for three minutes on how to deliver the line, "Yes, sir."

A few of the actors did not mind at all. Austin Pendleton, who plays Welles's son-in-law, got along with Welles simply by talking back to him.

"Are you sure you wouldn't like to say that line more slowly?" Welles asked Pendleton one day.

"Yes," Pendleton replied slowly. "I am sure."

But after a few days of shooting, many of the other actors were barely concealing their hostility toward Welles— particularly because of his tendency to blow his lines during takes. By the last day of shooting, when Welles used his own procedure, a lengthy and painstaking one, to shoot a series of close-ups, most of the people on the set had managed to tune out on the big, booming raconteur.

But Mike Nichols managed to glide through the two-week siege without showing a trace of irritation with Welles. And whenever the famous Welles eyebrow rose after one of Nichols's camera decisions, Nichols would turn to him and smile and say, "No good, huh? Where should it go?"

"Mike controlled the Welles thing simply by respecting Welles," said Austin Pendleton. "After all, if there's any one person who has a right to say where a cut should be made, it's Orson. Mike respected that. And Orson knew it."

At the same time, Nichols carefully smoothed the ruffled feathers among his company. And he got a magnificent performance, from Welles as well as from the rest of the cast. "The Welles situation, which brought a lot of people down, was almost identical to the tension that was written in the script," said Peter Bonerz, a young West Coast actor who plays McWatt in the film. "We were all under the thumb of this huge, cigar-smoking general, as written, and at the same time, we were under the thumb of this huge, cigar-smoking director. The discomfort that we were feeling was real, and I'm sure it looks grand on film."

One day shortly after Welles had left (taking with him his general's uniform, which he wore around Guaymas for two days until a costume man was able to retrieve it), Nichols sat in his trailer on the set. Outside, it was hot, dusty, and windy. But the trailer was air-conditioned, with an icebox full of brownies imported from Greenberg's bakery in New York, and Nichols sat eating one and talking about himself, his success, and the Welles episode:

"What I wanted to say to Welles was this—I wanted to say, '*I* know you're Orson Welles, and *I* know I'm *me*. I never *said* I was Mike Nichols. Those *other* people said that.' What I mean by that is that he's a great man. I know he's a great man. I never said I was. And, of course, you can't say such things.

"We were talking about [Jean] Renoir one day on the set, and Orson said, very touchingly, that Renoir was a great man but that, unfortunately, Renoir didn't like his pictures. And then he said, 'Of course, if I were Renoir, I wouldn't like my pictures either.' And I wanted to say to him, 'If I were Orson Welles, I wouldn't like *my* pictures either, and it's OK, and I agree with you, and what can I do?'

"I never said all that stuff about me. I'm not happy about this thing that's building up about me, because it has nothing to do with me. I mean, the things I've done are neither as good as the people who carry on say they are, nor are they as bad as the reaction to the reaction says they are. They're just sort of in-between. I'm not flagellating myself and saying I've turned out only crap, because I'm not ashamed of it and some of it I like very much. But Orson said to somebody that he didn't just want to be a festival director." He paused. "Well, I guess if you have the festivals and *Cahiers* and Pauline Kael and Andrew Sarris, you want to make pictures that break box-office records. And it also works the other way around.

"I was very moved by Welles. I knew what it felt like to be him in that situation, to come into a company in the middle, to have a tremendous reputation not to like acting, to be used to being in control—and I was sorry when people didn't see what that felt like. Where the camera is and what it does is so much a part of his life—how is he suddenly supposed to ignore it? Take somebody like Elizabeth Taylor—when she's acting, she knows where the light is and how close the shot is. Orson knows whether he's in focus or not. Literally. If you know that much, what are you supposed to do with it? You can't throw it out. And I know that if I were acting in a movie, it would be very hard for me not to say, 'I wonder if you would be kind enough to consider putting the camera a little more there so that when I do this . . .' How do you kill that knowledge?"

Nichols stopped, lit a Parliament from a stack of cigarette packs on the trailer table, and began to talk about what the Beatles used to call The Fall. "I almost can't wait for it to come," he said, "Because I'm somewhat upset by the Midas bullshit and also by the reaction to the Midas bullshit. I don't like a critic to tell me that I set out to make a success, because it's not true. There's enough worry in thinking that you set out to do the very best you could and came out with only a success—that's depressing about oneself. You know, none of the great movies has been a popular success. I can't think of any exceptions. But you accept that there's a great difference between yourself and the artists who make films. It's like when you're fourteen years old and you realize that Tchaikovsky would have liked to be Mozart—he just didn't have a choice. And I'm not even making a comparison there. But you have to go on as yourself. I'd like to be better, but I can't."

From outside the trailer came a knock, and a voice said, "Mr. Nichols, we're ready for you now." The water machine was working. The actors were on the set. And Nichols hopped out of the air-conditioned vehicle into the heat and began to walk over to the stone building where the cameras were set up. A few feet away, Buck Henry was having difficulty with a crossword puzzle. "Are there any Hindus here?" he was shouting. "One of your festivals is bothering me." A film is being shot here.

How to Succeed in Interviewing Elaine May (Try, Really Try)

Dick Lemon / 1970

From the *New York Times*, January 4, 1970. Reprinted by permission.

I have been interviewing Elaine May for three and a half years now. The first time I interviewed Elaine May was for the *Saturday Evening Post* in August of 1966, in a lavish hotel suite in New York—why I can't remember, because she had an apartment on Riverside Drive. We had coffee and small cakes and I enjoyed it, but the material, frankly, was thin, because whenever I went to make a note, she would abruptly look anguished, cry "What are you writing down?," leap up, and look over my shoulder. Then she would ask whether that sounded right for publication and we would talk about whether it did or not, while she paced and I held the pencil uncertainly.

Also, she was continually in motion, even when sitting down—eyes, ears, mouth, hands, feet, everything, so that I was distracted a lot. Then, too, she kept asking *me* questions, which is not in accordance with interview protocol. I, in turn, kept evading, which led to a stalemate. "You are the most evasive man I have ever met," she finally exclaimed.

Some time after this first meeting, I decided to write Miss May a letter:

"Dear Miss May: I enjoyed our meeting a few months ago, but about the only quote I have from it in my notebook is 'That's a nice horse,' which no longer makes much sense to me, and seems insufficient as the basis for an article anyway. I have an idea: Suppose I write you out a series of questions, one or two at a time. You would then answer them any way you chose and mail them back to me. I stipulate that if a question seems too stupid, trite, ponderous, whatever, you have the right not to answer it, or even to answer some other question, if one comes to mind."

Miss May called up immediately to say that was the niftiest offer she had had in a long time. So, delighted, I sent her a question, cleverly worded to force an in-depth response. Three weeks later, she sent back her answer:

"Question #1: Where were you born, and what has happened to you since then?

"Answer #1: Philadelphia, Pennsylvania. I have grown taller and learned to dress myself."

That left me with equivocal feelings. I was elated that I had gotten a firm answer. On the other hand, it was a rather short firm answer, and considering the time involved, I had a feeling it might take some time—perhaps years, or possibly a decade—to get a complete interview. So I quickly fired off three more questions designed to lead to a natural, relaxed discussion of the difference between writing and acting and the submergence of an actor's personality in his role. Three weeks later I got a letter, but it had no answers in it. She apologized, saying that she had been moving:

"I have tried to answer question #2 a little at a time, while choosing between cameo white, off-white, antique white and bone white (four whites which are indistinguishable to the naked eye but are, I am told, wildly different when seen on a wall). I have not finished question #2, but I have chosen bone white. The painter seems displeased about it but he refuses to say why."

It struck me that in what I had glimpsed of Miss May's world, you couldn't get anything out of anybody—Miss May, me, the painter, everybody was keeping mum. But she said she would be all moved in two weeks and would answer the questions, "which are very interesting and extremely answerable," at that time. I never got any more letters.

Then, several months ago, the *New York Times* asked if I would interview Elaine May. Her plays, *Adaptation / Next*—one written and both directed by her—were a hit Off Broadway, and she was directing a movie—a murder-comedy which she had written and was also acting in. So I went to East Eighty-Sixth Street to watch her directing *A New Leaf*, which had gone through about seven producers and was something like $1.5 million over its budget.

On Eighty-Sixth Street, there was a locked car in the way of the shot, and the assistant director kept hollering through a megaphone, "Will the owner of the maroon Grand Prix please come and inspect the damage?" There were also two Yorkshire terriers, an Afghan, a Great Dane, and two dachshunds hanging around. Miss May was waiting in an apartment between takes. She had on a leather jacket, Levis, and moccasins, and was smoking a little cigar, which she lit by striking a match on the underside of a coffee table.

"I read *Portnoy's Complaint*," she said at this time, "and discovered it was about food."

Later, I observed her in the process of directing. She was intensely casual but somewhat distraught, as reflected by her occasional muted swearing. Several times, she talked to Walter Matthau, the film's star, with the cigar sticking out of her mouth, and he would nod understandingly. On one of these occasions, without missing a nod, he took the cigar out of her mouth and tossed it in the gutter.

Our interview finally took place at Miss May's house near Riverside Drive. The house is four stories high, without an elevator, and she lives on the top floor. The floors underneath all appear to be empty. She started talking about touching comedies, and I asked whether *A New Leaf* was one. "Jesus, I hope not," she said. "I've gone out of my way to avoid compassion."

I started to make some notes. "Listen, let me just tell you about it before you start writing things down," she said. "Then we can figure out the interview." So she talked for about an hour, about the interesting and frustrating parts of the experience, and once in a while I would boldly announce I was putting something down.

"I really didn't know anything, but when I told them that, they thought that was my technique," she said. "You're supposed to be crisp. People would ask me where to put the camera and I'd say, 'I don't know.' The other thing you're supposed to say is 'Cut, print, beautiful, next set-up.' You're supposed to say it for the morale of the crew, like a captain on a ship. I couldn't say 'Cut, print, beautiful, next set-up.' I couldn't even say 'Action.'

"They kept saying this movie would be funnier than *The Odd Couple* and I didn't need to work so hard. I told Charles Bluhdorn, the head of Paramount, 'I'm not as good a writer as Neil Simon. It's not as good a script, so I have to work harder.' 'You *are* as good a writer!' he said. 'No I'm not,' I said. 'I'm not as funny.' 'Don't say that!' he said. 'You're *funnier!*'

"I had a nice makeup man who finally let me go without makeup," she added. "He was lovely. My hairdresser was marvelous. I used to fix my hair so that my ear would show through, and he'd stand there wringing his hands. But finally he'd let me do it. I wish we could figure out some approach for this interview."

I stared at her blankly. My approach is to try to find out what people want to talk about and write down what they say, and the only questions I know are desperation ones. "Why don't you ask some interview questions?" she said.

"OK," I said, skeptically, and sat up straighter—a bit of Method interviewing. "Miss May, did you find it easy, or was it pretty hard, directing this, your first film?"

She thought for maybe twenty seconds. "Pretty hard," she said.

"Which do you find more rewarding, acting or directing?" I asked.

She thought again. "They're both rewarding," she said.

"Only in different ways?" I suggested.

"Yup," she said.

"What have you learned from directing this film?" I asked.

"Not much," she said.

"Do you feel you broke any new ground in this film?" I asked.

"No, none. But I tripped over a lot of old ground."

"How would you describe this film?"

"It's adequate."

"Do you have any hopes of winning an Academy Award for your work?"

"Certainly not. It's not good enough for one. I'm just hoping that people will stay awake."

"Can you describe Walter Matthau's performance?"

"No, I can't."

"What directors do you most admire?"

"Arthur Penn. Mike Nichols. Truffaut. Whoever did *Loves of a Blonde*. Whoever did *Holiday for Henrietta*, which is one of the great movies ever made."

"Do you feel that American films are moving in a new direction?"

"No, I don't, as a matter of fact," she said. "I think they're exactly the same as they always were. My favorite movie is *Anchors Aweigh*, which I consider one of the great films ever made. I also like *The Wizard of Oz*. Of course I saw it when I was young, but I feel that I would feel exactly the same."

"Do you think the more liberal moral climate in this country gives filmmakers more latitude?"

"It doesn't give me more latitude. You mean sexy stuff and naked ladies?"

"Yes."

"Well if you're shooting sexy stuff and naked ladies, it gives you more latitude."

"Can you describe the plot of your film?"

"Well, it's the story of a very aristocratic young man from the South who falls in love with an arrogant, aristocratic, wealthy woman and they have this wonderful aristocratic life until the civil rights war breaks out and then he loses his plantation and after many events he marries the woman and they have this child who is killed horseback riding. Then he and the woman break up and he goes back to his land, which used to be run by slaves but is now going totally to seed because he can't afford labor. And he is literally starving and scrabbling in the earth for a radish. Then he decides he wants to get the aristocratic lady back and he doesn't want her to know he's lost his money, so he makes himself a shirt out of a drape. He nearly gets away with it until she notices his hands, which haven't been manicured, so she leaves him again. But it doesn't break his spirit and he feels he's learned something and he's still determined to get her back. I didn't want a pat ending."

"That sounds an awful lot like *Gone with the Wind*," I said.

"I never saw it," she said, with a hint of righteousness. "*Gone with the Wind* was about a woman and it was a period piece. From what I hear."

"Whom do you think you have more in common with, American directors or European directors?"

"I've only met two American directors, and I've never met any European directors, so I couldn't give you a really intelligent answer on that."

Here I got momentarily distracted because Miss May had taken a filter cigarette, broken the filter off, and then, after kneading the two parts for a while, dropped them both in the ashtray. "Did I ask you to describe your approach as a director?" I asked.

"No," she said.

"Could you describe your approach as a director?" I asked.

"On this movie, since it's the only one that I've made, first I set up the shot so the crew could light it when Walter came in," she said, simply but with authority. "Another thing, I try to get all the furniture in the right places without interfering with the lighting equipment. Then when Walter comes in—we'll call him the star, I think—I ask him if he knows what scene we're doing. If he says yes, I ask him if he knows the lines. If he knows all the lines, I have a bite to eat or make a few phone calls. Then he and I might rehearse the lines in the trailer, since we can't get on the set because they're still lighting. Then when they're done lighting and are ready for you, we go and rehearse the scene on the set. Then they light what we rehearsed while Walter gets into makeup and I have something else to eat."

She paused for a moment, to let me catch up on the notes.

"During this time, I explain to the producers why it is taking so long," she went on. "Or I might not, if they don't ask me. Or sometimes I will go in and ask why it is taking so long, so that everybody will know I'm a man of action. After a difficult technical explanation is given, I leave satisfied. Then Walter is called for again and we go over the scene, trying to get it just right so that the lighting will work. When everyone is satisfied that the lighting works, we shoot it. And then if I like the scene, I say, 'Print it.' And if I don't like the scene, we shoot it again."

I nodded in appreciation of this exposition. She was kneading another cigarette, not yet disassembled, so I leaned forward and lit it for her. "Do you prefer soft lighting or bright lighting?" I asked.

"For some scenes I like soft light. and then for other scenes I like bright light," she said.

"What sort of directions do you give to get the performance you want out of your actors?"

"Well, I try to aim for variety. For example, if they just said something very loud, I'll often suggest they try saying something very soft. And then the scene after that, neither loud nor soft, but a normal speaking voice. If they've been gesturing, I might ask them to stop or sit down. If an actor has been given a serious speech and wants something to do in it, I might suggest that since he's been serious for so long, he might try smiling or perhaps putting his cigarette out, if he's smoking. Or light one if he isn't. That way a scene never loses its pace."

"Do you use any ploys to get the emotion you want from an actor?" I asked. "For example, intentionally making an actor angry so that he will he convincingly angry in his scene?"

"No," she said, easily. "If an actor isn't getting angry enough, often I will say to him, 'Be angrier.'"

"Does that usually do it?"

She thought a moment. "It depends on the actor," she said.

"How do you get the mood you want on the set?" I asked.

"I don't terribly want any mood on the set."

"Will you do anything different in your next movie?"

She thought for some time. "Yes," she said.

"What?"

"Everything."

The Misfortune of Mike Nichols: Notes on the Making of a Bad Film

Frank Rich / 1975

From *New Times* 5, no. 1 (July 11, 1975): 58–61. Reprinted by permission.

When I was in California last summer, hanging around the old Selznick studio in Culver City where Mike Nichols was making *The Fortune*, I heard the word "wonderful" more times in ten days than I had heard it in my entire life. Everything was "wonderful," and some things were "very wonderful" or even "extremely wonderful." When Nichols finished a take, he was more likely than not to deem it "wonderful"; if people had been to a party the night before, that party was "wonderful"; the rushes screened each morning were invariably "wonderful." People could be wonderful, too— especially so in the case of *The Fortune*'s leading lady, thirty-one-year-old Stockard Channing, whose big break this picture was; when Channing finished her work for the day and went back to her dressing room to change, whispers of "She's very wonderful" or "Isn't she very wonderful?" usually filled the sound stage in her wake. Things were so wonderful out in Culver City last August that it never would have occurred to me or anyone else that all the wonderfulness might eventually produce a movie like *The Fortune*. *The Fortune*, I think, is pretty terrible—and it just goes to show that in California's flattering sunshine even disaster can have an alluring face.

I had gone to Hollywood because I wanted to watch a continuous stretch of work on a big American film—and *The Fortune* fit most of my definitions of big. In addition to the director, the production involved a full array of film-industry honchos: stars Warren Beatty and Jack Nicholson, screenwriter Carole Eastman (*Five Easy Pieces*), cinematographer John Alonzo (*Chinatown*) and art director Richard Sylbert (*Chinatown*, *Shampoo*, and all of Nichols's films); even Channing was not unknown to me, for I had seen and enjoyed her stage performances when she was appearing with local theatrical groups in my college town of Boston.

While Nichols notoriously fends off visitors to his sets (and even makes a point of discouraging still photographers from taking his picture), he agreed to let me watch him make *The Fortune*; we had never met each other, and I assume he extended the invitation in part because, as a critic, I have been a fairly consistent supporter of his work. I was glad to go, because the making of *The Fortune* looked to be an impressive exercise in Hollywood professionalism—as indeed it was. But professionalism is not necessarily the same process as artistic creation, and I came back from California with some unresolved, even troubling, impressions of the way *The Fortune* was put together. When, last month, I saw the finished film, and saw it with an audience who would never know how wonderful it had once promised to be, those jumbled impressions began to assume a somewhat coherent shape—as things tend to do when one has the privilege of hindsight.

The movie's principal set, a mangy old-time LA bungalow court, had been built at great expense on "40 Acres," the back lot of the studio, and one day Sylbert, who had designed it, took me on a tour of his handiwork. Sylbert is an engaging and literate man in his forties who has since gone on to become a production executive at Paramount; after explaining why he had made his various aesthetic choices in determining the look of *The Fortune*, he explained his succinct view of moviemaking in general. "Most movies have the good things and the bad things built into them," he said. "The point is to make the good things overshadow the bad so that people won't notice." Although the art director didn't say so, it was fairly clear then (and is, of course, abundantly clear now) that the bad thing built into *The Fortune* was its script—a script that Eastman had written for the male stars and which (according to Nichols) she had in part conceived as a good-natured "attack" on them. That script is a comedy—set in the twenties and decked out in period slang—about two low-life heels, Nicky (Beatty) and Oscar (Nicholson), who romance a Long Island heiress to a sanitary-napkin fortune, Freddie (Channing), so that they can bring her to California and get their hands on her money. (Freddie is in love with the already married Nicky, and so must marry Oscar to circumvent the Mann Act—a complicated plot point that the script must expend too much energy to establish.) While Eastman's screenplay sometimes trades in the madcap conventions of the old Three Stooges and Laurel and Hardy comedies (Beatty is the dashing, self-absorbed straight man; Nicholson the frizzy-haired, bumbling idiot), there's no denying that the story hangs largely on the comic attempts of the two heroes to murder the innocent and likable heroine; even the film's curious happy ending, which reunites the three protagonists in domestic near-bliss, doesn't effectively negate the nastiness of what has come before. *The Fortune*, like other Nichols films (*Who's Afraid of Virginia Woolf?*, *The Graduate, Carnal Knowledge*) that have focused on largely heartless characters, can only work if leavened by humor or, if possible, by charm. Unfortunately, the movie is not, except on scattered occasions, funny: Nichols, who rightly prides himself on going for "the element of truth rather than the gag," ends up leaning all too heavily on gags in this film (car collisions, collapsing deck chairs, food fights). And, except for brief flashes in Channing's ambivalent performance (she comes across as an uneasy mixture of Margaret Dumont and Betty Boop), *The Fortune* isn't particularly charming, either. As a result, the film's decidedly humorless premise overwhelms and finally wipes out its aspirations to farce—and much of the time *The Fortune* is cold, dead, and even a little ugly.

Eastman, an ex-actress who writes her scripts under the pseudonym of Adrien Joyce, was an aloof figure around the set. Her eyes hidden behind tinted glasses, she strolled stealthily about, occasionally speaking in brittle-toned whispers to her principal confidants, Nicholson and Channing. (The only time I heard her raise her voice was when, one day at lunch, she suddenly launched into an unsolicited tirade against critic Pauline Kael—who, I later learned, had mercilessly and astutely slammed Eastman's last script, for *Puzzle of a Downfall Child*, five years ago.) Since Eastman prefers not to speak to reporters, it was left to others to explain what her screenplay really meant. "In a sense," Channing told me, "these people all kind of belong together—they're married to each other. They're all they have, and Freddie just doesn't want to leave the two men; like people in a real marriage, she'll tolerate even physical violence. When they stay together at the end, they may try to kill her again, but she'll keep bouncing back. It's the genre of the Marx Brothers, but not as surreal. It's more multidimensional than that, more like the Italian comedies than American." Did Eastman intend *The Fortune* as a statement about sexism? "Well," Channing continued, "it is partially a story about shifting roles. The mousebed [the film's colloquial term for sanitary napkin] is a symbol of what men don't know about women, and it parallels the situation in the movie. If the boys had gone along with Freddie, she'd have given them anything, but instead they try to wrest it away from her. It's about role-playing between men and women. . . . The symbolism is always there. It's important that the fortune is from Freddie's mother, from the maternal side—there's a double meaning in that, because she has the burden of the fortune and the burden of the menstrual cycle, too. Mike said in rehearsal that it's like Freddie is the fortune and they miss it completely. She's like the goose laying the golden eggs, and they miss it. It's like raping Mother Earth—you can go on and on like that. . . ."

Beatty, who had just finished producing and acting in *Shampoo* and who seemed to regard the making of *The Fortune* as something of a lark ("This picture has been no work for me at all" is the way he put it), took a more down-to-earth view of Eastman's screenplay: "It's a lot of fun, really—a silly story about silly idiots. The men want this money and they want to kill her. They don't kill her and they don't really want to." In any case, the script, which reportedly ran four hours in its original draft, ultimately sustained only a ninety-five-minute film; whatever the screenwriter's original intentions, all that remains of her contribution to the film are those gags, the story, the viciousness of the male characters, and a related butch-homosexual subtext that surfaces most startlingly when Freddie gives a gratuitous speech about how she feels like "a real individual" when dressed in men's clothes and then, so dressed, makes love to one of the fellas.

Not in the habit of writing screenplays himself, Nichols has always been to some extent a prisoner of his material—though he sees his situation as being otherwise. "I don't know why I don't [write scripts]," he said. "I like the idea of two viewpoints pulling against each other. Or if not a pulling, then an overlay of one person's insight into something over another's; for me, it's parallax, it gives more of a 3-D effect. You get the viewpoint not of one eye, but of two eyes or four eyes. . . ." Maybe so, but in the instance of *The Fortune*, Eastman's and Nichols's points of view don't pull against or elucidate each other; instead, Eastman supports a dim view of human nature consistent with that of Nichols's other films—and doesn't bother to transmogrify the sourness into entertainment. Only one scene I saw being shot—one in which Nicholson's Oscar, a bundle of hysteria and sweat, unnecessarily confesses a murder plot to cops who are visiting him on another matter—was laughing-out-loud funny, and, coincidentally enough, the scene is also the funniest in the finished movie. Other scenes filmed that week seemed a bit lifeless—as Nichols himself was well aware. "You're seeing a running down of energy," he told me by way of explanation. "People are just tired, and it usually happens toward the end. You can't keep laughing and scratching and having a good time; you realize that the moments when you're rolling are the ones that really count and you work to preserve those moments." Ultimately, Nichols was less successful at preserving those moments than he might have hoped; the preponderance of two of the lengthier scenes shot while I was there—a seduction scene between Freddie and a barber who picks her up, a police-station confession by Oscar—found their way to the cutting room floor.

There was palpable tension on the set of *The Fortune*, but that tension did not derive, as one might think, from a sinking sense on the part of the company that the movie was going astray. Rather the tension came from Nichols and the manner in which he works—but it took me a while to figure that out. When, during the first afternoon of my stay, assistant director Peter Bogart told me that *The Fortune* was "the most emotionally taxing . . . the hardest . . . the most demanding" movie he'd ever worked on, I had no idea what he was talking about. My first impressions of the man who ran the show were just as benign as I had expected them to be: Nichols seemed very much the informal, witty, and unfailingly intelligent person that his comic voice had always projected. He is a little paunchier at forty-four than he had been on the record jackets of the albums he made with Elaine May, but he is still low-key and articulate. He hasn't gone Hollywood, proverbially or literally; except when he must work in the movie capital, he spends his time either in an apartment on Central Park West or on a farm in Connecticut (where he devotes a lot of energy to raising horses). When Nichols puttered around the set, checking details or conferring with Sylbert or executive producer Hank Moonjean or the members of his crew, he usually maintained a consistent, even-keel tone. If there was a lull in the filmmaking process, as lights were shifted or camera setups were changed, Beatty and Nicholson would retreat to their bungalows, but Nichols would hold down the fort, chatting with those around him about such favorite topics as the logistical nightmares of making *Catch-22*, Hitchcock films, and, inevitably, Elaine May. He was not averse to trading gossip—especially if it centered on New York City's *New York Review*–Random House literary axis—and only occasionally, when he talked glowingly of parties attended by Bianca Jagger or Michelangelo Antonioni, did his banter ever so fleetingly resemble that of the compulsive name-droppers he parodied in his old comedy routines, when he was still on the outside and on his way up.

Nearly always Nichols's face was fixed in an inscrutable, bright-eyed grin, his mouth slightly curled up to one side; in profile, he looked not unlike *Peanuts*' Charlie Brown. It is Nichols's quiet style, his willingness to sit and talk and his eager desire to laugh (sometimes until he cried) that actors tend to cite when they talk about working with him. "He's fun—very thorough, but without any kind of a power trip," Channing explained. "He's totally efficient, always there to discuss the tiniest little things, any actor's question—no matter how small. . . . You always feel his control; he's a wonderful audience, and he wants to give his approval and loves to laugh." According to Beatty, "Nichols is a very good audience. . . . One is constantly aware of a very receptive audience, and that's what a director is in movies." "Sometimes you want to let off steam with a minor tantrum," Nicholson said, "and, of course, it can get out of hand. But with Mike it never does. He disregards the small stuff and stays right with the work."

What Nichols's stars say is true, but so is that tension that Peter Bogart was getting at, and which I gradually came to understand. Nichols works almost too hard at maintaining a cool and breezy front, and, after a while, his success at keeping his feelings in check can become peculiarly rattling. Nichols bends over backwards to keep any displays of personal feeling out of his working life, and, in the end, he is so good at making that separation that to an outside observer such strict professionalism becomes a fetish in its own right. There were frequent instances during the time I was around *The Fortune* when technical snafus ruined takes or scenes just refused to come alive, and Nichols always kept his feelings in tight control. His response to calamity was always to drift off into an edgy silence, light another cigarette, and stare intently at the bustling technicians around him; such behavior seemed more unnatural than a shouting match or a temper tantrum would have under the circumstances. Nichols's working manner, his ability to project a smooth and usually affable presence no matter what he was feeling inside, soon became inseparable in my mind from that tension that informs his work. The frothy surfaces of Nichols's movies, whether a successful effort like *Carnal Knowledge* or a failure like *The Fortune*, may be, in the end, window dressing—a gloss designed to dodge a forthright expression of the misanthropic sentiments that underlie such projects. What makes *The Fortune* so unpalatable is that, when the jokes aren't there, this contradiction between style and content resolves itself: we suddenly find ourselves face to face with that darkness at the bottom of the filmmaker's soul. *The Fortune*'s hard substance has conviction, but its facile exterior does not.

"Fellini makes you realize what great filmmaking is," Nichols said to me one time. "He radiates waves of love from every inch of his body. He makes you want to sit in his lap." Because Nichols wants that affection, he packs *The Fortune* with slapstick—as if we might be cajoled into believing that the movie's coldness is actually warmth. That desire for affection may also be what's behind his determinedly unflappable demeanor, his willingness to be a good audience for actors, his looseness with the word "wonderful." The trouble is that Nichols wants it both ways, and while that is well within his rights, I doubt that anyone will want to sit in the lap of a man whose movies have such cruel, misogynistic heroes as those of *Carnal Knowledge* or *The Fortune*—no matter how eager he is to amuse. That doesn't mean that Nichols can't be a first-rate filmmaker, but his desire to please and entertain seems more than ever to be aesthetically incompatible with that festering at the pit of his stomach. The tension in his films and the tension on the set of *The Fortune* may not be healthy ones—for him, for the people who work around him, or for his art.

For all this, I liked Mike Nichols—or at least the Mike Nichols I was permitted to see—but I'm worried as well as fascinated by the way he presents himself to the world. In a conversation we had my last afternoon in California, he tied up the loose ends in my feelings about him—or at least brought the contradictions clearly to light. "I'm so confused by other people's responses to my movies," he said. "To me the people in *Virginia Woolf* have a pretty good marriage. They want more for the other one than for themselves. It reminds me of the end of *The Fortune*; the men treat Freddie badly, but, despite that, they're friends—they're bound together, the three of them. . . .

"I'm not sure my movies need to be linked together," he continued. "But in my mind they're almost the same picture over and over. They're all about friendship and making the best of a rough situation and not coming to any final decision about other people or one's self. . . ." In truth, though, I think Nichols has come to that final decision about people. He may prefer to believe that his movies are about friendship—that even *The Day of the Dolphin* is, as he puts it, about "the dream of finding a new friend"—but spiritually Nichols is not Fellini and never will be. His view of humanity is not an optimistic one—he is better off collaborating with an Edward Albee than with a Buck Henry or a dolphin—and he owes it to himself to face up to the fact, to stop distancing himself and his audiences from what he really has to say by putting on a clever face. Mike Nichols does have a vision; his job now is to let it flower—even if that means that there will be cracks in his own surface and that of his work, even if it means that he will be less professional, even if it means that everything will be less "wonderful" and that he will lose a few friends.

Elaine May: Too Tough for Hollywood? Or, The Benadryl Tapes

Michael Rivlin (interview by Leonard Probst) / 1975

From *Millimeter* 3, no. 10 (October 1975): 16–18, 46.

Afflicted by a bad cold and an interviewer who frequently missed the point, Elaine May, one of the more creative film directors at work in America, spoke in the auditorium at the New School for Social Research. The occasion was an evening meeting of a lecture course given by Leonard Probst, that bright-eyed, adorable television critic, to his class of predominantly middle-aged, affluent students who came to be entertained and titillated while pursuing a course of study referred to as "continuing adult education." It was an audience filled with those who believed that, were May to team up again with her former partner and perform *An Evening with Mike Nichols and Elaine May*, a state of bliss and enlightenment would descend like a gentle rain upon the earth. The odds for the night weren't good.

May, who looked oddly suburban in a blue terrycloth headband, bell-bottom jeans, and white deck sneakers, reached out continuously for either a tissue to blow her nose, a pack of long, white cigarettes which she smoked continuously, or a glass of red wine refilled graciously by Probst. Early in the evening, after answering one of his questions, she announced, "This is the Benadryl talking, not me."

Her voice was noticeably slurred at the start of the interview, and her replies slow and uncertain, but she picked up speed and clarity as the evening progressed, in contrast to Probst, who became increasingly disoriented and confused by his notes, a mass of yellow paper which began to spill off his lap and onto the floor. At one point, in a losing battle to maintain his air of mastery over the situation, he asked May the totally incomprehensible leading question, "Is comedy the opposite of boredom?" A surprised and amused May corrected him. "Interesting is the opposite of boredom, Leonard."

She took absolute control of the evening, and it was her ability to transform potentially tense and awkward moments into humorous ones that prevented the interview from turning into a disaster. But then, this is what we have come to expect from May, the gifted humorist who can illuminate the funny aspects of even the most tragic situations.

In fairness to Probst, May was no interviewer's dream. She dodged his questions whenever she could, feigning ignorance or a lack of understanding. "Repeat that," she would say. "I'm not quick." But behind her pale face with its spots of incompletely blended rouge, and behind her watery eyes, her mind was racing. Insightful, revealing statements dominated the evening, and her humor and sarcasm was less frequently unleashed. But every so often it broke through her seriousness, and May would once more become her more recognizable self.

When Probst stated that she seemed to spend much of her life hiding, she responded, "Well, I don't know why I shouldn't reveal myself to you. After all, we've known each other about an hour. What do you want to know?"

Some of Elaine May's other responses follow below.

I never wanted to be a director. Never. I never wanted to be one at all. I wrote this script, and I wanted to sell it for a lot of money so I could be richer. And at the time, I had just gotten a new manager. They were offering me an enormous amount of money. $200,000, I think. And he came back to me—he'd been my manager for two days—and said, "I've set a wonderful deal. I produce. You direct and write. And you get $50,000." And I asked, "What happened to the other $150,000?" And he said, "You can't expect to get that much the first time you direct." And I said, "I don't want to direct." And I think he said something like, "They can't afford it if you don't."

But I tell you, it's very frightening to give your stuff to a director, because you would not believe that a scene that seems as clear as day to you can turn out the way it does. And I was very frightened of that, because I'd already had trouble once. And I asked for director's approval. And they balked at that. Then I directed it, and here I am. I went way over budget, and I went over schedule and became a very hot director as the result. I think it has only to do with going over schedule, that, had I come in on time, no one would have wanted me.

When I started directing, some people said to me the first day, "Where shall we put the camera?" And I didn't know what the camera looked like. I thought it was one of the lights. And then they took me aside and explained to me quietly what it was. Then they said to me again, "Where shall we put the camera?" It was like a movie scene. There was a hush. There was a seventy-man crew which had been babbling incessantly. I have no idea how they heard. And everybody stopped in a row. It was like that movie scene when all the heads turn. And there was a long silence. And then somebody took me aside and said, "You make the crew"—the crew is spoken of as something sacred and for reasons which I don't know they are paid an enormous amount of money, and they're all sort of nice guys—"You make the crew nervous," they said. And I had been in a terrible movie in which I had watched this director who was so panic-stricken that they had to take him out of the bathroom just before a take. Literally. And I decided then that I wouldn't do that, and that if I just wasn't too cowardly to say, "Well, I don't know," then I'd be all right. The first movie, they thought I was insane. The second movie, after the first movie made money, they thought I had my way. "She has her special way."

They always think you really know. They figure, she knows. But you really don't. I'm sure that John Ford knew. I mean, there's twenty-five possible setups, and he did them all. I find that's an enormously helpful thing to cling to: I don't know. I find I say it less and less, because I now know those twenty-five setups, and they're really not interesting anymore. The interesting part is to figure it out.

(On the central issue of a movie script) That was the reason I wrote the movie. I wanted to see if I could get away with it. And they cut it out. Right to the throat. I mean, they do not cut out the peripheral stuff. They cut out exactly what you wrote the thing for. *(Pause)* They know, somehow.

In doing the first movie, *A New Leaf*, I realized it was quite an insane industry. And I was new enough to know it. If I could tell you—I don't have enough time—how a movie is done. You would not be able to open a fruit stand that way. I mean, they would laugh you out of town. And it seemed insane. By the second movie, I already knew the lingo, and, yes, I kind of took it for granted that, of course, you make a budget even though you don't know any of the prices. By the third movie, you're sort of a pro. And it becomes . . . I don't know what it meant in the beginning, but what it means in the end is that you have become without thought. That is what I now consider to be a pro.

I think there are problems with certain subjects because they're not considered commercial, but not because they're considered controversial. I think it's a very funny country now. Anything that will make money, no matter what it is, they will put on. I think there was a rock song about the SDS. If it made good money, Paramount would invest in it. If Hitler were alive today, as somebody said, I guarantee you, twenty million at the box office.

(Responding to a question about whether there was room for experimentation by a director of her stature) You just take a chance. You experiment, and you fall on your ass. The world does not offer it to you, no. This country does not offer it to you. It's a bad setup for people who are in the arts. It's really hard to work here. Mike Nichols once said that if you have a career, your career is diametrically opposed to your work. And that's true. It's like a credit rating. I mean, you just are really terrified if you miss a phone bill, because you know that someplace there's a computer that's recording it all and that someone will call up and it'll give you a bad rating. And that's a very hard atmosphere to go ahead and experiment in. So you just say, after a while, forgive me, "Fuck it. I'll do it anyway."

You can drink this wine straight, or you can drink it funny. You can kill somebody dramatically, or you can kill them funny. Funny is closer to life. This is not a direct quote, but someone once asked George Bernard Shaw how he knew something was funny, and he said, "When I laugh." There is no way to say what is funny. Certain things are humorous. If you have one person talk for a long time, a really long time, and then have a pause, and then have the other person say one short sentence, you'll get a laugh. And it doesn't matter what they say. But that's audience conditioning, and I don't think it has anything to do with humor. Humor is just a way of looking at things. I mean, you look at it this way, and it's a disaster. And you look at it this way, and it's funny.

The Heartbreak Kid didn't seem to be anti-Semitic to me at all. I was really surprised when it seemed that way to other people. It never entered my mind. It was written by Michelle Friedman,[1] who's a Jew. And it was scripted by Neil Simon, who's a Jew. And what would they write about? The Welsh? I think that Neil Simon is a very talented comedy writer. He's not going to make his character a hero, because then he won't be funny, nor will he be interesting.

I think that when Jews write movies, they are very concerned with being a Jew, because it's still a specific thing, just as being a southerner is. There are very few Americans who still have real cultures. I really don't think Hollywood would dare—even if they wanted to—to portray a Jew unfavorably. I don't believe they would portray anyone unfavorably.

Do you really want to know why *Mikey and Nicky* has taken six and one-half years to complete? Because I'm going to tell you now. And you must swear not to tell anybody. The sound! Somehow, something went wrong with the sound. And that's the truth. I wish I could say I was probing for artistic truths. Actually, I'm just trying to get it so you can hear it. And I just swung it last week. *(Audience claps)* Don't applaud. Wait'll you see it.

It's a funny thing to sit down and write or direct a movie. It really doesn't seem like life, which to me is really like working at Florsheim's. You're doing this peculiar thing which is you're writing a script. And then you're doing this funny thing on a set with a seventy-five-man crew. And no matter what you say about it, it's that strange thing that everyone makes fun of: Hollywood. It's the same thing with writing. You sit at a typewriter, and somebody's actually going to pay you. . . .

I guess it's sort of like you feel: Will they find out? I don't think it's that you enjoy it so much, as that it's something that's in your mind that you are going to impose or inflict on an enormous amount of people, and get paid on top of it. And every once in a while you think, "Well, gee, I'm getting away with it." But not because you enjoy it, but because it's better, God knows, than a lot of other things. It's not wild fun. But what is? What is? Did you ever think about that for one second? That's a horrifying thought. I guess if you think, it's about as much wild fun as anything else.

It's very long, hard work to direct a movie. Actually, the only thing you need—you don't need talent—you just need an enormous amount of stamina and physical endurance, and I'm very strong for my size. It's actually a rather tedious way of making a living. But not as bad as working at Florsheim's.

I'm working for exactly the same thing that everyone works for. They have something which they wish to say, and they wish to say it in such a way that the audience . . . It's like telling a joke. You decide that this joke is wildly funny, and you're obviously going to tell it to someone so they also think it's funny. But you've got to have something which you think is interesting. You can't just work for an audience. You've got to have something to tell them.

If the audience doesn't understand it, and it's meant to be understood, then they're right. Audiences are very smart and they're the best critics, because they want to be told a story, and they want to believe it. If they don't, then . . .

I never realized how different movies are from life until I saw this movie, and I had this longing for a cliché. Any cliché. You usually know what's going to happen next, and nothing at all happened in that movie that you thought would happen. And I realized that all movies have confrontation scenes in which, after the confrontation scene, something happens. And you realize that in life you have hundreds of confrontation scenes. Scenes in which you say the worst things you can say and in which you reveal yourself. And then, two hours later, you do it again. And you do it over and over and over. There is no such thing as a single confrontation scene.

I don't think that there's any proof that movies can show real or natural or truthful experiences. How could they? They're only an hour and a half or two hours long. They couldn't. How long would they have to be to be true? It depends on how long someone lives.

I really think it's best in any kind of directing not to say too much too soon. Explain too much too soon. Make it clear too soon. First of all, you want to see if an actor is right, because then you don't have to say anything. And then, if he's wrong, he usually knows it anyway if he's good. Then you try to figure out not so much what's right but what's uncomfortable. Then, when you're forced to, you say, "Do this." But by that time, they're uncomfortable enough to not simply do what you tell them. Because you can see that on the screen very clearly.

There are so many things that are boring that we sit through. We're used to being bored. Really. You cannot imagine how often you're bored. If you took a check, saying, "Am I bored now?" And I'm so grateful when it just picks up a bit

I tell you, when you direct, you do anything. You beg, you shout, you discuss, you say nothing, you kid. Sometimes you describe it. But you really do anything. It's like life: anything that works, you do it.

I'm not a pro as a director. I'm a pro at thinking about movies. I'm a pro at talking about them. You ask me anything about a movie and I can answer you in movie language: budget, schedule, gross, net, distribution. I'm a pro at that. And that's most of it, you know. If you can do that you can get hired anytime.

I'm not that artistic. I have nothing to say that everybody else doesn't know.

I was much smarter twenty years ago. I was much smarter in my first movie than in my second. I was much smarter in my first play than in my second. The only thing I think experience teaches you is what you can't do. When you start, you think you can do anything. And then you start to get a little tired.

Note

1. That is, Bruce Jay Friedman, author of "A Change of Plan," the story from which Neil Simon adapted the screenplay of *The Heartbreak Kid.*—REK

Elaine May: A New Film, but Not a New Leaf

Andrew Tobias / 1976

From *New York* magazine, December 6, 1976. Reprinted by permission.

If the world rated movies in terms of the trouble encountered in bringing them to the screen, Elaine May's forthcoming *Mikey and Nicky* would score a full five stars. Possibly five and a half. Considered all but unreleasable by certain Paramount executives just a month or two ago, it will open in Los Angeles on December 10, to qualify for an Academy Award, and in New York a month later. It will be by no means the longest film ever made, but easily one of the longest in the making: eight years in all, three and a half since the cameras actually began whirring. And whirring.

And whirring.

And whirring.

It took David Selznick 475,000 feet of raw film to make *Gone with the Wind*. Elaine May shot three times that much film—1.4 *million* feet—to make her little picture. All but ten thousand of those feet, like a vast stockpile of cooked but uneaten spaghetti, were left over.

With only a simple, first-rate script (her own), and not so much as a single mechanical monster to malfunction, or even George C. Scott (or an actor of similar temperament) to contend with, Ms. May managed nonetheless to direct a truly monumental behind-the-scenes disaster. The on-screen interplay of Mikey and Nicky (Peter Falk and John Cassavetes), however amusing, however deftly crafted, can hardly match the moment off-screen, a year ago, when May sold the nearly completed film—*Paramount's* nearly completed film, into which Paramount had already dumped $4.3 million—to another company for $90,000. She *did* that. And if it is funny that every place Nicky goes with his best friend, Mikey, the hit man keeps arriving just a few minutes too late (Mikey is setting Nicky up to be killed), well, neither is it easy to keep a straight face at the thought of a band of New York County sheriffs, dispatched by the court to retrieve Paramount's stolen reels of film, showing up at one door after the next to no avail.

But to appreciate this story, you have to appreciate Elaine May, which I first did when I was thirteen.

Deep Background

It is 1960, and I am convulsed with laughter, rolling on the floor by the hi-fi, pounding the carpet with my fists. I am listening to *An Evening with Mike Nichols and Elaine May*.

It is last week, the same album (different carpet)—and not a laugh has been lost.

"Arthur," May says to Nichols in their most celebrated sketch (they never wrote any of these things down; they just built them by improvising, over and over, take after take after take), "Arthur, this is your mother. Do you remember me?" She has been sitting by the phone for *days* waiting for Arthur to call ("Your father said, 'Phyllis, eat something.' I said, 'No, I don't want my mouth to be full when my son calls'") and she has finally decided to call *him*. At Cape Canaveral. Why, she wants to know, hasn't he taken a minute to pick up the phone and call his mother? Why? *Why?* "But Mom!" Nichols cries finally in plaintive, filial agony, "I was sending up *Vanguard*!" To which May replies: "I know. I read in the paper how you keep losing them. I think—what if they're taking it out of his pay?!"

It was apparent even to a thirteen-year-old that both Nichols—Michael Igor Peschkowsky (his father changed it when they got to America)—and May—born Elaine Berlin in Philadelphia (where *Mikey and Nicky* was shot)—were—together *or* separately—enormously, marvelously talented. And since their amicable parting in 1961, at May's suggestion, Nichols has gone on to direct, among other things, *Who's Afraid of Virginia Woolf?*, *The Graduate*, and *Catch-22* (movies); and *Barefoot in the Park*, *The Odd Couple*, and *Prisoner of Second Avenue* (on the stage). *Streamers*, at Lincoln Center, and *Comedians*, just opened at the Music Box Theater, are both his as well.

Elaine May, meanwhile, dropped out of sight. She underwent analysis; she married her shrink ("Why don't you just say I'm married to a doctor?" she suggested to Joyce Haber in an interview some years ago. Not only would it make her mother happy, she said, but "a psychiatrist is like a priest [in that he is not supposed to marry his clients]. If you mention him, it will take three of his patients four years longer to get well"); she did a little acting, a little writing—but her major reappearance came after ten years, in 1971, with Paramount's release of *A New Leaf*. She wrote, directed, and starred in this very funny picture (with Walter Matthau) and got high marks for all three.

More Background

Here is the story of *A New Leaf* (not the plot, the story):

Elaine May had written this great script. She enlisted costar Walter Matthau. He enlisted producer Howard Koch. And Koch enlisted Gulf & Western's Paramount Pictures.

As Koch was closing the deal with Paramount, he mentioned that May would take very little money for writing and acting if she could direct as well. She had never directed anything before. Koch wasn't recommending this, just mentioning it, but G & W chairman Charles Bluhdorn, who was even more involved with the day-to-day operation of Paramount then than he is now, leapt at the idea: "Stop the meeting, let's make that deal." Koch began to backtrack. "Listen, I don't know if I can handle her."

"Sure you can," Bluhdorn said.

May and Koch took just $50,000 apiece for their work, and Matthau a mere $250,000, figuring they could make the picture for $1.8 million and clean up on their profit participations. May got a clause included that if she were taken off the picture as director, Paramount would have to pay a $200,000 penalty.

After fifteen days of shooting, *A New Leaf* was twelve days behind schedule. On one two-minute scene alone—the one in which Matthau comes to borrow money from his "uncle," Jimmy Coco, who is feasting on a turkey leg (admittedly a wonderful scene)—they shot three miles of film.

Koch had arranged for a closed-circuit TV hookup so that May-the-director could watch those scenes in which she was acting as well. It backfired. She would do a scene brilliantly, watch the instant replay, become hysterical, and insist it be done over again. Endlessly.

Koch went to Paramount to have her taken off the picture, which he saw ballooning in cost and wiping out everyone's profit. But rather than can May as director and have to pay her $200,000 penalty, Paramount decided to bench Koch instead and send Stanley Jaffe in to work with Elaine. Jaffe was president of Paramount. Jaffe supposedly called Koch around this time and asked, "Howard, what's the matter? She's easy!" And then called back about two weeks later: "She's a f——ing maniac! Jesus, Howard, what am I going to do with her?"

Anyway, the picture shot eighty-two days instead of forty-two—which was a lot for a picture like this in the first place—and the cost topped $4 million. To date, *A New Leaf* has grossed around $6 million. But as Mario Puzo explained so eloquently in these pages not long ago, there are a lot of costs in the movie business besides the mere *costs* that have to be recouped before a state of profit can be declared. *A New Leaf* will have to gross $10 million or so before any of the participants begins to see a profit, and that could take a very, very long time.

But that's not the end of the story. Yes, they stopped shooting after eighty-two days. But having shot, one must cut. And the more one's shot, the harder that is. It is like trying to play memory (that card game gifted children play while the healthy ones play war) with five hundred cards face down on the table.

So May starts cutting. She is in the cutting room day and night, chain-smoking her cigarillos, cutting and editing and rejiggering and cutting—and ten months pass and she hasn't delivered the picture.

Ten months is an extraordinarily long time to take cutting a picture. (John Schlesinger managed the rather more complicated *Marathon Man* in six months. Sidney Lumet cut *Network* in two and a half.)

Paramount keeps saying, "Where's the picture? At least let us see a rough cut!"

And Elaine keeps saying, "I'm not ready, I'm not ready." She won't—forgive me—turn over *A New Leaf*. She is a genius and a perfectionist, and a little nuts, and that combination can be troublesome.

Finally Bob Evans, Paramount's studio head, managed somehow to get the film away from her (however he managed it, he should have kept notes—his technique became a lost art), and under his, Jaffe's, and Koch's supervision they finished the picture off. Two murders were dropped, and May's gruesome ending emerged bright and cheery. (Better we should leave the theater smiling.)

That Elaine May hated Bob Evans and Paramount for doing this need hardly be stated. Her worst paranoid images of money-crazed, aesthetically impoverished studio moguls had—in her mind, at least—materialized.[1] She disavowed the film. What's more, she sued to keep it from opening. (It opened anyway, at Radio City Music Hall.) And she refused to cooperate with the dubbing of the final scenes. The last five minutes, although you would never guess it, have someone else's voice coming from Elaine May's lips.

Now:

All this took place in 1969 and 1970, and into 1971. One might have expected a distinct . . . chill . . . to descend upon the Elaine May–Paramount Pictures relationship. And, indeed, May's next film, *The Heartbreak Kid*, was made elsewhere. But comes March of 1973, with Jaffe gone and a new man, Frank Yablans, at Paramount's snowy peak—but Bluhdorn and Evans still very much in evidence—and the trades announce that Elaine May has signed a deal with Paramount Pictures to make a movie called *Mikey and Nicky*. The budget is a familiar-sounding $1.8 million. (The title has a familiar ring to it, also. "Mike Nichols"?)

Koch calls Yablans:

"Frank, I don't believe what I heard."

"Howard, what happened to you happened to you; it's not going to happen to me. We've got an ironclad deal." According to this deal, the minute costs ran above $1.8 million, they would come right out of May's salary. The minute they were 15 percent over budget, Paramount could take over the film. And delivery had to be no later than June 1, 1974. "In this regard," the thirty-three-page single-spaced agreement stated, "time shall be considered of the essence."

Nothing was overlooked. The contract stipulated, among many other things, that *Mikey and Nicky* would be "in the English language"; that six (6) copies of a complete list of everyone connected with the picture would be rendered to Paramount, "including stuntmen, singers, airplane pilots, and puppeteers"; and that Paramount's distribution rights would include in-flight motion pictures, ships at sea, and even "U.N. expeditionary forces."

May had some special provisions of her own written into the agreement. She was guaranteed "final cut"—as coveted as "the last word" in a marital spat—and she would have to deal only with Frank Yablans. Which was a polite way of saying she would *not* have to deal with Bob Evans.

Yablans, meanwhile, enjoyed such a good relationship with Elaine, and was so enamored of this movie, that he decided to play the part of one of the gangsters in the film. The hit man, in fact. It was only after a couple of days' rehearsal in Philadelphia that Bluhdorn learned his subsidiary president was so engaged—Gulf & Western has always had trouble getting Wall Street to take it 100 percent seriously to begin with—and astute observers mark this moment as the beginning of the end of the Yablans reign at Paramount. (Replaced by Barry Diller in late 1974, he was quickly signed on as an independent producer at Twentieth Century Fox. His *Silver Streak* has gotten some good advance notices.)

Anyway, Elaine May and Paramount Pictures were in business together once again. And now Elaine had two movies under her turtleneck, the second made much more efficiently than the first, so maybe things would go just fine. After all, as she explained one day to the *New York Times*, when she started *A New Leaf* she "really didn't know anything." People would ask her where to put the camera (which at first, she says, she mistook for one of the lights), and she'd say, "I don't know."

"You're supposed to be crisp," she explained to the *Times*. "You're supposed to say, 'Cut! Print! Beautiful! Next setup!' You're supposed to say it for the morale of the crew, like a captain on a ship. I couldn't say, 'Cut! Print! Beautiful! Next setup!' I could not even say, 'Action!'"

But now, perhaps, things would be different. How hard could it be to make a movie about two guys out for a night in Philadelphia?

The Shoot

It's just damn hard to make a movie, even though it's about two guys during one night. Boy, let me tell ya! —Mike Hausman, producer of *Mikey and Nicky*

You can tell a lot about how *Mikey and Nicky* was made from the thousands of pages of legal documents, on both coasts, the enterprise generated. But to report the story properly one should really have been on the set. Only, who knew back in 1973 that this little picture would turn into *Gone with the Wind*?

So here we are indebted to Dan Rottenberg, who obviously has a nose for a story, and who, writing for the *Chicago Tribune*, was sneaked onto the Philadelphia set in workman's clothes to observe:

At this moment [he writes], Elaine May is standing in the middle of Front Street arguing with her producer, Mike Hausman. She seems gaunt and nervous in her brown shirt and tattered blue jeans, chain-smoking and gesticulating with bony hands. She looks like anything but an established show business celebrity. Shoulders hunched, head ducked, eyes staring soulfully, she resembles a teenager who has just been caught smoking on the stairs by the junior high principal. She is the meekest person on the set, and her voice is almost inaudible, but Hausman can be heard a block away.

"I can't promise to deliver that," he is screeching. "I just can't!"

May fidgets a bit. "You don't like the idea?" she mumbles.

"The idea is great!" Hausman moans. "I just don't think I can deliver it, that's all."

All May wants to do is move the scene from South Street to Front Street, around the corner. [. . .] The crew had spent several days on South Street putting up false storefronts and arranging the lights. [. . .] This change will require the crew to move the lights and create a few more phony stores [. . .] and to repave a stretch of Front Street. Oh, and if it isn't too much trouble, May would like all this done tonight, so a few takes of the scene can be shot before the sun comes up.

And so it went, night after night, 1:00 a.m. "lunch break" after 1:00 a.m. lunch break, from May through August, 1973.

Every scene in the script was shot and reshot—with three cameras, because Elaine doesn't believe in blocking out actors' movements too closely in advance and cramping their styles. But she remained unsatisfied. She was suffering from what Paramount later referred to as "subjective creative difficulties." They closed down the set in Philadelphia while Falk went off to film his *Columbo* series (each ninety-minute episode of which was knocked out in about two weeks), and resumed shooting in January in Los Angeles. (When they were in Philadelphia, they had gone to lengths not to make it seem too much like Philadelphia. In Hollywood, they did just the reverse.) Finally, in March, Elaine decided she had had enough. The forty-man crew had shot 120 days (nights) in all, and had accumulated enough film—where would we be without calculations like this to give life meaning?—to stretch, if not halfway to the moon, at least from New York to Washington and on over Key Bridge into Virginia.

The Cut

Into the cutting room rode Elaine May, who had chosen as her battleground the Sunset Marquis Hotel in West Hollywood. She occupied half the ground floor of this three-story establishment. Two rooms alone were devoted to storing and cataloging the film, for which a full-time librarian had to be employed. And the Sunset Marquis, known to New York transplants as "the Chelsea West," is not cheap. Eventually, the crew grew to about a dozen, working in two shifts to try to keep up with Elaine.

They were there, to the horror of the Paramount accounting department, for more than a year. Cutting.

I am reminded of my driver's-education instructor in high school, who would, at the critical moment in the parallel-parking exercise, render the following rapid-fire advice: "Cut-cut-cut-cut-cut-cut-cut." But, where I would settle for being within sight of the curb and not up on anyone's bumper, Elaine May, more power to her, pursued the ideal.

She was obsessed. You could walk by her rooms at two or three in the morning and there she would be with an editor, cutting. "We think she didn't want to finish it," says one insider, "because she had worked on it so long it had become her whole life. She loved editing it. She would take a scene and have it cut every way possible—playing with it." You mean, I asked, that throughout all this presumed torment she was actually having a good time? "A lot of people feel that's why she could never get to the final scene," my insider affirmed. "They would come down to the cutting room and she'd say, 'Today we're going to do the last scene.' But she'd never do it."

Terribly shy, she rarely ventured from the hotel. She would walk, eyes on the ground (and shielded by dark glasses), from her suite to the cutting room. She could be seen in the lobby on occasion, well past midnight, conversing with her close friends Falk and Cassavetes; but she rarely went out to eat, and, when she did, she tried hard not to be noticed. Thin, and younger-looking than her years (she is now forty-four), she subsisted mostly on a variety of pills and health foods. Her secretary would be dispatched periodically to Quinn's Nutrition Store on Melrose for yogurt, kafir, yeast—you name it—or else the crew would go out for dinner and bring her back a steak. "If you put any salt in the food," Elaine told one astonished waitress, "I'll die right here."

In the work areas the staff tried to organize her, but May's own rooms were hopelessly strewn with candy wrappers, half-eaten sandwiches, and, seemingly, months of accumulated cigarette butts. (She used film cans for ashtrays.) She refused to allow outsiders near her project, and that generally included the hotel maid service. Paramount executives, screaming to get a look at her progress, joked that the only way to get the film from Elaine would be to have the county health department come in and condemn the premises. The hotel management doubtless entertained a similar notion from time to time.

She was too preoccupied even to obtain a valid driver's license, and so was not set loose on the freeways. Occasionally she received visitors—her husband the doctor, her daughter ("the heartbreak kid"), novelist Peter Feibleman—but mostly she shut herself off from the bright world outside. She never used the pool or lay in the sun.

Apart from the sheer volume of film, and minor problems like the editing machines that would burn out from exhaustion or Elaine's cigarette ashes that would occasionally go astray ("She was always spilling them because of her little nutty, jerky movements," says the same insider), the major problem they were having was the sound. Someone had persuaded Elaine to record the sound on two tracks, one for each of the principal actors, for a variety of reasons that pale by comparison to the problems this caused. "Do you really want to know why *Mikey and Nicky* has taken six and a half years to complete?" May asked a New School audience in a rare public appearance a year ago.[2] "I wish I could say I was probing for artistic truths. Actually, I'm just trying to get it so you can hear it."

The tracks wouldn't mesh. And with two tracks for all that footage, the coding and cataloging got terribly confused. They didn't know where they were. Mouths were doing one thing; sounds were doing another.

The Chase

It is now May 1975, two years after filming of *Mikey and Nicky* began and nearly a year past the ironclad delivery date. Paramount has repeatedly pushed back contemplated release dates, and has been shelling out a great deal more money than the ironclad $1.8 million. (Lots of films go way over budget, of course, but most do it faster, and with more splash.) Yablans is gone; Barry Diller, Paramount's new chief, is beginning to lose patience. It is agreed that the film will definitely be delivered by September 15, 1975, and that costs will go no higher than $4.3 million. September 15 comes and goes.

On September 26, May lets it be known that she will need yet another $180,000 or so, and a little more time, to finish.

To May and her attorney it was a necessary and niggling 4 percent on top of the millions Paramount had already invested.

To Paramount it was the last straw.

May was informed that no further money would be advanced, that any further expenditures would be her own; and it was suggested that the film be transferred to Paramount's own lab where, under her guidance, Paramount's own technicians would complete the work for a great deal less than $180,000.

"Agh!" thought May. "They're trying to rape my film again!"

"Hardly," said Paramount.[3] "We don't want to cut your film; we wouldn't know *how* to cut your film; you are the only one who, possibly, *understands* your film. We just want to get it *finished*, already!"

At which point May turns around and sells Paramount's film to a little outfit called Alyce Films for $90,000 completion money.

Alyce may not have been granted rights to distribute to "U.N. expeditionary forces," but it did get the United States. Paramount was speechless.

Momentarily.

And then the lawsuits began flying. Paramount naturally sued May for breach of contract and for repossession of its film. May's attorney, no piker for Hollywood chutzpa, blithely sued *Paramount* for breach of contract, stating that Paramount's failure to advance the additional money required to complete the picture was (a) a plot to scuttle projects inherited from Frank Yablans; and (b) liable to cause the tremendous efforts of May and her crew over the past several years to go for naught.

A New York judge quickly ruled that, whatever the other considerations in the case, May could hardly sell Paramount's film to someone else, and that, by the terms of their agreement, Paramount was within its bounds to demand physical possession. A writ of seizure was issued, and suited-and-tied pistol-packing New York sheriffs were dispatched to a variety of addresses in search of the film.

(Who would be crazy enough to *buy* such a film, even for $90,000, knowing its origin and the unlimited resources of the Paramount legal department? It turned out that Alyce Films was none other than Peter Falk and a number of other May intimates who already had a stake in the film and who, presumably, assumed that some sort of settlement with Paramount would eventually be reached.)

Paramount did manage to obtain all but two reels of the nearly completed film. But unless they planned to release the picture with something like an eighteen-and-a-half-minute gap, all but two reels was not enough. (They could have called it *The Best of Mikey and Nicky*, or, perhaps, *Most of Mikey and Nicky*.)

Paramount had reason to think that the reels had been spirited off to the garage of a psychiatrist in New Britain, Connecticut—a friend of May's husband's, to whose abode the sheriffs had also paid a visit—but they had no authority to go beyond New York State in their search.

Friends of Elaine began attempting to intercede on her behalf. Warren Beatty called Barry Diller and wondered whether Barry couldn't just kick in the last stupid little $180,000 and get the thing over with. (They are all one big happy family in the movie business, when you come right down to it, anyway.) Diller said he refused to be blackmailed with stolen reels of film. She could finish her film, she could have her cherished right of final cut, but it had to be on Paramount's premises and she had to return the two stolen reels. "She is a brilliant woman and a wonderful woman," said Diller within earshot of a reporter, "but she can go to jail or the madhouse for *ten years* before I will submit to blackmail!"

The reels remained on the lam, and a contempt proceeding was initiated by Paramount's New York lawyers, Simpson, Thatcher & Bartlett.

Happy Ending

Eventually, with an important assist from Paramount vice-chairman David Picker—and only after a period of months and a great deal of legal churn and splutter—May and Diller have a telephone conversation in which he assures her: "Look, Elaine, return the film. This has gone on long enough. If you return it, I give you my word that things will go right for you. But I won't be blackmailed, and I won't put anything in writing. You have to trust me."

Shortly thereafter he gets another call. "Will you be in your office for fifteen minutes?" Elaine wants to know. "Someone will come with the film."

And sure enough, within minutes two reels of film in a box are sitting out in Diller's outer office. And, as this is written, May is working under Paramount's supervision to make her final cut in time for the December 10 opening in Los Angeles. In all, with legal fees, the film will wind up having cost Paramount close to $5 million. When it was originally offered to David Picker, then at United Artists, he turned it down because he thought $1.8 million was too much to budget for such a simple little film. Now he has high hopes for the picture, which he expects to be a critical, if not necessarily a commercial, success. Others at Paramount say the film looks as though it cost $500,000. There's nothing *wrong* with it; there's just not that much to it.

P.S. The judge never got Simpson, Thatcher's letter saying that all had been resolved—and when the two sides appeared for the contempt hearing they thought would be routinely dismissed, they found a judge who was not at all pleased with Elaine May for flouting his orders. Nor was he interested in the fact that the two parties had managed, finally, to work things out. She had still flouted the authority of the court by failing to deliver the reels of film as ordered.

May called Diller: "What are you doing? They're going to send me to jail! You gave your word."

Diller, shocked, called Simpson, Thatcher. They were sorry, they said, but in matters like this they had a dual loyalty—to their client, yes, but also to the court. And the court had instructed them to refile the contempt papers and go through with the action.

"Well, then, *you* go to jail," suggested Diller. "I didn't give my word to you. I gave it to Elaine, and I won't have it broken."

The case is still pending, but almost certain to die quietly.

P.P.S. I started researching this piece last June, in California (at the courthouse—May herself was too busy with the film to grant interviews). Over the summer I suffered "subjective creative difficulties" (I spent the better part of one month trying to dislodge a food particle with my tongue) and didn't get back to the piece until after Labor Day. I promised it, finally, for the end of October, which was a Sunday. Which I took to mean November 1. On that day, believing in heading off editors at the pass, I voluntarily called mine and announced I would be bringing in the piece November 3. But the election was interesting and I stayed up late, so I missed that deadline too. I sympathize with Elaine May! And, whether *Mikey and Nicky* proves to have been worth all this effort, she remains one of my all-time heroes. I'd just think twice before hiring her to direct a motion picture.

P.P.P.S. Having had a nice publishing success over the summer, during the period of my subjective creative difficulties, I am moving to an apartment on New York's fashionable West Side. The agent explained that it used to be one of those enormous ten-room apartments, but that it had been split into two enormous five-room apartments. My next-door neighbor, in the other five-room apartment, turns out to be Elaine May. Truth.

Notes

1. Such an image was neatly conjured last month by a *New Yorker* cartoon: "So, the creative people don't want to move to New Jersey, eh?" demands the table-pounding executive. "Well, then, let's get ourselves some creative people who *do* want to move to New Jersey!"

2. Highlights may be found in the October 1975 issue of *Millimeter*. [See pp. 80–85 in this volume]

3. Allowing here for a liberal paraphrase.

Mike Nichols

Jeffrey Sweet / 1978

From a series of interviews taped in 1974–77, published as *Something Wonderful Right Away: An Oral History of the Second City & the Compass Players* (New York: Avon Books, 1978; 5th Limelight edition: New York: Limelight Editions, 2003), 72–87. Reprinted by permission.

Mike Nichols began his association with [Paul] Sills and company when a student at the University of Chicago. For a while intent on pursuing an acting career, he appeared at Playwrights and Studebaker. But it was in improvisational comedy that he first made his reputation. Performing with the Compass Players, he established a special rapport with Elaine May, and within a few years they were recording hit records, appearing in the top clubs, and walking away with every television and radio program on which they were guests. Abandoning nightclubs, they appeared on Broadway in *An Evening with Mike Nichols and Elaine May*, which played to packed houses for a year. Shortly after, they split up the act to carry on separate careers.

Nichols quickly became one of the hottest directors in the history of the New York theater, scoring hit after hit with *Barefoot in the Park*, *The Knack*, *Luv*, *Plaza Suite*, *The Odd Couple*, *The Apple Tree*, *The Prisoner of Second Avenue*, *Streamers*, *The Gin Game*, and the star-laden revivals of *The Little Foxes* and *Uncle Vanya*. He has also directed a string of remarkable films: *Who's Afraid of Virginia Woolf?*, *The Graduate*, *Catch-22*, *Carnal Knowledge*, *The Day of the Dolphin*, and *The Fortune*. In addition, he produced the hit musical *Annie* for the stage.

Mike Nichols: I met Sills in the University of Chicago coffee shop when he was a busboy and I was eating the leftovers on the tables. There were two ways I could eat. One was to eat the leftovers on the tables of the coffee shop, and the other one was to enter the cafeteria backwards as if I were on the way out and had already paid.

I think that just about that time Sills was directing *The Duchess of Malfi* for the University Theatre. He got bored with it in the middle and rewrote some of it, and all of the university's great scholars were there but nobody noticed the changes. So we were fooling around in the University Theatre at the same time.

Q: Wasn't there a breakaway group you and he were involved with called Tonight at 8:30?

Nichols: Tonight at 8:30 was a "revolutionary" group, which just meant that the guys in Tonight at 8:30 didn't like the faculty head at the University Theatre very much. All it really came down to was that you had a choice between doing a play in some little place and calling it Tonight at 8:30 or doing it on a big stage in Mandel Hall. The first thing I ever directed I did at Tonight at 8:30. I directed my roommate Ed Asner in Yeats's *Purgatory*.

Elaine came along during the Tonight at 8:30 days. I was in a production of *Miss Julie*. Paul had taken over the direction from another guy toward the end. It was a pathetic, awful production. And a terrible thing happened. A man from the Chicago *Daily News* called Sydney J. Harris came to it, and for reasons of his own decided that it was wonderful and he wrote about it in the *Daily News* with the result that we had to play it for months. It was a huge hit and it was terrible. It got worse and worse.

And one night, there was this evil, hostile girl in the front row staring at me throughout the performance, which was in the round. I was about four feet away from her, and she stared at me all through it, and I knew she knew it was shit, and there was no way I could let her know that I knew it also. Oh, this was before the Sydney Harris piece because I remember a day or so later I saw Paul walking down the street with the hostile girl and I had just bought the *Daily News* and read this Sydney Harris thing, and I said, "Paul, look at this!" He read it and Elaine read it over his shoulder. She just said, "Ha!" and walked on down the walk.

She hung around school. She sat in on classes. She never registered. She once convinced an entire philosophy class that everybody in Plato's *Symposium* was drunk and that was the point of the *Symposium*. She used to go into classes and do things like that and then leave.

Q: How did you and Elaine finally become friends?

Nichols: One night I saw her in the Illinois Central station, which was the way one got from downtown Chicago to where we lived on the South Side. I sat down next to her and I said, in a German accent, "May I sit down?" And she said, "If you weesh." And we just started a kind of foreign-agent conversation for the few people on the adjoining benches and ourselves. And then I think I went home with her and she made me her specialty, which was a hamburger with cream cheese and ketchup that was the only thing she cooked. And then we became friends.

We both had big reputations on campus as being dangerous-to-vicious depending on the stimulus, and so we were both interested in each other from that point of view, as well as others. Once we'd had that meeting, there was that strange thing which is true to this day—that in some way we are safe from each other forever. We can't do each other any harm or say anything wrong to each other. But generally it was unwise for people to start trouble with her.

There was a bar called Jimmy's near the university where we all hung out. One day, the wind was blowing and her hair was wild, and as we walked in some guy said, "Hi, Elaine, did you bring your broomstick?" And she said, "Why, do you want something up your ass?" Without pause for breath or thought.

Q: What happened between your days at the University of Chicago and your involvement with Compass?

Nichols: I never graduated. I got a job on an FM radio station, playing classical music and talking in between. Then Paul started Playwrights with [David] Shepherd and Gene Troobnick, and they did a couple of plays, but I didn't want to give up my job at the radio station. They did *Wozzeck* with Zohra Lampert, who was sensational, and they did *Threepenny Opera* and a few other things. And then I was in *La Ronde*. Not too long after, I went to New York to study with Lee Strasberg.

It wasn't the Actors Studio, it was his class. I was with Strasberg for two years. By this time, I had no money at all and no possibility of any kind of work, and Paul came and said would I like to come back and be in Compass? It had already started while I was in New York.

The reason I think Compass was interesting was that you had a group of six or seven people and they were thrown onstage with no idea at all behind it. There was no plan. There wasn't even exactly a positive aim. There was the negative aim of doing something without a playwright. There were no tools or methods or technique, except Paul's spectacular theatrical imagination.

What I think happened was this—you had a group of people who were not actors, really, and didn't have a lot of theatrical experience, but who were very intelligent and, in some cases, highly educated. And they were thrown in front of an audience with very little help. What came from Shepherd was rhetoric, and what came from Paul were concrete and specific theatrical ideas. But I think what shaped it was the audience. I'd done improvisations with Strasberg, but none of us had ever been in a situation of having to improvise with the pressure from the audience. I think that over the months, and finally over the years, that pressure from the audience taught everyone to answer the unspoken question the audience asked—"Why are you telling us this?"

You learn various answers to that main question. "Because it's funny" is a very good answer. If you can't answer, "Because it's funny," then you'd better have a damn good other answer. You can't have *no* answer. I still resort to what I learned then having to do with what makes a scene. For instance, if we're improvising a scene and you choose a position, if I want to make it a scene, I've got to take the opposite position. If I agree with you, we don't have a scene.

We came up with certain vulgar rules. By vulgar I mean something to catch quickly. This one's vulgar in both senses: Elaine would say, "When in doubt, seduce." Because that was a scene.

You learned there had to be a core to a scene. It didn't matter how clever the lines were. If they weren't hung on a situation, you were only as good as your last line, which was never good enough. But if you could grab a situation, whether it was a seduction or a conflict or a fight, once you had that spine, then things could come out of it. And what was so good about it was that after doing it for months and months and years, it became almost a reflex. And there was a remarkable thing about Compass—whoever left, somebody would instantly rise to replace that person. *Anyone* could do it if he just did it long enough. When Barbara Harris first came to Compass, she didn't speak for two months. She couldn't do anything. But by simply doing it and doing it and doing . . . well, you know what happened. I was the same way.

I was a disaster! For a month I cried in scenes because that's what I thought I'd learned from Strasberg. That was my only contribution. I remember one night I was fooling around onstage with Elaine. We were doing a riding scene of two English people on a bridle path. Somebody went running into the bar for the guys who weren't onstage, shouting, "Come quick! Mike has a character!" And I guess my character was that I was English.

Q: If you were blocked for a month and Barbara didn't say anything for two months, what was it that allowed you to be kept on?
Nichols: Ah well, that brings me to Paul. The most striking thing about Paul is that he's one of the two people I've met who doesn't stratify people into important people, less-important people, unimportant people, people he likes, people he doesn't like. He takes everyone equally seriously. He'll get pissed off, but he'll get pissed off at anybody. He had terrible tantrums in Chicago. But he doesn't dismiss anyone ever. That attitude also extended to all his theater. Anyone could be in it and anyone could have any part. He didn't divide people into the talented and the less- and the untalented. Everyone was the same to him, and so everyone was equally gifted after a while. And people would walk in from the street.

In fact, that was how Barbara Harris joined the gang. She walked in from the street. She was fifteen years old and said, "What are you doing?" We were cleaning up a Chinese restaurant for Playwrights Theatre. We said, "We have a theater. Do you want to be in it?" She said, "Sure."

I remember I came back to Compass once after a vacation—every now and then you had to get away—but I came back and they were doing an incredible scenario about a personality course called *The Real You*. It was complicated and wonderful. I was watching it and Severn [Darden] was sitting next to me, and we were watching Andy Duncan do something and I said, "He's terrific," and Severn said, "Yes. I was supposed to play that part, but I went out for a cup of coffee."

It was Paul who made it possible for me and Barbara to stay. I kept saying, "I want to go home. I'm terrible." He'd say, "Stay, it's all right. You'll be fine." And it did happen that whoever stayed long enough was fine. I think it was a combination of this gift of his with people and the process, which was constant learning. As I say, there was no way to be onstage like that and not learn about the structure of scenes, about the connections with an audience.

And what it finally gave us, and something I felt with Elaine always when we were in front of an audience, was almost arrogance. A feeling that "I can handle you guys." I got to where I was completely comfortable with an audience. That has since left me to such an extent that I can't do anything in front of an audience anymore. I won't do a TV interview. I won't do anything as a performer because I've lost that feeling of connection and the ability to handle the audience as myself. I can do it with actors when I'm directing. But when I could perform like that, that had to do with the daily, weekly, monthly, yearly intimacy with an audience.

The great joy of Compass and then, after, working with Elaine was that once every six weeks you would be possessed. At the end of our show, Elaine and I would do an improv, like at Compass, and once in a while you would literally be possessed and speak languages you didn't speak. . . . I don't mean to sound mystical, but such things did happen. Like doing twenty minutes of iambic pentameter that we had not thought of but just came pouring out. That was thrilling, and you'd be drained and amazed afterward, and you'd have a sense of your possibilities.

At the time we were doing this stuff, somebody told me of some experiments they did in the paratroops which determined that there were two kinds of personalities— those who become less than themselves under stress, and those who become more. I thought about it at the time because we were doing improvisations and what happened after some time was that you had access to everything you knew and some things you didn't. You got so that under the stress of performing and improvising for an audience, instead of being crushed by it and made smaller, as one is to begin with, you could actually become more than yourself and say things you couldn't have thought of and become people you didn't know. Certainly not all the time, because for every one of those times there were, let's say, ten when you relied on certain tricks and certain things you'd done before and certain gimmicks you knew always worked. But that tenth or eleventh time when there was a dybbuk, when you suddenly didn't have to think at all, that was the most, the *only*, exciting thing about it.

Q: Do you have any idea what brought times like that on? Were there nights when you were about to go on when you just knew, "It's going to happen tonight?"
Nichols: Oh, quite the reverse. You never knew when it was coming. It had something to do with . . . You see, that was the difference between Elaine and me. She could do it with several people. I could always do it only with her. I never did a good scene of any kind with anybody else. I mean, I did some good group scenes. But for me

it depended on a certain connection with Elaine and a certain mad gleam in either her or my eyes when we knew something was starting and then the other one would jump in and go along.

Q: Do you remember the first really satisfying scene you and Elaine performed together?

Nichols: I guess the first complete scene was "Teenagers." I said, "Let's do two teenagers in the back seat of a car," and we did and it was a terrific scene, and then it kept changing and growing and we kept adding to it. It's hard to describe. It's just two kids screwing around in the back seat and getting their arms tangled up, talking about what they talk about, and it had the line in it when she says, "If we went any further, I know you wouldn't respect me," and I say, "Oh, I'd respect you like *crazy*! You have no *idea* how I'd respect you!" It was never recorded. The two best things we did were never recorded—"Teenagers" and "Pirandello." "Pirandello" was good. It was really something. And we fought about it steadily all the years we did it.

"Pirandello": I came out and said, "We would like to do something in the style of Pirandello, which has to do with reality. . ." And I'd get all mixed up describing it. "Holding a mirror to a mirror. . ." And I'd say, "We'll show you." We started out as two little kids. I was sick in bed and she did this staggering little girl—pulling on her dress and forgetting what she was going to say—and we started to play house. We got big laughs from insulting each other like Mom and Dad. You know—"Get your ass in here," and "What do you want, you drunken sot?" and "Be quiet in front of the kids," and all that stuff. Then we got quite angry with each other within the game. We had a Mom-and-Dad fight, and the angrier we got, we sort of slipped into *being* Mom and Dad, which was quite neatly done. You couldn't tell when it happened. Suddenly we were grown-ups yelling. Also big laughs. Then, at one point, I would improvise something. I would say something like, "Oh, that's very witty. I'm really shriveled," and she would say, "Yes, I've been meaning to talk to you about that," which would get a *huge* laugh, and I would get pissed off at her and start to say something—while she was talking—under my breath. And then we had a few more moments like that, and then the audience really got scared because it was clear we were having trouble with each other. And then we had a fight, but it was real. It consisted of a long pause and my saying, "My partner will now . . ." And then they were really scared, and she'd start to walk offstage, and I'd grab her. I'd grab her, and her blouse would rip and she'd start to cry. And then she'd say, "What do you think you're doing?" And I said, "I'm doing Pirandello." And we'd take a bow.

Well, we fought about this scene because I was always saying it was time to move on to the next point and, "You stretched this too long," and "We should have done that." I mean, friendly fights, but we argued about it, and we had a weird experience. . . .

We were out of town with the show we were going to bring to Broadway. And the one thing I thought wouldn't have happened did—the fight got away from us. I must have blacked out because I suddenly found that I had her by the front of the shirt and I had been hitting her back and forth for a long time, and my chest was pouring blood where she had clawed it open. And they brought down the curtain and we cried a lot. It never happened again. But that one time, it suddenly actually did take us over. When it happened to Ronald Colman in *A Double Life*, I thought it was bullshit, that that had nothing to do with acting. But . . .

A funny thing happened in Compass. You were not meant to repeat things. You had a new program every week or two weeks, a scenario and new improvisations. But Elaine and I found ourselves developing pieces and people would start asking for them, so we repeated and added to them. The more that happened, the more I wanted to keep doing the established pieces, and she wanted to do new things. I kept wanting to work on the ones we had already, because I'm a chicken and I don't really like performing and I don't like doing something new because what if it doesn't work? So she got bored with the old pieces and I kept wanting to do them. This always remained true, even when we had our own act.

One thing that distinguished Compass was that the people in it were not interested in being in the professional theater, at that time. I mean, right down to when Elaine and I auditioned at the Blue Angel, we knew we weren't going to be in show business. It was just something to make a living until we decided what we were going to do. For the first year, in which we ended up on television and everything else, we thought it was a big joke. Because everybody thought we were in show business, but we knew we weren't because we never could be. So that everybody back in Compass had that mentality of a group of . . . I don't know what . . . oddballs who didn't know what they were going to do, but they knew it wasn't going to be the theater because the theater was so dumb. We were snobs.

Q: Did this frame of mind help you be any more relaxed and/or daring with what you did, because maybe you didn't care quite so much?
Nichols: Well, Compass was, after all, a cabaret that was designed for a very parochial neighborhood university in-group. All the choices of subject, all the jokes, and all the serious things were based on a very specific and narrow frame of reference having to do with the University of Chicago. The frame of reference among these people had nothing to do with showbiz, Broadway, nightclubs, or anything like that. Also, as you say, none of it seemed to count very much. I mean, the worst thing that happened was that maybe we did a rotten scene and then we ran out the back door and down Fifty-Fifth Street and literally jumped in the lake. We would do that on some nights. If it was really terrible, the audience never saw us again.

Q: Could you give me some impressions of some of the people you worked with at Compass?

Nichols: Well, Severn always eats his handkerchief during rehearsal. He claimed that once, during a gigantic assembly at the University of Chicago, he stood up at the back and screamed at the top of his voice, "Mike Nichols fucks pigs!" He then managed to get "pigs" into as many sketches as possible: I would say, "Where have you been?" and he would say, "I've been in Africa—pig-sticking!" And of course, he got me to the point that whenever he mentioned pigs I would break up, which he took as an admission of guilt. He would try to use it as proof to the others that I did indeed fuck pigs. He would say, "The way you can tell is if you just mention pigs onstage, he'll go to pieces." That was Severn's little foible.

Once he went into the Ambassador East in a sweatshirt with a whistle around his neck and with a hard-boiled egg in a brown bag, and when they wouldn't bring him coffee to go with the hard-boiled egg, he stalked out under the marquee, blew the whistle, and Ted Flicker drew up in a Rolls-Royce, he got in and drove away.

I remember the first time Barbara Harris ever spoke onstage because it was extremely touching. As I said, she didn't speak for months. Well, we had a spot called "Story-Story." At the end of the show, we all lined up and somebody in line would begin telling a story. Then Larry Arrick, or whoever the director was that night, would stop that person and would point to you and you would have to pick up the story and continue it, and then he would stop you and point to somebody else. Then, after a while, at a certain point he would stop it and say, "And the moral of the story is . . ." and we'd raise hands if we had something and he would choose someone. With Barbara, the story would move on from her in a matter of seconds, and she would never raise her hand at the end. Till one night, she did raise her hand, and there was this whole line of people staring because Barbara had her hand up, and Larry called on her and she said, "Love is the key that opens every door." And we all went—*Aaah!*

Q: I read someplace that most of the material you did with Elaine was created during Compass and that you didn't do a lot of new long pieces after.

Nichols: Very few new pieces.

Q: Any idea why?

Nichols: Fear. The more we became the talk of the town, the more I was afraid to try something new when we had so many things that worked so well. I told you I'm a chicken. After all, other performers repeated their act. Why the hell should we have a new one every night? We did improvise every night. The last thing in the show was always improvised, where we got a first line and a last line and a style to play the scene in from the audience. We never skipped that. But we finally found that the safest thing was to stick with the set pieces, which changed a little bit anyway, do the improvisation, and then get off with some set thing we had prepared.

We did develop a piece on funeral parlors then. That was almost new. We'd done it in some club in Chicago for the first time and they said that if we ever did it again, they'd close the club and throw us out. And we did one about the emergency ward in a hospital that was new because Elaine had had it happen. She'd hurt her arm and went to the emergency room and of course they said, "Where's your Blue Cross card?" I'd say we did maybe four or five new ones, but not a lot.

Q: Can you talk a little about the chemistry between you and Elaine? Who was more or less responsible for what? Or was it such a blend that . . .
Nichols: Well, it *is* a blend. It's hard to sort it out except that by and large I would shape them and Elaine would fill them. It's still true in our work now. You can see it. What she's interested in is character and the moment. What I'm interested in is moving on and giving it a shape. I was always very concerned with beginning, middle, and end, and when it's time for the next point to be made and when it's time to move because, after all, we're telling a story. I was forced into that since she was a much better actor than I was. She could go on and on in a character. I could not. I could make my few points, I had my two or three characteristics, then I had to move on to the next point because I was out. I couldn't do anymore.

Q: How did the Broadway run happen?
Nichols: We did a concert at Town Hall which was a success, and then we decided to do concerts instead of nightclubs because we hated nightclubs so much. We went to San Francisco to do a show, and it was totally fucked up. We didn't go over, to our amazement. It was the first time anything had not been a success. We were so spoiled. We just assumed we would go do what we wanted and everybody would say it was great. Then we got to San Francisco, it didn't go well at all, and I charmingly blamed the manager and said that it all had to do with the sound system. At that point, Alexander Cohen said, "Let me be the producer and get you a sound system and help you with the physical part of the show and put it on in my Nine O'Clock Theater." We said, "OK."

Q: How long did the Broadway show run?
Nichols: A season or a little more. And then we stopped because Elaine couldn't stand it anymore. The longer you go, the harder it is. I now think, when I listen to our record of the show, that what happened is what happens to all long runs. It got so dehumanized and so unreal by the time we'd played it for a year. I listen to myself in the telephone sketch, and I'm not a person at all, just doing various voices and

squeaks and pauses and noises that you begin to do by rote. . . . I would start playing games like, "Let's see how fast I can make it go."

Q: In his book, *Ladies and Gentlemen, Lenny Bruce,* Albert Goldman says that Bruce wanted to write material for you and Elaine, but that you said, "No, thanks."
Nichols: Lenny Bruce, although he was a friend, never offered to write anything for us, so, of course, we never turned him down. The Goldman book is completely inaccurate about everything as far as I know but very "artistic."

Q: What did it feel like when you and Elaine broke up?
Nichols: We didn't break up when we closed the show, because we did some more TV and stuff like that. We broke up over Elaine's play. She wrote a play for me, as it were. It was also *about* me, which made part of the problem. We were meant to be in it together. Arthur Penn was going to direct it, and he wanted her to cut it and work on it. And he went to Europe saying, "I want you to do this and this and that," and Elaine chose to hire Fred Coe as a director, because he *didn't* want her to cut it. She then decided she would not be in it, that she would be better off if she could have the distance of watching it and judging me. It was disastrous. It didn't work for me, it didn't work for the play, it didn't work for her. If we had had Arthur, or somebody who knew how to work on a play, it might have helped us.

For the first time, Elaine and I really had a fight because we were so disoriented by no longer being together against everyone else. It divided us in some terrible way, and we never quite recovered from that. It's like that thing in *1984*—once they betray each other, they can be friendly, but it's never the same. And we did, in fact, betray each other. She was trying to get another actor. I was saying to people, "Get her to cut the play or I'm leaving." Once we'd gone through that experience of trying to screw the other one, out of panic and discomfort on our own parts, it was sort of over.

Q: How did you make the transition to director?
Nichols: It didn't feel like a transition. I was coming home in every way. Now this is theater direction I'm talking about. Movies felt very different and still do. But directing a play, it was as if I'd been getting ready for it all my life without knowing it. Here at last was the thing I knew all about. That was the feeling. It certainly wasn't true. But I came into the first day of rehearsal after all the years with Compass and Strasberg and Elaine and not knowing what I was going to do, and on the first day I thought, "This is what I've wanted to be without knowing it."

Q: Can you differentiate what you learned from Strasberg and Sills?

Nichols: As you know, everybody learns different things from people. What I learned from Strasberg has nothing to do with what he supposedly teaches. People aren't really very good at reproducing what he teaches. What I learned from Strasberg was much more about directing than acting. There are some good Strasberg rules that come up again and again when you're directing. For instance, he'd say to an actress, "The scene says it's after dinner. What about the dishes?" And she'd say, "I did them already." And he'd say, "Well, that's so uninteresting. Why not do them now?"

Another example: I mean, he never said it quite this way, but I came away from him thinking like this—I was talking to Lee Grant about a scene she was doing in *Shampoo*. In the film, Warren Beatty's just fucked Lee's daughter, and she said, "Warren wanted me not to know. What should I do?" And I said, "You should *always* know. There's never a time in a play or a movie or a scene when it's more interesting not to know something than to know it." The answer to "Should I know?" is always "Yes," but then maybe you have to dissemble "No," or maybe you have to do something about not showing you know. But you must always know. If someone's onstage and a second person comes onstage, of course they know. They see each other. It's stupid to pretend they don't know. If they're supposed to deal with it as if they don't know, the thing of it is to know and then find some reason to act as if you don't know. Such things come from Strasberg and they're basically useful ideas. Like about the dishes—it's always more interesting not to have done it before the scene or plan to do it after the scene. Do it now.

On the other hand, Paul never taught me, except as a person. There's a lot to learn from him as a man. But what I learned from the Compass has to do with dealing with the audience. Not catering to it, but understanding a story and telling a story to a group of people. You know, how do you tell a story? There's a thing you learn from Compass—if you're doing a play, or a movie, you have to say to the audience, first of all, "You feel fine, you're not worried. We know what we're doing. Everything is OK and you don't have to worry. It's not Judy Garland." You must do that in the beginning in one way or another. You must tell them that they're in a situation in which people have the confidence to begin the story they're going to tell.

Q: And then you hit them with "Pirandello" and you scare the shit out of them.
Nichols: Once you've reassured them.

Also there's the thing of finding the style for what you're doing. You have to find a way to tell the story that will permit the things that later happen to happen. If they're very bizarre or extreme things that happen later, you have to make that possible within the beginning.

Q: You mean to create a world or an atmosphere in which the events that follow are logical and consistent.
Nichols: Right. That's true for Strasberg and it's true for Sills. It's just true.

Q: Do you find that you use improvisational techniques much in your current work?
Nichols: Some. We improvised a lot for *The Graduate*. We improvised their whole childhood. In *The Graduate* we decided that Benjamin's father had had an affair with Mrs. Robinson, and we did some of the early childhood of the kids and the families together and stuff like that. And in some of Neil Simon's plays, we did a lot of improvisation, like the poker game in *Odd Couple*.

Q: Did you find things you ended up using?
Nichols: Yes. Not very much dialogue, because Simon had written that so well. Mostly behavior. I've never really used it to find dialogue, although there were some scenes in *Carnal Knowledge* that were improvised. Some short scenes. For instance, the off-screen stuff in the scene where Candy's laughing. I started them off on an idea, but then it was improvised. I don't think there was much other actual dialogue improvised. But sometimes behavior.

I've gotten more and more formal and controlled. I don't know why. Robert Altman is doing what I would have expected me to be doing. When it works for him, it's better than anything. When it doesn't work, as with all of us, it's not. Every time I decide that I'm going to go in that direction, something pulls me into a style that is much more spare and not so free.

As I've learned more about movies technically, I'm more and more interested in simplicity. I can be very excited by the kind of richness of texture of, say, *McCabe and Mrs. Miller*. I admire it immensely, but I'm just drawn in another direction. I can't explain it. But I don't seem to have any control over it.

Q: If someone introduces an actor to you and tells you that this person was really terrific in Compass or Second City, what do you automatically know about him?
Nichols: That he has what few actors have—a sense of character observed from without. The ability to comment on a character with some humor and a little bit of distance and, at its highest, with genius, like Elaine: to be able simultaneously to comment from without and fill it from within. That's Compass at its highest, to me personified by Elaine's best stuff—that she's doing both simultaneously. Being completely real, saying things for the first time. She's clearly just thought of them and she's really feeling the things, but also she's outside saying, "Did you ever notice this about this kind of person?" That's what I associate with Compass.

Q: Was there ever a time when you did a piece, with Compass or with Elaine, when you'd hit a target that jolted the audience?

Nichols: That we'd gotten too close to something about them?

Q: Yes.

Nichols: No. Because, as Elaine always claimed, if you were in the audience and I did you exactly, you would say, "I know somebody just like that." That was always the reaction. Elaine's mother always thought it was my mother we were doing, and vice versa. If you have a group of middle-aged Jewish ladies and you do the mother sketch, they all say, "I know a woman just like that."

You know, all the stuff Elaine and I did, everybody always thought we were making fun of everybody else, but of course we were making fun of ourselves. It was our attitudes we were kidding because we had nobody else to go by but ourselves. People would say that we were putting on this or that kind of person, but it was always us.

Mike Nichols: The Special Risks and Rewards of the Director's Art

Barbara Gelb / 1984

From the *New York Times*, May 27, 1984. Reprinted by permission.

Mike Nichols sits erect, arms folded, at a trestle table in a large-windowed, bare-floored rehearsal room, where he is directing a new play by David Rabe. Rabe sits slumped in a chair nearby, ready to leap protectively to the defense of any seeming slight to his precious words. The actors clutch their scripts—insecure, groping, desperate to please—watching Nichols for a sign of approval. Nichols, who is in a position more or less to have his pick of scripts and stars, has experienced both the joys of taking creative chances and the pitfalls of playing safe. He has been nominated for an Antoinette Perry Award for his direction of Tom Stoppard's *The Real Thing*; if he wins next Sunday, it will be his sixth Tony. And now—as he intermittently feels compelled to do—he has chosen to try a risky play.

While Nichols made a success of an earlier Rabe play, *Streamers*, in 1976, he is scared of Rabe's new play, *Hurlyburly*. He knew exactly how he wanted to stage *Streamers*: in a quiet, unoperatic style that made its theme of cruelty and violence doubly compelling.

But though Nichols is drawn instinctively to *Hurlyburly*, much as a lover struck by passion, he finds it somewhat elusive and mysterious. And Rabe, who writes from his unconscious, is not much help in explicating the motivations of his own characters.

Nichols is searching, as always, for what he calls, with emphasis, the "Event"—the truthful moment or series of moments—that will illuminate the author's meaning, that will reveal "real people living their lives."

It is a search that was inspired years ago, before Nichols had any thought of a career in the theater, when, at the age of sixteen, he attended the Elia Kazan production of Tennessee Williams's *A Streetcar Named Desire*. He remembers scenes from that production, he says, as well as or better than things that happened in his own life—"the scene between Blanche and Mitch, where he invited her to punch his stomach; the later scene where Mitch said, 'You're not good enough to bring home to my mother,' and Blanche said, 'Get out of here before I start screaming fire,' and she started to scream, and Mitch was terrified."

"What startled me so," Nichols says, "was that these people, although they were heightened and theatrical, were, simultaneously, in the course of *real lives*. I didn't understand what it was. I was mystified and excited.

"Later, when I had begun acting with the Playwrights Theatre in Chicago, I saw other plays Kazan directed—*Tea and Sympathy* was one—and I realized that we were just *saying lines*, and rather badly, while those actors in the Kazan productions were somehow conveying *life*."

Analyzing the invisible process by which Kazan created this sense of immediacy, Nichols realized it consisted of "getting the actor to physically express what the author, in his dialogue, gives only clues to."

Nichols nibbles on a bran muffin, sips coffee, chain-smokes (without inhaling), and nods encouragingly to William Hurt and Sigourney Weaver, who are about to rehearse a love scene. She is playing Darlene, a rootless woman, bruised by life, who has a vague career as a photographer. He is playing Eddie, a marginally successful Hollywood casting director with a drug habit. *Hurlyburly*, which is scheduled to open Off Broadway at the Promenade Theatre on June 21, is in an early phase of rehearsal and the two young actors, though they have practiced the love scene a few times, are still feeling their way into their roles, improvising. "Eddie and Darlene are talking about how it's lucky they didn't meet a year ago," Nichols explains, "Because, Darlene says, 'A year ago I was *crazy*.' And Eddie says, 'Oh, a year ago *I* was nuts.' Then *she* says they have to keep their hearts open, and *he* says they need time and space and no guilts. It's sort of like incantation."

Rabe's dialogue for the scene gives no hint of any accompanying action, and Eddie and Darlene could be sitting across a table from each other during their exchange. But Nichols wants to find a way to "physicalize" the "underneath," as his observation of Kazan taught him to do, "so that the clichés are heard in stronger contrast." And he has found his clue in the last line of the scene, a ribald—and in a family newspaper unprintable—suggestion from Eddie to Darlene that they immediately consummate their relationship.

"I felt that what would make the Event of the scene—the joke, or the irony—clearest, would be to have them—while they're in the midst of these clichés about *space* and *open hearts* and *no guilts*—be undressing each other and beginning to make love."

Sigourney Weaver slithers into William Hurt's lap, straddling him. Hurt, slouched into the sofa, begins fondling her. She pulls her sweater off.

"Once I'd decided it would be a good idea for them to partly undress each other and themselves, Sigourney said she wanted Darlene to be quite aggressive," Nichols says. "It was her idea to straddle Bill. And I said, well, if she was going to do *that*—and I liked it very much—why not do it on the line, 'I'm *scared*'?

"At one point, Eddie says, 'We need *time*.' And Darlene says, 'There's no rush'— whipping off her belt."

In the actor's lap, the actress unbuckles her belt and flings it away.

"We worked it out very carefully," Nichols says, watching approvingly. Weaver kicks off a boot. Hurt tugs off her other boot. In one swift motion, Weaver zips down her dress, wriggles out of it and drops it on the floor behind her. She finally is wearing nothing but silk panties and a thin, clinging, pink knit camisole.

Hurt hastily pulls open the buttons of his shirt and shrugs out of the sleeves, as Weaver yanks her camisole over her head and tosses it into the air. Naked from the waist up, the two embrace fervidly.

Nichols smiles with delight at his own handiwork and at his actors' adventurousness.

Sigourney Weaver is getting dressed. Moved by her daring, William Hurt says quietly, "You're very brave."

"You're brave, too," Nichols tells the actor, smiling one of his ferociously protective smiles. He ponders. "Leave it alone, now," he says, "get used to it, don't lose what you have. We don't need to lock it into one thing yet."

All of Nichols's comments are made after visible deliberation and they are made equably, even modestly. "Here's what I *think*," he says, prefacing a piece of direction, or "Why don't we try this?" And then, "Does it seem right to *you*?" He is equally demure when describing his work. "It seems to me," he says, and "I *guess* what I was trying to do was . . ."

After a recent slump in his otherwise highly successful twenty-one-year career as a director, Nichols has arrived at a new plateau of professional recognition, and he is as much in his element as an acrobat on the high wire: challenged, exhilarated, sure-footed. Last December saw the release of his movie *Silkwood*, for which he received his third Academy Award nomination. (He was also nominated for his 1966 production of *Who's Afraid of Virginia Woolf?*, and he won an Oscar for his direction of *The Graduate* in 1967.) *Silkwood* was followed a month later by the hit Broadway production of *The Real Thing*.

To watch Nichols at work is to perceive something about the making of a play that will never be discerned by its audience. To hear him talk about his work, as he did recently in full candor, is to perceive a good deal about the making of a director and the sources of his creativity—in Nichols's case, a blend of life experiences that he applies to every project, whether a genial comedy, like *The Odd Couple*, or a tragicomedy, like *Hurlyburly*.

The blend consists of that early, awestruck analysis of Elia Kazan's directorial technique; the assurance gained from years as a performer of improvisational comedy with his partner, Elaine May; lessons learned from classes with the renowned teacher

Lee Strasberg; the gift, as Nichols describes it, of "having been lucky enough to be born with an ear for comedy"; and finally—what is uniquely his own—an ability to draw upon his personal suffering to flesh out (and hold up to fond ridicule) the characters of whatever play or movie he happens to have fallen in love with.

"I have two kinds of affirmative responses," Nichols says. "One is, 'Yes, this will work,' as I felt about *Streamers* and—more recently—*The Real Thing* the minute I read it, long before seeing the London production. The other is, 'Let's give it a try'—as I felt with *Hurlyburly*."

Like nearly everything Nichols has directed, *Hurlyburly* is about sad and frightened people, self-pitying people unable to accomplish that most difficult of tasks, growing up. It is about people who say one thing and mean another and—more broadly—about comedy as an antidote to self-pity, which is at the core of Nichols's own weltanschauung.

The play is set in Los Angeles, where Rabe has spent several years writing movies. While Nichols loves the play, he assumes that it will—at least to begin with—have a special and limited audience. The Chicago production might be considered a workshop, remote from Broadway critics.

Rabe, who is present at all rehearsals, is perfectly frank about leaving the discoveries of his characters' motivations to Nichols and the actors.

"After a while," Rabe says, "you realize they'll come up with better ways of playing the lines than you could have thought of. Stage directions get in my way. I see them in my mind, but I see no point in putting them into the script. I fly very blind when I write. The less I know, the better off I am. If Mike takes on a play, he knows how to do it. The thing about Mike is that even when his advice to his actors turns out to be wrong, it's always *clear*."

Nichols often makes things clear for his actors by illustrating bits of motivation with incidents from his own life. "Partly, I do this because it's all I *know*, and partly because I very much want to encourage them to pour *their* lives into what they're doing. I believe that the process can illuminate a scene and it also lets us learn a little more about each other, so that we can work together a little better."

In a scene, for example, where Eddie manifests blind jealousy over a fancied betrayal by Darlene, and Sigourney Weaver is at a loss how to react, Nichols asks her, "Have you ever been with an insanely jealous person?" He is thinking of a year in his own life, and just such a relationship.

"I know a great deal about that kind of jealousy," he says. "If, for instance, we were watching a movie together and there was a woman on the screen, I had to sit very, very still, or I would be excoriated for a long time afterward. It was a *scalding* experience, and I learned from it that jealousy is entirely the problem of the person *undergoing* it, and it's not really attached to *you* at all."

And he gives the actress a startling image to think about: "Being with an insanely jealous person is like being in the room with a *dead mammoth*."

There are other aspects of *Hurlyburly* that Nichols can readily illuminate from his own life—aspects that spoke to him instantly when he read the script.

"The play is about men fixated at the buddy level," Nichols says, "about the early adolescent attitude toward sex and toward women as objects to be traded." Nichols himself has been twice divorced and frequently in and out of love affairs. He has become expert at staging lopsided, misbegotten love scenes, and he manages to see even the craft of directing as analogous to sex.

"You never see anybody else doing it," he says, meaning both directing and sex. "You're never sure you're doing it right." He chuckles. "I mean, everybody's always very polite about it when you ask"—a woman about sex, an actor about directing. Nichols speaks in the measured, somewhat nasal tones familiar to audiences of two decades ago, who relished the comic routines he improvised with Elaine May. And he still, quite often, lapses into mimicry.

"'Yes, yes, this is the way it's done,' they say. 'Don't worry.' 'Are you *sure*?' you say. 'Is this the way *other* people do it?'"

In fact, though, Nichols seems unconcerned whether other directors use the personal approach he favors. He will continue to reveal himself, thereby encouraging his actors to be revealing. "It seems to me a very important aspect of rehearsal," he says.

Nichols continued to work on the *Hurlyburly* love scene during the following weeks, making minor refinements in collaboration with his actors. (Darlene would become even more aggressive and would unbutton Eddie's shirt *for* him; she would, herself, take off both of her boots.)

He keeps at it until he has exactly what he wants—just as he did in the case of a memorable scene in Murray Schisgal's *Luv*, which won for Nichols the 1965 Tony Award. A scene opened with the character played by Anne Jackson seated on a park bench, complaining to her husband, played by Alan Arkin, seated by her side, that their marriage was a failure. Arkin, with wounded but naive disbelief, replied: "*Our* marriage a *failure*?" The line was meant to get a laugh, but it didn't play funny enough to suit Nichols during rehearsals, until he hit on the idea of opening the dialogue with Arkin sitting in Anne Jackson's lap. At that point, it became perhaps the funniest line in the play.

Nichols has been combing scripts for Events he can "physicalize" ever since 1963, when he directed his first Broadway play, Neil Simon's *Barefoot in the Park*, for which he won his first Tony. He is relentless in his efforts to convey what the author— in Nichols's view—intends to be "really going on." His ability to "get the actor to physically express what the author gives only clues to" so endeared Nichols to Simon that Simon asked him to direct three more of his plays—*The Odd Couple*, *Plaza Suite*, and *The Prisoner of Second Avenue*.

"Mike takes you so into the play," says Simon. "You forget you're in the theater. He made the big fight scene in *Barefoot* between Robert Redford and Elizabeth Ashley so real, I said to him, 'Let's get out of here, this is too personal.'"

"It's funny," Nichols says, "but when we were doing *Barefoot*, I was newly married, like the couple in the play." (The marriage was to his second wife.) That was when he began to use personal revelation to enhance his actors' consciousness. "The play was all about *my* marriage and honeymoon and the fights we had. And I told the actors about it," he says.

And then, he says, it was just a question of building each scene carefully, bit by bit, as he first learned to do when he studied acting with Lee Strasberg. Then in his early twenties, he had no thought of becoming a director, but, he says, "in a way, it was the most important lesson I could have had."

In class, Nichols watched two fellow students perform a love scene. Strasberg, as Nichols recalls it, asked the young woman what she was concentrating on to produce the required emotion. She answered, "Oh, you know, the spring, and, well, the longing, and loving him . . ." And Strasberg asked, "Do you know how to make fruit salad?" She said she did. And Strasberg said, "Tell me how you make it."

"You want me to tell you, here in class, how I make fruit salad?" And Strasberg replied, "Yes, please." "You mean it?" she said. He assured her he did. "OK," she said, "I take an apple and I peel it and I cut it into pieces. And I take a banana and I peel it and cut it into slices. Then I peel an orange and cut it into slices. Maybe I take a few cherries and pit them and cut them into slices. And then I mix it all together."

Strasberg said, "That's right, that's how you make fruit salad. And until you pick up each piece of fruit, one at a time, peel it, and cut it into slices, you don't have fruit salad. You can run over the fruit with a steamroller, but you won't have fruit salad. Or you can sit in front of the fruit all night, saying, 'OK, fruit salad!' Nothing will happen, though, until you pick up each piece and peel it and cut it up."

That lesson, says Nichols, was "the most useful metaphor I've heard, then or since, for working on a play. You do the first job as neatly as you can: *She comes in.* Then you do the next job: *He sees her.* And so on. It's an extraordinarily useful lesson."

When stage or movie characters cut up fruit salad under Nichols's direction, someone—metaphorically speaking—usually slips on a banana peel. What's more, if Nichols can possibly manage it, the character will end up laughing at his own absurdity.

The mechanics of the joke, however, will remain hidden. "You're not meant to say, 'Oh, look what the actors are doing!'" Nichols says. The audience is meant to laugh, but not to see the director's efforts. Nichols is simply describing the care every craftsman takes to prevent the seams from showing.

In movies as in plays, once Nichols finds the physical means to express motivation, he buries them, "either in laughter or development—so they don't stand out as a signal from the director saying, 'Get it? *Get* it?'"

He cites, as an example, the Event in *The Graduate* that leads to the scene in which Dustin Hoffman, as Ben, finally capitulates to Anne Bancroft, as Mrs. Robinson. This capitulation scene (Ben finally slipping on the banana peel) is very calculatedly preceded by the farcical business in which Ben's parents make him try out their gift of an underwater diving suit.

"It's *such* an Event," Nichols says, "that not only does he have to try the equipment *on*, which isolates him from everybody completely—he can't hear, he can barely move—but then he has to get in the *water*. You see it all from his point of view.

"And the parents continually push him *under*, and *smile*, and keep pushing him under. And then he just sits at the bottom of the pool, not knowing what to do.

"And from this, directly, comes his decision to call Mrs. Robinson; it's to free himself from his suffocating parents. While you are underwater *with him*, in the diving suit, you hear Mrs. Robinson say 'Hello?' on the phone. And in the next shot Ben is in a phone booth speaking to her, asking if she'd like to meet him at the hotel, and she says she'll be there in fifteen minutes. It's cause and effect." Nichols does not try to restrain his delighted chuckle.

He laughs a lot, as befits a man who has made his reputation on comedy, and his laughter is winning. But his smile is strange. Even when he appears to be at his most sanguine, it stretches his face in a grimace that seems almost pained. It's a smile that takes getting used to, but after a while nuances can be discerned: Smiles of amusement or delight—even of near-beatitude—give way to smiles of rue, of anxiety—even of exasperation. At fifty-two, he has grown a trifle jowly, and the pale, elfin good looks of the old Nichols-May days on television have been replaced by a ruddier and more Jovian visage. Yet he affects a boyish manner of dress, more Beverly Hills than Park Avenue; the well-cut jeans, low boots, and supple, caramel-colored suede pull-on that he wears to rehearsal suggest Rodeo Drive.

Having worked in movies almost as long as he has been directing in the theater, Nichols is firm about what will be effective as a film and what will not. "It's a very rare play that can *really* become a movie," he says. "A movie, to a large extent, focuses on *who* is experiencing any given moment, which character's experience is it? In a movie, the camera has to *choose one person*. That's one of the crucial differences."

Jules Feiffer wrote *Carnal Knowledge* as a play and sent it to Nichols. "Twenty-four hours later," says Feiffer, "Mike called me and said, 'I think it's a *movie*.'"

"It seemed to me," Nichols says, "it had to do with the expression in people's eyes. I wanted to be very close to them, especially to the men, when they did these monologues about how often they did or did not have sex. Because it seemed to me that the *despair* at being trapped in this macho role could best be expressed when you were *right into* those faces."

But according to Feiffer, Nichols had a moment of panicky doubt before shooting the bawdy and brutal bedroom scene between Jack Nicholson and Ann-Margret. "I'm afraid of it, audiences will hate it," Nichols told Feiffer.

"The behavior was so vicious on the part of the Nicholson character, I was worried that the audience would just reject him permanently," Nichols says. "And there was my fear that Ann-Margret didn't have the experience to sustain such a long, emotional scene; she is supremely talented, but up to that point, she hadn't done anything that demanding. It took us time to find the way for her to approach that scene.

"We tried it first after giving her a few drinks, but that just pulled the timing apart," Nichols recalls. "So the next day she was sober, and it worked. Jack has a great gift for going, without fear, to the middle of a role and taking us all *with* him—without considering whether he'll be liked or disliked. What he did became, finally, very touching. Because it was a scene of hatred and rage, I shot first Ann-Margret, then Jack—individually—as a way to express their separation."

Such a specific focus is seldom either possible or desirable in a play, Nichols maintains. "In a play, each Event consists of *all* the characters' participation. That's one of the problems with Chekhov on film. You're looking at a group of people, and you know that A is in love with B, and B is in love with C, and C is about to commit suicide.

"And the pain and fascination is that while *you* know all these things about all of them, *they* know only a few things about the situation. A knows he loves B, but he *doesn't* know that B loves C; and B, who knows she loves C, doesn't know that C is about to commit suicide. And so there's great tension and emotion in watching these people sitting around a samovar drinking tea. You're seeing them all at the same time, as in life. But if you have to see them, one at a time, through the eye of the camera, it's a different kind of experience."

If there is a gaping difference in the way a director selects and creates a movie and the way he chooses and brings life to a play, there is an even wider chasm between the social roles of the film director and the stage director. For Nichols, directing a film can be psychologically threatening, which may account in part for the eight-year hiatus between *Silkwood* and his failed 1975 film, *The Fortune.*

Buried within Nichols—by his own admission—is a demon infant, which he calls his "baby portion," and which, during much of his life, he has been trying to exorcise. When making a movie, Nichols says, "certain socially hierarchical things happen" that threaten to release the demon.

"On a movie, the director is king, there's no question about it," Nichols says. "It's one of the things that can be lots of fun. And although it's fun, and helps *sometimes* with the work—you can, for instance, keep the producer off the set—it can lead to things that are spiritually not very good for you." He laughs.

"Pretty soon there are a lot of people saying"—Nichols slips into a mock-officious voice—"'He wants his *banana* at *four.*' And, of course, you *don't* want the banana at four, somebody made that up. And then there's somebody else who says"—adopting a brisk, confident voice—"'Oh, no-no-no, he *never* sits on *that* side of the camera, he always has his chair on the *left* side of the camera, *do* what I'm *telling* you.'" They are catering to the baby-as-king.

"This comes with the territory, unless you dismantle it. And I *do* have to dismantle it *completely* to be able to work. I mean, it's perfectly all right to have somebody bring me a sandwich while I'm shooting or rehearsing, as they do the actors and the cameraman. I'm not saying that I need to live a life of great austerity, because I don't."

Clearly not. Nichols's material possessions are considerable: A two-bedroom co-op tower apartment in a chic, Upper East Side hotel; a handsomely renovated brownstone that houses his suite of offices; a Colonial farmhouse surrounded by sixty acres in Connecticut, where he spends weekends and summers; a 375-acre ranch in California, where he raises Arabian horses.

"I had a long time of poverty," Nichols says. "It's not that painful when you're young, but still . . . My mother had to take jobs in a bakery, in bookshops. And then, in college, where I went on a scholarship, I had to work my way through in weird jobs like night janitor in a nursery, and driving a delivery truck for the Post Office during the Christmas season. I never once delivered a package; I could never find the address." Everything about Nichols today bespeaks his expensive taste and the means to gratify it—his clothes, the Picasso and Matisse on the walls of his apartment, the soft leather upholstery of his chauffeur-driven Mercedes. He coproduces all of his plays and films and his earnings are legendary. He has, to date, made over $2 million just on *Annie*—a musical he produced, but did not direct—and he is currently earning $22,000 a week from *The Real Thing*. "Having fame is wonderful," Nichols says, if you can control its tendency "to make you feel like a baby."

The struggle with his baby feelings was at its most pronounced during Nichols's years as a performer, when, he says, his vanity all too often would take over and cause him to behave petulantly. "It's—you know—'I don't like the way the ads look,' or, 'One of the lights is out, I'm not being lit properly.' As a director, those things concern me for the *project*, not for *me*. When you're worried about it for *you*, that's something I'm very uncomfortable with."

Characteristically, Nichols dealt with the discomfort by parodying it (and himself). One of the funniest sketches in the Nichols-May repertory, originated in 1957 for the Blue Angel nightclub in New York, was a telephone conversation between a possessive mother and her rocket-engineer son.

The mother (Elaine May) whining to her son: "You were supposed to call me Friday. I sat by that phone *all day Friday* . . . *all day Saturday*. . . . Your father said to me, 'Phyllis, *eat* something, you'll faint.' I said, 'No, Harry, no, I don't want my mouth to be full when my son calls me.'"

The son (Nichols) reflexively guilty: "Mother, I was sending up Vanguard, I didn't have a second. . . . Mother, *please* don't worry."

And so on, the mother ladling out guilt and syrupy love in equal measure, until at last she is cooing: "You're my baby . . . and no matter how old you get . . . even when you're *eighty* . . . you're gonna be *my baby*. . . . So is it so hard to pick up a phone and call your Mommy, pu-leese?" By this time, the son has reverted, all too happily, to infancy, and is answering in baby talk, practically drooling down his chin: "I wuv you, Mommy, goo-bye, Mommy-nonnie-noonie . . ."

"I learned two things from improvising that turned out to be invaluable in directing," Nichols says. "One was to be confident with an audience. Being in front of an audience every night for three or four hours, you learned to think, 'I can take care of you guys.'" (Part of the routine was to take requests from the audience for a subject, around which to improvise.)

"But most of all," Nichols says, "you learned to damn well pick something that would *happen* in the scene—an Event. Elaine used to say, 'When in doubt, *seduce.*' So that if we had to do a scene about a laundromat, for instance, one of us would try to seduce the other. That's one possibility.

"Another was to have a fight, because, as we all know, *conflict* leads to a scene. As long as something is *happening*, you can continue to improvise—otherwise it's just chitchat."

With that lesson ingrained, Nichols learned to approach each scene of a play with the question: What's happening? "All this," he says, "became extremely useful in plays and movies, in terms of expressing the *unstated.*"

While he learned from performing, Nichols says he never took it seriously as a career, even when he and Elaine May were making what seemed to them "a *fortune*" at the Blue Angel. "We thought this was a great gag and we could keep doing this until we grew up and started our *real* jobs. We never took it as our actual *lives.*"

It wasn't until he became a director, Nichols says, that he began to outgrow the baby. It was the producer Saint Subber who offered Nichols *Barefoot in the Park*. Nichols recalls saying to himself, "'Well, let's try, let's see if I can do it.' And from the *first* hour of the *first* day I was *home*. Instantly, I knew that's what I could do. And I'd never thought of it or planned it. But I felt *adult* for the first time. This was a *grown-up* job."

Nichols, who has been in and out of analysis, has given the subject of maturation some serious thought. The process of directing makes him feel grown up because, he says, "It is in some ways like being an ideal parent."

"Kurt Russell and Cher called me 'Dad' while we were shooting *Silkwood*," Nichols says proudly. "And they still call me 'Dad.' Kurt gave me an award at the end of the picture—'to the all-around best Jewish Dad.'"

Jeremy Irons, the star of *The Real Thing*, uses a different image to express a similar sentiment. "Mike creates a very protective environment," he says. "He's like the best of lovers; he makes you feel he's only for you."

It is evident that this rapport with actors is of profound importance to Nichols.

"I know," he says, "that an actor needs, above everything, to be able to trust someone, because of the necessity to call on deep and sometimes frightening feelings.

He needs someone to say, 'That's OK, you're safe, nothing bad will happen from exploring those feelings. No, you're not making a fool of yourself'—or, 'Yes, you *are* making a fool of yourself *in the best possible way.'*

"I think the role of director satisfies me partly because I am creating a father that I miss. The great thing about playing an adult role, a father's role, is that it reassures *you* as well. It doesn't matter what *end* of the Event you're on, as long as it's taking place."

Nichols, in fact, lost his father at the vulnerable age of twelve. Born Michael Igor Peschkowsky in Berlin in 1931, his life was shadowed virtually from infancy. His father, a physician, had left Russia during the 1917 revolution for Germany, where he met his future wife, the daughter of Jewish intellectuals. With the rise of Hitler, Dr. Peschkowsky departed for the United States, where he requalified as a physician and assumed the name Nichols, an Anglicization of his patronymic, Nicholaiyevitch.

Nichols, seven years old, and his younger brother were sent for—their mother being too ill to travel—and Nichols remembers that when he stepped off the Bremen in New York into his father's custody on May 4, 1939, he saw a delicatessen bearing a Hebrew sign and asked, in wonder, "Is that allowed here?"

At ten, he was banished to boarding school. His mother, who had joined the family by then, was still ailing and not strong enough to care for two active boys.

"My parents had a lot to cope with," he says. "It was hard for them to have a fresh little kid around, which is what I was." But Nichols felt unwanted and lost at school. "I was quietly unhappy," he says. "I felt strange and solitary. I didn't fit."

The sense of strangeness was compounded by his appearance. Nichols had lost his hair at the age of four, and at school he was a natural target for bullying and derision.

"It was a reaction to a shot I got for whooping cough—it was rare, but it happens sometimes," Nichols says. "Everyone who went to school with me remembers. I was that little bald kid." He was as much remembered for his sense of humor as for his baldness. If he suffered inwardly, his defense was to be funny. He learned to laugh to save his life, in that special way that is part of the Jewish heritage, laughing through tears—what in Yiddish is called *lachen mit yashcherkes.*

After his father's death from leukemia, Nichols's schooling continued to be financed by scholarships and he always held part-time jobs, but he was often extravagant and his mother frequently helped him financially. He was both grateful and guilty.

"Oh, I suffered," Nichols says, when pressed. "And when I got to college I went to a shrink and got shrunk for free, in the way you could in those days. And I began to think, 'Yes, I had a tough childhood, I had all those problems—but enough already! Let's get on with my life, let's start *now.'*

"And then, the *miracle* of college. Everything was wide open, *everybody* was strange at the University of Chicago! It was paradise! I began to see there was a world that I could *fit* in. I was happy *and* neurotic. I found people who read the things I read— Yeats, O'Neill, E. M. Forster, Dostoyevsky —people who liked to stay up all night talking."

Nichols's gift for comic exaggeration is a heritage from his Russian father. "Being funny is inborn," he says. "Sol Hurok, who was a patient of my father's, once said to me, 'My boy, you're not as funny as your father was.' My father could rage, but he also told very funny stories and he used to dance for us in his underwear." His father, Nichols says, helped him to understand the men in *Uncle Vanya*, which he staged in 1973.

"Vanya and Astrov were both like my father," Nichols says. "Conversation was their entertainment. Even Vanya's kvetching was entertainment. And Astrov's 'save-the-trees' routine was a *number* he did, to get women."

Uncle Vanya is the only classic that Nichols has ever staged. "I want to do *The Three Sisters* and there are certain Shakespeare plays I think about doing," he says. "What slows me is that in order to do a play—or a movie—I have to feel I'm the best guy on earth to direct it. I have to feel I have some *insights* into its *secrets*."

That was the case with *Streamers*, the most successful serious play Nichols has directed.

"*Streamers*, it seemed to me, was less *about* Vietnam than a *metaphor* for Vietnam," he says.

"I wanted it to be shocking, in the way cruelty and violence and pain are shocking in life, in a kind of uninflected, unmelodramatic way. Because it seems to me that the really terrible things, when they come in real life, are quite flat and ordinary. It's part of their horror. And you never have any preparation for them. The emblem of *Streamers*, to me, was the moment when Carlyle, the black soldier, stabs one of the sergeants. The sergeant has cut his hand, breaking a bottle of beer to defend himself. He's looking at his hand, and Carlyle *stabs* him—walks up to him and *stabs* him. And the sergeant says to him, 'Wait a minute, will you, I cut my *hand*.' It's a truly horrifying moment, one that *I* identified with very strongly because of the ordinary, the non sequitur in the middle of death.

"Think of being semiconscious in the emergency room and hearing friends say, 'There's a Chinese place, I think, three blocks from here, but I don't know if they're still open.' Somehow, things go on. This is neither good nor bad. It's just the way it is."

Nichols is as instinctive about rejecting projects as he is about those he takes on.

"I turn down scripts about the Holocaust," he says. "I rejected *Sophie's Choice*. It's just . . . my problem. I *cannot* imagine sitting on a crane on the set of Auschwitz, saying, 'All right, let me see all the prisoners camera left.' I just can't *conceive* of my doing it. It's not that I read the script and burst into tears. It's that I'm physically incapable of dealing *technically* with those events."

He also turned down *The Exorcist*—for two reasons, he says. "One was that I didn't know what the hell it was *for*. And the other reason was that I was *incapable* of putting a little girl through that for four or five months. I couldn't imagine going to work, saying, '*Today* is the *day* that you *vomit blood*, and here's what you say. . . .'"

If Nichols is tender about children because he remembers the sad little boy he once was, he is also probably thinking of the children he has fathered—ten-year-old

Max and seven-year-old Jenny, whose mother is Annabel Davis-Goff, a novelist. Nichols also has a twenty-year-old daughter, Daisy, from his second marriage, who is studying art history in Paris.

After nine well-received plays and four movies, Nichols hit a creative lull in 1973. He directed two film failures (*The Day of the Dolphin* and *The Fortune*) and he abandoned a Neil Simon movie, *Bogart Slept Here*, after a few days of shooting, convinced it wouldn't work.[1]

"People said I was afraid of failure," Nichols says. "I really just felt dead mentally, jaded. I'd always *loved* rehearsing, but I could barely arouse my own interest. I must have been depressed without knowing it. I get more narcoleptic than scared when things aren't going well.

"I remember walking into my office in California and picking up the script of *Streamers* on the day we stopped *Bogart*. Everything changed for me on the spot. I called David and said, 'I want to do it.'"

Streamers was just a reprieve. After that, Nichols's theater career began to slide, too. He concedes that at this time he was at one of the "low points" of his life—a period that stretched through the production of Jean Kerr's *Lunch Hour* in 1980. He was sleepwalking through his work.

Not until the making of *Silkwood* did he regain his creative enthusiasm. "My interest began with Alice Arlen and Nora Ephron, who brought me a draft of their script," Nichols says. "I liked them both enormously and I liked what they had done. I was interested in the theme of being asleep and waking up. It was, in fact, the situation in which I found *myself* at the time. I saw that Karen Silkwood was a zombie, she was asleep during her work, and then she began slowly to wake up. That was my central image for the character.

"Waking, she said to herself, 'Where have I been? Why haven't I been paying attention?'

"And the pleasure of working with Meryl Streep! Her *joy* at getting to do the role, approaching acting with the attitude, 'What do I get to do next?' Like a child. That joy of hers is infectious. It reminded me how much I loved my work. I go to pieces when I talk about Meryl.

"It was, I suppose, the confluence of the group of us, the subject, the way we all felt about one another, the excitement about what we were doing. And I began to think, 'I'm pretty good at this, and it isn't as hard as I remembered.'"

After collaborating joyously with Ephron and Arlen and Streep, Nichols found himself just as happy in the company of Tom Stoppard.

"I take on the mood of the person I'm working with," Nichols says. "David Rabe and I tend to get gloomy. Tom and I had nothing but laughs and joy, working on *The Real Thing*. While David writes from his unconscious, Tom writes philosophically and intellectually. He has very definite ideas about how his plays should be done."

The fiercely verbal Stoppard does not deny this. "A writer arrives at rehearsals with strong prejudices about the *noise* his play should be making—how loud, how soft, how high, how deep, how fast, how slow the actors' voices should be," Stoppard says, sounding very much like the playwright-protagonist of *The Real Thing*.

"There was a particular scene, early on, that I thought should be taken in a very leisurely way. I thought the actors' speeches should be dropped into little pools of prepared silence. I said to Mike, 'I think this scene would be best if done very *slowly*.' And he said, 'Or very *fast*.'

"He was contradicting me, while appearing to agree. That was so typical of his cunning and courtesy. I loved him for that." (They did the scene fast.)

"Mike has relentless concern with every physical detail of a production. Once, during a technical rehearsal, when he was working on a blackout, there was a tiny flicker of light, no more than a glowworm would cast, and Mike called, 'What in God's name is that *searchlight* doing onstage?' Another time, he glimpsed a mere ghost of a shadow moving onstage and he said, 'Why is that *crowd* of people *milling about* in *full view*?'"

Nichols soon will be working in New York on the technical aspects of *Hurlyburly*. He and Rabe cut thirty-one minutes from the play in Chicago. Although he is excited about the play, Nichols still has doubts about whether he has solved all its difficulties.

Even after the play ended its run in Chicago, he was still tinkering with one of its major scenes, and he brought to it, as to earlier ones, several of his trademarked ingredients: Illustrations from his personal life, improvisational technique, and his skill at concealing the mechanics of the Event.

The scene, which runs about fifteen minutes, involves five of the play's seven characters—William Hurt; Christopher Walken, as his housemate; Harvey Keitel, as a former convict and bit player; Judith Ivey, as a nightclub balloon dancer; and Jerry Stiller, as an unsuccessful Hollywood hack. (The seventh cast member is Cynthia Nixon, who plays a nymphet.)

"I thought for some time," Nichols says, "about the fact that jungle and animal images are, to me, central to the play—the groping and crawling toward each other of these people, partly because they are stoned, partly because they are losing their humanity; but even more, because their *language* is the language of people who have been disconnected from human endeavor, almost entirely."

Nichols told his actors to think of themselves as drugged, lolling animals. Hurt begins the scene lying across the bar; Ivey begins by reclining in a chair; Walken lies on his back on the second-story platform, an arm dangling over the edge.

"I think he's a cat," Nichols says. "He takes random swipes at the people who move beneath him, sort of like a cat in a tree. I haven't asked the others what animals they are imagining themselves to be. All of them are prone, supine, or crawling."

Nichols says he experimented with drugs—marijuana and cocaine—during the time he was making *Catch-22*. "What happens when Judith Ivey gets her drugs is that she begins to slide out of her chair and go lower and lower, until she's on the floor; and Bill Hurt slides down the bar and *crawls* to her to give her more coke; and a little later, *she* crawls over to Harvey Keitel.

"The action is, I *think*, completely *hidden*, in the sense that I think you could see the scene several times and never say to yourself, 'These people are crawling, no one has walked for fifteen minutes.'

"We were on the way to achieving this when we first got to Chicago, and then it became a question of how to use the furniture, how to get them lower. You're not meant to say, 'Oh, look, they're all crawling!' It's meant to convey an atmosphere. It's supposed to give you a different *feeling* than if the words were being delivered by people sitting and chatting upright in chairs."

Nichols will continue to rehearse until the opening. *Hurlyburly* is anything but a "safe" play.

"Elaine May has a wonderful motto," Nichols says. "The only safe thing is to take a chance. I think she means that if you *stay* safe, and *don't* take a chance—don't do something that's different from the last thing, something that makes you nervous and holds dangers—if you keep trying to do the thing that worked *last* time, the encrustations of mannerisms begin to take you over. And pretty soon you're no good at all—and therefore not safe at all. The longer you play it safe, the less interesting is what you do."

After *Hurlyburly*, Nichols hopes to reward himself by working again with Meryl Streep, who said she is interested in the film version of Nora Ephron's best-selling novel, *Heartburn*. Absurdist that he is, Nichols is drawn to the heroine of *Heartburn* because she is "a woman doomed to be in the right—and, therefore, alone."

"My approach to a light comedy like *Heartburn* is the same as my approach to a tragicomedy like *Hurlyburly*," he says. "I don't think comedy is an escape from tragedy. They are both *life*."

All of the plays (and movies) he directs are, he believes, about the eternal comic-tragic self-delusion we all practice: "Life is hopeless—but it isn't; love is fleeting—but eternal; our personal lives are everything—but we are unimportant." These are ideas, Nichols says, that have a lasting life.

[Sidebar:] . . . And Elaine May

Mike Nichols says that his success as a director is due in part to his training in improvisation—first with the Chicago-based Compass troupe, which became the Second City company, and later as a nightclub act with Elaine May. Nichols and May split up professionally and personally in 1962, in a way that was very wounding to them both. Nichols seems to find it painful, still, to discuss the break. "Several things happened," he says. "One was that I, more than Elaine, became more and more afraid of our improvisational material. We used to make up several new things each night. We never wrote a skit down the first time, we just sort of outlined it: You be so-and-so, I'll be so-and-so. I'll try to make you, or we'll fight—whatever it was. That was it. *We actually improvised on national television!*

"But the bigger the nightclub we were in, the bigger the television show we were on, the more pressure there was to have the sketches we did be the best we had. She was always brave. But I became more and more afraid. And we found ourselves doing the same material over and over, especially in our show for Broadway. This took a great toll of Elaine. And I nagged the hell out of her. I was always saying, 'Can't you do that any faster?' and 'You're taking too long over this.'"

Nichols didn't realize it, but he was evolving into a director. (May says, "I always thought he'd be a wonderful director.")

"She'd fill things, I'd shape them. She had endless capacity for invention. My invention was not endless. But it taught me about beginnings, middles, and ends. I *had* to push the sketch ahead, because I couldn't invent as she could.

"Elaine wrote a play called *A Matter of Position*, and that's what fractured our relationship." Nichols played the leading role. "I was onstage, she was in the audience watching me, judging me." He gropes for a way to explain what, clearly, he would prefer not to talk about.

"As soon as we weren't in balance . . . equals on the stage . . . great angers . . . and things . . . arose. We flew apart." The play closed in Philadelphia.

At the time of the breakup, Nichols remembers walking down Park Avenue with his friends Felicia and Leonard Bernstein.

"Lenny had his arm around me and he said, 'Oh, Mikey, you're so *good!* I don't know at *what.*'" Nichols laughs. "It was a very Lenny thing to say. But I knew just what he meant. *I* didn't know at what either.

"It took years for Elaine and me to come back to each other after that. And what happened in those years was that we become two individual people, rather than Nichols-and-May. When she became wholly Elaine May and I became wholly Mike Nichols, we became the dearest of old friends." (In 1980, they acted together in *Who's Afraid of Virginia Woolf?* at New Haven's Long Wharf Theatre.)

"When Elaine and I split up—that was a shattering year for me . . . I didn't know what I was. I was the left-over half of *something.* We're very close friends now. I think now it's forever."

Note

1. *Bogart Slept Here*, with a revised script, became the 1977 Herbert Ross film *The Goodbye Girl.*—REK

Did Mike Nichols Squander His Luck on *Heartburn*?

Paul Rosenfield / 1986

From the *Los Angeles Times*, August 3, 1986. Reprinted by permission.

NEW YORK—Mike Nichols was improvising. The former improvisational comedian who (with Elaine May) brought psychoanalytic humor to America in the 1950s was at it again. Nichols was trying to explain *Heartburn*, the Meryl Streep–Jack Nicholson domestic comedy that has since opened to completely mixed notices. He was on the spot, in his own living room. And Nichols was taking his time with the answer. He might have been improvising the role of the English dentist he used to do onstage. (Leaning over the patient, who was Elaine May, the dentist said, "I knew before I met you I loved you. There I've said it! Rinse out, please.") Nichols has this forbidding way of looking at you, not unlike a demon dentist—or a shrink. He seems to be asking, "Did you get it? If so, how *much* did you get?" But before saying a word he takes a very long time.

Explanations are tricky, because *Heartburn* is nothing if not a roman à clef, written in the first person, and its players are alive and very visible. Nora Ephron, who based the book tightly on the breakup of her marriage to Watergate reporter Carl Bernstein, also wrote the screenplay for *Heartburn*—but Ephron isn't meeting the press. Bernstein has his say in the September *Playboy* now on the stands, but otherwise he is keeping unusually mum. (At least publicly.) The actors are hired hands. Nicholson only signed on for *Heartburn* one week into shooting, after the exit of Mandy Patinkin, who was to play the fictionalized Bernstein. Streep only came to the project shortly after finishing *Out of Africa*. So it's largely up to Nichols to explain *Heartburn*.

Why explain? In anticipation of what the critics might say. If *Heartburn* were to get unqualified raves, Nichols would only have to improvise a bow. But the reviews have since run a gamut from hate to love that even an analyst might have trouble with. *Time*'s Richard Corliss: "True and painful and funny." *People*'s Peter Travers:

"Streep and Nicholson have never opened up more emotionally on-screen." And then there was the rave-of-the-week from the *Washington Post*'s Paul Attanasio: "A masterpiece [. . .] and something of a summing-up for Nichols, who more successfully than any other American director, has staked out the terrain where men and women meet as his own."

Then there was the other camp, *Newsweek*'s Jack Kroll: "*Heartburn* doesn't seem to be about anything." The *Times*' Sheila Benson: "Thin stuff from rich talents." *USA Today*'s Mike Clark: "Too scattershot to make sense." The movie opened strongly—$5.7 million in three days at 843 theaters—but it is too soon to determine its staying power.

Director Nichols, a critics' darling since his debut play *Barefoot in the Park* and his debut picture *Who's Afraid of Virginia Woolf?*, isn't used to defending himself. So improvising was in order. Questions were invented to help him along: Is *Heartburn* about the failure of a two-star marriage? Is it about yuppie love? Is it about jealousy? Two years ago, Nichols explained that *Heartburn* was about "a woman doomed to be in the right, and therefore alone."

Now he had a variation on the theme: "*Heartburn* may be about squandering your luck," he said as if the answer had finally come. "It may be that we don't get lucky that way—with love—very often, and to squander it is to take a big chance for the man. And for the woman, too. She does a certain kind of squandering, of a different kind maybe, but . . . *Heartburn* is also about what Carly Simon (who did the film's score) calls 'coming around again.' With any luck in life we do come around again."

If devotees of Ephron's novel are having problems with Nichols's movie, Nichols has his own explanation: "I don't know a great deal about Nora's story," he professed, sitting very still and erect in the tree-lined, book-lined living room that faces Central Park. (Ephron cowrote *Silkwood* for Nichols after the breakup with Bernstein.) "*Heartburn* is fiction, after all," defended Nichols, "and with a work of fiction we don't know everything. We don't really know the basis of most fictions. If you talk to spouses of major novelists through time, what would you learn about their private lives? Are novels disguised reality or not? And if so, how much disguised?"

When it's mentioned that the Carl Bernsteins were not as notorious as, say, the Richard Burtons or the Sean Penns, Nichols nodded. "I know what you mean. The movie is meant to show little bits of people we know, and to tell a larger story than Nora's own. All we know for sure is that certain people know about some of the events. It's like real life, yet it's no truer to real life than (Proust's) *Swann's Way*. The point of view of the picture is not what really happened, but what *will* really happen. Ideally, this story will connect to your own life."

And if not, not. Nichols has what appears to be (and has been acknowledged to be) a laissez-faire attitude in the midst of chaos. Example: When Patinkin left *Heartburn*, there were no leaks to the press as to why, no public explanations. (The movie could be called a top-to-bottom Sam Cohn project. Cohn, the Manhattan-based ICM agent, represents Nichols, Streep, and Patinkin.) Ask Nichols now about Patinkin's disappearance, and he will say, "Let's talk about Jack. Let's talk about how Nicholson is a master of bringing life to every scene." But what about Patinkin? "The chemistry was better between Meryl and Jack. Period."

To really change the subject, Nichols went so far as to credit Nicholson with creating "my first painless experience shooting a movie, on *Carnal Knowledge*. I always loved the preproduction work on movies, and I loved the editing process. But I abhorred the actual shooting. I was terrified. I would always sigh with relief," sighed Nichols, "when something was finally shot. Most people would give anything in the world to make a living the way I do, and they are right. But not until Nicholson, on *Carnal*, and Meryl, on *Silkwood*—and then the two of them on this—did I love the actual shooting."

Nichols not enjoying movie making? Even after his celebrated debut (*Virginia Woolf*), after winning an Oscar for *The Graduate*, and after becoming the first star director to command a six-figure salary (for *Catch-22*)? In the late sixties, Nichols found himself barely thirty-five and stuck with the nickname Midas. ("A journalistic figment," he calls the label now.) But for a solid decade he had almost owned Broadway (*Luv, Plaza Suite, Apple Tree*), if not Hollywood (*The Graduate, Carnal Knowledge*). Then ten years ago, after the failure of his Warren Beatty–Jack Nicholson film, *The Fortune*, Midas Nichols vanished. In 1976 there was a shutdown during the first week of production on his Robert De Niro–Marsha Mason–Neil Simon comedy called *Bogart Slept Here*, and Mike Nichols didn't make another full-scale movie until *Silkwood* eight years later. (*Gilda Live* was docucomedy and doesn't count.)

In person Nichols is like an intellectual Puck, curious and yet almost completely protected by serious people at this point in his life. Nichols, who briefly studied pre-med and wanted to be a psychiatrist, could easily have become one of those specialists one goes to in extreme moments. His intelligence is not an improvisation—it's not something he pastes on each morning like eyebrows. His choices, especially in the sixties and eighties, are object lessons in how to launch and maintain a show-business career. Like almost nobody else, he's used actors (Ann-Margret, *Carnal Knowledge*) and playwrights (Tom Stoppard, who rewrote *The Real Thing* for Broadway, and for Nichols) and opportunities (he jumped in with enough last-minute funding for *Annie* that he could rename the Broadway musical "Annuity"). In other words, Nichols can probably outsmart almost anyone on either coast, which would almost bestow on him a noblesse oblige attitude.

But for years the question has been, Did Mike Nichols abandon Hollywood or was it the other way around? In 1983, Nichols made *Silkwood* and got Oscar-nominated. The popular thinking was that Hollywood had either forgiven Nichols his commercial failures—*The Day of the Dolphin* and *The Fortune*—or forgotten them. But the Directors Guild of America didn't nominate him for *Silkwood*. So maybe all was not forgotten. At any rate, he remained in New York (and in Connecticut, at his sixty-acre farm). Traditionally, wunderkind directors—names like Elia Kazan and Joseph Mankiewicz—would return from Hollywood to the East with bodies of work behind them. But Nichols even now is only fifty-five.

"In California," said Nichols slowly, "I always feel I'm missing out on something. I pick up those trade papers, and I feel other people are doing things I don't know about." The look in Nichols's eyes was conspiratorial, a glint. As though he wasn't sure anyone knows he has a 375-acre horse ranch near Santa Barbara—even if he is ambivalent about California. (He is also private—if not reclusive—about the details of his multiple marriages or his children.)

"California is a swell place to live if you imagine yourself an anthropologist," he decided. "It reminds me of . . . well, it's like when Elaine (May) and I were performing. And I would worry about things like 'Is this the best dressing room?' or 'Did you check our billing on the marquee?' That's the baby part of me, and in California I take a little slide toward the baby part. I find California easier for living, but it's also easier there to avoid real life."

Yet again Nichols had almost maneuvered his way out of a question, or had he? "Had I had it with the movie business after *The Fortune*?" Nichols asked himself out loud. "No . . . and it wasn't movie people I didn't like. One of the lessons of *The Fortune*, in my view, and God knows who else's view, is that it's not enough just to put together good people. You have to have an idea. You can't just wait for the idea. I don't believe in picking fruit before it's ripe. But you have to either find an idea or forge one eventually."

Who's Afraid of Virginia Woolf? would seem to have been the ideal idea, for starters. Yet to tackle Edward Albee's catharsis play as a debut film was one of those gambles that only in retrospect looks inevitable. Tyro Nichols came to Warner Bros. facing not only Elizabeth Taylor, who was set to play the fiftyish Martha, but also the late Jack Warner, the waning tycoon of the lot. *Virginia Woolf* was one of Warner's own swan songs, the most expensive black-and-white movie shot to that time, and Mike Nichols was not yet thirty-five.

"Do you think *Virginia Woolf* was a gamble?" he asked coyly. "That's funny. A very bright woman friend of mine said it was not enough of a challenge. She said it was a sure thing. . . . Actually, for me it was a learning film. You can see me learning as we go along."

Example: Nichols demanded the title sequence be shot in Northampton, Massachusetts, "because I had this crazy notion that a sound stage wouldn't look authentic. And they indulged me, because I felt so strongly." Here Nichols's boyish-modest front appeared: "They indulged me" is not unlike his *Graduate* acceptance speech at the New York Critics Awards when, after thanking his associates, he added, "I can't really tell you who did what. I hope I did some of it."

Under the boyish-modest attitude, however, are more revealing admissions. "God, the things I didn't know about movies!" Nichols confessed. "I had to check a print of *Virginia Woolf* recently for one of those Lincoln Center tributes, and I took one of my kids along. We saw the first three reels, and I thought, 'This is not what my kid wants to watch. . . .' Then I realized it got better as it went along, because I was learning. On that movie I was like a kid taking things for granted, making things up, diving in. Kids do things relatively unquestioningly. I was diving in."

But to direct Elizabeth Taylor and Richard Burton the first time out? "Elizabeth was set before I came along, but Richard wasn't; he needed to be suggested, which seems impossible now, but it's true. Richard and I once shared an alley on Broadway. *Camelot* was at the Majestic Theatre, and *An Evening with Nichols and May* was at the Golden Theatre. He was a pal, and Elizabeth I was getting to know pretty well, and . . ." (Almost unknown is the fact that Taylor insisted on Nichols. During her Roman fracas on *Cleopatra*, and the publicity surrounding the Burton-Taylor affair, Nichols was one of the only friends to fly to Italy to be with the couple. The stars didn't forget.)

And Nichols was launched in Hollywood.

The follow-up film, the one that got him the Oscar and a generation of devotees, was *The Graduate*. It made Nichols a culture hero because Nichols made Southern California look like another planet, sexy and rich and full of new chances. Especially for Benjamin Braddock (Dustin Hoffman) and Mrs. Robinson (Anne Bancroft), if not the clones they inspired. Two years ago Bancroft told Calendar, "I never worked harder in my life! Mike's theory about Mrs. Robinson was very clear: All grown-ups were bad and all kids were wonderful."

Now Nichols disputed this notion. "I don't remember telling Anne Bancroft that," he said thoughtfully. "What *The Graduate* is about for me is something very different. The movie always was, and still is, about finding yourself surrounded by objects and people who are concerned with objects. It's about saving yourself from becoming an object, through passion and, if necessary, madness."

Nichols admitted that, yes, Doris Day had been sought to play Mrs. Robinson. ("I believe we did ask her, and she turned it down because of the love scenes, but my memory is not so strong now and wasn't even then.") The very married, very available Mrs. Robinson struck nerves, and sent lots of American youths to California, in search of seduction. "Mrs. Robinson," said Nichols, "is a person who did not like what she let her life become. She's angry at herself, and therefore angry at others. And then there's Benjamin, who felt he was drowning in things. He determines to become prouder of himself and his whole situation by going as far as he can. He hits bottom, then bounces back. That's what usually happens, in life and movies, and it's dramatic to see it."

But what happens next? A sequel to *The Graduate* seems if not inevitable, then intriguing, and Nichols doesn't disagree. Some time went into speculating over who and how and in what way a sequel could be done. Would Ben and Elaine (Mrs. Robinson's daughter) return to Beverly Hills? Would they split like the couple in *Heartburn*? "Partly you don't want to tamper with it," reasoned Nichols. "Also it's hard to know where they all are. But let's think about it: Do they all forgive each other? And in what manner? They can't go on, you know, until they forgive each other, which is true in life as well. But do they have Mrs. Robinson over for dinner? I mean, here you have this seductive mother-in-law . . . I don't know. Maybe it ends like *Down and Out in Beverly Hills*."

The irony of Nichols and Beverly Hills is how little time he'd spent there before so accurately catching it on film. "But it was there to be caught! Those were the days: (Production designer) Dick Sylbert and I spent six months looking and preparing. We were obsessive. We'd ask each other questions like 'What would you see from a helicopter?' Answer: You'd see a pool behind every house. That means the line of the bathing suit strap has to be just right because these are people who spend a lot of time by their pools."

No tan lines for Nichols, however. Before, during, and after his Hollywood stay, he worked consistently on New York stages, and won six Tonys for directing. His output might seem compulsive to anyone not versed in show-business compulsion. A-show-a-season (or sometimes two shows) seems almost to have been his motto. "I suppose it looks like I've been working all the time," he admitted. "But I have to tell you, I am also happy and capable of just hanging out." Yet while editing *Silkwood*, he directed *Hurlyburly* on Broadway. While editing *Heartburn*, he directed *Social Security* on Broadway. "I like the process," he said simply. "I like taking the stuff that happens to us and pulling it in to something worth watching."

A case can be made that Nichols's career as stage director was charmed from day one. In 1962, after his breakup with Elaine May, he was "the leftover half of a comedy team." But only months later he got a $500 offer to direct a summer-stock production of a play called *Nobody Loves Me*, starring Robert Redford. Nichols still claims he "backed into it. There was no plan or purpose. But then there never was a plan ever. When Elaine and I were working together, people used to ask us, 'What kind of work do you kids do during the day?' We never knew what to say. Working in improvisation, as I was with Elaine, meant I was working with a director's point of view. Improvisation gives you that; it gives you the elements of a scene, the need for conflict, and the tools that keep an audience interested."

Becoming a director "may have been a conscious act, and it may have been luck," Nichols claimed. "What if (producer) Saint Subber hadn't asked me to direct *Nobody Loves Me*? The play became *Barefoot in the Park* (and won Nichols his first Tony). But if Saint Subber hadn't asked, I might never have directed. But also I *might* have. Yet from that very first day of rehearsal I knew I liked directing. It fit. I liked being asked *how do you do this?*

Nichols was asked to recall his first day directing, and his laugh was mysterious. "I remember Redford. There were altogether six days of rehearsal because this was summer stock. So my direction consisted of saying, 'You stand here, Bob,' and 'You go over there, honey,' and 'Your arm is exposed.' I was meticulous in a superficial way. Did I see a larger career for myself? No. Then one day Redford did something."

To demonstrate, Nichols stood up and mock-flipped his collar to improvise a man wearing a topcoat and simultaneously lifting a body. "I remember telling Redford, 'The first thing to know is that being onstage is like being in a battle, and the first thing you do is admit to being in battle.' Anyway, Redford and the other characters in the play have just come back from a Greek restaurant, and they've walked up five flights of stairs. And Bob said something smart. He said, 'What if I carried the mother-in-law up the stairs?' He was right, and it got an enormous laugh. Then I said to Bob, 'I think your character might have a head cold.' You don't have weighty discussions with a six-day rehearsal period. But Redford was, and is, such a good actor that he suddenly had a cold. I don't mean he went home for two days and worked out a head cold. I mean he got a cold then and there. I think at that moment I decided I loved what I was doing."

The joy (or power) came relatively late. Late, that is, if one subscribes to a Nichols Theory of Life. The theory: "There are people to whom all good things happen in the first part of their lives—and then there are the rest of us." Nichols, who admits he was not particularly happy in his first half, was a German immigrant who arrived in America by ship at the age of seven, accompanied only by his younger brother. (He spoke only two sentences: "I do not speak English" and "Do not kiss me.") The brothers' doctor father died only a few years later, leaving very little cash. It would seem a grim saga, but Nichols, as usual, is surprising. And, again, improvising. He was suddenly remembering the Bremen, the German boat that brought the refugee brothers to America. By screwing up his face Nichols became seven years old. A very forbidding seven years old.

"That little boy on the boat wasn't so unhappy," he said, attempting a Jack Nicholson grin. "I remember now looking for the prow of the boat, or was it the bow? I remember asking a fellow passenger, in German, where was the tip? I meant in which direction. He pointed to the tip of my nose. And I said, 'No, no, no, I mean the front of the boat! Don't kid around!' Well, he wasn't kidding around. . . . And I was looking ahead, even then. And you know what?" Nichols was about to revise his theory. "I now think there are people who are happy as children, happy in high school, and happy straight through life. Isn't that depressing?"

The Road to *Ishtar*: How Warren Beatty, Dustin Hoffman, and Elaine May Made a Farce in the Desert for Just $40 Million

David Blum / 1987

From *New York* magazine, March 16, 1987, pp. 34–43. Reprinted by permission.

Warren Beatty just earned $6 million from Columbia Pictures, but he doesn't really think that's any of your business.

These days, the forty-nine-year-old actor-director-producer is especially upset about the weekly *Entertainment Tonight* segment in which the relentlessly chipper Mary Hart usually recites the top five movies—ranked according to earnings, not artistic merit. The public, to his thinking, gets as wrapped up in the competition for first place in movies as it does in professional football, which is his own passion.

Beatty is deeply concerned about the obsession the public seems to have with the inner workings of the studios—who's on top and who's about to be fired.

"I think to some extent it might be good to let these very cautious and very intelligent businessmen take care of their own business," Beatty said recently, in his first magazine interview in almost a decade. His baby-soft voice climbed several decibels to make this point "And if things cost too much and they don't make a profit, they won't do it anymore. They'll lose their job." It should also be noted that Beatty—the producer of four big movies (*Bonnie and Clyde*, *Shampoo*, *Heaven Can Wait*, and *Reds*) and no flops—doesn't think $40 million is too much to spend on a movie.

"Everything in the movie you have to measure in relation to the return on it," he said. "Saving money per se is not any particular skill."

Beatty's own next movie just happens to have cost $40 million, out of which comes his $6 million salary. It's called *Ishtar*, and it's set to open all over the country on May 15. Almost since the day it was announced, *Ishtar* has been regarded as a potential *Heaven's Gate*—the classic $44 million bomb that brought about the downfall of a movie studio and helped focus moviegoers' attention on budgets. It's a comparison that Beatty deeply resents. "What you're hoping for is that an audience will go in for an hour and forty-five minutes and have a nice time," he says.

Before you decide whether Beatty is right or wrong, you might want to consider the Case of the Perfect Camel, and the Flat-Desert Brouhaha.

The Case of the Perfect Camel: It was September 1985, and production was about to begin on *Ishtar*. A contemporary road picture in the style of the old Hope-Crosby movies, it stars Dustin Hoffman and Beatty, who also produced it and brought in his old friend Elaine May, a fifty-five-year-old writer-director, to write and direct. Hoffman, forty-nine, and Beatty play two down-and-out singer-songwriters who've gone to Morocco for a nightclub gig and get caught up in foreign intrigue. Much of the movie was set to be shot on location in North Africa, where the two superstars were to ride across the desert on a camel.

So one of the first things the production needed to buy was a camel.

Specifically, it needed a wide-eyed camel that would look blind on-screen. A couple of production staffers were dispatched to Marrakech with a blank check to find a Perfect Camel and four stand-in Perfect Camels.

In a matter of minutes on their first day of talking to camel dealers and salesmen, they found a Perfect Camel for about seven hundred dollars. It also happened to be the first camel they looked at.

So they didn't buy it.

"We had lots of time to spend, and lots of money," recalls a production source close to the camel. "We didn't want to go back to the office and say, 'Elaine, guess what. We bought the very first camel we looked at!' We figured what the hell, we'd keep looking. We told the camel dealer, 'Thanks a lot. We'll get back to you.'"

Two days went by. The camel buyers continued their search through the Sahara for the Perfect Camel and the necessary backups. But every camel they looked at suffered by comparison with that first, exquisite camel. The humps would be too large or too small. The facial hair would be beige or brown. It was always something. (It's important to know that a camel search is no cheap date. Every minute of a production staffer's time on a location shoot—at union wages, with costly travel and hotels—is worth money, and days of it can cost thousands of dollars.)

Finally, they figured they'd been looking long enough. "Let's see if we can buy that first camel we looked at," the buyers agreed. So they went back to the dealer who'd showed them that lovely specimen.

"Remember us? We'd like to buy that camel of yours that we looked at the other day."

The dealer shook his head. "Sorry," he said. "We ate it."

The Flat-Desert Brouhaha: Dunes, Elaine May thought. Dunes. I want big dunes in my movie. I mean, *Ishtar* is a movie that takes place largely in the African desert, so shouldn't there be some big dunes in it?

So her production designer, associate producer, and other key people went looking for big dunes. It wasn't just a matter of finding any old big dunes either. They had to find big dunes alongside a luxury hotel, so that the director, stars, and crew wouldn't have to trek several hours each day across the desert to shoot the movie.

It was not easy to find a luxury hotel in the middle of the African desert.

After several weeks of searching through several countries, Paul Sylbert, the production designer, finally found some big dunes to his liking in the south Moroccan Sahara—with two comfortable hotels right nearby. "It was a miracle that somebody had built those hotels," Sylbert says. They booked the necessary fancy suites for the stars, and proceeded to set up production.

But once Elaine May arrived and took a good look at the dunes, she started to think: Maybe I don't want only big dunes. People have an image of what a desert looks like—endless and flat. Maybe I should shoot some of the movie on a flat desert.

"You want to shoot on a flat desert?" Paul Sylbert asked. "But we've got *dunes* here. You wanted *dunes*."

"No," May said, "I think I want a flat desert."

So Sylbert had to hire several people at union wages and spend about ten days, but he did it. He took a square-mile area in the vicinity—right where all the big dunes were—and had his team of workers scrape away the dunes. After nearly two weeks under the hot desert sun, Sylbert managed to turn a desert full of big dunes into a flat desert.

"It was incredible," Sylbert remembers. "Right there, right smack in the middle of all those dunes, I'd built Elaine a flat desert." Sylbert is an amiable fellow. If someone wants to turn big dunes into a flat desert, that's fine with him.

In ancient times, "Ishtar" referred to the Babylonian goddess of love and war. In Elaine May's script, it refers to a country that appears to be Morocco. (For several months last year, Columbia Pictures tried to think of a different name for the movie, but after coming up with more than forty alternatives, including "Blind Camel" and "Ishtar Hotel," they gave up.)

May's shooting script is a classic buddy picture—focusing on two very different men joined for comic purposes. It begins with a standard movie premise—ordinary people trapped in an extraordinary circumstance—and never veers very far from that formula. In this case, it's two American singer-songwriters in Morocco for the only gig they can get (aside from one in Honduras); they suddenly find themselves ensnared in a complex political intrigue involving a secret map, a beautiful left-wing terrorist (played by Isabelle Adjani), and a bumbling CIA operative (Charles Grodin).

What separates May's script from, say, *The Man with One Red Shoe*—the Tom Hanks remake of the French comedy-thriller about a violinist caught in a spy caper—is a level of satirical bite and intelligence that is rare in contemporary movies. May's script has the occasional gem that may send viewers into convulsions. And while her brainy humor may elude some moviegoers, it also takes an exhausted movie genre and wakes it up a bit.

The most talked-about plot element of *Ishtar* will almost certainly be the fact that May decided to play the two stars against their public personas—Hoffman is the handsome rake and Beatty is the nerdy nebbish who can't attract girls. In fact, there's the faintest hint of homosexuality in Beatty's character; Adjani, who is a girlfriend of Beatty's in real life, doesn't fall for him in the movie.

The physical distinctions between the two actors will be obscured somewhat by age. Moviegoers who haven't seen Warren Beatty since *Reds* will notice crow's-feet around the eyes and a slightly pasty complexion. Hoffman may benefit by comparison: Though he looks older than Beatty (he's actually the same age), there's still a boyish quality to his narrow face and compact physique.

The first third of the movie takes place in New York, where May shows the two performers at rock bottom: Hoffman getting stared off the stage on open-mike nights for bad Jewish jokes; Beatty working as a Good Humor man; Beatty talking Hoffman out of a suicide leap. They go to a singles bar (shot at Amsterdam's), where Hoffman coaches Beatty on how to pick up girls. By the time they decide to accept their agent's offer of a booking in Morocco, their characters have been more fully developed than those in any Hope-Crosby picture.

In Ishtar—the country where they get stuck on their way to Morocco—the story becomes hopelessly complex. Without Hoffman knowing, Beatty gets himself enlisted as an agent for a leftist terrorist group; and Hoffman, without telling Beatty, starts working for the CIA. Pitted against each other unwittingly, the two men set off on a trip through the desert on a blind camel, leading to a wild, incomprehensible windup in an Ishtar nightclub where Beatty and Hoffman sing happily ever after.

Through it all, they spend most of their time trading Elaine May barbs:

"Look at the birds," Hoffman says, awaking in the desert after a brief fainting spell. "Are those vultures?"

"Yeah," Beatty replies. "You fainted. I guess they thought you were dead."

"You mean," Hoffman says, "they're here on *spec?*"

That'll get a big laugh at the Loews 84th Street, but will freelance-writer jokes play in a Nebraska shopping mall?

Last November 16, J. L. of Sherman Oaks, California, asked this question of the "Personality Parade" column in *Parade* magazine, read by more than thirty-one million people:

"What has really happened to *Ishtar*, the $30 million movie with Warren Beatty and Dustin Hoffman, scheduled for release this Christmas? They say it has been rescheduled for the spring. But one hears that the comedy is so disappointing, Columbia is keeping it under wraps indefinitely. True?"

"Not true," *Parade* replied. "*Ishtar* obviously is not ready for Christmas release and requires more postproduction preparation."

There is something in the movie business called Word of Mouth. It is usually heard well before a movie's release—often within weeks after shooting has stopped—and it is transmitted alongside water coolers, in meetings, at Russian Tea Room lunches, and everywhere else that obsessive movie people gather. *Platoon* had Good Word of Mouth, which means that beginning last September, people started saying to one another, "I hear good things about *Platoon*"; and by November, people were saying, "I hear *Platoon* is surefire Oscar material." Of course, most of these people had never seen *Platoon*—they were merely repeating Word of Mouth.

Ishtar is a textbook definition of a movie with Bad Word of Mouth.

Ever since the first news of a collaboration among three of the most temperamental, idealistic, and creative forces in show business—Beatty, Hoffman, and May—people have been suggesting it was a doomed project. Then, when they heard its cost had shot up to $40 million, they were *sure* it was doomed. Until the day *Ishtar* started shooting in October 1985, most people assumed the cameras would never roll. And then, after the release date was pushed back from November 26 to May 22, everyone—from the top ranks of movie executives to the readers of *Parade*—started to believe that *Ishtar* might qualify as a genuine disaster.

Officially, Columbia Pictures has said nothing about the movie at all. The public announcement of the postponement came in a two-page ad in the *Hollywood Reporter* last August. One page carried the word "*Ishtar*" in white, Arabic-style lettering against a black background; the other page said simply, "National release May 22, 1987." Columbia yanked from theaters trailers that promised *Ishtar* for Christmas, and Beatty insisted that it wasn't a postponement at all—merely an official announcement of the release date. As of January, Columbia Pictures flacks were still authorized to offer just one sentence about the movie to the public:

"*Ishtar* is a comedy-adventure starring Warren Beatty, Dustin Hoffman, and Isabelle Adjani, produced by Beatty and directed by May, scheduled for a May release."

Beatty productions are typically cloaked in secrecy, but none more so than *Ishtar*. Many big-budget movies seek advance publicity, but no journalists were allowed on the *Ishtar* set—not even friends of the stars. All production workers were instructed not to talk to the press. For months, magazines were under the impression that Beatty would honor interview and photo requests, but for the most part, he has remained elusive. He had been rumored to be planning all sorts of promotional gimmicks. One nationally syndicated Hollywood column reported that he would appear in the Macy's Thanksgiving Day Parade, riding a camel.

"In a way, I'd rather ride down the street on a camel than give what is sometimes called an in-depth interview," Beatty said, referring to the kind of questioning he abhors most—about his private life. "I'd rather ride down the street on a camel *nude* . . . in a *snowstorm . . . backwards.*" May agreed to talk over the phone but declined to say anything. "If you can," the press-shy director said sweetly, "I'd appreciate it if you didn't mention my name in your article."

And Columbia chief David Puttnam has distanced himself from the project.

"It was agreed prior to my joining Columbia that I won't involve myself in the release of this particular picture," Puttnam wrote in response to an interview request last August. "It's all too common in this industry for incoming heads of studios to take the credit or blame (!) for work negotiated by their predecessors. I don't want to be guilty of this."

Puttnam's arrival at Columbia couldn't have been welcome news to the people making *Ishtar*. The British filmmaker had publicly criticized both stars—Hoffman for his work on *Agatha*, which Puttnam helped produce, and Beatty for *Reds*, which Puttnam attacked as an example of overspending. As a result, Beatty felt no need to push the pace of production just to give Puttnam a Christmas release for 1986. (To date, Beatty hasn't even let Puttnam see the film.)

In the end, of course, it is entirely possible that *Ishtar* will turn out to be a comic masterpiece. May has been regarded as a comic genius ever since her partnership with Mike Nichols first made her famous in 1960. Her movies, in particular *The Heartbreak Kid* and *Mikey and Nicky*, have reflected a quirky brilliance and led many to feel her full talents have yet to be realized. Her reputation as a difficult perfectionist has plagued her since she went to Hollywood in the sixties.

"If Elaine May keeps her name on *Ishtar*," one production executive pointed out, "it will be one of the first times she has ever done that willingly in her career as a director. She'd be happiest if she could keep *Ishtar* in the editing room forever, and never release it."

The facts support that widely held assumption. A Broadway-bound play she wrote in 1962, *A Matter of Position*, closed in Philadelphia because she refused to make changes. She went over budget on her first movie-directing effort, *A New Leaf*, in 1969—and finally tried to remove her name when Paramount Pictures took it away from her. May refused screen credit on the 1971 Otto Preminger film, *Such Good Friends*, for which she wrote the script. And stories of her inability to complete work on *Mikey and Nicky* are legendary; she filmed it in 1973 and approved an authorized cut of the movie in 1985.

At this moment, May is still making changes on *Ishtar*. A few weeks ago, she got an inspiration about restructuring the movie, and that has meant another round of late-night editing and mixing for the dozens of people required to put *Ishtar* together. "It's brilliant," said one production source, "but it's thrown everything into turmoil."

By May 15 of this year, no matter what happens, Columbia Pictures has promised a finished version of *Ishtar*. And it will deliver one, regardless of the final product's quality. The advent of home video and cable has made it possible for major films, particularly those with world-famous stars in them, to make back their money without being huge hits. That must have been Columbia Pictures' belief when it spent $40 million to make *Ishtar* and still is—but nevertheless they'd like the film released in May.

Is the making of *Ishtar*, as some believe, a triumph of a brilliant director over the skeptical Hollywood establishment? Or is it, as others argue, further evidence that studio movie budgets have become bloated beyond all reason—meaning that in the long run, fewer movies will be made?

By 1964, Warren Beatty had met the two people who would ultimately prove necessary to get *Ishtar* produced almost a quarter century later. One of them was his young press agent, Guy McElwaine. And the other was an immensely talented young writer and actress, who shared Beatty's disdain for most of the movie projects offered her, by the name of Elaine May.

Beatty was then one of America's leading sex symbols. He'd befriended a producer named Charles K. Feldman, who was pushing Beatty to make a movie based on Beatty's lifestyle. It was to be about a young man who couldn't help but attract beautiful women, and Beatty was to star. But they needed a screenwriter for this project, which they were going to name after Beatty's own trademark telephone whisper: "What's new, pussycat?"

At that time, Elaine May and Mike Nichols had reached the pinnacle of their fame as humorists.

Nichols was already moving toward a career in theater directing, and his partner seemed more inclined to write and act. In 1964, Beatty approached her as a possible screenwriter for the "Pussycat" project. She turned him down (Woody Allen later got the job), but they became close friends and sometime collaborators.

In 1978, they did *Heaven Can Wait*, a remake of the 1941 comedy *Here Comes Mr. Jordan*. That credit—on what turned out to be a $120 million hit—revived May's sagging career and brought her frequent assignments as a script doctor. She did considerable uncredited rewrite work on Beatty's next movie, *Reds*, which was nominated for the Best Original Screenplay Oscar. And despite all the arguments over who wrote what for *Tootsie*, no one disputes the fact that May contributed Bill Murray's character to the script.

"Elaine is the exact opposite of everyone else in Hollywood," says her friend Charles Grodin. "She's always fighting to get as little credit as possible, to keep her name off movies, to *not* be invited to the parties. She's happier without any of that."

Following the enormous success of *Tootsie*, Beatty, Hoffman, and May began to discuss a three-way collaboration. "I'd said to Elaine that if she wanted to write a movie, that she should write a movie," Beatty says. "I said that we should try to make a movie that she wrote and directed. I said I would produce it for her."

Beatty makes it sound so simple; and in Hollywood, when Warren Beatty wants to make a movie, it usually is that simple. "I've never been a person who runs around making a lot of movies," he says. "I've never been able to get interested in that. I read the script. I thought it was funny. I decided to do it." So at that point, Beatty approached his former press agent, who'd since become head of Columbia Pictures.

McElwaine didn't really know May, but he knew quite a bit about her reputation as a difficult, expensive director who had trouble finishing her movies. But he also had the same awestruck admiration for Beatty that most of his colleagues do—enough to cause temporary blindness, if not outright insanity.

"All you have to do is look at Beatty's track record as a producer-star," says McElwaine, who left Columbia shortly after shooting finished on *Ishtar* and now works as an independent producer on the Columbia lot. "You have to be very careful if you're going to say no to something of Warren's, because his record as a producer-star is almost 1,000 percent. It probably *is* 1,000 percent in terms of just recouping on a per-picture basis, cash."

In spring 1985, Beatty and May met with McElwaine at his Burbank office and pitched the notion of *Ishtar*—at that time just the barest bones of a plot, and the casting concept of pairing Hoffman and Beatty. Afflicted with Beatty Blindness, McElwaine gave a go-ahead on one of the most expensive comedies in the history of the movie business.

Ishtar came to life one Sunday afternoon in 1985 in the house in the Hollywood Hills that is sometimes Beatty's home.

To read the script of *Ishtar*, he assembled a group of trusted friends—an odd amalgam of actors and writers who had become a private support group for one another, for a decade or more in some cases. Because most of them were nowhere near as famous as Warren Beatty, their friendship with him had remained private and unobserved.

Among those present that day were Herb Gardner, the playwright whose *I'm Not Rappaport* had just opened on Broadway; Peter Feibleman, a writer and the executor of Lillian Hellman's estate; David MacLeod, a cousin of Beatty's and the associate producer of *Heaven Can Wait* and *Reds*; Marlo Thomas, a longtime friend of Elaine May's; Charles Grodin, who starred in May's *The Heartbreak Kid*; and Dustin Hoffman, whom May had worked with on *Tootsie*.

Once everyone had assembled in the living room, May passed out scripts and the reading began. Parts had been assigned, and most people had been given several different ones to read.

"It was very clear that we were hearing a terrific script," one participant said much later, "one that should and would get made into a movie. It had problems, but it was very, very funny, and very *Elaine*."

It was also clear that if *Ishtar* got made, it would be at a lavish price.

"Elaine May is a woman of many words," says one of her closest professional colleagues. "However, the word 'cut' does not happen to be among them." On a frigid day in early 1986—actually, it turned out to be two days because of May's particular vocabulary affliction—two busloads of extras, three enormous cameras, thousands of feet of wire and cable, dozens of technicians, and two movie stars crammed into the subterranean confines of the Trax nightclub (now defunct) on West Seventy-Second Street to shoot an early scene of *Ishtar*. Had everything gone according to plan in Morocco, this scene would have been in the can for months.

They were already well beyond the $27.5 million budget originally set for the movie. And this shoot was costing even more than most filming done on location in New York, because they were using an Italian camera crew—headed by Vittorio Storaro, who won an Academy Award for *Reds*—which meant, according to New York union rules, that the production had to hire a New York "standby" crew. whose job was mostly to sit around, eat doughnuts, and read the *New York Post* while earning scale and overtime and getting meal penalties.

And now the musical segments of the movie were about to be shot—which meant two big stars doing something they'd never done, and a hundred people earning huge hourly salaries to do whatever May instructed. The scene involved the two would-be singers performing their own composition, "Since We Left 'Nam," at the open mike with a large and stone-silent audience watching them.

"Dustin and Warren would do a take, and Elaine would watch them or look at the video monitor and say, 'Fine, let's do it again,'" a production staffer recalls. "Once or twice they didn't mind. Five times. Ten times. But by the time they got back from lunch, and after stopping to rehearse the song again and again, they were tired. But Elaine didn't want to stop. 'Let's do it one more time,' she'd say, and do it ten times. She never gave them any directions, never said to do it again this way or that way. It was always 'Let's do it again.'"

She ended up shooting more than fifty takes of the same scene, with three cameras rolling at all times.

Until then, Beatty and Hoffman—both known for their difficult temperaments on movie sets—had been models of good behavior. Hoffman spent much of his time between takes telling ethnic jokes to the extras and crew; Beatty, though more reserved, still had an aura of cooperativeness and good nature. "They were so aware of their reputations as difficult perfectionists themselves," said G. Mac Brown, the movie's New York production manager, "that they were obviously trying extra hard to be easygoing and friendly."

Hoffman's reputation has been widely chronicled over the years. On *Tootsie*, he was reported to have fought bitterly with director Sydney Pollack over scene after scene. But on the set of *Ishtar*, he was as gentle and kind as could be. He memorized the names of extras and always offered a kind word. He entertained the crew with jokes, riddles, and puns. "He was exactly the opposite of what we'd been led to expect by the hype," said a colleague of Beatty's. "He was a good person, a friend to everyone."

A friend, most particularly, to Beatty—whom he hadn't known well before their *Ishtar* collaboration. They almost instantly became comrades, seen together around town at bars and restaurants. What might have been at first an actor's instinct to work on his part grew into a genuine friendship, one that colleagues say has lasted well beyond the end of shooting. And for Beatty—who is often considered diffident and private on a movie set—that marked a significant change.

But tensions were bound to show. After lunch on the second day at Trax, Beatty and Hoffman were visibly angry; May's deliberate pace seemed finally to be getting to them. "OK," May said to the two actors late on the afternoon of the second day, after they'd finished the fortieth take of the same shot. "Let's do it again. We didn't quite get it."

"Elaine," Beatty said wearily, "we got it before lunch."

By the end of the second day, the production *had* to move on, and May knew it. So she wrapped up the scene as best she could, though everyone watching felt she was still dissatisfied, still wanting to shoot it again.

"I think that if Elaine could have her way," said one person who had been on the set, "she'd *still* be shooting that movie."

To understand why Elaine May had not worked behind a camera in over a decade—and why it took the collective star clout of Beatty and Hoffman to get her another job—it is necessary to flash back to *Mikey and Nicky.*

It was very late at night, probably past three in the morning, in the summer of 1973. A camera crew stood on a Los Angeles street as May continued to work on an exterior shot.

It was the first night for the camera operator; May had already gone through several cameramen on the movie, which was way over budget with hundreds of hours of film in the can. He'd been shooting a conversation between the two main characters in the movie—John Cassavetes, a two-bit hood with a contract out on his life, and Peter Falk, an old friend who'd been given the job of setting up the killing.

The movie had been largely improvised up to this point, in the style of the movies Cassavetes himself directs, and often the camera rolled for hours as the two men talked to each other in and out of character about whatever happened to be on their minds.

But at this particular moment, the two stars were not talking to each other at all. Falk had walked down the block to talk to a friend, and Cassavetes wandered off the set entirely.

Still, the camera kept running.

And running.

After several minutes of shooting film of a scene with no actors in it, the new camera operator called "Cut!" and turned off the camera.

May, who'd been sitting quietly behind the cameraman, suddenly jumped from her seat.

"Why did you turn the camera off?" she yelled. "You don't say 'Cut.' I say 'Cut.' *I'm* the *director*, and only the *director* says 'Cut.'"

"I know," the camera operator replied, "but the actors left. They walked away!"

To which May answered, "Yes . . . but they might come *back*."

May ended up shooting 1.4 million feet of film for *Mikey and Nicky*—possibly a record ratio (140 to 1) of film shot to film shown, since the finished product was only 10,000 feet. The average ratio is around 20 to 1. *Gone with the Wind* was made from only 475,000 feet of film.

After taking two years to edit the film from a suite at the Sunset Marquis Hotel in Los Angeles, May refused to let Paramount Pictures distribute the movie because it *still* wasn't ready. Finally, after lawsuits started to fly, May took two reels of the movie from the Paramount lot and stored them in a friend's garage in Connecticut. So the movie (or at least, the part of the movie Paramount still had on hand) was shown for a few days to fulfill contractual obligations, though it was never given a real release. Still, it was in theaters long enough for the *New Republic*'s film critic, Stanley Kauffmann, to rank it as one of the ten best American movies of the decade.

(The movie was finally released last year in an edited version approved by May— ten minutes *shorter* than the Paramount version. Go figure.)

Last fall, the Museum of Modern Art honored *Mikey and Nicky* as part of a directors' series, and after an early-evening showing one November day, May wandered over from her editing room at the Brill Building, at Forty-Ninth Street and Broadway, to make one of the few offstage public appearances of her life.

"I was sued," she said softly, "and the movie studio gave it back to me with the words 'Here.' I think I was sued because they so hated the movie. The guy leaving the studio [Frank Yablans, now an independent producer] told the guy coming in [Barry Diller, now chairman of Twentieth Century Fox] that it was a comedy for the summer."

Standing nervously in front of a microphone and looking for support from the sea of admiring faces, she talked about what *Mikey and Nicky* cost her.

"It was difficult for me to get directing jobs because I seemed sort of crazy," she said. "They accused me of taking the negative. But then I wrote *Heaven Can Wait*, and everything was all right.

"Hollywood," she concluded, "doesn't care what you did as long as you're making money for them."

Here's how it was supposed to be on *Ishtar*, and how it turned out. Production was supposed to begin in August 1985. It was supposed to involve eight weeks of shooting in Morocco, a couple of weeks off, then six weeks of shooting in New York. Almost all the Morocco shots, as well as the New York ones, were to be done on location. It was supposed to finish shooting by Christmas. Editing was supposed to begin after the New Year, and a rough cut was supposed to be available for screenings by August or September 1986. Beatty and Hoffman were supposed to go to California in September to shoot a music video to help promote the movie. Editors at *Esquire* believed Beatty would pose for the cover of the magazine.

The movie was supposed to be in theaters by November 26. And, of course, it was supposed to be nominated for several Academy Awards.

It worked out a little differently.

Production began in October 1985. It took about three extra months to make the necessary preparations. The script went through several changes as time wore on. Casting now became a matter of finding bit actors who could block out an entirely different period than had originally been planned; the same held true for the production team.

Ishtar lost one major member of that team right away—its original cinematographer, Giuseppe Rotunno, for many years Federico Fellini's camera chief, who couldn't change his schedule to accommodate the delays. So when he quit, Beatty hired Storaro, whose experience at shooting a comedy was minimal. Probably the funniest movie he'd worked on before *Ishtar* was *Last Tango in Paris*.

Once work got started, everything took a little longer and cost a little more than it should.

"This was the kind of movie where nobody would say, 'Sorry, we can't afford that,'" says Mac Brown, who monitored the budget. "Not that people were spending wildly. But you never had the feeling that money was the main issue—creativity came first."

When it was discovered that a camera-repair piece was needed from the United States, a New York location coordinator was flown to Morocco with it—for fear that if it were shipped as a package, it might get lost or held at customs. The production paid for the coordinator's plane ticket and put him up in a hotel room in Morocco for a week.

And when it was discovered that suitable locations for three important indoor sequences could not be found in the Middle East, the production shipped pieces of one set back to New York and built others from scratch at an additional cost of $250,000.

Then there was the scene that involved Beatty and Hoffman standing on the seventeenth-story ledge of a New York apartment building. Because the production was behind schedule, the scene was being shot in winter instead of spring, and because conditions were icy, the location was switched to a six-story building with a substantial scaffolding that would ensure the safety of the stars (that change must have pleased Beatty, who has a mild fear of heights anyway). It was also discovered that the musical numbers, a fundamental part of the movie's comic premise, simply weren't ready. From the beginning, people were worried that the songs, written by songwriter-actor Paul Williams, weren't quite right.

"When we were in Morocco," remembers Paul Sylbert, "we'd be eating dinner and Paul would run in with his latest and sing it for us while we ate. And believe me, it was not the kind of music you wanted to eat to."

Of course that was partly intentional; Beatty and Hoffman were supposed to be bad songwriters. But the songs had to be *just* bad enough yet *just* good enough, and so did Beatty's and Hoffman's performances. And the more May shot of them singing, the more it became apparent that the two stars simply needed more time to rehearse. So in late February—already way behind schedule, with no end in sight—the production halted for several days so that Beatty and Hoffman could have a chance to get their act together.

"Some of us on the set thought Columbia was actually about to shut down production on the movie, what with all the rumors," said one low-level production staffer. But instead, Columbia continued to pay everybody, as it was contractually obligated to do, after production came to a halt, and Beatty and Hoffman feverishly practiced their musical numbers.

By all accounts, it turned out to be worth it. Their climactic scene in the Ishtar nightclub, Chez Casablanca—designed by Paul Sylbert to be a parody-replica of Rick's Café in *Casablanca*—is supposed to be a howler with the two performing several of their original numbers.

"It is," Charles Grodin assures, "a hilarious movie."

Propped up against the walls of the Kaufman Astoria Studios, one or two miles away from the movie theaters that will be showing *Ishtar* in just two months, is a folded-up version of Chez Casablanca.

That is where the final sequence was shot over several days and nights. It's also where—on the night of the Academy Awards presentation last year, which turned out to be the last night of shooting—Warren Beatty gave a huge bash with wide-screen television sets, so that the cast and crew could watch the Oscars without leaving. At 10:12 p.m. on March 24, the production officially shut down. A pool had been put together so people could bet on the exact time and date that *Ishtar* would finally wrap; everyone in the crew had participated in it, at five dollars a bet. When the winner of the pool was announced, it prompted a cynical shrug from everyone else—it was, appropriately but unfairly enough, the production accountant who guessed right.

It is now almost a year since that night. May and her team of editors remain huddled in the Brill Building, working feverishly to finish the movie in time for its May release.

Production staffers report that the process has taken so long because of May's perfectionism. She works on a different schedule from most people's—showing up at about 11:00 a.m. and keeping her editors at their machines until late at night. It's all part of her obsession with the minutest details; once on *Mikey and Nicky*, when a sound timer made a slight error, she is supposed to have crawled across the screening-room floor, rolled up the timer's pants leg, and bit him. She intended the gesture as a joke.

May has recently started to show rough prints to her close friends (not including anyone from Columbia Pictures of course), and some of them have found the plot a little confusing. So she has been thinking of writing a short speech for Charles Grodin to make near the end, to clear things up. That will require more editing, more mixing.

The other day, Mac Brown got a call from the Astoria Studios about what to do with the Chez Casablanca set. It's not unusual to keep the set intact for a little while, just in case the director decides to reshoot something. Brown figured it had been a year—enough time to know whether there'd be any more reshooting.

But instead he was told, *Don't* destroy that set just yet. We're still not done.

Mike Nichols: A New Feeling about Films

Charles Champlin / 1988

From the *Los Angeles Times*, December 27, 1988. Reprinted by permission.

It seems like only yesterday that Mike Nichols and Elaine May were the freshest voices in comedy—he the love-struck dentist, she the patient in a wonderful send-up of *Brief Encounter*, one among their many deft little skits. But they broke up the team nearly thirty years ago.

It seems like only the day after yesterday that Nichols was the hottest young director on Broadway, commencing with the Tony-winning *Barefoot in the Park*, but that was in 1963.

And it seems only the afternoon of the day after yesterday that Nichols was loitering nervously on a cavernous sound stage at Warner Bros. during a set party Jack Warner himself gave to launch the production of *Who's Afraid of Virginia Woolf?* (1966).

Many a triumph (*The Graduate, Carnal Knowledge*) and an occasional near-miss (*The Fortune*) later, fifty-seven-year-old Mike Nichols is an ungrayed eminence of stage and screen. His recent production of *Waiting for Godot* with Robin Williams and Steve Martin at Lincoln Center was a sellout. His latest film, *Working Girl*, with Melanie Griffith, Harrison Ford, and Sigourney Weaver, looks to be one of the substantial hits of the Christmas season.

Nichols, briefly in Los Angeles for the premiere of *Working Girl*, was saying that he now feels a good deal less like a director on loan from the stage to a dubious film industry.

"I used to find making movies painful; I no longer do. It's now entirely pleasurable, even the shooting, which people used to say was the boring part after all the creative work had been done in preproduction.

"It all shakes down to people," Nichols says. He has built a team. Sam O'Steen was his editor on *Virginia Woolf*—it was O'Steen's first film as well—and has edited for Nichols ever since, with an editing room in Nichols's New York house. Costumer Ann

Roth, whose dresses for Weaver and Griffith are meaningful as well as decorative, is another regular.

On the other hand, says Nichols, "I am less sanguine about the theater audience. It astounds me that they pay forty or fifty dollars for a ticket and then start trying to read the *Playbill* as soon as the lights go down. They're suburbanites terrified of being at home alone with each other for an evening."

Godot required an institution, with subscribers, which creates its own problems. "The blind trustingness of subscribers leads to an audience who can't be *in* the moment, can't surrender to it. . . . People who like the theater have been lied to so often—'You'll *love* it'—that they're forever on guard."

Movie audiences are another matter. "I love them. They have no preconceptions about Life or Art." (You could hear the capitals.) "Give them an experience and they're yours."

The problems of the stage are not entirely the audiences' fault, Nichols adds. "The theater and the audience have inhibited each other. Injuries have taken place. Yet the troubles can be blown away by a powerful experience. The John Malkovich performance in *Burn This*, for example. It happens every ten years or so and it takes care of the lethargy."

Virginia Woolf was a baptism of fire, almost but not quite searing enough to put a man off making movies thenceforward.

"I had to be political with Jack [Warner] and strong and overbearing with everyone else. Five days before shooting, Jack said New York said it had to be done in color. I said that that would give away Elizabeth Taylor's aging makeup. He persisted. I said, 'I'll go home; you do it in color.' Jack relented, then he invited me to dinner every night. I made excuses not to go." (It was obvious to Nichols that Warner had not given up hope of color.)

"Two days before shooting the cameraman said, 'Why don't we shoot it in color and print it in black-and-white.' I realized where his loyalties were and I let him go.

"After the first shot, I heard the assistant director murmur, 'It's just another picture,' and I fired him on the spot. I felt like a Jew in the merchant marine. It was very lonely. It's much nicer now; there's no longer that kind of opposing pressure."

It would be difficult to describe Nichols's feelings about the old-time major studios as mixed, but in fact they are. "I defy you to say what it was that the barracudas *knew*. And while I'm loath to quote Bill Goldman favorably, he rightly said, 'The thing about Hollywood is that nobody knows anything.'

"But what those guys knew had something to do with the public, with having *absorbed* the public. I don't want to idealize them, but they had powerful appetites. They wanted a lot of everything—power, houses, girls, food, money. Power. And this led them to want movies to deliver powerful experiences.

"What we've seen since is the committee approach, which gives you homogenized experiences. That's why I admire Barry Diller at Fox (which did *Working Girl*). He's one man who can say, "We'll do this or we won't. Right or wrong, this is what I want to do.""

In its day (1967) *The Graduate*, for which Nichols won an Academy Award, was not simply a coming-of-age comedy; the coming of age was taking place in a time of radical (but not necessarily permanent) changes. A younger generation was rejecting the material values of its parents, along with various side values that smacked of hypocrisy.

Working Girl is, like the earlier film, a brilliantly constructed and suspenseful comedy with charismatic performers delivering crisp dialogue. It also has as much subtext as you care to dig out of it. It is about the aspirations of young women in an arena dominated, ever less securely, by men who are for the most part terrible role models, mean and treacherous—if we are to judge by the women who emulate them. (And Nichols and scriptwriter Kevin Wade do suggest that that's how we ought to make the judgment.)

"My concern," Nichols says, "was that it should be about equalness." They worked particularly hard, he says, on a street conversation when Griffith and Ford agree to crash a wedding to advance her scheme.

"She sees, as people do when things are tough, that he's just a boy as she's just a girl. No feet of clay; he's just as worried and vulnerable as she is. She gets this sense of his honesty, and his ordinariness. Their personal and business interests are joined from that moment."

Things do change, and it is clear from her diction and from the suited chic of her later costumes, that Tess, the Melanie Griffith character, has exchanged her Staten Island origins for what Nichols calls "a grasp of Manhattanness." The question beyond the credits is whether Tess will also grasp the ruthlessness that had overtaken her former boss, Weaver.

Nichols is an old hand at leaving questions beyond the final crawl. The memorable last shot of *The Graduate* holds on Katharine Ross—she in her wedding dress—and Dustin Hoffman, as the bus rumbles away from the ceremony from which he has rescued her. The shot holds on and on and on, and the joy seems to drain from their frozen expressions.

I once asked Nichols if he ever speculated on what happens next. "They ride on for another five minutes," Nichols said, "and then she says, 'I haven't a thing to wear.'"

The more things change, the more they only change a little.

Nichols, May Honored by TV, Radio Museum

Jane Hall / 1992

From the *Los Angeles Times*, April 17, 1992. Reprinted by permission.

NEW YORK—It was a scene that called for Jack Ego, the unctuous radio talk-show host who called everyone, including his buddy "Al" Schweitzer, a "very close, very personal friend," and for Barbara Musk, the eager Hollywood starlet who was making *The Big Sky*, the life story of God—whom Ego immediately claimed as a very close, very personal friend.

Mike Nichols, who played Ego to Elaine May's Miss Musk in one of the many memorable sketches created by the comedy team of Nichols and May during their heyday on TV and records in the late 1950s and early 1960s, was trying to encapsulate their art to a sea of sound-bite-seeking reporters from *Entertainment Tonight* and other entertainment-news TV shows.

Nichols and May—who, it is still surprising to remember, *improvised* scenes that are still considered some of the wittiest comedy turns in American humor—have performed only a few times together since their professional breakup in 1962. They were being honored for their TV work on Wednesday night with a tribute by the Museum of Television and Radio in New York.

"What was the secret of your success?" a TV reporter asked.

"You know, I'm just not good at that kind of self-analysis; I'd be the last to know," Nichols replied.

Quietly, May, sixty, a dark-haired woman once described by Carl Reiner as "either the funniest sexy woman or the sexiest funny woman" he knew, appeared behind the cameras, facing Nichols, sixty-one, and causing him to laugh, just as she often had broken his actor's facade with an ad-lib onstage. May posed with evident nervousness for the photographers.

She was more relaxed when she was facing only a reporter's notebook a few minutes later.

"I'm truly phobic about this," said May, who rarely has been interviewed in the past twenty years. "But I'm not scared to wing it onstage."

It was that ability to wing it onstage that created sophisticated comedy (a kind of psychoanalytic shtick) about the neuroses of the post-Eisenhower, pre-Kennedy era—and made Nichols and May heroes to a generation.

"Whenever I wanted to be cool and hip in the outer reaches of South Dakota," NBC anchor Tom Brokaw recalled during the tribute, "I'd light a candle in a Chianti bottle and listen to [the comedy albums] of Nichols and May."

"They were the quintessential class act of television," recalled Jack Paar, who cast the then-twentysomething Nichols and May, an improvisational comedy team from Chicago, on *The Tonight Show* in the late 1950s. "They became the intellectual Fibber McGee and Molly."

NBC, Paar said, erased many of the videotapes of the pre–Johnny Carson *Tonight Show* that Paar hosted from 1957 to 1962 in New York. But, he said, thanks to the controversy his show sometimes generated, a number of kinescope recordings of the program had been saved for evidence in potential lawsuits. These kinescopes, recently discovered in storage, yielded a number of Nichols and May routines that the museum plans to add to its collection for viewing.

The formally dressed audience at the Waldorf-Astoria Hotel, some of them too young to have seen Nichols and May before, laughed with great appreciation as some of the sketches were shown on a giant screen.

> "I'm Miss Loomis, your grief lady," May says to a bereaved Nichols in a sketch satirizing the funeral industry and the high cost of dying. "Would you like some extras for the loved one?"
> Nichols: "What kind of extras?"
> May: "Well, how about a casket?"

In one Kafkaesque sketch that went on for many minutes, May played several different telephone operators, all of whom failed to return Nichols's last dime. In another lengthy sketch, Nichols, playing a rocket scientist who has been too busy launching rockets to call home to his mother, was slowly irrevocably reduced to blithering baby talk by her guilt-invoking phone call.

But the one that seemed most hilarious—and most harrowing—to the audience was one in which Nichols played a high-school boy trying to get to first base with May in a parked car. It was funny at first, with Nichols grabbing May so quickly that they had to blow their cigarette smoke to the side of kissing lips. But their roles reversed when May—asking plaintively, "Do you really like me?"—began to undress.

Such scenes, Nichols said in an interview, were largely improvised. "I never knew what she was going to say onstage," he said. He also said that they are considering updating and re-releasing one of their comedy albums.

May, asked to speculate about the state of comedy, said: "*Saturday Night Live* and Second City [the Chicago-based improvisational troupe] are doing satire, but sometimes today, it seems that reality is beyond satire. And language has so deteriorated in this country—it takes four words for one, and people use phrases like 'vertically disabled' . . . A kind of Newspeak takes over. That may have an impact on satire."

Since they went their separate ways professionally—Nichols has said that the demands of maintaining their standards of high-wire improvisation, plus his moving toward becoming a director, were among the reasons for their splitting up; the separation was said to have been painful, although they are close friends today—both Nichols and May have become film directors. May's credits range from the successful *The Heartbreak Kid* to the flop *Ishtar*, while Nichols's include *The Graduate*, *Who's Afraid of Virginia Woolf?*, *Silkwood*, and the recent *Regarding Henry*, a critical and financial disappointment.

In their brief remarks at the conclusion of the tribute, Nichols said that they were so delighted and encouraged by the event that, "We have decided to go back to performing together." All they need, he said, is to update their name for the 1990s: "We're going to be called 'Ishtar' and 'Henry.'"

Who's Afraid of the Big Bad *Wolf*?

Peter Biskind / 1994

From *Premiere*, March 1994. Reprinted by permission.

Mike Nichols is waiting for Jack Nicholson. He is sitting in a director's chair before the entrance to a dank underpass that is supposed to be situated in the southwest corner of Central Park, opposite the Mayflower Hotel, but is actually on a soundstage at Sony Pictures Studios in Culver City. It is clear something very unpleasant is about to happen. "Mike, do you want to go wide or tight?" asks an assistant.

"Both," replies Nichols, without cracking a smile.

In this scene Nicholson's character, Will Randall, is menaced by three muggers. Having been bitten by a wolf earlier in the picture, Randall is well along on his lupine journey and more than a match for his attackers, whom he routs with an unexpected, preternaturally athletic leap. While the star is in the makeup trailer, getting tiny hairs pasted on his face by effectsmeister Rick Baker, Nicholson's double is catapulted some ten feet into the air by a spring device.

Nichols stands up. He is tall, six feet or so, and wears a blue windbreaker over a blue-and-white tattersall shirt. "Good jumping," he murmurs, in a soft, cultured voice with only the faintest whisper of irony. Then, aside: "Harrison [Ford] says movie acting is 50 percent running, 20 percent falling down." He thinks for a moment and looks over his shoulder at the makeup trailer with the expression of a man who expects to be disappointed. His eyes light up.

"Jack's here." Indeed, Nicholson has arrived, looking only slightly more wolflike than usual, in a blue oxford shirt, gray sports jacket, and corduroy trousers, and smoking a cigarette. The set is swept by an imperceptible quickening, as if, at last, real work can begin. "What am I matching?" he demands, heading for the video monitor to inspect the work of his double. "Why is the camera so high?"

"I raised it a little. You looked so Orsonian."

Nicholson is supposed to pick up where the stunt jump ends, land on a mugger, lift him up, swing him around, and bite his face. And so he does.

"Is it possible, while you're flailing around, to maintain apparent contact with his face?" says Nichols, half apologetically, as if it is his fault that the scene is not quite right.

"Yeah."

Nicholson shoves what appears to be a chocolate truffle into his mouth, then falls on the mugger again. As he performs the lift and swing roundel, he adds a couple of grace notes. Throwing his head back and rolling his eyes upward, he emits a chorus of growls, barks, and yips, then takes a big bite. "Oh, shit! Fuck that shit!" screams the mugger. Nicholson spits out the truffle, which turns out to be Baker's best shot at the mugger's nose, spraying a pink spume of bodily fluids. "How was it, Nicky?"

"That spritz was too much water."

Nichols picks up the nose off the ground, examines it closely. "Isn't there a middle ground between a well-shaped nose and a piece of red meat? Where's Rick Baker?"

Wolf began its life more than four years ago as a conversation between novelist Jim Harrison and producer Douglas Wick on an airplane. Harrison likes Wick; he is one of the few producers in Harrison's experience who "has read whole books from front to back," as he puts it, and so he was happy to entertain him with a description of a "lycanthropic" episode he once had in the thick forests of Michigan's Upper Peninsula. Wick, holding Harrison in high esteem (it didn't hurt that he's a close friend of Nicholson's), was happy to listen as the barrel-shaped writer whispered his tale in a hoarse, Jack-like drawl. "Where I live is extremely remote," croaked Harrison. "There are wolves up there. I dreamed that one of them had been hit by a car. When I picked it up, it went into my mouth and into my body, which is uncomfortable, 'cause at the time I was on yet another diet, and now I'm full of this bitch, ya know? One night, I thought someone was coming into the yard, so I hopped out of bed, tore off the doors to get at whoever was out there, and my face was covered with hair—ya know, the usual. It meant the dog wouldn't have anything to do with me for about a day and a half. I don't care for that kind of thing. I'm a very ordinary person."

Instead of suggesting that Harrison seek professional help, Wick told him it would make a good screenplay. Harrison agreed, and after nearly two years of noodling the concept, showed a script to Nicholson in Paris. Nicholson committed, and the nightmare began.

Nicholson being the eight-hundred-pound gorilla, the choice of Nichols as director was pretty much up to him. Wick had produced a Nichols hit, *Working Girl*, and liked him. "I always hated werewolf movies," says Wick, "because I couldn't relate to the character. But we felt that if you took the audience in teeny increments, all of a sudden you'd find yourself in an extreme place. We wanted to tell the story in quarter inches. Hence the choice of Mike Nichols. He would make it about details."

Actually, Nichols is more at home with chocolate truffles than red meat, which made the pairing with Harrison odd at best. Harrison's script derived from Native

American myths in which the souls of sick humans enter animals for therapeutic purposes. "Then you either come out or you don't," he explains. "If you have to stay a bear, you'd be quite happy about it. Unlike the Inuits, we think we would miss going to Zabar's." Which was precisely the problem. To Nichols, Mr. Broadway, witty and sophisticated, Harrison's conceit seemed no more than the old romantic notion of the noble savage—the idea that redemption lies in the heart of the beast—a notion with which he was uncomfortable. "This is a story about somebody who loses his humanity, and you can't say that's something to be desired," says Nichols. "It's a sentimental lie." To him it must have looked more loopy than lupine: *Dracula* in suits.

"There were stages where I thought, Are we crazy?" recalls Nichols. "If it's about anything, it's about male sexuality. You know, a beast at night, a nice English gentleman by day. That interested me, and the idea of Jack being the man who is becoming a wolf, because he's already partway there."

Harrison did two scripts for Nichols, then, discouraged and angry, went home to the company of wolves. In came Wesley Strick, who did *Cape Fear* for Martin Scorsese, to do a quick polish. ("Working with Marty was like going to the best film school in the world," he says. "Working with Mike was like being at the best cocktail party!") But bringing in another writer was tricky. "Mike always referred to it as the Jim Harrison movie, because there was a need to appease Jack," says Strick. Nichols, in Strick's words, "was a bit baffled by it. He was always asking unsettling questions like, Why is he becoming a wolf?"

As Nichols got into it, Strick's quick polish turned into a thoroughgoing rewrite. And in wrestling with the script, Nichols unexpectedly found himself grappling with profound cultural and ethical themes: How fragile is the veneer of civilization, how black the human heart, how thin the thread of redemption, how difficult it is to grasp it. "Terrible things are happening," says Nichols. "Yesterday I got home and saw the news about the guy shooting people on the Long Island Rail Road. You know those Yeats lines everybody's always quoting: 'slouching towards Bethlehem.' But the line that kills me—the line I think of every week, from the same poem—is: 'The best lack all conviction, while the worst are full of passionate intensity.' It's the line of the century."

The moral and emotional freight of the plot, in addition to Nichols's doubts about the script, made it difficult for him to commit. "He's the kinda guy who's prone from one project to the next to feeling that he's completely forgotten how he ever made a movie," says Strick. "He has exquisite taste, but his fear was that taste in this kind of material might not win the day." It didn't help that Michelle Pfeiffer had already turned the script down several times. ("It was 'the girl,'" she says. "I hadn't done that in a long time.") Nichols was in; Nichols was out—but always, he was drawn back. "There was a time when I called Jack and said, 'Listen, I've got to withdraw, because they want to start shooting in a couple of months. I have no script, and I can't shoot a meeting.' With one flick he says, 'Sorry, guys. It's Nichols or Kubrick—which one do you think is faster?' And suddenly I have more time."

When Nichols is in script trouble, he goes to one place: Elaine May. She enhanced the love story and punched up "the girl" to the point where Pfeiffer, who was eager to work with Nichols and Nicholson, committed. Says Pfeiffer of her character: "She was a vet, she was a nurse; basically it became this sort of device to make her look as if she's someone important. I finally said, 'It's Jack's movie. It's better just to not pretend—to make her somebody who really can't find a purpose, the black sheep of the family, and a kind of wanderer. At least that's something that's playable and real.'" In this last stage, ironically, Nichols abandoned some of the ideas he had explored with Strick and returned to Harrison's original concept.

Whether the mating of Harrison's inspiration to Nichols's sensibility will be successful or not remains to be seen. But it was a mischievous match, and the mischief runs deep. Nichols, by an accident of birth, had already gotten a look at the wolf, close-up. He was born in Berlin in 1931: Michael Igor Peschkowsky, the older son of a distinguished Jewish family. His father, a doctor, had left Russia during the revolution and, with little historical foresight, made his way to Germany. His mother's mother wrote the libretto to *Salome* with Richard Strauss.[1] His mother's father was a prominent radical who was arrested in 1919 and beaten to death in jail.

In the late 1930s, with Hitler threatening war, his father fled again, this time to New York, where he Anglicized his Russian patronymic, Nicholaiyevitch, to Nichols. Mike and his brother, Robert, followed. His mother, ill, stayed behind. "The reason that we got out was the Hitler-Stalin pact, which lasted two years," Nichols says. "If not for that, none of us would ever have lived. I have a very sharp memory of getting off the boat here and opposite the dock was a delicatessen with Hebrew letters in neon, and I said, 'Is that allowed?'"

Their mother finally did arrive, but the marriage turned bad. "As my mother later explained to me, Jews in Nazi Germany didn't have marital difficulties," recalls Nichols. "It wasn't possible to concentrate on such luxuries." He was sent to boarding school while his parents fought and separated. "When they would fight, I would think, Not me, man. I'm going to the movies. I'm going to the movies became, Screw this and screw you." Nichols's parents never did get divorced, because Nichols *Vater* died of leukemia, leaving the family with nothing. Working at odd jobs, his mother scraped together enough money to send the boys to college. "The moment I got there," he says, "my life began."

After attending the University of Chicago, Nichols fell in with a band of inspired crazies: young, rebellious actors who lived on the fringe of the campus community. Among them was Elaine May, a "dangerous wit" and famous neurotic. "You wouldn't dare fuck with her," recalls Nichols, "because she was right back so fast, people fell left and right."

Nichols and May became a comedy act, casting a cold satirical eye on the foibles of middle-class America, raising improvisation to a fine art. Recalls United Artists head John Calley, a longtime friend: "You could say, I want this to be the first line, this to be the last line, and I want you to do it as though it were written by Kierkegaard, and they would do it. Brilliant as they were separately, they were more brilliant together." In 1960, at the peak of their powers, Arthur Penn directed them on Broadway. They were so well known that a letter from Nichols's paternal grandmother addressed simply to "Famous Actor Mike Nichols, USA" actually reached him.

But Nichols and May were too incandescent to last. "Elaine was more interested in taking chances than being a hit," Nichols once said revealingly. "I was more interested in making the audience happy." And before long, he was doing just that, directing Robert Redford and Elizabeth Ashley in a Neil Simon comedy on Broadway, *Barefoot in the Park*. It was a hit. More hits followed. But Nichols knew he was cruising. He had mastered the knack of entertaining out-of-towners with Neil Simon, but there had to be more to life than that. When Elizabeth Taylor asked him to do the movie version of Edward Albee's scabrous *Who's Afraid of Virginia Woolf?*, he jumped at it.

Virginia Woolf—a drama in which a small-college history professor and his wife, lubricated by rivers of alcohol, generous amounts of self-loathing, disappointment, and sexual frustration, cannibalize each other for the edification of the Broadway audience—was strong stuff. But the movie was a critical and commercial success, and it showcased Nichols's greatest gift: getting the best performance an actor had ever given or, in many cases, would ever give. Critics had scoffed when Taylor took the part, but somewhere in the bitter depths of her soul, Nichols discovered Martha and helped her get out. Taylor won her second Oscar. Nichols was nominated for Best Director.

Despite his skyrocketing career, Nichols suffered from the Woody Allen disease: anhedonia, the inability to experience pleasure. "It's a tax that you pay for being obsessive," says Nichols. "At every opening night there's something you can fasten on that's ruined it." Still, he showered himself year after year with the things he was told would make him happy. He bought a sixty-acre farm in Connecticut, on which he raised Arabian horses. He bought a 375-acre ranch in California, on which he raised more Arabian horses. He bought a Rolls-Royce. He bought art—a Matisse and a Picasso. He braved a blizzard of dinner parties, where his charm and wit invariably dazzled. As Anthea Sylbert, his costume-designer-to-be, put it, "Mike was always the smartest guy in the room."

When Nichols began casting his next movie, based on a novel by Charles Webb called *The Graduate*, he read Robert Redford and Candice Bergen for the young leads. But something was wrong. "What I said to Redford was that he could not at that point in his life play a loser, because nobody would ever buy it. He didn't understand, and I said, 'Well, let me put it to you another way: Have you ever struck out with a girl?' And he said, 'What do you mean?' It made my point." Nichols decided to turn Benjamin Braddock into a Jewish kid from Beverly Hills, and in a bold stroke cast an unknown—Dustin Hoffman.

At this juncture, it's hard to recall how powerful *The Graduate*'s impact was. Stanley Kauffmann dubbed it "a milestone in American film history." The *New Yorker* ran a twenty-six-page essay by Jacob Brackman that called it "the biggest success in the history of movies" and a "cultural phenomenon." In its first six months, the film grossed in excess of $35 million (about $150 million in today's dollars).

Nichols was now the toast of both coasts. He was voted Best Director by the New York Film Critics Circle and the Directors Guild and finally won his Oscar. Still, in those dark, private moments, he was filled with doubts; the thrill of Oscar night left him feeling empty. He worried that he would get out of touch. His youngest daughter once said to him, "Dad, you have no idea what people are like, because everybody kisses your ass." Nichols longed for the failure that would free him from the obligations of success. In *Catch-22* he found it.

Joseph Heller's book, which managed to be both a cult novel and a best seller, was a nervy choice. Everyone had read it, everyone loved it. Hot young actors hastily volunteered to follow Nichols into battle: Richard Benjamin, fresh from *Goodbye, Columbus*, Paula Prentiss, Alan Arkin, and Jon Voight. Orson Welles played General Dreedle. Nichols built an air base near Guaymas, Mexico, and assembled the biggest air force in Latin America. The budget soared to a reported $15 million. Back in LA, with the editing nearly finished, Nichols and Calley went to a sneak of *M*A*S*H*. Recalls Calley: "When the lights came up, we looked at each other, and we knew that Bob Altman had gotten the essence of what we had wanted to do, and had done it in a much simpler way." *Catch-22* played to indifferent business. But even the most tepid reviews were respectful. Worse would lie ahead.

Even as film editor Sam O'Steen struggled to get *Catch-22* under control, Nichols was in a small screening room, watching a newcomer in an unusual character study, *Five Easy Pieces*. It was Jack Nicholson, of course, and Nichols liked what he saw. "I was amazed at this strange Jack thing in which his sexuality wasn't kept in a drawer for dates," recalls Nichols. "The rest of us have to sort of go through a gear. A little wine, candlelit dinner. Jack is in that gear all the time." He wanted Nicholson for a script by Jules Feiffer called *Carnal Knowledge*. An unsparing look at male arrogance, self-delusion, and sexual plundering, *Carnal Knowledge* was easily as original and savage as *Virginia Woolf*, but it lacked even the whisper of affirmation that saved *Virginia Woolf* from total bleakness.

Once again, the director got stunning performances out of actors no one took seriously—Candice Bergen and Ann-Margret—and a nonactor, Art Garfunkel. *Carnal Knowledge* was well received and did respectable business. It stands as perhaps Nichols's greatest film, up there with the best of the early seventies: *The Last Picture*

Show and *Five Easy Pieces*. Calley says: "It changed my life and the lives of many friends. It wasn't this runaway hit that seemed to catch a generation in the palm of its hand like *The Graduate*, but as a—forgive me—work of art, it was very, very important."

Nichols had set an impossibly high standard for himself. His next two films were failures: *The Day of the Dolphin*, an espionage thriller that Pauline Kael called "the most expensive Rin Tin Tin picture ever made," and *The Fortune*, a comedy with Nicholson and Warren Beatty. On his next project—another "safe" bet, a Neil Simon script called *Bogart Slept Here*, starring Marsha Mason and Robert De Niro—Warner Bros. pulled the plug after two weeks of production. For the first time, Nichols's career was in real trouble. Not only had he lost his golden touch, but the critics had abandoned him, and he had gained a reputation as a free spender who would suspend shooting merely because an actor had the wrong color tie while costumers scoured New York for the right one. The near-imperial power accorded the director on the set unleashed the baby inside him—as he put it, "the-baby-as-king."

Except for a Gilda Radner concert film in 1980, Nichols didn't do another picture for seven years, until Nora Ephron and Alice Arlen came along with the script for *Silkwood*. He *was* busy in the theater in those years, with Trevor Griffiths's *Comedians* and David Rabe's *Streamers*. Still, he walked down the aisle with script after script—*Melvin and Howard*, *The Last Tycoon*—but would never tie the knot. "Numerous people said that it was fear," says Nichols. "If it was, it didn't feel like fear. It felt like, This isn't it, over and over."

Silkwood, the true-life tale of a working-class whistleblower at a nuclear materials plant in Oklahoma, finally struck a chord. Says Nichols: "As I began to talk to Nora and Alice about it, I got interested in it being about an awakening and discovered that it was my own awakening."

Nichols was determined to turn *Silkwood* in on budget and schedule, but the old baby Mike would occasionally demand his bottle. According to one source, he had his own blend of coffee flown in from New York and had it brewed in a Proctor-Silex labeled MR. NICHOLS, next to the coffee machine for the rest of the crew. Needless to say, a crew member with tools hanging from his belt did a double take, ostentatiously sampled a mouthful, swished it around in his mouth like a wine tasting, and spit it back into the pot. But according to line producer Michael Hausman, Nichols tried hard, even with the crew. And he did turn in the film on schedule and under budget.

"I only saw him relaxed once," says Hausman. "I was at his horse farm, and there was, like, Man o' War—some horse that was worth maybe $5 mil. Six guys carried it around; it never walked anywhere. I took a little stroll with him, and we went to a paddock that had a couple of colts. He put his foot up on the railing, and just for a moment he let his guard down, fleeting, off in his own world, just admiring that little colt."

Silkwood was a hit, and better, a terrific movie. Once again, Nichols launched the film career of a nonactor, Cher, and drew a powerful performance from underachiever Kurt Russell. He inaugurated a three-picture association with Meryl Streep. Streep, Cher, Ephron and Arlen, Sam O'Steen, and Nichols were all nominated for Oscars.

Since then, Nichols's output has been uneven. *Heartburn* was basically a disappointment. Nichols called on Nicholson to replace Mandy Patinkin, whom he fired after the first day of shooting. "Jack's loyalty is frightening," he says. "When I called him, the first thing he said to me on the phone was, 'If you need me, Nick, I can be there in two days.' Then comes the bill, and it's very high, but that's also part of 'If you need me.' Because you can read it 'If you need *me*.' And that's fair; the price is the price. And God knows, he's worth his price."

In the late eighties, Nichols had a *crise de conscience*, triggered, he says, by a severe depression brought on by Halcion, a sleeping pill. He would begin to feel he was subject to some vague retribution "for having escaped, for no particular reason, the Holocaust. That my whole life is on borrowed time. Last summer I was at a party at the Doctorows, sitting next to a wonderful woman, and it turned out that we left Germany the same year, at roughly the same age. She said she'd been to a shrink about it and told him about her guilt, and he said, 'We've been looking for you for a long time. It appears then we've finally found you.' And she said, 'What are you talking about?' And he said, 'We've found the person responsible for the death of six million Jews.' She said it, and I burst into tears at the dinner table. It was extremely embarrassing. It never occurred to me, you know, it's fifty-odd years that I've felt this guilt.

"I was once very close to doing *Sophie's Choice*. I tried to picture myself on the crane saying 'OK, all you Jews: Camera left. SS guards on the right.' And I knew I couldn't do it. I don't think I can deal with the Holocaust. It's not . . . I don't think I can."

When Nichols emerged from his dark night of the soul, he changed his life. He got rid of many luxuries, including his beloved horses, and divorced his third wife, Annabel. "He has taken a real amount of time to think about his human responsibilities," says Anthea Sylbert. "Mike is someone who probably gives himself a grade about how he's behaved in the course of the day. Probably because he knows that he's capable of behaving not so well sometimes." He has quietly donated to charities and is known for helping his friends without being asked. Once, he slipped a struggling writer friend a $20,000 check and asked not to be paid back.

Nichols met Diane Sawyer in 1986. "I was at the airport; he had seen me on the morning news, and I knew instantly who he was," she recalls. "I'd been up three nights in a row, and I kinda didn't really want to meet him, so I kept backing away—went behind a plant. Finally, he had me cornered, so I said hello." They married two years later. Nichols simply says, "I'm happier now that I'm married and I don't have horses and I don't collect paintings."

Last year, Nichols left his longtime agent, Sam Cohn, and moved to CAA. He is taking a more active role in shaping his career, developing material, producing as well as directing. He and Calley had a modest success producing *The Remains of the Day*, and he is passionate about Cormac McCarthy's *All the Pretty Horses*, for which he has a shootable script he wants to set up at UA. *Pretty Horses* is a wonderful but difficult novel to adapt—*Lonesome Dove* without much plot—a drawback that Nichols will have to overcome to make it work as a movie.

For *Wolf* to be a success, much depends on whether the perplexities that plagued preproduction have been resolved—whether Nichols has found the right tone and style for a movie that is part thriller, part romance, part gothic horror story, part comedy, and whether the "quarter inch" approach can make the premise believable. As Pfeiffer puts it: "I would ask throughout shooting, 'What is this movie about?' As soon as you say 'Jack Nicholson becomes a wolf,' people laugh."

Wolf was an expensive picture, with a hefty above-the-line; it nudged the $25 million mark, with script development alone accounting for $2 to $3 million. By all accounts, it was a very tough shoot, with a lot of night work. Nicholson did not relish the four or five hours it took to make him up. "It was hard for Jack," says Nichols. "Not only physically, but to keep all those things in your mind: He's falling in love, but he's also turning into a wolf, and he's lost his job. Where are we now, you know?"

"Was it a hard shoot?" comments Nicholson. "Well, I don't know what an easy shoot is. Yeah, it was a hard shoot—as opposed to making a story about a guy who survives a bath in radioactive waste, or who is the devil. It's not such a new area for me."

The picture went ten days over, triggering the $150,000-a-day penalty clause in Nicholson's contract. But if there was pressure, the actors never felt it. "No matter what happens to Mike Nichols, he will always be a director that anybody wants to work with," says costume designer Ann Roth, "because he lets you be free to try something, and if you screw it up, he has that great sense of humor. He is the creative person's best friend."

"It was so relaxed, I never really believed the camera was going," says Kate Nelligan of her experience on the *Wolf* set. She plays Will Randall's wife. "My character read as unpleasant, cold—the bitch from hell. I said, 'Mike, you gotta tell me what you want me to do.' He said, 'I want you to make the case for her.' A good director only has to say the one thing you need to hear. The case for her was to take her out of the fucking fur coat, put her in a regular coat. It's so much more interesting to make a thing contradictory."

Nichols is sensitive to the charge, as well he might be, that he has never lived up to his potential, that he did his best work in the first five years of his twenty-eight-year career. When this point was raised by Bernard Weinraub in the *New York Times*, Nichols lost his famous cool. "It's not fair," he snapped. "Why should I have to defend myself? Why do I get punished for making two or three or however many great movies?" Calley points out that "Mike is not a screenwriter. He is in a sense a victim of what he gets. I don't think he's lost an iota of his gift. He's as capable on any given picture of knocking it out of the park as he ever has been."

Why indeed does Nichols have to defend himself? There is no doubt that he is supremely gifted, that he can always, given the right material, hit one out of the park. Nichols's "problem," if there is one, lies elsewhere. Perhaps he was never the kind of director we thought he was. In the days of *The Graduate*, he was hailed, with typical media hyperbole, as America's auteur, our answer to Truffaut and Fellini. But he never really made "personal" movies. Although he built his career by transforming the material of his life into biting comedy, as a filmmaker he turned his back on improvisation. Perhaps Altman, who built improvisation into his method, not only bested *Catch-22* with *M*A*S*H* but also went on to have the career we expected Nichols to have. Perhaps, with our obeisance to "sincerity" and "authenticity," we are more forgiving of our less commercial filmmakers.

Nichols has been smart on this subject, as he is about most others. He considers the "art film" or "auteur" period of the sixties and seventies an aberration, a dead end. He points out that movies have always been a popular medium, and likes to cite the case of Larry Adler, who could play Bach on the harmonica but forces us to ask: Do we really want to hear Bach on the harmonica? Wouldn't we prefer "Oh! Susanna"? There is some truth in this. Certainly Bergman was a dead end for Woody Allen.

But there is an irony too. For all that the ship of celebrity is awash in a sea of schadenfreude, there is always the hope that a new Mike Nichols movie may be a special gift, because, God knows, there are precious few out there, and he has done it before. Nichols says that "the miracle is that anyone survives at all." But it would be distressing indeed if, in the autumn of a career as distinguished as his, we can expect no more than survival. It *is* a jungle out there, and maybe Nichols needs more "Screw you" movies and fewer "Like me" movies. Maybe he has to discover the wolf inside himself. Maybe, with *Wolf*, he has.

During his Halcion episode, Nichols says, "I was afraid the story would end badly. Then I realized there is no story. As Lawrence says in *Lawrence of Arabia*, 'Nothing is written.' It's never over until it's over. All things are still possible. That was a source of great happiness."

Note

1. Nichols's maternal grandmother, Hedwig Lachmann, published a translation of Oscar Wilde's *Salome* that Richard Strauss adapted as a libretto for his opera of the same title.—REK

They All Have a Secret

Patrick Goldstein / 1998

From the *Los Angeles Times*, March 15, 1998. Reprinted by permission.

Mike Nichols has a secret.

Actually, the fabled film director has lots of secrets. As soon as he is alone in his Bel Air Hotel suite, Nichols drops his voice to a conspiratorial hiss, swearing a visitor to silence, a bad idea when the visitor is a reporter. Nichols should know better. After all, his new $65 million movie, *Primary Colors*, which stars John Travolta as a Bill Clinton–esque presidential candidate, is based on a reporter's juicy literary caricature of Clinton's campaign trail travails.

Nichols is even married to a journalist, ABC News' Diane Sawyer, who, as bad luck would have it, is the person he wants to keep this particular secret from. "Don't tell my wife I'm smoking," he says, lighting up the first of many cigarettes. "I officially quit two years ago. But with the movie coming out, having to do all this press and promotion, I've been backsliding."

For Nichols, secrets are integral to the creative process. Asked how he and screenwriter Elaine May plotted out *Primary Colors*, due this Friday from Universal Pictures, he explains, "What we really did was endlessly discuss its secrets—the levels and levels and undercurrents of this story."

Most of the sixty-six-year-old director's movies are about secrets, in particular the messy concealments that come from sexual conflict. A scroll through his credits finds amorous discord everywhere: The marital gamesmanship of *Who's Afraid of Virginia Woolf?* A college-aged boy's clandestine affair with his girlfriend's mother— the legendary Mrs. Robinson—in *The Graduate*. The erotic twists and turns of *Carnal Knowledge*. Love and betrayal in *Heartburn*. And the many-layered sexual identity shifts in *The Birdcage*.

So it's hardly surprising that *Primary Colors* appealed to Nichols. The best-selling novel focused on the exploits of Jack Stanton, a womanizing southern governor whose presidential bid is punctuated by bimbo eruptions, marital spats, and hardball spin control.

For Nichols, the story's web of seduction and betrayal offered a perfect subject for a film—a satiric morality tale about political sex and sexual politics. When Nichols bought the book, it even had its own secret—an author who went by the pen name of Anonymous. Months would pass before he was unmasked as Joe Klein, who'd covered Clinton's first presidential campaign for *New York* magazine.

Making his pitch to buy *Primary Colors*, Nichols wooed Klein's literary agent, Kathy Robbins, by saying he was drawn to the novel because it was about honor. When Robbins relayed this pitch to Klein (then still publicly denying his authorship of the book), he told her Nichols was right. *Primary Colors* was about exactly that: honor. There were other bidders willing to match Nichols's $1.5 million offer, but Klein chose Nichols.

And why not? With Nichols, you feel as if you're traveling first class. Even in rumpled black slacks and a houndstooth jacket, he looks like a man in an Armani tux. Warm, courtly, and a wonderful raconteur, adorning his anecdotes with quotes from Oscar Wilde, Woody Allen, and longtime pal E. L. Doctorow, he has the soothing air of a psychiatrist who understands his patients far better than they understand themselves.

"Mike's probably the smartest guy I've ever met in my life," says Billy Bob Thornton, who plays a grits 'n' gravy political consultant in *Primary Colors* modeled after James Carville. "One minute he'll be talking about Russian theater in the 1930s, the next about some philosophical debate. When we had rehearsals before shooting the film, it was like a therapy session. One night I asked Diane Sawyer, 'Do you ever find yourself nodding your head and agreeing with him all the time because you have no idea what he's talking about?'"

Like so many successful film directors, Nichols is a great salesman. When wooing Klein, he talked about honor. But now, with *Primary Colors* arriving on the heels of a new presidential sex scandal, Nichols sees the film from a different angle.

"This isn't a movie about politics," he says firmly. "It's a movie about our problems dealing with the sexuality of our leaders. Why is everyone allowed to ask the president if he's had a sexual relationship? You can't ask me that, or ask your friends that. But we judge politicians differently. We expect politicians to be the superego. They're supposed to control every circumstance and control themselves, even though everything this country has taught us is that sexuality is beyond control—that's the whole point of sex, isn't it?"

He casually raises an eyebrow. "Do you know the woman in England who is the subject of most men's erotic dreams?" The answer isn't Helena Bonham Carter or Minnie Driver or even Emma Thompson, although Nichols liked Thompson's work so much that he hired her, British accent and all, to play Susan Stanton, the governor's strong-willed, Hillaryesque wife.

"It's the queen," Nichols explains. "What could be a clearer statement about the intimacy of our erotic fantasies? In America, we're the same way with the president. It's something Puritan America is very unrealistic about, that excess and empathy can reside in the same person."

Nichols fishes for another cigarette. "You know, on my horse farm, I have a lot of well-behaved horses. But the stallion everyone wants is the one you can't control around the mares. It goes with the vitality of leadership."

Just after the Monica Lewinsky scandal broke, John Travolta was on location in downtown Los Angeles, shooting scenes from the upcoming film *A Civil Action.* Early one morning he walked over to producer Scott Rudin to ask his opinion: The scandal seemed like a bad break for Bill Clinton. But what about *Primary Colors*? Travolta asked. Would it help the film or hurt it?

Travolta wasn't the only one worried. At Universal Pictures, studio head Casey Silver was on the phone with Nichols the morning after the scandal made headlines. Silver insists the uproar had no impact on the film's release. "I've read about all these hand-wringing sessions we've supposedly had, which is just ridiculous," says Silver, who paid Nichols $5 million to produce and direct the film, as well as reimbursing him for the book rights. "We already knew the movie tested well before the scandal. I called Mike and said, 'Hey, I think we should stay the course.' And he agreed. It was unanimous. You sell what you've got, and when what you've got is good, you stand tall."

On the other hand, it's possible moviegoers might avoid the film, feeling satiated by weeks of headlong media coverage. "Truthfully nobody knows," says Nichols. "I see encouraging signs. Never have so many friends begged me to get them into a screening. I was in an elevator when someone badgered me, saying 'I've got to see it! I just can't wait.'"

For Nichols, the most encouraging sign was that his all-important "definitely recommend" preview scores, which he says were high to begin with, went up another ten points at the screening held after the Lewinsky scandal broke. "The sympathy for Emma went up," he says. "In fact, all our women scores were higher, especially for older women which, tragically, means women over the age of twenty-five."

Nichols has trimmed several scenes from the film. But he insists the cuts were made based on preview audience feedback, not at the behest of any Clinton emissaries. "Those are complete fantasies," he says. "I keep reading these stories that say, 'It was reported that Mike Nichols made cuts after a phone call from . . .' But nobody checks to see if the 'report' is accurate. These days, a tabloid prints a story, and by the third time it's printed, suddenly it's true!"

So he hasn't had any pressure from the White House at all? "Not at all," he replies, a tad grumpily. "I have final cut on this picture, which means nobody can change anything, not even the president."

Nonetheless, the *Primary Colors* creative team is top-heavy with unabashed Clinton admirers. Nichols and Elaine May performed at a 1992 Hollywood fundraiser for the Clinton campaign. Nichols and Sawyer frequently socialize with the Clintons at summer gatherings on Martha's Vineyard. Being from Arkansas, Thornton has known Clinton for years—when Thornton's house burned down, he got a condolence card from the president. He freely admits asking for Clinton's blessing via mutual friend—and Clinton crony—Harry Thomason before he took the part. "If he'd had a problem with it, I wouldn't have done it," Thornton says.

Travolta has not only met Clinton, but received an unsolicited offer of presidential help in the religious persecution battle between the German government and the Church of Scientology. After US diplomats raised the issue, Travolta was briefed on the outcome by no less than national security advisor Sandy Berger.

Conservative columnists had a field day, speculating that Clinton's actions were more about influencing Travolta's portrayal of the president in *Primary Colors* than any sudden sensitivity toward Scientology. It's a weak argument—the movie was practically finished by the time Travolta met with Clinton.

"We never spoke about the film," Travolta says. "It's ridiculous to correlate the two issues. He has a lot more important things to think about."

But Travolta, like Nichols, is pretty starry-eyed on the topic of Bill Clinton. "I just feel that he's completely genuine," says Travolta. "He really impressed me. He's smart and caring and he's a great communicator. He always hits the right note when he expresses himself."

Before filming began, Travolta watched Clinton speeches and documentary films. "For me, I was playing Jack Stanton, a great character who's southern and gray and overweight," he says. "But I know there's a lot of Clinton there. He was the blueprint for the illusion."

Maybe that's what gives *Primary Colors* such a voyeuristic charge—it's hard to say where Clinton ends and Jack Stanton picks up. Like the president, Stanton is a man with insatiable appetites. He's always grabbing folks' elbows, inhaling doughnuts, talking politics. When he hears a hard-luck story, his eyes well up with tears. Call him the ultimate political narcissist—he's moved by his own emotions.

Before Travolta took the part, Nichols had offered the role to Tom Hanks, who he'd known since sharing a honeymoon—by chance—with their wives in Saint Barthélemy. (Nichols's marriage to Sawyer is his fourth.) When Hanks dropped out of the part, citing scheduling difficulties, there was considerable speculation that he'd bailed out in deference to Clinton. "I think a bigger reason was that Tom just couldn't identify with the character's promiscuity," says Nichols. "He didn't know how to play a man who was like that."

Nichols is no political junkie—the first thing he cut from the book was its inside-the-Beltway campaign material. But he's endlessly drawn to promiscuity, and how it drives men like Stanton—and Bill Clinton. For Nichols, it's one of life's primal secrets, dating back to a childhood experience that seems to have fueled his fascination with sexual misadventures.

"I have a Freudian response," he says when asked about the romantic entanglements in his movies. "I've never talked about this before, but when I was a boy of five or six in Berlin, I had a gym teacher who'd give me rides from school on the front of his motorcycle. And I remember with awful clarity, a scene with my gym teacher and my mother, and realizing they were lovers. She was a beautiful woman, and I remember her quarreling with him, and he ripped a necklace off her and threw it out a window and she went running after it."

Nichols shuts his eyes for a moment, as if using his directorial skills to organize these chaotic images into a coherent narrative. "So my earliest memories are of my parents and their secret relationships. I suppose I've spent a large part of my life trying to sort it out. And when you do, an awful thing happens. Because along with the sorrow, you get a kind of a kick out of it too. And even when you've sorted out the painful stuff, the kick remains."

After seeing Nichols weep uncontrollably on the set of his movie, Emma Thompson has come to the conclusion that men are more sentimental than women—especially when the woman in question is Elaine May.

"We'd been doing a particularly emotional scene," Thompson recalls. "And Mike would be standing behind the video monitor, these huge tears rolling down his cheeks. And Elaine would be right behind him, staring balefully at the monitor. And when the scene was over, Mike would be wiping his eyes and Elaine would say, quite impassively, 'For the next take, I think [the actors] should move slightly to the left.'"

Of all the relationships in Nichols's films, none are more complex than his real-life partnership with May. They met in the early 1950s at the University of Chicago. Born in Germany, Nichols had come to America as a childhood war refugee. May worked as a child actor in the Yiddish theater, where her father, Jack Berlin, was a prominent director.

Together, they helped form the Compass Players, an improv comedy group that was the forerunner of Second City. In 1957, Nichols and May moved to New York and launched what became the defining comedy act of their time. They were New Frontier pop royalty: playing to packed houses on Broadway, performing at JFK's legendary forty-fifth birthday (where Marilyn Monroe sang "Happy Birthday" in a clinging, flesh-colored gown). Their routines, crackling with edgy, neurotic wit, would influence Woody Allen, James Brooks, and countless comic minds to come. As Nichols's old friend, Sony Pictures chief John Calley, once put it: "Mike and Elaine were so intimidating—they were a combination of Robin Williams and Dostoyevsky."

When the duo split up in 1961, Nichols became a Broadway theater director, where he did many of Neil Simon's early plays. He broke into film in 1966 with an adaptation of *Who's Afraid of Virginia Woolf?* A year later came *The Graduate*, which helped usher in a new era of youth-oriented movies.

Nichols was a golden boy—nominated for an Oscar for his first film, winning with his second. May made her film directing debut in 1970 with *A New Leaf*. She later worked with Warren Beatty on *Heaven Can Wait* and the now-notorious *Ishtar*, before settling into a successful career as a top Hollywood script doctor.

It took years for the two to reconcile. For Nichols, the icebreaker came when he ran into May at a party, and later overheard her say to her then-husband, "See, I told you Michael was wonderful." Nichols began using May to punch up his scripts, which you could say were penned by May stand-ins—razor-sharp comic wordsmiths like Carole Eastman, Nora Ephron, and Carrie Fisher. "Elaine would always come in and save my ass," Nichols says. "On *Heartburn*, she came in and just by talking to Nora, got her to come up with the best line in the movie, where her character says, of men, 'You want fidelity, marry a swan.'"

May's first screenwriting credit for Nichols was 1996's *Birdcage*, the biggest box-office hit of his career. Nichols sees May and himself as a strange set of inner twins. "She has all my references," he says. "She's the person to whom I have to explain nothing. In the fifties, we were two hot, headstrong adolescents. Now we're two infinitely courteous, almost Japanese diplomats."

While making *Primary Colors*, they lived in adjoining houses and drove to the set together each morning. "It's like I told Elaine once, we haven't said anything personal to each other in thirty years," Nichols explains. "No confidences, no truths. That's our relationship after our relationship. We never confide in one another or speak about the people we've loved. We know so much about each other that we don't have to talk about it at all."

When starting a script, the two first map out a rough outline of their story, then May goes off and writes. Before filming begins, Nichols oversees several weeks of rehearsal which have the air of a group therapy session. "I tell slightly embarrassing stories about myself to get us to a more intimate place, so we can say anything to each other, as trusted friends," he says. "It's a way of getting the unconscious into acting. We never complete a scene in rehearsal. We do it part of the way, then leave it alone and let the unconscious do the work."

On the set, the Nichols and May dynamic was as complicated as ever. Travolta says that when he couldn't get his way with Nichols, he would recruit May as his ally. "Mike and I are two indulged, big babies, so if I couldn't convince him of something, I thought, 'I'll go to Mom,'" he recalls. "Once she'd agreed with me, I'd tell Mike, 'Elaine said I could do this.' And Mike would go, 'She did? Elaine! Is this true?'"

Travolta laughs. "They have an incredible bond. You know, if Elaine was in Paris and couldn't figure out what to wear to dinner, Mike would fly out from New York and help her pick out the shoes."

May was on the set every day with a laptop computer, ready to rewrite. Thompson says her favorite line in the film was one May came up with on the spur of the moment. An emissary from New York is visiting the Stantons in Arkansas. Eager to talk turkey with the governor, he says to Susan Stanton, "You don't mind us talking business?" Catching his patronizing tone, Susan coolly responds: "No, no. How else will I learn?"

However, for Nichols it's an image, not a line of dialogue, that crystallizes the theme of the film. Midway through the film, the Stanton camp is in a crisis, one precipitated by the governor's excess libido. His aides huddle into the night, nervously debating solutions. And where is Stanton? At a Krispy Kreme doughnut shop, patiently listening to the night manager pour out his troubles—feeling his pain.

"It's the first thing I saw in the movie," says Nichols. "To me it's like a dream. It gets at the heart of Jack Stanton. That's where his nature takes him in a crisis."

So what are we to make of Jack Stanton? Should we trust someone who believes, much like Bill Clinton, that no matter how cynical his actions on the campaign trail, he'll do the right thing once he gets into office? It seems like a steep price to pay: to do good things as president you have to do bad things to get the job.

"That's the central question of the movie," says Nichols. "What do you lose when you drop things on the way up? I'm still shocked when I hear Jack Stanton say that Abraham Lincoln was a whore too. But it's true—that's how you get elected. You can only reveal who you really are by what you do after you get elected."

For Nichols, politicians are like everybody else—they're entitled to keep their secrets. Perhaps that's why it's so difficult to figure out what keeps Jack and Susan Stanton together. What kind of understanding do they have? In all of *Primary Colors*, you never see them alone together—there's always a scrum of campaign aides in the room. The moment they are by themselves, Nichols cuts the scene, leaving everything to our imagination.

Perhaps it's another one of Mike Nichols's secrets. Emma Thompson says she was struck by the sense that, with Nichols, something is always hidden.

"When I think of Mike, I'm reminded of an acting lesson I learned years ago," she says. "You always have to walk onstage with a secret, something the audience doesn't know about. It's a great thing, because it magnifies you. It makes you more interesting, even if you never figure out what the secret really is."

Of Metaphors and Purpose: An Interview with Mike Nichols

Gavin Smith / 1999

From *Film Comment* 35, no. 3 (May/June 1999): 11–31. Reprinted with permission from the Film Society of Lincoln Center and *Film Comment Magazine.* © Film Comment 1999.

Q: How did you start out in your career?

Nichols: I sort of backed into it. That is to say, I did some plays in college, and then I became part of a theater group that Paul Sills started in Chicago called Playwrights Theatre. At that point I had a job as a disc jockey in a classical music station, which is how I supported myself. I would occasionally go to New York and see plays directed, for instance, by Kazan, and I became more and more curious about how he worked. I saw *Death of a Salesman* and *Streetcar* when I was in high school, in the same year, and I had already seen another great production, *The Heiress*, directed by Jed Harris. All these seemed to me 100 percent real and simultaneously 100 percent poetic. I was extremely excited about this and wanted to learn more about it, so I started to study with Strasberg in New York.

[Yet] I never thought I would be an actor, because when I would occasionally try to cast myself in something, I couldn't; I didn't ever find a part that fit me. So I thought, Well, I'm not going to be an actor—I'm not sure why I'm doing this. I'd been through all the usual jobs of waiter, busboy, night clerk in a hotel, janitor in a nursery, and so forth, and I was running out of those jobs when Paul Sills again offered me a job in Chicago at what was then called Compass, which was an improvisational cabaret. And that's where I began to work with Elaine May, who I had known before. I was very bad at it for months, and then I became better, and then I became better, and then I became pretty good. Elaine was very good at it.

Q: How did you meet and what was your impression of her?

Nichols: We met at the University of Chicago. My first impression of her was of a beautiful and dangerous girl that interested me enormously, scared me. We were both what was known on campus as dangerous. We were introduced and then we oddly met in the Illinois Central railway station on the way back to the South Side of Chicago where the university was. I said, "May I sit down?" and she said "Eeef you vish," and we were in an improvisation—we did a whole long spy mystery improvisation for the benefit of the other people on the bench. That's how we met.

We became very close; it's a very difficult thing to describe, but what was true then is true now in our most recent version of collaboration, in which she writes the script and I direct it: what one of us doesn't think of the other does, and we define the things that are involved in drama and movies in a similar way. And what was true when we were a team—namely, that I would tend to make the shapes and she would tend to fill them—is still roughly true for us now. Each of us has learned quite a lot about the other's, let's call it specialty, but we still tend to work that way a little bit.

Q: Why were you both "dangerous"?
Nichols: We were both seductive and hostile people, and we were both very much on the defensive with other people, and we both had big chips on our shoulders. Chips that we've in different ways whittled away at during the course of our lives and reduced the size of. We had very dissimilar backgrounds. Elaine was from Los Angeles; I was from Europe and then New York. My family was all doctors; Elaine's family was all Yiddish theater actors, and Elaine started in the Yiddish theater playing little boys who grew up to be doctors. It was different.

Q: You had a few experiences as a professional actor in late-fifties television, including something called "The Red Mill," and something directed by John Frankenheimer.
Nichols: "The Red Mill" was an all-star version of an old musical, with Elaine and me and Harpo Marx and Shirley Jones and Elaine Stritch and Donald O'Connor, and it doesn't bear thinking about, at least our part of it. The other was a *Playhouse 90* called "Journey to the Day." Elaine quit, as I recall, and I was very unhappy in it—not for any reason to do with the piece, which was good, and Frankenheimer was a very good and very helpful director. We just weren't equipped as actors to just step into a TV play. It was about [some people] in a mental institution in group therapy, with Arthur Hill as the therapist. It was very good—I just would have liked to take me out of it and I thought it would have been better still.

Q: Why do you say that?
Nichols: I just hadn't figured out enough about acting, about how I would do it. It's funny, it's as though you imagined yourself ice skating and you'd never done it, and you fall on your ass and then you spend the next thirty years coaching ice skaters. And then somebody asks you if you'd like to ice skate again, and you say, "Well, that would be very interesting." And that's what I did: I acted in a play in the National

Theatre in London by my friend Wally Shawn, directed by David Hare, and I was OK, I was good. I had figured out how I could act by then. It would be tantamount to going out on the ice and finding that you don't fall on your ass after thirty years of thinking about but not doing it. And that was a very interesting experience.

Q: And that became the film *The Designated Mourner*.
Nichols: Yes, which is another story.

Q: Why?
Nichols: The film didn't make me happy, because the play was a very specific event that transpired between the three of us actors and the audience, the living audience. The film had the tremendous problem of not being able to have that event and that process. I had a very specific process in the play, in which I played a monster who was able for a while to charm the audience, and just as they began to realize that he was a monster he could get them to laugh one more time and then they'd say, This is really it, you're really beyond the pale, and then I would say, Come on, one more laugh, it won't hurt you. During the course of that process, to some extent, they began to wonder if they were in any way like this monster, which was both the purpose of the play and the fun of the performance. Now if you take that process away and don't have the time to substitute something satisfactory for that process, the film isn't a complete film. But the play was a complete play; it was an experience.

Q: Didn't you and Elaine May work on a play in the midsixties?
Nichols: It was a play called *A Matter of Position*, written by Elaine, in which she didn't perform but I did. It was pretty much an unmitigated disaster, not because of the play, which remains a very interesting play, but because we who had always been onstage together were now in an impossible situation in which I was performing and she was in the audience sitting next to the director watching, and it just imploded under that pressure.

Q: And didn't Arthur Penn direct both of you on Broadway?
Nichols: Arthur Penn did direct us in our own evening, that was basically our act on Broadway. He helped us turn it into an evening in the theater, which of course it had never been—it had always been cabaret. But this had two acts, and it had an intermission and it had a build before the intermission. It had our best piece, really, something we could never do in a cabaret or on television. It was something called "Pirandello," in which we started as children and then grew up and then turned into ourselves fighting, that was very flashy and worked very well. Because [Arthur Penn]'s a very good director, he kept leading us back to ourselves and our initial impulses, and how these pieces had come about and what they were. He was in this particular case more of a friend than a director—an eye and an intelligence that we could trust

absolutely. But it was material that we had done for years, literally. He helped us in the same way that I helped Whoopi Goldberg put together her evening in the theater, [created from] stuff, pieces, that she had done at various times in other places.

Q: How did you make the transition from performing to directing?

Nichols: Improvising was a wonderful training, as it turned out, for theater and movies, because you learn so much about what the audience expects in terms of action and events. When you're improvising, an audience basically is saying to you, Why are you telling me this? and you learn over the months—and in our case over the years—some answers to that question. "Because it's funny" is an answer, and if you don't have that as an answer, you're going to have to have a good, clear answer. And improvising teaches you the elements of a scene. If you and I are improvising and you say "black," I'd better say "white" if I want a scene. And then we developed certain rules, Elaine and I, just for improvising. When I teach acting, I still fall back on some of those rules. "What is happening?" is the first question you have to answer. Conflict is good and a seduction is good, but something has to happen or you're just sitting there making up lines. You have to create a situation, an event.

Q: Why were you so successful together?

Nichols: I have no idea. We had done it for so long in Chicago; it never occurred to us that we would do anything further with it—we just did it because that was how we were making a living. And we were sort of surprised to be so successful in New York. We were at this nightclub and that nightclub and then we were on television. We were in a long segment on a show called *Omnibus* that was a very big deal at the time; we were very famous the day after, there were big headlines about us, and Elaine says that I called her at four in the morning and said, "What do we do now?" Because we thought it was something we would do to make a living until we grew up and started our lives as adults. Well, that apparently wasn't going to happen, because now we found ourselves doing this all the time, and doing it on television. Finally we did it in a theater for a year, and then when Elaine felt it was enough and didn't want to do it anymore, I really didn't know what I was or what I was going to do. I was half of a comedy team.

And then a theatrical producer called Saint Subber suggested I might want to try directing a play. And he gave me a play called *Nobody Loves Me* by Neil Simon, and I said, "Well, let's do it in summer stock and see if it works and see if I'm any good at it." In the first fifteen minutes of the first day's rehearsal I understood that this was my job, this was what I had been preparing to do without knowing it. It had literally not crossed my mind as far as I was aware. Everything I learned from Strasberg, from improvising, from performing with Elaine, was preparing me. I felt what I never had felt performing: I felt happy and confident and I knew exactly what I wanted to do.

We changed the name of the play from *Nobody Loves Me* to *Barefoot in the Park*, and from that point on it went very fast—by which I mean I directed a lot of plays.

I loved movies, and I saw many movies, some over and over. Movies had always been very important to me even as a kid. I remember going to movies in the afternoon after school, but I didn't think particularly about making them until I heard that Elizabeth Taylor, who was a friend by that point, was going to do *Virginia Woolf*, and I said, Oh, I could direct that. I had a very powerful response to the play and I felt that there were many things I knew about it and things I'd like to do with it as a movie.

I can't say that I had the same sense immediately as I had with directing a play— Oh, this is what I was meant for—because at least for me it was too vast a possibility; it's too daunting for that. The thing about movies is, you're there looking all the time at the great movies that great directors have made, so it's difficult to jump into it and say, Oh, yeah, this is made for me and I'm made for it. It was a kind of total immersion in the process that seemed not difficult to learn, in the sense that I'd read Orson Welles saying "you can learn all the technical aspects of movies in one day"—which is not quite true, but you can learn a great deal about lenses and dollies and montage and so forth, and of course, you've been learning about all that seeing movies all your life. I think you can actually see me learning during the course of *Who's Afraid of Virginia Woolf?*, because we shot it in sequence.

I did know—and this is very rare for me—that it was something that I could never use up, that was going to be endlessly fascinating and exciting to me. It was a process the tools and possibilities of which are infinite. You can take them further and further, but you can also simplify them more and more, and over a very long time it can become as simple as your own grammar. It's something I knew I could never tire of, and one of my problems is that I do wear things out and want to go on to something else.

Q: Was that a problem with working on the stage?

Nichols: It was, because I was doing plays for such a specific purpose: I was making Broadway hits, and that was a process of rehearsing, and then previewing out of town, and sharpening the play and the performance and improving them and standing in the back and making notes, and making it better over a period of weeks and sometimes months. It was a process I enjoyed, but it was also in a way finite. You have two simultaneous, different problems. One is, doing each performance as though it were for the first time, fresh and alive—this has never happened before. And the other is just finding the highest expression of that particular text. A movie is a very different thing. It's far more mysterious. A play is a little like coaching a team, making your plans for your plays, working with the quarterback, being the quarterback really, devising your strategy and then practicing how to make that strategy happen. A movie, although it's very technical in the shooting stage, really puts you much more in touch with your own unconscious and the unconscious of the audience. Which is, I think, the great hold that it gets on us all.

Q: Isn't it also a question of control? In the end, in the theater, you have to let the actors take it away. With film, you can keep your fingers on everything almost until it's going through the projector. Yes, there are degrees of control, but ultimately it's more control-oriented.

Nichols: I think that's very true. I remember in *Barefoot in the Park* we were a tremendous hit, and somebody told me some weeks after we opened that one actor said to one of the others, "When is Mike ever going to leave us alone?" Because I kept coming back and giving them notes and re-rehearsing things—I couldn't give up control, I couldn't let it go, I wanted to continue to control it for every performance. And of course that's impossible.

As you say, in a movie you do have control of it, but the thing that you don't ever control after you choose [a film] is the central metaphor that is the movie. It seems to me that, to a greater extent than a play, a movie's artistic success, success as an experience, depends on the power of the metaphor that is the central engine of the movie. If you have a powerful metaphor, if the audience knows why they're there, you can soar very high. If you don't have that metaphor, no amount of cleverness with the camera or talent on the part of the actors can lift it, because the engine that is the metaphor is everything. I believe that now as much as I did when I began.

Q: Is that central metaphor something that you can impose, or is it inherent in the material?

Nichols: It's in the story—it's as simple as that. The story either contains it or it doesn't. In between there are gradations. There are stories that seem to convey them but can't stand the pressure of the process or confrontation by the audience, and certain metaphors crack under that pressure. I said to [Anthony] Minghella, when I'd seen *The English Patient*, that I'd never seen a New York audience so still, so absolutely silent, during a movie. It was a very strong experience to be in that audience. And he said, "Yes, well—they sense purpose." That's a wonderful thing to say. And we do, as an audience, sense purpose. If there's a purpose inherent in a story, in the metaphor that is a given story, we do sense it and we can be tamed by it. An audience is a ruthless, heartless, and unruly monster, and if it doesn't sense purpose then get out of its way, because it's going to be difficult—difficult to get the attention of, difficult to make laugh, difficult to carry along on the journey that is any particular story. But when your purpose is high and strong and an audience can sense it, they'll go pretty far with you. So that all the mysteries of choosing a story—what does it mean to you, what does it *really* mean to you, what does it mean to you that you're not even aware of? How can you communicate on that level, of which you are not necessarily even aware or which you cannot necessarily articulate, to an audience? All these things reside in the power of the metaphor, and there you just have to get lucky. You can't invent, create, carpenter, that metaphor if it isn't there. Sometimes Hollywood people say, "If you can say it in two sentences it's a hit; if you can say it in one sentence it's a blockbuster." That's a relatively shallow formula, but it has some truth to it.

Q: Since as a director, part of your work is to work with the writer, aren't you, at that very early stage, doing something to direct the metaphor?
Nichols: It's already too late. Let's say we're going to do a musical. One of us says to the other, "I have an idea: sixty people audition, six make it." If I gave you that idea, or you gave it to me, the other one would say, "Oh, I'd like to work on that." That's it, it's done. We could have all done *Chorus Line*; we might not have done it as well as Michael Bennett and his collaborators, it's very likely we wouldn't have done it as well, but we could have done a pretty good job because that one sentence is so powerful, it leads to so much that is story, tension, development, conflict, resolution, emotion, that you can make a pretty good show out of it. Now that sentence doesn't seem like such a big deal, but go find another one. Michael Bennett couldn't. All of us can spend decades of our working lives and not find such a powerful central sentence to a story again.

About a month into working on *Barefoot in the Park*, Neil Simon and I were walking down the street after rehearsal, and he said, "I have an idea for a play about two men who are separated from their wives and they room together and they begin to treat each other as they did their wives." I said, "I want to do that play." And he wrote it and it was *The Odd Couple*, and I knew from the sentence that he uttered in beginning to think about it that it was a brilliant idea for a play. Those acorns are precious, and they're very rare; they don't come to an individual that often, and in some ways our working lives are a process of trying to seed and fertilize the field, trying to grow something that will produce those ideas. But it is the most difficult part of it, because it is the part that you have to pray for—you can't make it come. You have to pray that another one will be dropped on you.

Q: Have there ever been instances when you weren't sure of what the true central metaphor was and yet you were still able to see it through? And have you ever gone ahead with something that didn't satisfy the criteria you describe?
Nichols: Yes. All those instances. I think what happens is, you see all the signs of the central metaphor and you try different names for it, but it's always there, you're always describing it in different ways. You can also be in the middle of something and realize that there's a serious flaw in the central metaphor. I realized very early in *Wolf* that the metaphor of vampires is very powerful, it speaks to all of us, we all know a great deal about it, but the metaphor of werewolves is not—it has never

worked, never will work, because it doesn't echo anything that happens to people. People are and do become vampires, people are preyed upon by vampires, this is something that has infinite resonance. Give me a vampire picture and I'll make you a better picture than *Wolf*. Because although a lot of very good work went into *Wolf*—from Nicholson and from Elaine May, who rewrote the script, and I did some good work—it didn't really matter because the metaphor just didn't sail, it didn't travel on its own. We had to start pushing and pulling, and once you have to start doing that, it is usually too late.

Q: In some ways *Wolf* is almost a mirror image of *Regarding Henry*. Both are stories of transformation, of discovering a new self.

Nichols: Well, yes, all my pictures turn out to be all about transformation, actually. Transformation and awakening are very powerful themes in our lives. But this was not a conscious . . . I didn't send agents out to look for stories of transformation; this is what I was drawn to. What drew me to *Wolf* was working with Jim Harrison on a story about some atavism in men. But it turned out that it was an incomplete metaphor. And that was probably true of *Regarding Henry*, too, that it was an oversimplified metaphor, and therefore gave itself away.

I suppose there are ways of avoiding those . . . finally you'd have to call them mistakes . . . but if I got to do it all over again I'm not sure that I would avoid them, because it's a way to learn. This unconscious part of it that we're talking about, and the metaphor aspect of these things, are sufficiently mysterious, simultaneously mysterious and powerful, that you can't make a formula, you can't make it problem-proof, you can't test it. It's sort of like finding out about your boat when you're in the middle of the Atlantic—you have to commit yourself and jump in and set sail and then somewhere several hundred miles from Newfoundland you discover whether your boat is sufficiently seaworthy or not. You have no idea how it will turn out, but you have inklings. You always come to it with infinite hope while simultaneously testing it and attacking it and being its enemy, to make sure it's as strong as possible. While you're doing those two things, you can lose track of reality. And reality is a very simple thing: reality is the first time it's in front of an audience, and then it's almost always too late.

Q: Which films came out closest to your initial inkling of them?

Nichols: It takes me a while to know whether I see anything. I can love a piece of material, but [not] know for some time whether I see it as a movie, whether I literally see things that'll be in the movie. When I begin to see those things, it's always a moment or a scene that is the hook that pulls me into it. Sometimes it becomes so specific that the movie in the end is very much what I saw in the beginning. That's certainly true of *The Graduate*, *Virginia Woolf*, *Carnal Knowledge*. *Primary Colors* is very much what I saw from when we were close to finished with the script. *The Birdcage*, of course, was not the first or second or even third time that the story had been told, but once we began to imagine that plot, which Elaine and I both loved very much—a perfect metaphor for what the movie is about, which is family—once we began to see it in this time and found the exact right place for it to happen in this country, it came out very much the way I imagined it.

Q: In what way did the dangerousness you talked about sharing with Elaine May carry over into movies for you?

Nichols: By the time I was a director, it had more to do with choice of subject and the events of any given story than with either of our lives. The anarchy, the carp swimming at the bottom of the sunlit pond, has been in terms of the subject and the subtext of the pieces. Flaubert said, "Live the most bourgeois life possible and put your wildness in your work."

Q: Was the most scathing side of your sensibility manifested in *Carnal Knowledge*, *The Graduate*, and *Catch-22*?

Nichols: Yes. Whatever satire is, our anger and our feeling of not belonging, which is sort of a sine qua non for an artist, I guess, did go into the satirical/angry aspects of more of the pieces we did than not.

Q: Did your way into *Who's Afraid of Virginia Woolf?* have anything to do with that "dangerous" chemistry?

Nichols: That was never our personal relationship. With the exception of the rough part in the middle, when we stopped doing the act and Elaine got married, and a long difficult stretch in our friendship during which we just didn't see each other, and then picked up again after some years. With the exception of that, the difficulty of any team breaking up, it's always been pure pleasure and always only increased [each of us]. However, both as individuals and as participants in other relationships, we do know quite a lot about the people in *Who's Afraid of Virginia Woolf?*, not least because of where we began, the University of Chicago. The set of the movie was based on [the home of] a couple that Elaine and I both knew in Chicago, and we knew quite a lot about the backyards and the bedrooms and the bars of academe, and we lived different but parallel lives.

Q: How was it when you and Elaine May played George and Martha in a 1980 production of *Who's Afraid of Virginia Woolf?*

Nichols: Well, it was OK, we were fine. There wasn't the time or scope to do it completely properly. We did it with two other very good actors, Swoosie Kurtz and James Naughton, and I got sick in the middle of performing it. There were times when it was perfectly all right, but I wouldn't call it the highest achievement of the play that ever was. It was an interesting experience. To some extent we did it to find out what it was like. I wanted specifically to know what it was like to be directed, and I found out. It was very tough for both the director and me because I did know so much about it and I disagreed so much with some of the just plain staging of the play. We hadn't set it up wisely for that reason.

Q: It seems an incredibly loaded situation.
Nichols: It was too loaded.

Q: How did *The Graduate* come about?
Nichols: It was a book that Larry Turman, the producer of the movie, sent me before I did *Virginia Woolf*. I liked it, and we arranged to do it, and then *Virginia Woolf* came along, and I said, "Would you mind if I did this first?" and he didn't mind. It helped in many ways, because we had several scripts that I was very unhappy with, and then while I was shooting *Virginia Woolf* in LA I met Buck Henry, and I said, "I'd like Buck to do the script." He'd never written before; he'd been a member of another improvisation group, Premise, but I thought that he would do a brilliant job, which he did.

Q: Given that *The Graduate* was a film that turned out the way you wanted it, what for you was the defining moment?
Nichols: There's a moment that I thought was at the very heart of it. In fact, I told Anne Bancroft about it, and then when we got to shooting the scene she left it out, and I [reminded her], and she said, "Oh, oh, oh, I forgot, let's do it again." So it was more important to me, although Anne did it.

It was when Benjamin and Mrs. Robinson are in bed and he says, "We never talk, let's talk." And she says, "All right, what do you want to talk about?" And he says, "Well, you suggest something." And she says, "All right, art." And he says, "Art, that's a good topic, you start." And she says, "You start, I don't know anything about it." And somewhat later in the same scene, when he's asking her about her early life, she's talking about college and he says, "What was your major?" And she says, "Art." He says, "Art . . . oh, well I guess you kind of drifted away from it," and she says, "Kind of."

I thought that was the very heart of Mrs. Robinson, and therefore of the movie: namely, her self-hatred and the extent of her sadness about where the exigencies of her life had taken her, as opposed to where she had originally wanted to go. And that was very important to me. These hooks into the person who's making the movie or writing the play are so invisible and mysterious to other people. It's very personal and strange, but that was the first thing I understood about the people in *The Graduate*, and it was the beginning of the process.

Now, I don't want to compare myself to Bergman, because he's The Man, but his description of how he writes a screenplay is very beautiful. He says that he imagines a black leather satchel with a little piece of red thread sticking out of it, and he pulls on the thread, and keeps pulling and the thread keeps coming, and it's tied to a string and he keeps pulling, and the string is tied to a rope which begins to come out of the satchel. It's very beautiful and accurate. That moment of Mrs. Robinson was the little red thread sticking out of the satchel, and I just kept pulling on it.

Q: You don't identify closely with Benjamin; you seem to view him from a distance.
Nichols: And yet the parts of me that did identify with Benjamin predominate in what I did with the movie. By that I mean, I didn't cast Redford. Dustin has always said that Benjamin is a walking surfboard. And that's what he was in the book, in the original conception. But I kept looking and looking for an actor until I found Dustin, who is the opposite, who's a dark, Jewish, anomalous presence, which is how I experience myself. So I stuck this dark presence into Beverly Hills, and there he felt that he was drowning in things, and that was very much my take on that story. When I think of Benjamin, there are many things that come from my personal experience. His little whimper was my little whimper when Jack Warner would tell a joke; in fact, people had to tell me to try not to whimper when he told jokes, that he was going to notice. And that was the direct source of Benjamin's whimper. To me, one of the most alive scenes in the movie is when he wants to leave the hotel room and Mrs. Robinson is putting her stocking on and now he can't. A lot of these things come from inside of us, and I think that the characters that speak to us, that express us, will never be apparent to anybody but ourselves because the outsides of people are so different, but the insides, especially people who feel themselves to be outsiders, are really similar.

Q: What you notice about yourself as an outsider is not what everybody else notices, anyway.
Nichols: That's it, exactly. So that you identify with people that are objectively not like you at all. Thomas Mann's distinction in his short story "Tonio Kröger" was very important to me, both when I was growing up and when I was starting to do plays and movies—the difference between oneself and the blond, blue-eyed people. Well, I was a blond, green-eyed person, but I could never see myself that way. I identified with the dark outcasts.

Q: The use of compositional space in the film is strange: full of forced perspectives and foreground objects and figures blocking the frame, shooting Benjamin through the negative space of a person in the foreground, shooting through somebody's leg, or arm. How did you arrive at that and what were you trying to express?

Nichols: Well, I talked a lot to Robert Surtees, the DP, and to the art director and to the actors about expressions of isolation and estrangement. Glass, plastic, windows, fish in tanks. Depersonalization. It sounds so pretentious, but it was meant to be our secret, which is I think what you do with the theme in a movie. You choose it and you express it and it should be secret, there's no need for people to walk out of the movie talking about it. But it is nevertheless the spine on which you hang the rest of the body of movie. In this case it was drowning in things, and the danger of becoming a thing, the danger of treating yourself or other people as things. So that preoccupation led to the choices of the compositions of shots and where the camera was and how isolated he was.

Q: *Catch-22* was considered to be an artistic failure at the time of its release, but I think it's one of your best.
Nichols: It was in some ways a failure. I ran it for Stanley Kubrick and he was very nice about it. I don't remember the good things he said, but he did say that people might have some narrative problems with it: where are we, what's happening, and because it was all circular, you weren't really sure when a given scene was taking place. Which I don't mind, but it did bother some people. I think I made some mistakes. I should have scored it—I think it would have helped. It was sort of arrogant not to score it. And it should have been funnier. The strange thing for me about that movie is it kicks in about the middle, in the dark part, in Rome. And then it gets pretty good. I didn't really find a completely successful way of translating the surrealism of the novel. It came and went. It was like one of those Von Stroheim follies. If I could do it again, I would like to think it could be funnier and have more heart. It was very cold, too. What I like very much about it are its ambitions.

Q: Do you feel *Carnal Knowledge* presses the cynicism of *The Graduate* even further?
Nichols: Oh, I think so. *Carnal Knowledge* is the darkest movie I ever made. It's the only one I ever see again. I'm very impatient, and in looking at it I'm very annoyed by its pace. Because I was so hung up on not cutting and doing everything in one, I just think it's slow. In the beginning especially, I just think, C'mon, let's go, let's go. And then indeed it does get moving, in the middle, and then I think it works—I like it very much. It's a mannerist film, and that's both what I like and don't like about it. It was written as a play, and I said I thought it wasn't a play, actually it was a movie. I think without planning to, it was in some ways reminiscent of Feiffer's panels, when he draws his cartoons. It was somehow connected to that.

Q: In the end the film underestimates the female capacity for duplicity and manipulation and underestimates men's naivete. Nicholson's character is so completely in control, and the women are really just objects of manipulation and abuse.

Nichols: That's the form at the outside of it, but the concern of it is with the interior experience of the object. That's what I still like about it. People thought it was an antiwoman film. I never thought that was true. It was a film about the underclass and what its members suffered. The main thing to remember about *Carnal Knowledge* was it was about a specific generation of men. I don't think those men exist now, and I think feminism has changed everyone to some extent. But what you said is absolutely true, that we all think of men as the liars. Well, of course, women, like any underclass, are liars, too—they're just better liars, because their lies are part of a necessary strategy. I think some of that is in the movie; we probably could have used more of it.

Q: *The Day of the Dolphin* was a departure for you. What drew you to it?
Nichols: What drew me to it was the dream of a friend which we usually express in terms of people from outer space, but this was the dream of a friend right here on earth, of an equal to human beings. We keep trying to find somebody to talk to, literally. I think we ran into some trouble because of the comedy aspects of that, if it's a dolphin, but I think it's a perfectly legitimate dream. It didn't adequately express that dream, to get past the conspiracy thriller outside that contained it. It really came about because I needed to find something to get out of my contract with Joe Levine. Polanski, who had been planning to make the movie, dropped it, and I picked it up. On the first day of shooting, he sent me a jar of gefilte fish with a note that said if only he could speak. That's my strongest memory of the movie.

Q: Your next film, *The Fortune*, was again not well received.
Nichols: It doesn't work. *The Fortune* has one hilarious scene where Jack breaks down. There's nothing to be said about it and too much to be said about it. The writer giving me a 325-page script without an ending, which I had to carve like a block of ice. It was really a case of three good friends [Nichols, Warren Beatty, and Jack Nicholson] who wanted to work together, and we didn't wait until the script made sense and was right. I don't think I helped it, with the long takes. The trouble with *The Fortune* was that it wasn't like anything. You couldn't compare it to anything in life. I think that just put it right outside; we were too far outside of it at every point. It just didn't ring true. It had some hilarious Jack scenes, and Stockard [Channing] was wonderful.

Q: After *The Fortune* you took a seven-year break from movies. You've said that you couldn't find anything you felt like doing. Was that all there was to it?
Nichols: I think what happened is that I was a little like those cartoon characters that run off the cliff. I was quite arrogant about plays at that point. I said, "Give me any play that's reasonably good and I can take it out of town long enough and I can make it work." And I did movies and they worked pretty well, and then they worked

very well, and then they didn't. And I hadn't had that experience. They kept calling me Mr. Success, which made me very nervous. I was on a plane once where the pilot said, "Just a minute," and we were all panicked, and it went into a steep bank to go back to the airport. And a woman way down the plane turned around and looked at me and said, "What do we now, Mr. Success?"

Catch-22 was the first failure. Instead of being dashed by it, I was very interested in both the experience and its aftermath. As my friend George Wolfe pointed out, you don't learn anything from a success, you learn from failures. I think I had stopped paying attention enough. In the theater there's always this terror as the audience is approaching. And you work out of a panic. In the movies I think you can be lulled into thinking, This is how we do it, and we like the process and it's always all right, and then suddenly it isn't all right. And I think without really naming it or knowing it at the time, I needed that time to pause and begin again. Pay a little more attention. And then, there really was nothing that seemed strong enough for me to feel like I needed to do it, for those years. And then with *Silkwood*, I like very much what it was about.

Q: Which to you was what?

Nichols: It was entirely about an awakening. And it turned out in my life to be about me awakening also. I was galvanized by [Meryl] Streep. I was stunned by what she brought, not only in terms of her part, but what she brought to the others just by rearranging her soul a little bit. What happened to the whole group meant a lot to me. And in the years in between, the grammar of movies had become a part of me. I no longer stopped and sent everybody away for an hour while I tried to figure out how to shoot it, I just shot it. And I was finally through with long takes and the sort of hubris of not cutting.

I'm a big believer in learning about things while you're not doing them, not even thinking about them. Something is going on by itself. It's my retake theory of acting, which is this: you do a scene and it takes you three days, and finally it's OK, and then the next day they come and say, "Bad news, they screwed up at the lab, this footage is lost." And you say, "Oh no—all right, we won't worry about it now, we'll reshoot it at the end of the picture." At the end of the picture you say, "Oh, God, we have to redo that scene," and the scene that took three days takes fifteen minutes. It's just ripened on its own, while no one was thinking about it, or working on it. There were a number of such scenes in *Virginia Woolf*, where we fought to get them, and shot and shot, and then had to do them again and we just did them. In the seven years in the desert, without particularly thinking about movies, something happened, I learned some things. I always say to acting students that time is one of the things that's been taken away or curtailed as a working tool, and whenever you can give yourself time, know the lines for a long time or leave something alone for a few weeks, sometimes that brings things that no amount of whacking away can do.

Q: Which plays represent your best work?

Nichols: I feel my best work was on *The Odd Couple* [1965], *Streamers* [1976], and *The Real Thing* [1984]. I think I brought the most to those plays, and those were the productions that I guess I'm proudest of. The sort of sheer wild comic invention in *Barefoot* was a lot of fun at the time and is still fun to remember, but it was very much of then. I think *Streamers* is a great play, and we worked on it for so long, really for eight months between doing it at Long Wharf and stopping and redoing it in New York. By the time we were through it really was a wonderful thing.

Q: Do you see *Silkwood* as your most conventionally realistic film?

Nichols: Yes and no. *Silkwood* was so much about being in a daze and looking around one and thinking, Oh my God, I haven't been aware of what's been happening, and what's been happening is very bad. And it was so much about people who don't spend a lot of time talking about relationships, talking about what's wrong, so that there was a constant obbligato, a kind of underside of what's really happening between the people. And that's what I liked about working on it, that what is going on between the people is still quite visible even when they don't talk about it.

It's also what drew me to the theater to begin with. You find ways to express the underneath without words; sometimes it's the opposite of the words, or a tangent of the words. I think *Silkwood* has a lot of those things—unexpressed undercurrents that are palpable.

Q: How do you feel about *Heartburn*?

Nichols: I think *Heartburn* needed one more element, which would have been the equivalent of the female character's voice in the book. We had come to a point where narration seemed somehow stiff and not integrated. There's a sort of moment in movies where narration became a crutch instead of a tool. I'm always uncomfortable with it, although we know it can be great; I've never found the way. I think what disappointed some people in *Heartburn* is it didn't express his experience as well as it did hers, although I felt it did, because I thought Nicholson was so eloquent. I thought it was always clear what was happening to him, but it wasn't manifest enough, I guess. But it does have a real ease, and these two great actors working with one another was a nice thing to watch.

Q: *Biloxi Blues* was the first film you did with Neil Simon, even though you collaborated with him a lot in theater. How did that come about?

Nichols: I'd been sick. I had a sort of breakdown for six months, which turned out to be caused by Halcion, which some doctor had given me as a sleeping pill. It made me basically crazy. I was in a depression and nobody knew what it was, and by the time it turned out to have been the Halcion, six months had gone by. Then in stages, I stopped taking it and I was me again. But I still felt rather shaky, and *Biloxi Blues* seemed an ideal thing to work on, because Simon and I understood each other so well and because I knew how to do his work. When we started, I thought, Oh look, I can still do my job, I know where I want to put the camera, and it's going to be OK.

Q: And then you did *Working Girl* back to back.
Nichols: We took what started out as, how shall I say it, not a completely original plot. Let's say a classic plot. And because of going detail by detail—what is the makeup really like of the women on the Staten Island Ferry? It's one of my favorite questions in work, "What is this really like?" We did a lot of that in *Working Girl*, both with how people looked and with the sort of tics and behaviors of the workplace. And as we began to pile up these details, it became very pleasurable.

Q: It's your most class-conscious film.
Nichols: Class is still one of the great subjects of drama. Whether it's expressed more in its subterranean aspects, whether it's expressed in a code of unwritten rules that have to be learned, each world has its unwritten rules.

Q: Do you see it as a fantasy of crossing over?
Nichols: Very much. It interests me in everything. It interests me so much in Hollywood, the lines that can be crossed and the lines that are never crossed. No brilliant production manager, no matter how much he knows about making movies, has ever become a powerful producer. He's "below the line." The guy who takes the option on the material for fifteen hundred dollars and has no idea how you make a movie, but does know how you fight for a producer credit, has a better shot than a below-the-line guy. And those glass ceilings and distinctions are extremely interesting.

Q: *Postcards from the Edge* goes to the other extreme—a very hermetic world where reality doesn't intrude.
Nichols: I think *Postcards from the Edge* is really a woman's picture, in the way that Barbara Stanwyck and Bette Davis movies used to be. Which is why I put the big fight on the staircase. I thought it was an honorable tradition.
    I also like the little movie-reality gags.

Q: Which refer to a larger question about the struggle to separate an authentic self from an illusory one.
Nichols: It's about a special place that doesn't exist anywhere on earth, in which reality has been long ago left behind. Willingly, by everyone—not just the stars, but the people who think there is such a thing as a star. It's a place in which reality is only to be imitated in work. It's not much use in life. Hollywood was and is a place in which how you are perceived really does come first. It's the reason that it's difficult to live there for any length of time. It's a virus that's very hard to immunize yourself

against. For people who've been there for generations, perception is everything. If one were to do *Postcards* now, it would have to be more and more of a farce. What can you do with perception being number one except make some good jokes about it?

Q: A theme you return to in *Primary Colors*. What were you getting at in the final shots, the dancing, panning across the campaign workers and coming to Henry (Adrian Lester), the protagonist?

Nichols: I wanted it to be ambiguous. It seems to me that the very concept of selling out is dead, it doesn't exist anymore. It's in fact George Stephanopoulos's dilemma: does he live very simply and teach at Columbia and keep faith with the assumptions about taking such a job, or does he take the $2.4 million and write an excellent book and forever after make some people think that maybe it would have been wiser not to? People go now where the power is. It's just what's happening. And it's not that there aren't millions and millions of people who do everything by their own lights and are unable to betray anyone or anything, because that's going to go on. People don't change. Fashions change. Right now the most effective thing is to go towards the greatest power, the most money, and then you can afford a shrink.

The dilemma of *Primary Colors* interests me because we are now in a time when so-called current events have largely replaced fiction as the primary metaphor. So that as we go from chapter to chapter of the big soap opera, from O. J. to Princess Diana to Clinton and Monica, they have crowded out the metaphors that were in fiction, they've sucked up metaphor into them so that they're the main story. They're the story that everybody's watching in the way that everybody used to read Dickens and Dostoyevsky in serialized form. *Primary Colors* is confusing because it's fiction and reality at the same time. That's why it interested me, and that's why I think there were certain problems in looking at it. That mixture is happening in our lives as well as in more and more pictures, but the most interesting thing about the big soap opera is that what we are following are not the actual events. There are the things that go into Nexis, and once it's gone into Nexis it's happened, whether it's really happened or not. At the same time, we're looking at movies about worlds further and further into space and more and more of the imagination. What sort of seems dull now is just ordinary people's lives. Every few years we still get a picture about ordinary people and you think, Oh, isn't that interesting!

City of Angels

David Ansen and Marc Peyser / 2003

How in heaven's name do you describe *Angels in America* without taking up this entire magazine? After all, this is a play about Jews and Mormons, gays and straights, New York and Antarctica, the ozone, Ethel Rosenberg, AIDS, African Americans, Reagan Republicans, *Cats*— and we haven't even mentioned the angels, or a devil named Roy Cohn. When *Angels* opened on Broadway in 1993, it blew the roof off American theater. Here, at last, was a play that wasn't afraid to take on the whole world—and the afterworld—with thrilling language and stagecraft, and wicked humor that would have made Oscar Wilde proud. Tony Kushner, then only thirty-six, won a Pulitzer Prize and two Tony Awards. See why we're afraid we can't do it justice? Which is why we've enlisted some expert help. On December 7, HBO will debut a six-hour, $60 million TV version of *Angels*. Directed by Mike Nichols, HBO's *Angels* features a dream-team cast headed by Al Pacino (Cohn), Meryl Streep (one of the Mormons), and Emma Thompson (one of the angels). How dreamy are they? For one thing, they help this *Angels* stand shoulder to shoulder with the play. Brutal, hilarious, and deeply moving, the movie is like a bonfire that never stops giving off heat and light. At a time when TV movies make news for all the wrong reasons, *Angels* is political, passionate—and better than almost anything on the air. Last week these all-star actors joined Nichols, Kushner and Justin Kirk, who plays an AIDS patient named Prior Walter, in discussing the film with *Newsweek*. Excerpts:

Newsweek: So Justin . . .

Justin Kirk: I knew it! [*Laughter*] Clearly I have a role to play here today.

Newsweek: What's your role?

Kirk: Coffee-getter.

Newsweek: Is that your way of saying you were intimidated coming into this project?

Kirk: Nope.

Newsweek: Not a bit? This is a fairly legendary cast.

Kirk: Yeah, of course. The people in this room, you know, are certainly of note. But I think the biggest burden was the play, because it wasn't just a great script. It was a previously hugely celebrated separate entity. And my friend Stephen Spinella played the role on Broadway to great acclaim, so I certainly felt the burden of that.

Al Pacino: That was sort of all of us. We all came in with that feeling.

Emma Thompson: No, *I* didn't have that because I'd never seen it. That was sort of both a blessing and a curse, really.

Kirk: Emma was on the receiving end of our neuroses.

Thompson: A great privilege it was, too.

Newsweek: What kind of neuroses are you talking about?

Kirk: You know, deadening self-doubt and fear.

Meryl Streep: Oh, I had that. I had that, too. [*Laughter*]

Pacino: That comes and goes.

Kirk: I don't believe you. You pretended to have it one day, and I thought you were just doing it to calm me.

Streep: I was. [*Laughs*]

Newsweek: Mike, you've said that you wrote down your dream cast when you decided to do this movie.

Mike Nichols: This certainly was it. There was no one that any part was offered to that we didn't get. That was a nice start.

Thompson: It's nice not to be the thirty-fifth person on the list as well. That's quite rare.

Nichols: As an actress once said to me, "Thank you so much for my part. Usually five or six people have to die before I get cast." [*Laughter*] But in this case it was obviously a piece that everybody knew and loved. They're great, great parts. And I think actors also sometimes like to do things for too little money.

Streep: Oh? Do you think so? [*Laughter*]

Nichols: Because it feels like art.

Newsweek: Tony, a lot has changed since *Angels* first appeared. Here was a play about the eighties that came out in the nineties, and now we're ten years further along. One of the things that made the play of its moment was that it was about gay liberation, and now it's showing next to *Queer Eye on the Straight Guy*.

Tony Kushner: *For* the straight guy . . .

Newsweek: What did I say?

Kushner: *On* the straight guy . . . Well, that happens, too.

Newsweek: What does that do to the play? What's changed for you?

Kushner: Well, I mean, of course, the world has changed enormously since the play was written, and thank God. But I was scared about that in terms of the film. I thought, "Is it just going to be very old hat?" But the way Mike has made it, it doesn't insist that you go back into the period by shoving it at you. "This was back then, when things were like this." It simply uses the basic tool of drama, which is empathy and compassion, and says, "This kind of suffering was the consequence of this kind of oppression." After all, you can immediately sympathize with what Nora is going through in *A Doll's House*. You don't need to be in a prefeminist era. You get it because the play *makes* you get it.

Newsweek: And obviously CBS just learned—the hard way—that people still care passionately about the Reagan era. How do you feel about the flap over the miniseries?[1]

Kushner: I don't know, because we don't really know what happened. But it does sound to me like CBS put the kibosh on this because of pressure, and I think that's appalling. I was struck by a line in the *New York Times* editorial today that warned, "While the former president is suffering from Alzheimer's . . ." Of course, anybody who's a human being feels sorry for anyone who's suffering from Alzheimer's, and for any spouse who has to take care of them. But I don't think that a president of the United States can be safely exempt from public criticism, in art as well as in other forms, because of present-day debility. I wish his suffering were eased, and I don't have any desire to see *her* suffer. But they ran the country for eight years, and, in my opinion, did great damage.

Newsweek: Do you think CBS's decision will have a chilling effect on political art?

Kushner: I think it's going to boost the ratings for the thing through the roof when it turns up on Showtime.

Thompson: Yeah, I can't wait to see it.

Newsweek: In your film, I was startled at the scene in Brooklyn where Mary-Louise Parker is on the roof and you show the World Trade Center.

Nichols: Well, it's correct for the era.

Newsweek: But kind of gutsy. Don't forget, people were editing images of the Towers out of movies and TV shows after September 11.

Kirk: That didn't last for long, though.

Newsweek: But you didn't *have* to create that image.

Nichols: It seemed important to me that it was there then and it's not there now. And that's part of the way in which we're looking at this film. What was there then, what's not there now. What *is* there now that wasn't.

Kushner: One thing that sort of produced the play in the first place was a feeling of apocalypse, which is now very much with us.

Streep: I wanted to ask you, Mike: what made you think this could work? I thought the play was amazing and in its time and place it just sort of radiated heat. But it was a theatrical experience I thought could never, ever be achieved in any other medium. It's such an act of bravery and of recklessness—sort of a young man's challenge, you know. Not that you're not young in every sense, in your mind and in your outlook, but I'm in awe of that starting place that says, "Yes, I think I can do that."

Nichols: It's not entirely different from how you feel reading a play or film script for a part. There are instinctive responses. Something in you begins to stir when you read certain portions of things. And then there's the experience I think we all had that brought us so wonderfully together and became the tone of every day's work, which was: "There's too much to understand." You could never, *I* could never, understand all six-and-a-half hours, you know, in time to shoot it. I mean, I'm not that kind of scholar. And we're *still* arguing what the play is about. On the way to the premiere last night, my wife [Diane Sawyer] said, "You keep talking about what it's about, but only I know what it's about." I said, "OK, if you're so smart, what is it about?" She said, "Being Jewish."

Kushner: Seeing it last night, I realized it's completely a film. The language is not in any way naturalistic—it's very large; it's written for the stage. But it's so completely effortless how that trip from a stage play to the film was made.

Streep: It makes me think we're not ambitious enough on film.

Pacino: We're caught in that naturalistic language thing.

Thompson: We're *actors*, you know. The point is not to be just like everybody else. One is to give a performance, and that's what's so glorious about this opportunity.

Newsweek: Why did you have actors play multiple parts, as they did on the stage?

Kushner: The first time that Mike and I met, we had lunch to talk about this. And the very first thing he said was, "I want to do the doubling." It never occurred to me that anybody would do that. And I immediately thought, "OK, this is the person that should make this." It's celebrating the artificiality of the event, and it's scary for people in film to do that. You know it's Emma again, in another role. You know it's Meryl as another person.

Nichols: Something happened in America quite a while ago—far less in England—it's the idea that acting is *feeling*, which is such nonsense and so useless and leads us into a corner of unintelligible people muttering.

Newsweek: It's the ultimate perversion of Lee Strasberg and the Method.

Nichols: That's right. It *is* a perversion.

Newsweek: When I started to watch the show, the old rabbi came on and I thought, "Onstage this part was played by a woman." I couldn't figure out who this terrific old guy was. Only at the end when the credits came on did I realize it was Meryl.

Streep: That's good.

Kirk: All the extras that day, the same thing. They knew Meryl was in the movie, and as she took off her costume, they were all buzzing.

Newsweek: Have you played a Jewish character like that before?

Streep: Oh, Nora Ephron [in *Heartburn*]. She was very high-church Jewish. [*Laughter*]

Nichols: You know, when it comes to Meryl's curtain call, where it shows all the characters she played, I wanted to throw in the black woman singing the gospel song. [*Laughter*] And then say, just kidding.

Newsweek: Emma, was it intimidating to do all those characters in front of the queen of accents?

Streep: [*Sighs*]

Newsweek: You don't like to be thought of that way?

Streep: [*Even more wearily*] It's OK.

Newsweek: You hate it.

Streep: Yes. It's like saying, "I really like you because of your feet."

Nichols: That's a very good simile.

Streep: It's just, it's so—I mean nobody means to be insulting but . . . it *is*. I mean, if I only played people from New Jersey, it would be such a limited career. [*Laughter*] But it would be honest.

Newsweek: Laurence Olivier could never really do a good American accent.

Nichols: Or a Jewish accent, God help us.

Newsweek: That whole generation of English actors couldn't do American. But they didn't grow up with television.

Thompson: That's exactly it. My mom and dad both went to theater school, always expecting to do Shakespeare. They were required to do three accents at drama school.

RP—you know, Received Pronunciation—a country accent and then maybe Irish or Scottish. You know, that's all you needed. Now you practically have to know the f——ing US postal district.

Newsweek: Al, we've heard that when Robert Altman was planning to make a movie of *Angels* years ago, your name was mentioned to play Roy Cohn even then.

Pacino: Yeah, Altman contacted me.

Newsweek: Did you see Ron Leibman play Cohn on Broadway?

Pacino: I saw Ron and I saw F. Murray Abraham. I remember the effect they had on me, but fortunately I saw it a long enough time ago. There's something about seeing someone do something that you're going to play that gives it—it's almost a model. I did *American Buffalo* that way. I did *Pavlo Hummel* that way. It's almost like, "Somebody did it, so therefore it can be done." It sanctions it for you. And even though you don't copy the model of it, it gives you a kind of confidence that at least it can be done and done really well, so you've got something to go for.

Newsweek: Meryl, you've worked with so many great actors in your career. What was it like to work with Al as compared to Dustin Hoffman or Bob De Niro?

Streep: Same. The same. They're all alike. [*Laughter*] It was great. We've known each other for thirty years and I'd never worked with him.

Newsweek: Why? Were you avoiding each other?

Pacino: She doesn't work that much.

Streep: His leading ladies are much younger. I'm kidding.

Newsweek: Justin, what was it like *not* to work with Al Pacino? You have no scenes together.

Kirk: It's like a horrible joke. You get to do a movie with Al Pacino and never work with him.

Newsweek: Al, do you think you made Roy sympathetic?

Pacino: I don't think you set out to do that. I think it's innate in the characterization that Tony has made. It's impossible to do that character without getting to the humanity of it. He's already done that work, and so it's up to you to sort of find it in yourself and follow his lead.

Thompson: You know, what he made me think of when I first read the play was Satan in Milton's *Paradise Lost*. That's who he *is*. And you're so fascinated by Satan, he's the best character.

Pacino: I played him once [in *The Devil's Advocate*].

Nichols: I thought it worked. I quite liked it.

Pacino: As a matter of fact, I did read Milton when I was playing that part. It was very helpful.

Thompson: It's amazing, isn't it? I haven't read it for a long, long time, but my God, that's sort of who he is.

Kushner: But the great trap is that when you fall in love with the devil you're recapitulating the fall of the human race. That's why we fall.

Thompson: And that's the point. It's so fascinating. You desperately want to be with him.

Nichols: There is something to be said for the idea that one of the actor's main jobs is to make the best possible case for the character. Al does that playing a villainous person.

Streep: I always loved that idea—defending a character from the judgments that are made right off the bat. We certainly did with Hannah, the Mormon mother who's lost in New York. You make a decision about this character that maybe she's someone who's ignorable. In an airport you see millions of these ladies in mauve coats with white hair and features that sort of blend into their clothing. They're like walking errata. They're lost, you can't find them, and you wouldn't be interested in them. But Tony's interested in Hannah and the possibility of her, the size of her journey. And *this* one [*points to Pacino*]. I mean, you took this character who is so reprehensible, and . . . even I was touched.

Newsweek: Really?

Streep: No. [*Laughter*]

Nichols: The first time I ever saw Meryl was in a play called *Taken in Marriage*. It was about the reunion of some women in a small theater, which is where we were.

And there were these people onstage, some women acting quite well and speaking a not-very-interesting text. And out came this person who clearly, it seemed, had been allowed to invent her own dialogue. And she said whatever came into her head while the other people were all stuck with the text. That's the difference. It was as if she was improvising. The accents are great, but as you say, they're beautiful feet.

Newsweek: Emma, how do you play an angel? There's not a lot of precedent.

Thompson: No, you just have to let your imagination run riot, don't you?

Pacino: She's the sexiest angel I ever saw.

Thompson: It's my Farrah Fawcett angel.

Newsweek: Did you have any control over that hairstyle?

Thompson: Yeah. I looked at pictures of angels, and then I remembered that I had received a Christmas card from Elton John. With an angel on it.

Nichols: What an inspiration.

Thompson: I thought a Christmas card of an angel from, you know, the queen of England, basically. It was one of those wonderful little Renaissance angels with wispy hair. And Mike, you wanted a proper angel.

Newsweek: This *is* a very sexual angel. You get to seduce both Justin and Meryl.

Thompson: The sex! It was just such a wonderful thing to play. It's a kind of sexuality that's like fire. Because I think that part of the play is fantastically erotic.

Newsweek: This is the first time you've acted with Meryl and you get to have a cosmic orgasm together. In midair.

Thompson: Our breastbones were literally tied together; there were like six inches between us. And our glasses knocked as we put them on to look at the monitor. We were shrieking with hysteria.

Newsweek: We've been talking about this as a film, when in fact it's a television show.

Thompson: It's not, precisely.

Nichols: Well, it's a film on television. What is a television show? It's something with a host.

Newsweek: There are some shots that you would rarely see on TV, like that long, wild tracking shot that goes from inside an elegant bar where Roy Cohn is putting the make on a guy, through the window across the street and then into the Ramble in Central Park.

Kushner: What I love about that shot is it goes zooming and then it stops for traffic.

Nichols: I was just obsessed with the fact that this was not only simultaneous but that they were within hailing distance of each other. The guy was f——ing somebody in the a—— not that far from the Plaza, and that seemed to me a crucial part of it. I think it's worth it just to remember that about New York, that twenty yards from the fanciest hotel is a kind of jungle.

Newsweek: Mike, do you feel that these days you can actually do bolder things on television than you can in film?

Nichols: I do, yes. It has to do with HBO, it's as simple as that. We love HBO and we love the freedom that there is on HBO, and the power. And what is that power? It's economic. You know, we're run by market forces—the fact that an outfit can make a billion dollars a year just sitting there collecting its subscriptions. It's an economic basis that affords us this freedom.

Newsweek: The budget was $60 million?

Nichols: Yes. But, that's like three movies—and with visual effects! So it's $20 million per movie—which *is* a lot for television. [*Laughter*] But look at the budget of any Disneyesque Cinderella movie where little sparkly things appear on the screen and there are fairies and so forth.

Thompson: You see a lot of these movies?

Nichols: Well, I have a granddaughter.

Kushner: Sparkly things and fairies. It's sort of a good description of our movie.

Note

1. The miniseries referred to is *The Reagans* (Robert Allan Ackerman, 2003).—REK

Elaine May in Conversation with Mike Nichols

Mike Nichols / 2006

From *Film Comment*, July/August 2006, online exclusive: http://www.filmcomment.com/article/ elaine-may-in-conversation-with-mike-nichols. Reprinted with permission from the Film Society of Lincoln Center and Film Comment Magazine. © Film Comment 2006.

Following a sold-out screening of her unfairly maligned 1987 comedy *Ishtar*, writer-director Elaine May took to the stage of New York's Walter Reade Theater for an hour-long interview with her former collaborator and old friend Mike Nichols.

Mike Nichols: Clearly we were all sitting here thinking the same thing. How were you so prescient? Where did your Orwellian vision come from? Because you invented the perfect metaphor for the behavior of the Bush administration in Iraq.

Elaine May: Well, oddly enough when I made this movie, Ronald Reagan was president and there was Iran-Contra, we were supporting Iran and Iraq. We put in Saddam. We had taken out the shah. Khomeini was there. I remember looking at Ronald Reagan and thinking—I'm qualifying this, this was just an idea, I didn't really believe it—I thought, he's from Hollywood, he's a really nice man. It's possible the only movies he's ever seen about the Middle East are the *Road* movies with Hope and Crosby, and I thought I would make that movie.

Nichols: Well, it's true. This is a *Road* movie about the Middle East. [*To the audience*] How many people have never seen it before? Everybody?

May: If all of the people who hate *Ishtar* had seen it, I would be a rich woman today.

Nichols: That leads me to the subtext of all this. We have to talk about studios and how we work with studios and what your experiences have been with studios. What is your feeling about a) the machine that has to be gotten together for a movie and b) the relationship to the studio?

May: Every movie I made except for *The Heartbreak Kid*, the studio changed regimes in the middle of the movie.

Nichols: How funny, that's happening to me. Not one but two studios. I'm working on two movies and two studios: the regimes are changing as we speak. One is happening actually over this weekend.

May: It's not a great thing because whoever is coming in doesn't like you a) because you have been chosen by someone else and they don't really know whether they want to take responsibility for it. So it's not a good thing to have happened. But I've never made a movie, except for *Heartbreak Kid*, in which it didn't happen. With this movie, the guy who took over Columbia was David Puttnam. Actually I prepared for tonight, because I knew about it three weeks ago—first the breast implants and then I actually looked up this stuff. When David Puttnam came in, he was a guy who, when Warren Beatty did *Reds*, I think he did *Chariots of Fire*, and they were up against each other in the Academy Awards. And he wrote something that was published in the paper that said Warren should be spanked because he was profligate. But underneath the article it didn't say in italics like it does after other letters, that he was a competitor for the Academy Awards, that he had an agenda. They just printed that article. And everybody adored him. In fact even today, one of my dearest friends said to me: "He was really rotten to you, but he's a great guy." So people do seem to like him. You like him.

Nichols: Well, let me say that I think that both in our work and in our life, function determines character. When you run a studio, you change. I think after David Puttnam ran the studio he turned out to be a very nice guy. But he talked a lot when he ran the studio. And I think *Ishtar* is maybe the prime example that I know of in Hollywood of studio suicide. In that it had a great preview.

May: It had three great previews.

Nichols: And then this really strange thing started to happen, which was that stories began to appear with studio sources about what a problem it was.

May: And many of the details were not true. This is a really embarrassing thing to say, but it's just us, so I know it won't go any farther, but I left almost immediately for Bali. The film was political and it was a satire but it was my secret. When these articles started coming out, I thought—only for five minutes—it's the CIA. I didn't dream that it would be the studio. For one moment it was sort of glorious to think that I was going to be taken down by the CIA, and then it turned out to be David Puttnam. I think this man was unique in that way, in that he was going to redo Hollywood and make it a better place. He was going to work from the inside.

Nichols: It doesn't want to be a better place. It's like Las Vegas. From the very beginning there's been the problem between the executives and the people making the movies. And it's a problem because the process of making movies is not something that can be apprehended from without. A guy that works in the studios, a very nice, often very intelligent executive, thinks that expressing an opinion in a meeting is a creative act because that's all he gets to do. And that's as high in the creative scale as he can ever hope to get. And the problem with it is that the opinions expressed often bear no relation to the work that's being done. Would you say you agree so far?

May: Except . . . yes, I do agree.

Nichols: I've convinced her. Here's where it gets to be a problem. They say: "But it's our money." But here's the funny part. It's not, of course. It's GE's money, or it's Sony's money. Who is "us"?

May: It's funny that you say that because Charles Grodin, the CIA agent in this movie, who is a very funny man and a great actor, defended it when it came out. It was attacked because they kept saying it's so much money, it's so much money. And it was actually not.

Nichols: Well, if nowadays you say what it cost, I'd love to make a movie for this. It was like $33 million, right?

May: Thirty. And he said one day, as I recall, to the people who were saying it was so much, he said, what do you care? It's not like you're going to get the money. It's not like if the movie were $20 million you'd get ten of it. You'll never see it. What do you care how much money it is? They're not going to give it to schoolteachers.

Nichols: God forgive me, it's also interesting to look at their salaries. Their salaries stay the same no matter how the movies do.

May: That's right, isn't it? I've never thought of that.

Nichols: Sometimes people get fired because their movies have done badly. But those people have gotten $12 million a year for the years they have chosen movies unwisely. It's not a tragedy when one of them goes to another studio. Because they keep changing off and going to different studios.

May: This is really correct. a) You realize later in life that you've chosen the wrong job, and b) you think it's about making money, but I believe it's really about keeping your job. Whether the movie makes money or not is really way down on the list.

Nichols: I agree. I also think that there's a whole probably larger subject: which are the movies that live on and why? It's very mysterious, why *The Lady Eve* or *The Palm Beach Story* is completely alive now and why *Ishtar* is hilarious and alive and in some cases it seemed almost improvised tonight. Who knows what movies will live and what movies will die as time passes?

May: Well, yours will live.

Nichols: Well, you're very kind.

May: Yes, I am.

Nichols: But I don't think we know. I don't think anybody knows. And the whole thing of a movie catching the wind and sailing off. And nobody understands the winds of fashion that strike movies. Although I begin to have a theory. It's the Hollywood Foreign Press. Here's my theory: the people in the Golden Globes are not exactly reporters—they send something in once every two weeks to the *Bulgarian Weekly*. And they don't have all that much to do. And they are masters of fashion.

May: So far this sounds right.

Nichols: And in their deep understanding of what the coming fashion is, they will choose a movie, let's say for instance *Brokeback Mountain*, which is a wonderful movie, but nevertheless, it's a nice movie to vote for because it makes you feel so very, very human and understanding of all different kinds of people. And yet you could have a fugitive thought seeing that movie—Boys, you could move to California. They have sheep, they have cows. You would be fine in California. There are many like you, they would understand you. You could have friends. So I think we are all fashion-ridden. And because the Golden Globes are first and because they really have nothing to do but call the fashion, they tend not to confuse things, but crystallize them.

May: What about the Weinsteins? Do you think that they influence the Golden Globes?

Nichols: Yes.

May: Then what will the Golden Globes do now?

Nichols: Do you think that Weinsteins will stop influencing the Golden Globes?

May: [*May fiddles with a chain attached to her clothing*] Nothing matters to me except the fact that I was trying to keep this chain in place all day long and now it's a goner. And now I'm just going to whip it off.

Nichols: Will anything be revealed?

May: Just those implants.

Nichols: Now tell us a little about the people who you made your movies with. People like our friend Anthea Sylbert, who was a great costume designer and an inspiring and remarkable person—how important is a person like that?

May: There's about five of them. And when you meet them, they're sort of like friends, you want to keep them. On *Heartbreak Kid*, I had no idea what these people would wear. Anthea said: "White cotton underwear is what the girl would wear, that's what those blondes wear." She was just perfect. She was just a true artist. And in *A New Leaf*, she said: "Have you thought about what's in your purse?" Man, I hadn't thought about my part. I had no idea. And every once in a while you get a fantastic art director, and Sylbert was wonderful. I do miss that. Those wonderful people who work with you on a movie, and who tell the story with you. That's the best part of making movies, I think. It's the only thing where you can work in a group where five or six people all tell the same story in their own specific voice. The music person has a voice. The makeup person makes you up to tell the story. . . . And they all tell the same story. And I miss that because you can't really do it on the stage.

Nichols: I never thought of it that way. But there's a moment in which many people are putting in something that no one else could contribute, and if you're the leader, if you're lucky you have found an idea that you can communicate to them, because people love an idea. It should be a very simple idea. But whatever the idea, it should be something that everybody can say: "Yes, oh, I see what you mean. I get it." And that's the joy of it, of course: that you can inflame some remarkable people. I have a story about Anthea that I guess you know.
May: I may not.

Nichols: I stopped making a movie once on the fifth day.[1]
May: This is a great story, I do know it.

Nichols: What happened was that we got five days into it, and I hadn't really prepared, I hadn't really been paying enough attention, and the script needed work. I said, "Could I see all the dailies of everything we've done so far?" And I was with the editor and the producer, and we looked at the dailies. And I said, "This is shit, this is no good." Everybody said, "No, don't be silly," and the editor said, "I'll put it together," and the composer said, "You have to do music." And I said, "Well, let me think about it," and I went into my office. And Anthea came in and she said, "You're right. It is shit." And I said, "I thought so. What should I do?" She said, "Stop." I said, "Stop? In the middle of making a movie? How can I do that? It's already cost $3 million." And she said, "Well, is it better to spend $6 million? If it's no good, it's no good." And I went to the head of the studio, who luckily was my best friend [*May laughs*], and an exception to what we were saying earlier, and he said, "Well, it's terrible, but I mean, if you really think it's no good, we'll stop." And we actually did stop and years later that script had been worked on and was made into a very successful movie. And it should be possible to do strange things, because movies, like any art form, are strange. They're strange all on their own. And we should be able to do odd things to fit in with them. But once time is gone, and time is now going, because everything is so expensive. . . . People don't have time to figure out, "Well, maybe this scene has to be redone, maybe this is a bad place for us to go, maybe, God forbid, we've got the wrong actor here." These things . . . nothing can be reconsidered.

May: It seems to me that the thing that costs the most money in a movie, the thing that you can't *not* spend money on, is publicizing it. Because even if you make a movie for $10 million, it costs $50 million to get somebody to come see it. And I always thought that what all artists who are pissed about this—and I know very little about business, so this is probably a really bad idea—but what I thought they should do is get together and buy a theater, one theater in key towns. And if they have a movie that they really think is good, but that nobody's going to spend $60 million to publicize, they could show it. You'd always have people coming. Movies don't cost that much anymore. There are digital movies. Because now when you make a movie, they come to you from the publicity department. And they say, "We just don't know how to publicize this. We don't know what to say about it." And sometimes the movie gets turned down because of it. But I always thought that that would be the best thing to do, to suddenly just have one theater. They aren't that expensive to run.

Nichols: Well, there are wonderful things happening. People like Steven Soderbergh, who made a movie, I think, for fifteen thousand dollars in Ohio with real people. He released it simultaneously in theaters, on DVD, pay-per-view, and some fourth way that's been invented that I haven't heard about yet [*he and May laugh*]. You have to break it up. He also operates his own movies. I mean, I give up, you know. I can't do that. I can't do a movie for fifteen thousand dollars and also operate, so—

May: Oh, you could if you wanted to, but you—

Nichols: I'd need thirty, thirty-five [*laughs*]. But the fact that a) we have to remember how young they are, and b) there are remarkable people now—

May: But he's not that young, Soderbergh. He's made many movies, and he was young, but he's not anymore [*laughs*].

Nichols: Well, he's young enough.

May: Younger than we are, but he's really not that young.

Nichols: Well, he's forty, if he's a day.

May: Well, that's not—forgive me—young [*laughs*]. Yes, it's a terrific thing that he does, but he's done it after he's had a lot of very successful movies. So it's almost whimsical to do this. When people are starting out, and they have some movie, and they really want it to be seen, they aren't that clever. They can't say, "I can, you know, you can look at a DVD, I can push it into your mind and shove it up your ass," or whatever, however you look at movies now, you really want it to be in a theater. I really don't know why that hasn't happened. You think I'm wrong?

Nichols: No, I don't think you're wrong. There's a dozen ways to see a movie now, including on your computer or in the back seat of your car.
May: But it's not as good as a theater.

Nichols: It's not as good as a theater, but it's another way. And there's something very nice about everything disintegrating, and this is certainly a time when you might say that. More things are possible. You know, *we're* thinking about doing a movie for, if not fifteen thousand dollars, for half a million dollars.
May: Yes, so close to it—

Nichols: And it's the one I look forward to most. Because I already know a lot of things I want to do. For instance, improvising and shooting twenty pages in one day, or half the movie in one day. And we also know that when you have a small group of people that you really trust and you understand and they understand you, and you know what you're doing together, you can do remarkable things. And you don't need the 125 people who come with the big trucks. We don't necessarily need the big machine every time.
May: You also are somebody who, whatever movie you make, is going to find a way for it to be seen and shown. Because you're very famous and very good. But people who are beginning and people who don't have the clout that you have, they have no place to show their movie. And probably only one out of thirty of them is that good, but one out of thirty is not bad. There's stuff you do, all of us do, that we really feel hopeless about. I once went on a cruise, and I said I would lecture one day. And everyone in the audience wanted to write a screenplay—

Nichols: They all sent them to me, I know [*laughs*].
May: And I said, "Write a three-page summary of this and give it to me, and I'll read it." And people said, "Are you crazy, are you insane, are you nuts?!" And not one came in, because no one wanted to take the time to type up three pages of their screenplay. So not a lot of people will do this, but there are some people who have a real dream and a real goal, and it's so overwhelming to think, after you finish it, what do you do, and then where do you go? It's such a big world now. It's so hard to do anything. It's so hard to get anyone on the phone. It's so hard to return a piece of furniture [*laughter*]. It's almost impossible.

Nichols: Yes, it is.
May: So there has to be some way where you can have some kind of control, where everything is not such a terrible, terrible problem. And look how quickly we all get used to eating shit. Really, about seven years ago, if somebody had answered the phone saying, "We really value your call. Please hold on for the next hour and twenty-five

minutes," we'd have hung up. We get used to it very fast. We get used to skim milk very fast. Whole milk tastes like cream now. We adapt very quickly to being treated very badly [*laughter*].

Nichols: I do think that you put your finger on what is central about making movies, what makes it something that you—that I—never want to stop. Just as you never want to stop seeing them. There is something that happens among people and what it finally is, is a sort of melding of unconsciouses. When you do your best, you're depending to a large extent on your unconscious, when you've done this for some length of time, because you're waiting for the thing you can't think of. You're waiting for the surprise of shooting that day. And when a large group of people is waiting for today's surprise, and they're all in the same place, and you have the people that you do it with every time, and you love them and they love you, something begins to happen. Over the weekend I went to see Oprah do a thing she does in a theater, telling people how to be their best, live their best life. And she charges a lot for it, and the money goes to the charity of the town in which she's done it. And she has this *gift*, she can *hear* twenty-five hundred people sitting in the dark. She can connect with what they're thinking.
May: Yes, she's amazing.

Nichols: And in hearing them, remarkable things happen. She says remarkable things, and funny things, and so forth. But, in a weird way, we need the unconsciouses and the souls of the people that are making the movie to make some kind of connection with the unconsciouses of what Gloria Swanson called "those wonderful people out there in the dark"—we are those wonderful people out there in the dark—and that connection still lives, even as everything says to us, "Your call is important to us." Which is a lie. I mean, everything is a lie.
May: Everything is.

Nichols: But the unspoken things are not all lies yet.
May: But don't you feel—and you, too [*to the audience*]—don't we all feel that we actually now can choose what to believe? I mean, if I see a really great commercial, I know this car isn't going to change my life, or whatever it is, and still—I know it's a lie—but I really think about buying it. And when this girl—Jessica Lynch, was it? Is that the young girl who was in the Iraq war? Was that her name?

Nichols: Yes.
May: There was a story about her that she was a hero, and they abused her in the hospital. . . . And this girl finally said, "It's not true. That's not what happened."

Nichols: Well, she told the truth at every point.

May: She told the truth at every point. And she went on Diane's show, and they made a television movie out of it, and it totally ignored what she said, and they made it about what was in the papers. I said, "Well, this is just bullshit, isn't it?" And somebody said to me, "Well, it's such a better story." [*Laughter*] And that was very scary.

Nichols: Well, it's so weird what you said. a) Yes, and b) I have that with cars, but I have it another way. [*May laughs.*] I had a Mercedes for a long time, and then I had a Mercedes, and it was always in the shop, and they no longer understood how to fix it. [*Laughter*] Literally, you know, it was so complicated they didn't know what to do, so they would put it out in the back where the cars gathered dirt. And then after about two or three weeks, they would say, "Come and get it," and it would be just as busted. And then I switched to a BMW, because it was rented, everything is rented. The same thing happened with the BMW. So then I got a nice Lexus and everything is fine. But when I see the gorgeous commercials for the beautiful new Mercedes, the beautiful new BMWs, I sort of think it's like a hooker with clap. [*Laughter*] You know?

May: Yes. [*Laughing*]

Nichols: I know too much. They can't get me with the pictures anymore, because I know they don't work and there's nobody to fix them.

May: Yes. But, still, this hooker-with-clap image, this beautiful hooker-with-clap image . . . [*Laughing*]

Nichols: Yes, thank you, thank you. I'm a poet, basically. [*Laughing*]

May: I'll always remember it now. [*Laughing*]

Nichols: Should we quickly take a few questions from the audience?

Audience Member: When you made *The Heartbreak Kid* and *The Graduate* and *Carnal Knowledge*, we had a society that was unfolding, and you helped to disinhibit it and put it on the right track. And somehow it hasn't maintained itself. So there must have been a joy in discovering themes that you were going to be working on. What has happened now? Where do your themes come from? Is there a joy? Is there content you're preoccupied with to tell?

May: I only made one of the pictures you named, but this is a very good question. I want to answer it with this odd thing. When psychoanalysis began, Freud used to take very repressed people and try to break them down, break their structure down so that it would all come out. It has now changed so that what psychoanalysts try to do is take very broken-apart people and repress them and put them together, really, and structure them, because people just come in and they don't know what they're talking about. [*Laughter*] And it is a little like that with movies. You think, How can I shock? What can I say? What truth can I tell that's as good as this lie they believe? Because the thing about what I choose to believe, the fact that we feel—maybe it's this administration or the world or television—but the fact that we kind of feel that we can choose the truth. A friend of mine called today and said, "I read a story that when you made *Ishtar*, you got to the desert, and you said, 'What are those hills?' and they said, 'Dunes,' and you said, 'Flatten them.'" And I said to him, "Well, do you believe that?" And there was a long pause, and he said, "Well, no, but it's *such* a great story!" And it's like that. It makes it hard to do a movie, because you think, What can I possibly choose, when people can so irresponsibly say anything, people will do anything, nobody is ashamed of anything—you're just lucky to get it on television, whatever this repression is? It is hard to find a theme. It's really hard to find something and to say it in a way that will get people's attention. So I have no idea, do you, Mike?

Nichols: I'm afraid I'm still so in love with the, for want of a better word, process, and the thing I love most about movies and that I love most about other people's work is the *small* things. You think about your favorite thing in a movie or in a play or in a performance . . . it's always something very small, it's so small that you can barely tell other people about it, but it just makes you gasp, because it's like a little pebble of something true. And harvesting them—because, after all, the acting is done by other people—is still something that I think is so thrilling. I think the thing is just to keep doing it because with luck you can catch that wind, it can still be done.

May: Yes, I think the question really is, those tiny moments—the small things you remember—where do you choose to put them in? What do you choose to make this process about? Because you can make this process, I think, about almost anything. From any small thing you can make a million truths.

Nichols: No question, and for me—because I teach once a week I had to sort of try to think of a couple of ideas, and one of them is that in working on something, and also in the thing itself, if it's a movie, the question always is, "What is this *really* like?" Not what is the convention, not what do people always do in this case, not what happens in a ribald comedy or a tragedy-comedy or a film of lysergic unhappiness, you know, or whatever, "What is this *really* like?" And in the search for what it's really like—something that you [*points to May*] do instinctively, every time you write—it answers the question "What is this really like?" Every line reminds you of a living person and the funny things we do and the silly things we do and, sometimes, the nice things we do. That's the answer to the question "What is this really like?" It can be expanded a little bit to "Where are we really at now? What is this like? What in the hell is happening?"

May: That's a very good question.

Audience Member: The little things, are they part of a big picture? Or are you holding onto the little things for their preciousness?

May: I don't know . . . There's a little thing that I believe is the most horrifying thing that I've ever heard, and it's like what you [*points to Mike Nichols*] said: "What is it really like?" How different life is from the movies. . . . Is this a book that you [Nichols] gave me? This woman who worked in a Nazi concentration camp and was up for trial, and they said, "How could you do this? Knowing that these people were being sent to the gas chambers, how could you participate in this, with these beds?" And she said, "You don't understand, we had such a limited amount of beds. They were filled so quickly. We had to keep them moving." And she said it with absolute sincerity. She had narrowed her vision down. She was not evil. I mean, she was evil, but she wasn't evil in the way we really think of evil. She just had a small German accent. [*Laughter*] She had just narrowed her vision down to this, to filling the beds. And somebody, I think it was Warren, was telling me that when you have a lack of imagination and you do harm—I think this is from T. S. Eliot—that you don't do harm to be mean, you do it to get the job done, and you are totally unaware and unaffected by the harm you do. And I always thought, How would you build a whole movie around that moment, a moment that would repel everyone in the audience. But when you speak about having moments that are really like life—"What is it *really* like when you lose someone? What is it *really* like when you're happy?" There are very few moments like that in movies. They're all pretend. When you see a real moment in a movie, it's almost shocking, isn't it?

Nichols: It is shocking, but, as we know, it still happens. And we all revere it, and we see movie after movie, hoping for it, and sometimes finding it. It still happens in movies from here, movies from there. It still happens in plays. You just have to wait a long time. [*May laughs*] There's almost nobody you can trust. I mean, people are forever sending me to plays, and I say, "Son of a bitch, they've done it again! Somebody I thought I could trust sent me to this piece of *shit*!" [*Laughter*] I get really angry. Forget the papers, I'm not talking about reviews. It's harder and harder to find somebody who sees theater the way you do. We're flying apart, like the universe, in some way. But now and then, by hook or by crook, you see something on the stage that's also alive and remarkable. And the whole question—here we are in the place we are in, that we all know, that your picture [*Ishtar*] predicted—surely we have to find hope, and we have to act on our hope. We have to *wake up*. And start to do stuff, and be citizens, and speak up.

May: Well, let me ask you something. I speak for the whole audience. Now, stop me if I'm wrong. What do we do?

Nichols: [*Shrugs shoulders*] You're asking me? [*May laughs*] I told you about the interview with Cher that I heard?

May: No.

Nichols: It was so wonderful. The interviewer said, "Hey, what do you think about this whole Middle East thing that's happening?" And she said, "Listen, I'm Cher." [*Laughter*] "Please," she said, "Ask me about showbiz." You know, I love her. She always tells the truth, and I'm Cher, too.

May: But Cher has never said we have to have hope, as you just did. [*Laughing*]

Nichols: Well, we have to look for hope, of course we have to look for hope.

May: You're not really Cher. [*Laughter*]

Nichols: Well, I mean, a very simple thing that we all know about: the congressional elections are coming up. Let's get off our ass, let's get something done, let's make everybody get off their ass, let's do something. And please not just by e-mail. I don't want to get any more e-mails from groups. I want individuals to talk to each other and say, "Who are you voting for? And is this an OK Democrat? And who do we work on and what do we do?" That's the next thing we have to do. Does anybody have a better idea? Please tell us now.

Audience member: Hi, I'm just responding to some of the comments that you made, Mike, about theater that seems to be flying away from you and about the fact that we choose the facts or truths that we believe. To me it seems to correlate to a dumbing down of our society. It seems to be more of an interest in just sheer comedy, less in drama, less in something that's important; people don't care, they don't have the time or the intelligence to care. I am wondering a) if you agree, and b) if that's the case, how is it to be a creative person working in a world where the audience doesn't really care to be elevated anymore? They want to be sort of dumbed down.

May: Well you have to remember most movies are made for sixteen-year-old boys. Maybe that's changing, but sixteen-year-old boys have truly had a poor education. Really the point is that people want to make too much money. If you want to make a movie that's going to make a $100 million, you need all those sixteen-year-old boys and their dates. You have to start saying, "How do you think smaller?"

Nichols: Well, people are thinking smaller. That's what's great about this year. What could be smaller than *Capote*? I'm talking about money spent. It's a modest movie that's reaching a lot of people. *The Squid and the Whale, Brokeback Mountain*. These are small movies that to begin with are aiming to reach a small audience. I mean Weinsteins are Weinsteins, as we all know, but they also are the ones that started pushing smaller movies for awards, so that the small movies would make a medium amount of money. Everything is still possible. The fact that everyone does seem hypnotized in some way is unnerving and I have a boring theory that has to do with everyone on their iPods and their BlackBerrys and their Trios and their back-seat-of-the-car TV screens, and we are behaving like a person who is avoiding the truth, is avoiding something. What's the word?

May: Hypnosis.

Nichols: We're behaving like hypnotized people, but we're somnambulant. I hope we can wake each other up. But please, one at a time. There's so many things, "Your call is important to us"—how do you know who's calling? It's the goddamn generalities that make for those tapes on phones and annoying e-mails from a group. The individual—there's not enough money in the individual. And we have to—person to person—fight for it a little bit.

May: Let me ask you something. To simply actually stop. I'm just taking this "Your call is important to us" thing as an example because, having visited a large corporation, some executive is getting a hundred million a year and saving money by *not* giving some woman a job for thirty thousand a year. And he says we don't want to take the shareholders' money. And you say, well, you pay it, deduct it. But there's no way to enforce that. We all know that that's true, we all know that that's bad, and we all know that there's something about the tiny things in life happening to you that devalues you, that lessens you, that makes you numb. You have to become more and more numb not to get offended. And pretty soon you get pretty thick. And it seems to me—because I'm really a much more negative person than you are, you're the lightness, I'm the dark—

Nichols: Bragging.

May: But it seems to me, at some point what you really want to say is I won't deal with a company that doesn't have a real operator. For one day, I'll make them lose that much money. For one day, I won't go to a bookstore where the guy says, "Huh, I don't know." For one day I won't say, it's so hard. I won't run home to a rerun of *Cheers*, I can't bother with it. For one day, you'll take the trouble to make trouble for someone else, because it's the only thing that keeps you from getting thick, from sort of retreating. I think that's what dumbing-down kind of is. It's too much trouble. And there is such a thing as too much trouble.

Nichols: It's hard to find the line, because if you're a snob like me, and somebody says, "What is this in *regards* to?" I'll say it's in regards to Broadway. If you want to know what this is in *regard* to, tell your boss I want to borrow a lot of money. Where do you start, where do you stop, when are *you* the pain in the ass?

May: That's a very good way to start. You've got to start tiny, as Giuliani said, "Don't go after the big guys, get the pushers off the street." I know he did a lot of bad things, but I remember when you couldn't walk around New York after five o'clock, and now you can. So with all of that, you really do start with tiny crimes. I think they're like crimes, they're like little insults that you get all the time.

Audience member: Earlier in the day, I had the good fortune of seeing *Mikey and Nicky* for the first time. It's every bit as breathtaking and astounding as I'd heard it was. And it occurred to me talking with my friends and wife afterwards, it's a piece that is so at home in the period of the seventies, where independent filmmaking seemed to come out of a studio system. The period of Altman and Scorsese and your film, Mr. Nichols, *Carnal Knowledge*. Having said that, what happened? The stories about its mishaps are almost as legendary as *Ishtar*. As recently as the Terrence Rafferty piece in the *New York Times* this weekend. About exposing as much film as was exposed for *Gone with the Wind*, and hiding the negative from the studio. I'd like to know how much of that is hyperbole and why it got such short shrift in terms of release.

May: Really, this is true. The studio changed heads. The guy who was in charge, Frank Yablans, left, and a new guy, Barry Diller, came in the middle, and he thought it was a comedy. But we screened it and it wasn't. And they stopped it. They pulled it. We were two-thirds done. I don't even know how we finished. I once told John Cassavetes he'd have to actually shoot his own death scene, because he was so wonderful with the camera. We had no one. It was really a very difficult thing to do because it wasn't that the studio heads involved really didn't like each other. They were really not happy with this movie because it was not a comedy. Actually the first time it was previewed I said to the guy in charge—he was the vice president of something at Paramount—"Please don't put my name on it because people will think it's a comedy and they'll hate it in the end." And he tried not to, but they did. And they laughed all the way through, laughed. And in the end when the guy got shot, there was the most stunned silence. And then boos, loud boos. Somebody said, "Are they cheering?" "No," I said, "They're booing." I should have just said this is a sad, dark movie that no one will enjoy, and do you want to do it. But no, we had names and it seemed to have a few jokes, and there was a lot of politics involved. And it could just be me because I've had trouble with every movie I've done. I had trouble with *A New Leaf*. They took a murder out of it. I wanted to do the first comedy in which somebody got away with murder. I had trouble with *Mikey and Nicky*. I didn't have trouble with *The Heartbreak Kid* because I was hired for it. But with every movie that I have done, I may just be a pain in the ass.

Nichols: I've thought about this a lot. If you recall the very first person who was a line producer for you, a friend of both of ours, there was the famous story of when you did process for the first time, bluescreen, I believe it was. And this person who you hired—he was a professional—got you a blue car. Bluescreen means everything that is blue disappears and what remains is what is not blue. So they shot all these scenes in a blue car and the people were all sitting in the air.

May: It wasn't even that. We just couldn't shoot, which cost an enormous amount of money. But the point is the studio wasn't in back of it. It just had one screw-up after another. You know when I started. the first movie I directed, I really didn't want to direct [*A New Leaf*]. But they wouldn't give me director approval. And the guy who represented me, Hilly Elkins, said they won't give you director approval but they will allow you to direct it. And I said, I know nothing. I actually remember calling you and I said, "Well, how should I say action? Firmly or . . .?" I began sort of on one foot and just continued that way.

Nichols: I think the real secret of movies is putting a crew together. And it takes about twenty-five years to get it right. That's not an exaggeration. And you have to do it steadily because you can't ask anyone. Everybody will say about everyone you ask, "He's a very good man." Nobody will ever tell; you have to find out. And when you have that many people that you can depend on, everything changes. And some of them are here tonight. And we're family, and we can depend on each other, but it took forever.

May: Yeah, it's like friendship. Who's left after the others burn out? Actually you started with Anthea and gave her to me. And she lasted . . .

Nichols: It takes a whole bunch of Antheas. They save you even when you screw up. Let's take one more question.

Audience member: *A New Leaf* was a great movie and your performance was Chaplinesque. I have this fantasy of winning the Mega Millions, and that I would give you the money to add the scenes that you wanted—you wanted to make it longer, didn't you?

May: I had a murder in it.

Nichols: But you shot it, it exists?

May: I shot the murder. It exists. It was a wonderful scene.

Audience member: Well, if I win the Mega Millions, it's yours. But you could talk a little more about making *A New Leaf*? It's a very underappreciated movie.

May: I started out with a short story in an Alfred Hitchcock omnibus. I liked it because I realized the guy, the hero, was going to kill this woman. And he actually kills somebody else. And I thought he's going to kill her and he's not going to realize that he likes her. Reading the short story I thought, what an interesting thing to do in a movie. So I wrote it. I said I have to have director approval, and they said you can direct this. I couldn't get it on without Walter Matthau, who started out as a regular person. And then they wanted to have Carol Channing play the woman, and I said, no it has to be someone who really disappears. It's the guy's movie. I said, "Can I pick the person?" And they said, "No, but you can play it. And all for the same money." And on the first day, when we began, it was a very tough movie for me. I knew absolutely nothing, I barely knew what a camera looked like. Really, I struggled through. This story is almost unbelievable. I had written screenplays and I could write great-looking scenes, but I didn't know there was such a thing as coverage. Does everyone know what I mean? Surely now everybody's got a camera. I didn't know that you have to shoot two people in order to cut.

Nichols: Call it a master. Shoot a master first.
May: No, no. I didn't know you had to shoot anything but one thing.

Nichols: That's the master.
May: Even if you shot one person . . .

Nichols: Oh, I see. You thought just one thing per scene.
May: Yes, one thing per scene. I thought that you picture the scene and if it's just one person you do that. Nobody told me because they didn't want me on the movie and they wanted me fired. I was way ahead of schedule. In the first week I had jumped four weeks ahead of schedule with no coverage. And I was very proud. And they wanted me to go in and cut it. And I said, "Well, this is too long. Let's take some time out." And they said, "Well, we can't." This is how little I knew, I mean kids with a camera know more than that. And I learned that weekend that you had to cover. So I went back and immediately fell behind six months. And on this movie, the only thing I knew anything about was acting. And I had my cast in the movie. I had my actors. I had been an acting teacher. I directed. And I knew how I wanted it to look. And I would say things like I want them to be full-figure but not tiny. Because everyone said you don't have to know about lenses, you know, little girl. And finally somebody took me aside and told me that there are long lenses and wide lenses. You've never seen a movie with that many mistakes in it. My editor was a really nice man who had a drug problem. And the first cut he did, he did flash-forwards, so that I would watch the scene and there would be a piece of the next scene in it. He'd never edited. It was his first movie. And I said, "There's a piece of the next scene in this," and he said it's a flash-forward. I didn't know what to do. And fortunately, well he didn't OD, but he took too many drugs and left, and the apprentices and I sort of took out the flash-forwards. But I did—because the story was so good, and because the cast that I had were my people, and because I had Anthea Sylbert—and the crew was not very good, but I hired D. D. Ryan. And I managed to learn on that movie, while shooting it I made so many mistakes that I actually learned a little bit about how to make a movie. I didn't learn—I had such a good focus puller I didn't know there was such a thing as focus until the next movie. There's no way to know unless someone teaches

you or you screw up. And when you start a movie by someone saying, "You can't pick a director, but you can direct it," you really start knowing nothing. And that was the story of that movie. Every day became about trying to remember just what it was about and not screwing up too badly. Because if anybody can screw up badly . . . I give you this blouse as an example. It was just a hair-raising experience, but I had such a strong story that it was hard to screw it up. And what you're saying is right. If you have some story that you want to tell, it's almost hard to make it not work, even me.

Nichols: Let me tell you a quick story about why *A New Leaf* is so great. I was supposed to do *American Beauty* for DreamWorks. One day I was getting ready to fly to an island, and there's a storm. And my little cell phone rings and it's Steven Spielberg, and he says, "Where are you?" And I said, "Well, it's funny, I'm on a plane waiting for a storm to clear up. We're about to take off." And he said, "Well, what kind of plane?" And I said, "A Citation Ultra." And he said, "Well, your plane is too small." And I said, "Thank you and you called because?" And he said, "Are you going to do *American Beauty* or not? Because if you're not we have Sam Mendes." And I think he's trying to tell me something, so I said, "Sam Mendes is great, you should do it, do it with Sam. I have to wait for this other picture I have to make. Go ahead and take Sam." So they did and so I saw the movie and it was great. And I said to my wife, you think I should have done it? She said, "No, the reason it's great is Sam's excitement about making his first movie." And she was right, and she was right about you and *A New Leaf* because with all that you were still so excited about making your first movie. And we see it. It's alive.

May: Yes, I think that is what experience does. It just teaches you what you shouldn't do. But in the beginning you think you can do anything because you don't have any experience and that really does give you a lot of energy.

Nichols: Do you remember what you said to me about *The Exorcist*? I also turned down *The Exorcist* because I didn't want to do that to a little girl for six months. And it was my best friend again, the head of the studio, and it opened and it was a gigantic hit. He took me to see the line. He said, "You personally lost $30 million by not making this movie." And I said to Elaine, "I'm trying to feel bad because John [Calley] said I lost $30 million by not doing *The Exorcist*." And Elaine said, "Don't worry, darling, if you'd made it, it wouldn't have made that kind of money."

May: It wouldn't have. You would have made it human and real.

Nichols: We have time for one more question.

Audience member: There are maybe four, five, or six women making Hollywood films—whatever the number, it's relatively few. Can you talk a bit about the difficulty being a woman director?

May: Part of the difficulty with *A New Leaf* was, Walter, whom, incidentally, I came to love, would call me Mrs. Hitler among other things. I didn't want to frighten anyone, and people would leave me saying, she's a nice girl. What is this big thing about? She's a nice girl, and the thing is, of course, I wasn't a nice girl. And when they found this out, they hated me all the more. And I think that's what really happens. It's not that they're women. It's that as women they think, I want to show that I'm a nice person. I'm no one to be feared. I'm not one of *those* women who are not nice women. And in the end, when it comes down to it, you're just as rotten as any guy. You'll fight just as hard to get your way. So I think the real trick is, for women, is they should start out tough. They don't start out tough. They start by saying, "Don't be afraid of me. I'm only a woman." And they're not *only* women, they're just as tough as guys. In that way I think I did have trouble. But only because I seemed so pleasant.

Note

1. The project was then titled *Bogart Slept Here*. The revised script became *The Goodbye Girl* (Herbert Ross, 1977).—REK

Elaine May Salutes Mike Nichols at the AFI Life Achievement Award

Elaine May / 2010

From *38th AFI Life Achievement Award: A Tribute to Mike Nichols*, June 10, 2010; extended version published by the American Film Institute on YouTube, October 8, 2010: https://youtube/AgjBxiDmJyU. © 2010 Courtesy of American Film Institute.

Elaine May: This is a very emotional night for me because ten, twenty, thirty years ago tonight I bought this dress.... I bought it for Mike's first lifetime achievement award.

And at the time, he promised me that from then on he would only do mediocre work so that I wouldn't be inconvenienced again, and then year after year after year after year, he consistently broke his word.

So here I am tonight. And I think that tonight, my speech for Mike will have a Yiddish theme.

Because as Howard said, not only is Mike a wonderful producer, a remarkable actor, a brilliant director, he's also, really Albert Einstein's cousin. It is true! It's on a show on PBS, that is hosted by—[*looks at hand*] I can barely read my hand—Henry—ah, Robert Gates Junior—I have always suspected this, because years ago, I was leafing through a Gutenberg Bible that Mike keeps on his coffee table. And I found a letter, one page of a letter, it was a letter obviously written by Einstein. I don't know to whom it was written because it was the second page.

I took that letter, and a few other little things that Mike will never miss. I have that letter with me tonight. I'm going to read it.

[*Reaches into bra*]

I just don't want to take out the wrong thing.

It's the second page.

[*Reading*]

"Agitated, I moved away from the dinner party, and wandered into the kitchen, where Little Igor [*Mike Nichols's birth name was Mikhail Igor Peschkowsky*] was finishing his mashed potatoes and peas. He ate the peas one at a time. On impulse

I said to him, 'How can I explain to dinner guests that relative time equals distance over speed, without sounding pedantic?'

"Little Igor paused over his pea. He said, 'A mother is forced to send her little boy away. Sitting on the train the boy is grief-stricken. Suddenly he looks through the window and sees that there is another train standing still on the track beside his. And a little girl is looking at him through the window and smiling. For a moment the boy's grief is lifted and he smiles, and then we pull back [*gestures camera move*] and we see the heartbroken mother watching the two trains, which are actually racing away, but to the children smiling at each other, through the window, the trains seem to be standing still, because they are both traveling in the same direction, at the same speed.'"

And here Einstein writes, "It was at that moment I gave up my dream of being a director, and decided to stay with physics."

And the last line:

"I said to the boy, 'I had no idea where you were going with that story,'" and this is as far as this letter goes.

But I knew immediately that Little Igor was Mike, because of course I know that his name is Igor, and that's the way he still eats peas. But I, like Einstein, never know where Mike's story is going, either. I watch his movies, and I have no idea where they are going to go, and then when they get there I think, oh well, yeah, of course.

I watched the Graduate kill himself for this girl, and then defeat her mother, and then he tears her away from some guy at her own wedding, and then when they're on the bus and he's won, he has nothing to say to her.

And you think, oh well yeah, of course.

If you kept the camera on the prince after he put the glass slipper on Cinderella's foot, what would he say to her? He would say, "Nice shoes."

You don't know where *Carnal Knowledge* is going because there are no clichés. You can go crazy, your mind can't drift, you can't get popcorn, you don't know what's going to happen. And *Working Girl*, well, you do know what's going to happen, because Melanie Griffith is going to get Harrison Ford and she's beautiful and he's handsome and they're both in business. And they have something to talk about on the bus, because, they're in the market.

They're probably one of the corporations that are funding this evening.

These scripts are all written by terrific writers, but if you're a writer, you really want Mike to direct your screenplay. Because you know that every shot and every costume and every piece of furniture and every shoe, and everything you see is going to tell your story. And never give it away.

I have to go back to my Jewish theme now, because I don't want to not be thematic. And here it is:

Albert Einstein was a very sad man when he died, because he had never achieved a combined field theory and that's gotta be depressing. But in whatever super extreme sixth dimension he may be in, if he's watching the show tonight, I think he'd probably be immensely cheered up to discover that he is Mike Nichols's cousin.

Blind Camels, Idiot Execs, and Five Other *Ishtar* Revelations from Director Elaine May

S. T. VanAirsdale / 2011

From *Movieline*, May 18, 2011. Reprinted by permission.

"Either you like the movie or I'm very sick." And thus the actor, writer, director, and comedy legend Elaine May greeted her warmly welcoming audience Tuesday night at New York's 92nd Street Y. The occasion: An ultra-rare screening of her infamous 1987 comedy *Ishtar*—made all the rarer by exhibiting, for the first time ever, May's own director's cut of the film.

Featuring Warren Beatty and Dustin Hoffman as a hapless songwriting team embroiled in CIA/terrorist/Cold War intrigue after innocently attempting to find steady work in North Africa, *Ishtar* has become synonymous with Hollywood bloat, ego, and cutthroat studio maneuvering since its tortured production (and even more tortured release) a quarter-century ago. It's also found a groundswell of critical and cultural support for its revival, with devotees arguing the film was never given a chance upon completion and that its satire is as funny—and relevant—as ever in this era of upheaval, espionage, and various American political actions in the Middle East.

By most accounts of the *Ishtar* fans on hand, there wasn't much separating the studio-sanctioned version from May's own cut, which she viewed with her audience. "I thought it was funny—which is a terrible thing to admit about your own movie," she told moderator David Schwartz. "But whenever I see it, I think of those people who try out for *American Idol*, and how certain they are of their talent, and how touching they are."

Among the evening's other revelations from *Ishtar*'s troubled production, its fraught legacy, its imminent Blu-ray release and May's twenty-five years of post-*Ishtar* silence:

1. *Ishtar*: The First Film Jointly Influenced by Bing Crosby, Bob Hope . . . and Ronald Reagan

"I had seen the *Road* movies," said May, referring to the Crosby/Hope comedy franchise of the forties and early fifties, "and Warren and I wanted to do something together. And he's very good musically. And at the time, I think I saw *Road to Morocco*. We, America, were backing Iran *and* Iraq—one against the other. We were in Lebanon. We were of course in Afghanistan, as we always are. We were all over the Middle East, and everyone I knew was in the CIA. The CIA was everywhere. And I thought, 'If you did a *Road* movie today, if you really sent somebody . . .'"

Which would have been enough inspiration even *without* the guy in the White House at the time. "At that time, Reagan was president, and I met him," May said. "And he's an amazingly naive, innocent, charming guy who really, really cared about show business! In the nicest way, really. He knew Mike's and my albums. He could quote them—he memorized them! He did our 'Telephone' routine. So he was the president. And nobody really knew what was going on, actually. I thought, 'Really, there's something very endearing, if terrifying, about this kind of innocence, this kind of naivete.'"

2. Filming in the Sahara Is Just as Tough as It Looks . . .

Most of the film's final third takes place with Hoffman and Beatty—and their blind camel—lost in the desert. Challenging much? "It wasn't really a blind camel," May explained. "I don't exactly remember how we did it, but it acted like it. It was a great actor! We tried camels out; a lot of camels came. But this camel had it, and we cast him."

Also among May's gifted discoveries on location: A flock of hungry vultures and an ensemble from the indigenous Berber population. "They were great sports because Dustin had to lay in the sand, and the vultures wouldn't come to him unless they put raw meat on him. And he said, 'Are these vultures going to know where the raw meat ends and I start?' And he did it! It was a hard shoot. [. . .] The guys who were in the auction scene were real Berbers. They knew no English. They just got them from the hills—all of the extras, all of the people were from around there. And they were fantastic, these Berbers. I have no idea how they understood sort of exactly what to do. They just sort of followed Warren. It was a very hard shoot, but I really liked it. I actually have an affinity for the desert."

3. . . . But It's Nowhere Near as Difficult as Dealing with Then-Columbia Pictures Chief David Puttnam

If *Ishtar* is famous for anything, it's the legend of going millions of dollars over budget before Columbia put the brakes on May and Beatty. "This is like a curse," May said. "In the middle of this movie, *Ishtar*, they changed the head of the studio—Columbia's head of the studio. David Puttnam came in. David Puttnam was a guy who was up against Warren Beatty for the Academy Award for *Reds* [in 1981] with . . . Oh . . ."

A few audience members jogged May's memory: "*Chariots of Fire!*"

"*Chariots of Fire*," May repeated. "About a—and I don't want to sound bitter about it—but about a Christian and a Jew who *ran*. But [Puttnam] had written a piece before the Academy Awards saying Warren was self-indulgent and should be spanked. But nobody mentioned that he was the competitor! They just wrote it as though it was an op-ed piece, because he's English, and we respect that in Hollywood. He then had a falling out with Dustin, and he said that Dustin was a brat and was troublesome and also some childlike person. And this is a guy who then became head of our studio!

"When the movie came out, we had three previews, and they went really well. And [former Columbia owner] Herb Allen said, 'This is fantastic! Thumbs up!' So I went to Bali, because I thought everything was fine. I hit Bali, and Warren calls and tells me that the day the press came, an article came out in the *Los Angeles Times* in which the head of Columbia wiped us out—David Puttnam. It was the same thing he said before: That we should be spanked, that there was too much money, that he was going to reform Hollywood! Because the British film industry made so much money? I had *no* idea. I was pleased to hear he's now in Parliament. He's running England, which is doing so well.

"But it was really sort of unforgivable what he did. He attacked his own movie; he was the head of the studio. And Mike Nichols, my partner, said it was like an example of an entire studio committing suicide. They all just *went* with him.

"So when the press junket came, the next screening of this movie, which had sort of gotten really good word of mouth, there were no laughs, and people kept saying how much money it cost. Because he—David Puttnam—had done something that no studio had never done: He actually *released* the budget, or his version of it. So Charles Grodin, who plays the CIA agent, was at a screening. I was told about this: The entire audience was saying, 'It cost so much money! It cost so much money!' And he finally said, 'What do *you* care? It's not *your* money! It's not like if it didn't cost that much money they'd give it to you. It's [corporate parent] Coca-Cola's money! Coca-Cola would keep it! What do you care? Your tickets don't cost any more. Your tax dollars didn't go to it. Why are you—you people in cloth coats—complaining about how much money it costs?' And it occurred to me that that's sort of true, when people complain like that."

4. She's (Mostly) Used to Your *Ishtar* Jokes by Now

"The thing about *Ishtar*," May said, "is that there are so many gags about it. *The Golden Girls* is being replayed, and I saw some episode of it, and *they* made a crack about *Ishtar*. Somebody quoted me as saying this, but I really did say it: If *half* the people who had made cracks about *Ishtar* had seen it, I'd be a rich woman today. [. . .] I think *Ishtar* is just an easy thing to make fun of. I think it really made me think that maybe before I jump on the pundit bandwagon, I should actually look at what I'm making fun of or insulting."

5. She Never Wanted to Direct in the First Place

"I've had a lot of trouble with all my movies," May acknowledged. "I'll just admit that. I didn't want to direct—I wanted director approval [as a writer]. And I had this guy representing me who was like the last of the crazy agents. His name was Hilly Elkins, and he said, 'They won't give you director approval, but you can direct.' I really didn't want to. I wanted to write. And they said they'd pick the director. And I couldn't have actor approval, but I could be the girl. Or else they'll use Carol Channing, who is really good, but I thought wrong for this. So I said I would direct.

"I knew about acting, but I knew *nothing* about film. I thought one of the big lights on the first day of shooting was the camera. It was a really screwed-up production. It really was. One of the guys said, 'The camera isn't here yet.' [. . .] And I didn't know you were supposed to cover a movie. I had written my shots out brilliantly, but I didn't realize you were supposed to shoot two angles in order to cut. I thought you just took the film out of it. So at the end of the first week of shooting, I was four weeks ahead of schedule. I went into the editing room and said, 'This scene is too long; take that out.' And he said, 'I can't; there's no coverage.' Then the next week I was four weeks behind schedule. [. . .] I must say, if you screw up enough, you really learn a lot."

6. Despite All Appearances, She's Still Working—Just Not Directing

May briefly confirmed her contribution to *Relatively Speaking*, a triptych of one-act plays with fellow writers Woody Allen and Ethan Coen and director John Turturro (it opens this fall on Broadway), but added that she has no filmmaking prospects on the horizon.

"It's hard," she said. "You'd have to be offered a movie that's worth your time and your struggle, and I haven't been. Once in Los Angeles, years and years ago, I was in a restaurant where a lot of stars go. And somebody said to me, 'What are you doing now?' It was some actor. And I said, 'Nothing.' And they looked at me as though I'd said I had cancer. They were *horrified*. No one had ever said that; no one had ever said 'Nothing.' No one had ever said, 'Well, I didn't get a good enough film.' So I'm telling you now: I haven't been offered a film I'd want to direct, and that's why I haven't directed any."

7. The Long-Awaited *Ishtar* Blu-ray Is on Its Way. Promise!

Despite—or perhaps because of—its notoriety, *Ishtar* has never been available on DVD or Blu-ray. Even an announcement last year that Sony had the latter in the works for early 2011 has yielded zilch. May insists she has nothing to do with it. "Earlier today," she said, "somebody said that they had read on the Net that the impending [Blu-ray] release of *Ishtar* had been delayed by my 'people.' And I was so thrilled to think that I had 'people'! And that my 'people' had power! And I thought, 'Who are they?' They could only be the Jews. I have no other people."

Indeed, it's up to Sony, which bought Columbia in 1989, to pin a date to its imminent *Ishtar* video release. And it *is* imminent, according to May. "They tell me now—Sony—that they're going to release this on Blu-ray, and it will really look wonderful and sound wonderful. If they don't, you'll be the last eighty or ninety or however many people to see this movie in this particular version. [. . .] If you all clap your hands and believe it! They say they want to and they'll do it soon, and I have great faith that they'll do it."

Who's Afraid of Nichols and May?

Sam Kashner / 2013

From *Vanity Fair* 55, no. 1 (January 2013): 94–106. © 2013 by Sam Kashner. Reprinted with the permission of the author; all rights reserved.

"She's not like other people," Mike Nichols e-mailed me when I first approached him about being interviewed with his legendary partner in comedy, the soulfully offbeat and intensely private Elaine May. "As you know she ignores publicity but we'll see." John Lahr profiled Nichols for the *New Yorker* in 2000, but May declined Lahr's offer to do a similar profile of her. The last in-depth interview she gave was to *Life* magazine in 1967, six years after her and Nichols's professional breakup. She has mostly held her silence ever since.

But there it was in an e-mail from Nichols later that night: "Elaine says Yes. So sharpen your pencils and your tongue and we will commence."

Judd Apatow, the guest editor of this issue, who yields to no one in his admiration of Nichols and May, reminded me that it's been fifty-one years since the pair walked away from their comedy act at the height of their popularity, in 1961—Nichols to become a stage and film director, and May to become a playwright, screenwriter, director, and occasional actress. Their partnership lasted just four years, beginning at the University of Chicago, moving to nightclubs, then to television and radio, and culminating in a Broadway run and three top-selling comedy LP albums, all of which established Nichols and May as the freshest, most inventive, and most influential social satirists of their day. And then—we're still scratching our heads about this—it was over.

They first worked together as members of an improvisation group called the Compass Players, founded by Paul Sills and David Shepherd. Shelley Berman and Ed Asner were early members of the troupe, which later evolved into Chicago's Second City, the launchpad for, among others, John Belushi, Bill Murray, and Harold Ramis.

When Nichols first met Elaine, he was dazzled—and intimidated—by her sheer inventiveness and dangerous wit. Their first improvisation happened offstage, at a chance meeting in the waiting room of Illinois Central's Randolph Street Station.

Mike, pretending to be some kind of Russian spy, sidled up to Elaine: "May I seeet down, plis?" Elaine instantly went into character: "If you veesh." Nichols: "Do you haff a light?" May: "Yes, zertainly." Nichols: "I had a lighter, but . . . I lost eet on Fifty-Seventh Street." May: "Oh, of course, zen you are . . . Agent X-9?"

Both were primarily actors at first. Nichols would leave Chicago to study the Method with Lee Strasberg in New York; May studied acting with the Russian character actress and teacher Maria Ouspenskaya. But their improvised skits for the Compass were so outside the box and so hilarious that they soon attracted an enthusiastic audience of students, faculty, and other intellectuals who hung around the University of Chicago.

Before then, comics had just stood up and told jokes—jokes that were usually written for them by gag writers. Think of Bob Hope, Jack Benny, Milton Berle. But a new generation was taking comedy to the edge: Mort Sahl, Lenny Bruce, Sid Caesar and Imogene Coca. Nichols and May combined the political and social satire of Sahl and Bruce with the inspired comic skits of Caesar and Coca. "Individually, each one is a genius," says Woody Allen. "And when they worked together, the sum was even greater than the combination of the parts—the two of them came along and elevated comedy to a brand-new level." You might say there would be no Steve Martin, no Lily Tomlin, no Martin Short, no *Saturday Night Live* without them.

Soon a national audience was listening to Nichols and May on the radio, television, and record albums, their voices nasal, earnest, and full of intimations of mortal, adult absurdities. Their skits mined everyday situations and mundane characters, stretching them to the breaking point of comic possibility: the woman psychologist left frustrated and weeping when her favorite patient announces his decision to spend Christmas with his family ("Merry Christmas, Doctor"); the officious operator in "Telephone," who drains valuable seconds from the desperate caller's last dime trying to spell his party's name ("*K* as in knife, *P* as in pneumonia . . ."); the jealous doctor who asks his nurse in the middle of an operation, "*Is there somebody else? . . . It's Pinsky, isn't it?*" ("A Little More Gauze"); the Cape Canaveral rocket scientist whose phone call from his overbearing, guilt-tripping mother leaves him regressed and babbling ("Mother and Son").

I grew up listening to them on the radio from the back seat of my parents' car and on shiny LPs, which my parents played for friends after they'd all come back from dinner out and the babysitter had been sent home. My parents thought I was asleep in bed, but in fact I was hiding behind the door in the next room relishing the forbidden adult sophistication of it all. So it was incredible for me to see Nichols and May more than fifty years later, together in the same room, at Nichols's Manhattan apartment, like one of their album covers come to life. I could easily see why men have fallen like bowling pins for Elaine. For our meeting she was dressed in a black-and-white-striped shirt and skinny black pants, her dark hair still worn long. The first words out of her mouth were "Your name is Sam. Can I assume we're all atheists here?" We first had a lunch of mushroom risotto, but Mike noticed that Elaine wasn't eating much. "You didn't eat anything, Elaine. Don't you like your lunch?" he asked.

"It's absolutely tasteless. It's good for us." She then handed me the salt, explaining, "We can't have salt. You might need this."

"I'm worried about Jewish narcissism, Elaine," was Mike's opening gambit. She assured him that he had nothing to worry about. He then asked her which recent movies she'd seen, but she couldn't think of any. What about TV? Nichols asked. He thought the best work was being done there, in such shows as *Breaking Bad.*

Elaine hadn't seen it. "With my addictive personality," she said, "I'm afraid to start watching a TV series, but I love *Law & Order*—it's so straightforward and has no plot. It's a real pleasure."

Mike mentioned Steven Spielberg's *Lincoln*, giving it a thumbs-up. "I'm a pariah at dinner parties," Elaine responded, "because I don't get all this about Lincoln. It's not like he wanted to free all the slaves right away. And all that death. Why didn't we just stop buying cotton?"

But when we moved into the living room to sit in big comfortable armchairs at either end of a large coffee table, Elaine looked as if she were about to flee. "We had so much fun at lunch," she said. "Now look at us. I'm nervous and terrible at this."

"That makes two of us," I told her. "Would you like to see my questions?"

She took my List of Questions—a number of them supplied by Mr. Apatow—and proceeded to take over the interview. Holding onto the list for dear life, she read the first question: "Did you have any ground rules for improvisations at the Compass Players?"

Nichols answered, "The greatest rule was yours, Elaine: when in doubt, seduce. That became the rule for the whole group. And looking back, because I did teach acting for a while, we figured out over a long time that there only were three kinds of scenes in the world—fights, seductions, and negotiations. Do you remember this?"

"But we also discovered that the scene that always works is a blind date," May said.

One of their most famous sketches, "Teenagers," is not so much a blind date as a look at two high-school kids parking by a lake. She is shy and vulnerable and giggly, taking occasional nervous stabs at intellectual profundity: "Have you noticed the lake at all? It's just suicidally beautiful tonight. . . . You look at that lake out there and you think, what is it? . . . And it's just a lot of little water, and then you put it all together, and it's this entire lake, you know? That just knocks me out." He's a callow jock trying desperately to make out with her. When she demurs, he says, "I know exactly what you're going to say. You're going to say that I wouldn't respect you, right? Look . . . I want to tell you right here and now that I would respect you like *crazy!*"

Locked in a long kiss, Elaine exhales smoke out of the side of her mouth. You can see the same inspired moment in *The Graduate*, directed, of course, by Mike Nichols, who reprised the joke with Anne Bancroft as Mrs. Robinson.

"The second scene that always works is a card game," May continued. "And the scene that never works is a scene about divorce."

She moved on to the next question: "What do each of you bring to the partnership?" She answered it. "Well, I brought a kind of rough, cowboy-like attitude, and Mike was very attractive and groomed and . . ."

Nichols laughed.

"What you brought," he explained, "is that you always knew the character that would not be the theater choice, but the real-life choice, and therefore the comedy choice. Do you remember when we did the whorehouse scene and you were the madam? And you were like somebody's aunt. When the guys were through with the girls, you would say, 'It was lovely to see you. Please say hello to [your wife] Edith.' You did a clubwoman for the madam and you did a madam for a clubwoman."

Elaine jumped in. "We were very similar. I mean, he was a Method actor, and I was Method. One of the big strengths was that we really, actually, worked the same way. We found the same things funny; we were both mean and Method. So that was the strength. Also, I found him hilarious."

"I found her hilarious."

One of the delights of their performances was how often the two broke each other up—you can hear it in their recordings. "Once during 'Teenagers'—I still remember it—during the kissing, we either hit teeth or something, and we began to break [into laughter]," recalled May. "And we stayed together in the kiss until we could pull ourselves together, and then we parted and something happened, and we broke up again, and we couldn't stop. At first the audience laughed with us, and then they began to get a little annoyed. I remember during intermission, Mike said we had to pull ourselves together—these people have paid an enormous amount of money to see us, and we have to be professional. So we went back onstage and just fucked the second act. We laughed, and we couldn't stop."

Nichols remembered that when *Forbidden Broadway*, a New York satirical revue of current and classic theater, did a send-up of Nichols and May all they had to show was "the two of us walking onstage, beginning to speak, and then breaking up. And then we would try to say something else and break up again. And then, after the third time, one of us turned to the audience and said, 'You'd laugh too if you knew what we were laughing at.' It was brilliant."

"When Mike did break up," May recalled, "he would say this terrific line to get me off the hook. He would say, 'Go on without me.'"

May described Nichols as "an amazingly good actor, really good, who constantly says he isn't." This is a conversation they seem to have had often over the years. Nichols countered that there were "a couple of parts I'm really good at, but—remember when I quit *The Sopranos*? I was [supposed to be] the shrink [Dr. Krakower] that [Carmela Soprano] goes to. And there was a reading with about forty people sitting around many tables put together, with a lot of spaghetti behind us, and we read that week's script. I was the only person at the table who had to act. Everybody else *was* their character. And already I loved it. [Show creator] David Chase and I got to be friends after that, but I said, 'I'm sorry to tell you, I'm the wrong Jew. You need a whole other kind of Jew for this doctor. I'm miscast, forgive me.' And I took myself away. I can only do certain parts. I see the words and I say, 'Oh, *this* I can say, no problem.' But when I can't, I'm no good, because I'm not an actor. It's a fluke, I'm telling you."

"It doesn't mean you're an actor if you can act," Elaine corrected.

"Oh, I thought it did."

Nichols was once offered the role of Hamlet to open the Guthrie Theater, in Minneapolis. "I said, 'I don't have the speech for Hamlet, I don't have the carriage for Hamlet, I can't fence, I don't look like Hamlet, I can't possibly do it.'"

"But here's the thing," Elaine explained. "One of the reasons that it would be easy for you to do Hamlet was that you would by the second week see how hilarious Hamlet is—thirty years old, still in college, obviously drinking a little bit, hanging out with those two other guys, doesn't really do anything. Pretty soon, as you delved into him—even maybe a little potbelly—you would start finding out what it was really like."

Elaine moved on to another question from the list: "Your improv comedy that came out of the University of Chicago has been credited, blamed, in parentheses, for changing comedy from stand-up comics telling jokes to actors creating satiric skits. Yes?"

"Yes," Mike said, "with some others. We were not alone. There was also . . ."

"Oh, don't babble on."

"I'm sorry."

Elaine read the next question: "Who are your comic or satiric heroes?"

Mike answered, "Sid Caesar and Imogene Coca . . . and Lenny Bruce. Lenny Bruce opened for us for six months in that nightclub that we were in."

"I thought we opened for him?"

"He opened for us, Elaine. And I watched him every night, and he was more than a genius. He was a great spirit, and he was, for want of a better word, very innocent and sweet. Every time he made things up, which was every show, it was the best. He changed the face of comedy by saying the unsayable, and it was hilarious. And then many people began to do that, and it goes further and further, and it gets more and more elegant. For instance, Chris Rock isn't more shocking, but he has more style while doing the same thing. He's taking it to a new place."

"But I think the guy closest to the satire that is being performed now," Elaine said, "was Mort Sahl. He was really sort of like Jon Stewart, but he made it up every day all by himself, without writers, from the newspapers."

I asked Nichols if there was anything he missed about doing comedy. "I miss terribly the ability to get revenge instantly," he answered.

Elaine read the next question, "Is *The Daily Show* really satire or just revenge?" and immediately answered it: "It's satire, but satire is revenge. Lewis Black is less satirical; Jon Stewart can really put a jab in, as can Stephen Colbert, but oddly enough Lewis Black, because he's so angry, can't. I mean, that doesn't mean that he's less; it just means that his anger means 'I'm helpless.'"

She shrugged.

"I think the main thing about comedy and humor is that it's impossible and always was impossible to define," said Mike.

Elaine asked, "Do you remember the show *Omnibus*? It was that English guy, whose name I don't remember . . ."

"Alistair Cooke?" I interjected. It's one of the few times I spoke up: just saying his name made me feel smart.

"Yes, Alistair Cooke," Elaine answered. "He was having a discussion about humor—what was funny—on Steve Allen's show. And while they were speaking Alistair Cooke took a pie and smashed Steve Allen in the face with it, and the audience fell to fucking pieces, and I thought, This is an amazing demonstration of humor. I don't know if it would have been funny had it not been Alistair Cooke."

"Yes. The whole point about laughter is it's like mercury: you can't catch it, you can't catch what motivates it—that's why it's funny," added Mike.

Elaine returned to the list: "Did I ask you what the point of humor in society is?"

"No."

"What is the point of humor in society?"

"Well, it's not hard to answer."

"Oh. Of course not. Go on, Mike."

"It's the expression of freedom. The only way I know that this is still a free country is when I watch Jon Stewart's show, and Stephen Colbert, where you can say anything you damn please."

Elaine with the next question: "What have you learned, Mike?"

"I've learned that many of the worst things lead to the best things, that no great thing is achieved without a couple of bad, bad things on the way to them, and that the bad things that happen to you bring, in some cases, the good things. For instance, if you grow up odd and—what is it when you're left out? You're not an extrovert—"

"Introvert?"

"No, when you grow up—"

"Peculiar?"

"Peculiar. Different," Mike continued. "The degree to which you're peculiar and different is the degree to which you must learn to hear people thinking. Just in self-defense you have to learn, where is their kindness? Where is their danger? Where is their generosity? If you survive, because you've gotten lucky—and there's no other reason ever to survive except luck—you will find that the ability to hear people thinking is incredibly useful, especially in the theater."

The film critic David Thomson observed of Elaine May, "The air of Jewish fatalism is always there in her work." Born in Philadelphia, she spent her childhood traveling with her father, Jack Berlin, who performed in a Yiddish theater company, where she sometimes played a little boy named Benny. Around the age of ten, when her father died, she gave up the role. ("I developed breasts, and our people do not believe in breast binding," she told *Life* in 1967.) At fourteen she dropped out of high school in Los Angeles—where she had moved with her mother after having attended something like fifty schools during her itinerant youth—and at sixteen she married Marvin May, and had a daughter, Jeannie, who, as an actress-screenwriter, would take the family name of Berlin. The marriage broke up, and after a string of odd jobs (private eye, roofing saleswoman), Elaine looked for a college that would take her without a high-school diploma. The University of Chicago apparently said it would, so, with seven dollars in her pocket, she hitchhiked to Chicago, where instead of enrolling she just showed up at classes and attended theater productions on campus, where she met Mike.

In *A New Leaf*, one of the films Elaine later cowrote, directed, and starred in,[1] the character of the painfully shy botanist Henrietta Lowell comes close to self-parody. Like Henrietta, Elaine was famously disheveled, wearing mismatched clothes generously sprinkled with the ashes from her cigarettes. Like Henrietta, she was brilliant in some academic and artistic fields, but clueless in others. As one wag pointed out, "She knew about theater and psychoanalysis. She didn't know about anything else. She didn't know if Eisenhower was a Republican or a Democrat."

As for Mike's outsider status, when he and his brother, Robert, first arrived in New York in 1939 on the *Bremen* and saw a delicatessen with Hebrew letters on the window, Mike, then seven, turned to his father and asked, "Is that allowed here?" His family had just escaped Nazi Germany, where Jewish culture was being decimated. One of Mike's grandfathers, a prominent writer and a leader of the Social Democratic Party named Gustav Landauer, was close friends with Martin Buber and was killed by German soldiers in 1919. Mike's grandmother Hedwig Lachmann also established herself in society circles, having translated into German Oscar Wilde's play *Salome*, which Richard Strauss later adapted as a libretto for his opera of the same name.

"American society to me and my brother was thrilling because, first of all, the food made noise," recalled Nichols. "We were so excited about Rice Krispies and Coca-Cola. We had only silent food in the old country, and we loved listening to our lunch and breakfast."

His father, a physician, died when Mike was twelve; Mike lived with his brother and his mother, Brigitte, in a kind of dreary poverty in Manhattan's West Seventies, in "one of those tiny apartment houses with podiatrists on the first floor," as he told John Lahr.

It was Paul Sills who introduced the two outsiders to each other. Elaine remembers that Sills said, "'I want you to meet the only other person on the campus of the University of Chicago who is as hostile as you are.' And I think we were that hostile because we could hear people's thoughts. But also, the other thing is, let's face it, we were peculiar and geeky—but we got much nicer. But we're also richer and more successful. I don't know what we'd be like if we weren't."

Elaine went back to reading the list: "What is important in life and art?"

"Love and babies," Mike shot back. "That's my answer. What's yours?"

"I can give you Freud's answer."

"What's that?"

"Love and work."

"Yes, I love his answer, always did. What's yours?"

"Money and success."

"In life and art?"

"Oh, sorry," Elaine continued. "My mind wandered. I just read the word 'important.' What is important in life and art? You know, when I was very young, I thought it didn't matter what happened to me when I died, so long as my work was immortal. As I age, I think, Well, perhaps if I had to trade dying right now and being immortal with just living on, I would choose living on. I never thought I would say that. I feel it's so unethical and wrong."

Mike jumped in. "I'm very weird about survival because the older I get, the more I think that the life that I started with—I was insanely, unfairly, ridiculously lucky. All Jews went to the camps, but we not only didn't go to camps, we were allowed to leave the country. We got to America, and everything that happened was luckier and luckier. I didn't finish college. I just stopped going to class, and I got a job on the radio. I didn't know anything. I couldn't get a diploma in anything! Over and over I was luckier than I had any right to be. I found the love of my life [Nichols is married to broadcast journalist Diane Sawyer]. How many people do that?"

"Luck is very strange," Elaine answered, moving to the edge of her chair. "I'm lucky in that I met the guy who said, Go to the University of Chicago, and I hitchhiked there. Then I met Paul Sills, and then I met you. My few pieces of luck."

"No, there are others—it goes on and on," Mike said.

"One piece of luck spikes to another piece of luck, spikes to another piece of luck. I don't want to embarrass you—I think you know you're so intelligent and you're so talented that, without those things, what the fuck good would your luck have done you? Do you think Diane would have married you if you were some putz?"

While at the University of Chicago, Nichols not only acted in plays but also found work and a measure of celebrity as a daytime radio announcer at WFMT, an eclectic FM station that played mainly classical music. He eventually dropped out of school and moved back to New York to study with Strasberg, while May stayed in Chicago, where she was acting and trying to develop a film treatment based on Plato's *Symposium* in which everyone was drunk. ("That's the only way it makes sense," she explained.)

Nichols returned to Chicago in 1955 and joined the Compass Players, where his real collaboration with May began. The Compass later opened an outpost at the Crystal Palace, in St. Louis, and Nichols, by then married to his first wife, singer Patricia Scott, continued to perform there with Elaine. In his book *Seriously Funny*, Gerald Nachman quotes Jay Landesman, who ran the Crystal Palace, as saying Nichols and May "were so good, they eventually threw the company off balance." After a brief skirmish among the Compass actors, Mike and Elaine headed east in the fall of 1957 with forty dollars between them. In New York, they auditioned for the theatrical manager Jack Rollins.

Two months later, they were famous.

"Gentleman Jack" Rollins was a legend in New York, known as "The Dean," "The Guru," and "The Poet of Managers," according to Janet Coleman's *The Compass.* If he hadn't already existed, you could have found him in the pages of Damon Runyon: a cigar-smoking gambler given to two-dollar bets on the ponies who was also an intellectual and a devotee of fine wines. His career began almost by accident, after he met folk singer Harry Belafonte flipping hamburgers in New York. (Unbutton your shirt, Harry, and sing calypso!)

Rollins, whose clients would come to include Woody Allen, David Letterman, Robin Williams, Robert Klein, and Billy Crystal, met with Nichols and May among the samovars and year-round Christmas lights of the Russian Tea Room, near Carnegie Hall. Over borscht and beef Stroganoff, they manically ad-libbed skits that they "not only had never rehearsed but had never even thought of until that desperate minute," Nichols once recalled. The two were so broke at the time that they were as thrilled that Rollins paid the bill as when he offered to sign them. "I was stunned by how really good they were," Rollins remembered. "I'd never seen this technique before. I thought, My God, these are two people writing hilarious comedy on their feet!"

Rollins got his friend Max Gordon, who owned the Village Vanguard, in Greenwich Village, and co-owned the Blue Angel, on East Fifty-Fifth Street, to give them a chance. They went on at the Blue Angel as an afterthought to the Smothers Brothers, in their matching red jackets, and sultry singer Eartha Kitt. Their skits went over so well that Gordon let them open for Mort Sahl at the Vanguard.

Mike asked Elaine, "Do you remember that some nights [Mort Sahl] would feel the crowd was ready and say, 'They're not going on tonight. I'll go right on'? We were very pissed with him because we'd be ready to go and he'd say, 'No, no. Skip them—I'm ready.' But he was very funny."

A few days after they opened, they moved back to the Blue Angel, where the *New Yorker* caught "their little dialogues" and enthusiastically, if oddly, compared them to the famous theatrical couple Alfred Lunt and Lynn Fontanne. *Variety*, more to the point, called them the "hipsters' hipsters."

If Rollins had worried that they were too intellectual for a mainstream audience, the *New York Times* wrote that they had "both snob and mob appeal," like Chaplin and the Marx Brothers. Rollins booked them into Town Hall, and they filled it twice, to adoring reviews. The *New York Post* enthused, "Nichols and May have mastered what appears to be a new comedy form—improvisation [. . .] the way jazz musicians will throw a phrase at each other and 'make up the music' as they go along."

"The best [show] we did was in Town Hall," Mike said, looking a tad nostalgic. "Was there any record of it?" He turned to Elaine and asked, "Why didn't we stick with the act? It was your fault. You wanted to stop. We should still be doing this."

"We can do it again," she offered.

"It would be different."

"We'd have to drop 'Teenagers.'"

"No, don't," I protest.

"No, certainly not," Mike said. "It would be funnier."

Looking back, perhaps there was just too great a physical and emotional toll, such as the night their "Pirandello" sketch got out of hand. "We scared the shit out of everybody," Mike recalled. "You clawed my chest bloody. How can you not remember this? And somebody tried to save us by applauding."

"In Chicago?"

"No, it wasn't. It was in Westport [Connecticut]. We were on the way to Broadway."

"Thank God it was not on Broadway."

"I had you by the front of your shirt, and I had been slapping you back and forth for quite a while, and my chest was pouring blood. You don't remember this? And they brought down the curtain. They didn't wait for our announcement or anything. We fell into each other's arms sobbing. This is one of my strongest memories of all time."

"Well, I'd like to remember it. It's a great memory," Elaine said.

Their success in New York clubs and at Town Hall got the attention of television executives, and Nichols and May were invited to do their brand of improv on Jack Paar's *Tonight Show*. They bombed.

"It was the first nightmare I ever experienced," Mike recalled. "We started and realized the audience had no idea what we were doing. And after not very long, Jack Paar said, 'Hurry it up, kids.' It was the worst experience in our lives, you remember? We were a catastrophe."

"It was awful."

Rollins realized they needed the luxury of time—which *The Tonight Show* didn't give them—so he got them booked on *The Steve Allen Plymouth Show*, where they did

"Disc Jockey," in which "the very wonderful, very talented Barbara Musk" is interviewed by radio DJ Jack Ego. That got the attention of *Omnibus*, the Sunday-afternoon show hosted by Alistair Cooke. *Omnibus* gave them fifteen unedited minutes, after which "the world broke open for them," Rollins's partner Charles Joffe recalled. There were lines around the block for their shows at the Blue Angel. Milton Berle couldn't get in, which symbolically marked the end of one comedic era and the beginning of something new. Even Jack Paar came around, telling people he had discovered them.

More TV shows followed: *The Dinah Shore Chevy Show, Perry Como's Kraft Music Hall*, even a Ginger Rogers special. But their stint on a game show called *Laugh Line*, with Dick Van Dyke, proved a rare disappointment in their brief, shining television career.

"It was the absolute nadir," Mike recalled. "We were supposed to improvise captions from seeing cartoons. You cheated, Elaine. You read the captions. You always read from what you had prepared."

"*Laugh Line* was sort of the way I am at interviews. I could think of nothing."

"Did you guys do other game shows?" I asked.

"Well, we only did one," Mike answered. "We were mystery guests on *What's My Line?* and they didn't guess us. You remember?"

"It was disappointing."

(The tricks memory plays: as you can see on YouTube, Random House publisher and man-about-town Bennett Cerf had little difficulty guessing "Mike and Elaine.")

"Was it fun doing commercials?" I asked.

"It was the most fun doing commercials, I think, for us both," Elaine answered.

Their dozens of ten-second animated cartoons to advertise Jax Beer still sound contemporary, with their offbeat, deadpan humor, such as the following:

ELAINE: I have something to tell you, darling.
MIKE: Fine, darling. Can I have a beer, please?
ELAINE: Of course, darling. Here is a glass of cold, extra-dry, sparkling Jax Beer.
MIKE: Thank you.
ELAINE: You're welcome. Phyllis shaved the dog today.

TV was making Nichols and May famous, but it wasn't making them happy. Eventually, May said, "I have no sense of mission about our work. I have nothing to tell people." She hated giving interviews even then and sometimes teased her interlocutors: "I will tell you something," she told one reporter, "but I warn you, it is a lie." They quit *Laugh Line* after three weeks and turned down, in Nichols's words, at least ninety-nine shows offered to them—"husband-and-wife situation comedies, brother-and-sister situation comedies . . . panel shows, quiz shows, musical comedies. No one offered us a Western."

They crowned their career on television with an outrageous stunt on the 1959 Emmy Awards telecast, in which May presented an award for "the Most Total Mediocrity" in the industry, accepted by Mike Nichols as "Lionel Klutz," a flashy television producer who bounced onstage and gave her a big, wet kiss on the mouth.

"Oh, God. It was great," Mike recalled. "Mediocrity—it was the award for mediocrity, for 'year in and year out producing garbage'! I came out and I said, 'I'm very proud, but how we managed to do it is . . . no matter what suggestions the sponsor makes, I take them. And most important of all, I think I am trying to offend no one anywhere on earth. In ten years of producing, we have received not one letter of any kind.'"

The apotheosis of Nichols and May's performing career was *An Evening with Mike Nichols and Elaine May*, which opened on October 8, 1960, at the John Golden Theatre, on Broadway's West Forty-Fifth Street. Opening night was a gala, preceded by a buffet at Sardi's. Carol Channing, a young, skinny Richard Avedon, Sidney Lumet, and Gloria Vanderbilt were among the guests. The producer, Alexander H. Cohen, arranged for an armada of Rolls-Royces to bring guests from Sardi's to the theater, a block away. A Ferris wheel was set up in front of the theater to celebrate the opening; fans danced in Shubert Alley after the curtain fell on the first night. Nichols and May presented their usual sketches and only one improv a night, but the audience went away feeling that everything was improv. When the audience threw out suggestions, Nichols and May were ready for every literary style—Faulkner, Beckett, Tennessee Williams. In one sketch, Nichols parodied Williams as "Alabama Glass," who drinks deeply while describing, in a honeysuckled southern accent, his new play (*Pork Makes Me Sick in the Summer*), complete with a Blanche-like heroine who "has taken to drink, prostitution, and puttin' on airs," and a husband who has committed suicide "on bein' unjustly accused of not bein' a homosexual."

An Evening with Mike Nichols and Elaine May was a triumph. The duo had caught the zeitgeist, and the public had fallen in love with them. Rollins was turning down something like eight TV offers a week. "It was amazing," Elaine said. "Our opening night was the worst performance I think we ever gave because our friends were there. And they were terribly nervous for us. And it only seemed to show how nervous we were."

"That's true."

"We were absolutely certain that we had failed totally."

The show ran for nearly a year, with 308 performances.

And then they just walked away.

Elaine read the next question: "Did you walk away from the partnership and your brand of satire because America was changing with the Kennedy White House, and it seemed less important to push back against a society that had loosened up a bit?

"Yes, that was it! That was it. Yes."

"No, we stopped because Elaine got sick of it. That's the truth. You didn't want to do it anymore."

"Don't you see, Mike, the opportunity this question gives us for a little depth?"

"Please let me give my answer. My answer is the truth for a change. I also think it's such a wonderful reason."

Elaine continued reading: "Or did you both just want to break out into wider spheres—acting, writing, directing?"

Mike jumped in. "Can I answer that? Well, there's two things: One is that Elaine, when I met her, was already a writer. You were forever writing and dropping your pages. I was this guy who did improvs, to my own surprise. I was going to start my life later. And we both had a plan—not to be in show business." As he told Gerald Nachman, "It was just a handy way to make some money until we grew up. Everyone thought we were in show business, but we knew we weren't—we were snobs. We kept thinking, How the fuck did we get *here*?"

Mike did go on to direct, and by 1965 he had three hit shows running concurrently on Broadway: *Luv, The Odd Couple*, and *Barefoot in the Park*. Elaine continued to write, creating a full-length play in 1961 for him to star in, *A Matter of Position*, which didn't get off the ground, closing at the Walnut Street Theatre, in Philadelphia, after seventeen performances. It must have been strange for Mike alone onstage, with Elaine in the audience, watching and assessing his performance. In any case, their working relationship ceased after that, until 1996, when Elaine adapted *The Birdcage*, from the French film *La Cage aux folles*, for Mike and, two years later, was nominated for an Oscar and Writers Guild Award for her screenplay adaptation of Joe Klein's *Primary Colors*, directed by Mike.

The Golden Theatre was near the Majestic Theatre, where Richard Burton was starring in *Camelot*. "That's how I got my first job in movies, because I got friendly with Richard," Mike recalled. Burton and his wife, Elizabeth Taylor, chose him to direct *Who's Afraid of Virginia Woolf?* "So it's just opportunism. I got close to a star and I made it pay off. That's my advice to the young people, if you possibly can."

Nichols's directing career has never stopped: *Who's Afraid of Virginia Woolf?* was nominated for thirteen Academy Awards, winning five. Burton, who starred in the movie with Taylor, wrote in his diaries, "The last man to give me direction which I found interesting . . . and sometimes enthrallingly brilliant was Mike Nichols and that was in the comedy sequences of *Woolf*."

Nichols followed that up with *The Graduate*, in 1967, the iconic, generation-defining film of the decade, for which he won the Oscar for Best Director. (He cast Anne Bancroft to play Mrs. Robinson because, in part, she was the same kind of dark, sardonic beauty as Elaine.) *Catch-22* followed, and since then he's worked with America's greatest actors in films such as *Silkwood, Working Girl, Carnal Knowledge, Heartburn, Closer, Charlie Wilson's War*, and, for television, *Wit* and *Angels in America*.

Throughout it all, he's continued to return to the theater: in 1988 he directed Steve Martin and Robin Williams in Samuel Beckett's *Waiting for Godot*, and most recently he did *Death of a Salesman*, with Philip Seymour Hoffman as Willy Loman. He has won seven Tony Awards for Best Director.

May continued to work on screenplays, most often as a script doctor. There was trouble with Paramount over her 1976 movie, *Mikey and Nicky*, starring John Cassavetes and Peter Falk, which she wrote and directed. (She secreted away a few reels of the film when the studio complained about how long it was taking her to edit the four-year-overdue final cut.) The industry began giving her the cold shoulder, until Warren Beatty, a friend and admirer, rescued her by giving her the chance to cowrite *Heaven Can Wait*, in 1978, earning her an Oscar nomination and a Writers Guild Award.

What few people know is that she was also the coauthor of *Reds*, *Tootsie*, *Labyrinth*, and *Dangerous Minds*—all uncredited.

Looking down at the sheet of questions, Elaine asked herself, "Don't you like credit?"

"What a brilliant fucking question," Mike shouted. "What is your answer?"

"Well, I didn't have any control."

"There you have it."

"Yes. You can make a deal if you're going to do the original writing. But if you're going to do the original rewriting, you can't. You're a hired gun. No matter how much you write, what you write, you're still a hired gun, and you have no control."

"That's a perfect answer."

"Well, it's sort of the truth. Not hilarious, but—"

"In a sense, the truth is the perfect answer."

"The only time I really ever took credit was when I worked with Mike."

"That's actually true."

"Because I knew him, and I thought probably he won't fuck it up."

"Or fuck you up. [As a rewriter] you have nothing at stake."

"It's like when the [studio] guard is bringing you coffee and glances at a sentence you wrote and laughs, then leaves. You change everything in the script but that one thing that the schmuck who brought coffee laughed at. It's sort of like that."

"But the best thing," said Mike, "after having total control, is having none. I think that's accurate about the movie business. You have more control as the schmuck that wanders in."

"But the other thing you have when you don't take the credit is great control because you can say your name isn't on this. I'm getting nothing out of this."

May did get credit for writing two original screenplays—*A New Leaf* and *Mikey and Nicky*—and the blame for *Ishtar*, the 1987 mega-bomb she wrote and directed. She directed the hilarious comedy *The Heartbreak Kid*—the first one, in 1972, costarring

Charles Grodin and Cybill Shepherd, in which Jeannie Berlin, her daughter, is funny and touching as the abandoned, sunburned bride with cold cream on her face.

Nichols has filed more than a few amicus briefs on behalf of *Ishtar*, which, although much critical ink has been spilled over it as a kind of cinematic bridge to nowhere, is in fact a charming, if not downright prescient Reagan-era *Road to Morocco*. ("If all of the people who hate *Ishtar* had seen it, I would be a rich woman today," Elaine said.)

In perhaps the most Pirandello-ish turn of their careers, in 1980 Nichols and May played George and Martha in a six-week run of Edward Albee's *Who's Afraid of Virginia Woolf?* at the Long Wharf Theatre, in New Haven. Frank Rich reviewed their reunion, noting that "this legendary pair [. . .] transform a Strindbergian duel of the sexes into a knockout battle of wits." Rich noticed that the two managed to find the play's biting humor. "We arrive expecting to watch two rusty stand-up comics do a novelty act," he wrote. "We leave having seen four thinking actors shed startling new light on one of the great dark plays of our time."

"Do you know my theory about *Virginia Woolf*, which I think I only developed lately?" said Mike. "It may be the only play—certainly the only play I can think of, including Shakespeare—in which every single thing that happens is in the present; even the beautiful reminiscences of the past are traps being set in the present, sprung in the present, having violent effect in the present. It's why you can't hurt it. It always, always works. It's now. It's the one thing plays have the hardest time with."

I still hadn't asked The Question, the one everyone wanted me to ask. (I was so shy about it, I'd even left it off The List.) Had they ever been romantically involved? People who knew them back in the days of the Compass believed that maybe, perhaps, for a few days, they had—but that they put it out of their lives fairly quickly.

In fact, Nichols and May have each been married repeatedly—to other people (Mike to Patricia Scott, Margot Callas, Annabel Davis-Goff, and Diane Sawyer; Elaine to Marvin May, lyricist Sheldon Harnick, her then psychiatrist, Dr. David L. Rubinfine, and her current partner, the great director Stanley Donen). "We both found the love of our lives," Mike said.

The two continue to have a long and deep friendship, and after fifty-eight years they can still make each other laugh. So I apologize, first to Mr. Apatow, who, like me, always wanted to know. Not only did I lose my nerve, but sitting there between them I thought they were entitled to keep a secret like that.

"We were fools to give it up," Mike said of their partnership.

"We were," Elaine answered.

Mike leaned in to tell her, "Very slowly life gets better and you learn that there is another way to respond to people. You've changed more than anybody I've known in my entire life. You changed from a dangerous person to someone who is only benign."

"What a vicious thing to say!"

"But it's true! If you can't say anything nice, you don't say anything. You never ever attack people to their face, or behind their back. You're the most discreet person about other people that I have ever met in my life. I haven't heard you be unkind for fifty years. You have done a complete 180-degree turn—don't you know that?"

"That's such a horrible thing of you to say."

"I'm really sorry—"

"I feel exactly the same way about you, too."

"Bitch!"

They suddenly broke into laughter, just as they had in the Golden Theatre fifty years ago. Certainly one of the happier moments of the twentieth century was the sound of Nichols and May laughing, and here they were, laughing again.

Note

1. *A New Leaf* (1971) is the only film Elaine May wrote, directed, and starred in. Her screenplay is based on a Jack Ritchie short story.—REK

A Lovingly Obsessive Tribute to Mike Nichols, by Elaine May

Richard Brody / 2016

From the *New Yorker*, web-only content, January 29, 2016. Reprinted by permission.

Among the greatest tragedies in modern cinema is the fact that Elaine May hasn't directed a feature film since *Ishtar*. Now she has something new on display: a documentary. She directed the *American Masters* tribute to Mike Nichols (who died in 2014), and that's appropriate: the two became famous together, in the late 1950s, as an improvisational comedy duo. So May herself is a part of Nichols's story, but, for the most part, she lets him tell it.

But first, before Nichols gets to open his mouth, May begins with a swift comic touch: the title card, "Mike Nichols: An American Master," set to the perky strains of *Eine kleine Nachtmusik,* dissolves to a clip of Adolf Hitler bellowing a speech. That's because Nichols was born in Berlin but, as a Jew persecuted under the Nazi regime, immigrated at the age of seven to New York. Nichols tells that story, as he tells the story of the rest of his life and work, in the form of a talking head against a murky black background, the work of a filmed interview from sometime in his later years, conducted by the producer Julian Schlossberg.

Most of the film's fifty-two minutes feature Nichols in this one filmed interview, which is punctuated only by a few snippets of interviews with others (including Meryl Streep, Renata Adler, Robin Williams, Tom Hanks, and the director Stanley Donen, who is May's partner) as well as a handful of archival stills, newspaper clippings, and film clips. But these punctuations feel unusually judicious and brisk; what's noteworthy about the film, besides Nichols's own reflections, is the fact that May leaves him on camera talking in close-up, without musical or graphic adornment, for surprisingly extended periods. The movie (which airs on PBS tonight at 9:00 p.m.) isn't a major contribution to May's filmography; her singular and original artistry doesn't take utterly free flight here, but the show is nonetheless distinctive in its sparseness, its fixed and almost obsessive concentration on Nichols's face and voice.

Beyond the substance of the film, its very form is May's highest tribute to Nichols: she can't stop looking at him and listening to him.

Nichols discusses his happenstance matriculation at the University of Chicago as the crucible of his work. It was there that he became fast friends with Susan Sontag and other young illuminati (including Ed Asner and Zohra Lampert), took a desultory interest in the theater, studied with Lee Strasberg, and then—with no sense or dream of a vocation—got involved with the Compass Players improv company. With the group, he developed unexpected skills that, in his partnership with Elaine May, took off, completely beyond his expectations. ("We were so surprised; what were they all carrying on about?" he says. "We were so, sort of, dazed by it.")

A clip of the pair's performance at the 1959 Emmy Awards suggests what everyone was carrying on about. But, Nichols says, their success was bewildering to him and May, and, perhaps even worse, "neither of us could understand this *thing*. [. . .] And then Elaine and I were on Broadway. A big fuss was made almost immediately. We were very successful [. . .] and we felt nothing, because it was what we had done for quite a while."

May plugs onto the screen an article headlined "Egghead Comics Score Hit." It was the late 1950s, May and Nichols were not yet thirty, and they were slightly ahead of the times. A decade and a half later, intellectualizing comedians, led on different fronts by the *Harvard Lampoon* and by Woody Allen, would press to the forefront of entertainment. The youth revolution, such as it was, was also the revolution of the college-educated. Yet Nichols and May would make their enduring mark on those later times separately. The lack of novelty, despite the perpetual surprise of improvisation, was what drove the act, and the friends, apart:

> It wasn't hard on me at all, and it was strangely hard on Elaine. [. . .] I kept thinking, What is she talking about, it's less than two hours out of every twenty-four. [. . .] Cute people want you, we're famous, we have money, we just do our own thing. [. . .] But Elaine wanted to do more. [. . .] We stopped because Elaine said, "I don't know if I want to keep on with this."

When the act broke up, in 1961, Nichols says, "Not only had I lost my best friend, I lost my work. I was the half of something." He appeared in a play in Vancouver; when he was invited to direct a play, he did so, for lack of anything else to do, and then was asked to direct another play, one by Neil Simon called *Nobody Loves Me*, soon renamed *Barefoot in the Park*, starring a young Robert Redford. As Nichols says, when he began directing, "I knew instantly what to do." At that point, he realized, "This is my job. [. . .] This is what I was preparing for."

Nichols may have been an "egghead," but he had, in his telling, a pretty tough shell. Called to Hollywood to direct *Who's Afraid of Virginia Woolf?*, his first film, he not only faced down the studio head Jack Warner with a nervy threat to resign but also treated him with a contemptuous standoffishness. It was May who broke up the act because she had other plans, but it was Nichols who realized his plans first. Quickly becoming the toast of Hollywood (*Virginia Woolf* was nominated for thirteen Oscars and won five), he then made *The Graduate* and followed with *Catch-22* before May made her directorial debut, with *A New Leaf*, in which she also costarred. (Hers was a brilliant but troubled start; her conflict with the studio over the film's reediting ended in court—and it was only the first of her great yet conflict-riddled productions.)

Nichols tells the story of how he shot himself in the foot the old-fashioned way— he made a couple of flops and went back to directing plays until reestablishing himself, in 1983, with *Silkwood*. By contrast, May, after her one great commercial success, with *The Heartbreak Kid*, made *Mikey and Nicky*, a film with a famously rocky and contentious path to completion, and one that's as great an artistic achievement as it was a commercial flop. She wrote scripts, she script-doctored, and then she got another chance at directing, thanks to Warren Beatty's loyal devotion; the result was the even greater, even more maligned *Ishtar*. Meanwhile, Nichols returned to the business with a new luster, directing movies until 2007. (May features a brief clip from his final film, *Charlie Wilson's War*, which bears a surprising resemblance to a scene from *Ishtar*.)

May caps the tribute with a clip of Nichols sharing his assessment of cinema history—an assessment that's laced with resentment at his unbeloved place in it, his ranking among the unoriginal entertainers of the time rather than alongside May as one of its prime cinematic artists. It's in this editorial touch—the placement, at the film's apex, as its climactic moment, of Nichols's lacerating allegations of critical misjudgments—that May tips her directorial hand. His culminating spew of bile wrenches the show out of the merely anecdotal, out of autohagiography, and into the twisted guts of an unquiet soul who went to the grave resentfully despite the worldly rewards ("we're famous, we have money") that he earlier thought would be enough.

As death approached, Nichols thought of that other kind of immortality—that of the work—and here he takes critics to the court of God and makes his case. Nichols complains that he saw *The Graduate* right after he completed the television production of *Angels in America* [2003], and found it "surrealistic," like the adaptation of Tony Kushner's play. He then complains about the label "generation gap," which had been affixed to the earlier film: "I'd never thought of generations. I was thinking about material things, material objects, somebody drowning in material objects, trying to free himself from death by material, through madness, which is what ultimately happens." Then he cuts loose, saying, "The people who describe all our work to us often don't know what they're talking about. They're wrong." May offers visual reinforcement, showing a poster for *Bonnie and Clyde* along with a phrase from Bosley Crowther's pan of it in the *Times*, then a poster for *2001: A Space Odyssey*, with a phrase from Pauline Kael's pan of it: "It's a monumentally unimaginative movie." (The film misattributes the line, though—it appeared not in the *New Yorker* but in an essay that she wrote for *Harper's*.)

May follows this with a mockup of an essay called "Auteurs and Their Influence on Hollywood," which matches the next phase of Nichols's cheerful rant. "They are people, literally, people who think that expressing an opinion is a creative act," he says. "The auteur stuff—I think there were these French guys with cigarette ashes all over them and that they basically misunderstood the whole thing." Matching a stereotype with a stereotype, Nichols mocks the French taste for Jerry Lewis (insulting Jerry Lewis en passant), and continues,

> Howard Hawks was a wonderful director, but he was not the greatest director Hollywood ever knew. The guys with the cigarette ashes on them ignored our greatest directors and humiliated George Stevens, Willie Wyler, Billy Wilder—Billy Wilder not so much, he became fashionable again. But the tragedy of Willie and Stevens and Fred Zinnemann, these were great men, but they just weren't part of the froggy conspiracy.

Renata Adler offers a reason why Nichols might have been denied "auteur" status: the fact that he did "so many different sorts of things worked against it, because it wasn't so clearly Mike's work." Stanley Donen, James L. Brooks, and Steven Spielberg come on board briefly to criticize the notion of the auteur, and then Nichols returns: "To say it's the work of one man is to completely misunderstand a quite mysterious process, and the only answer to it is, it's different with different pictures." He proceeds to assert the crucial importance of scripts and screenwriters.

It may not be the work of one man, but May's films, at least, are certainly the work of one woman (all the more so in that she's among the best screenwriters as well as directors of her time). And, of course, the rebuke to critics, though coming from Nichols's mouth, is all the more pertinent under May's editorial touch, given that her career, not his, was buried by critical incomprehension, indifference, and derision.

May rounds off the film with a few seconds of her own public tribute to Nichols, from her speech at the 2010 AFI Life Achievement Award ceremony in his honor, which is a comic masterwork in itself. The film concludes with her voiceover, in which she calls Nichols's work "oddly underrated" and pulls out four of his films as his best—*The Graduate, Carnal Knowledge, Silkwood,* and *Working Girl*. These films show that "every three years, American culture undergoes a complete change," she says, yet "they're not about it, they're about us." In a splendidly gracious and loving way, she distinguishes Nichols's great talent, his enduring artistry, with what comes off as royally—and, I believe, unintentionally—faint praise. That, too, is the mark of an artist—as Robert Bresson said, the artist is someone who is unable to do things as others do them. Nichols succeeded—all too well—and May, to this day, stands out because she doesn't fit in.

Additional Interviews and Profiles

Braun, Michael. "Mike and Elaine: Veracity-Cum-Boffs." *Esquire*, October 1960.

Champlin, Charles. "And Not a Sign of Mike Fright." *Los Angeles Times*, July 28, 1965.

Jennings, C. Robert. "Mike Nichols: Playboy Interview." *Playboy*, June 1966.

Johnson, Kevin M. (i.e. Elaine May, under the pseudonym Kevin M. Johnson). "Elaine May: 'Do You Mind Interviewing Me in the Kitchen?'" *New York Times*, January 8, 1967, https://timesmachine.nytimes.com/timesmachine/1967/01/08/83571386.html?pageNumber=103.

Jennings, C. Robert. "That's the Catch to *Catch-22*." *Los Angeles Times*, May 18, 1969.

Thompson, Howard. "Elaine May Spends Her Summer Knee-Deep in Film." *New York Times*, August 26, 1969.

Gemlis, Joseph. "Mike Nichols." In *The Film Director as Superstar*, 265–92. Garden City, NY: Doubleday, 1970.

Gussow, Mel. "Mike Nichols for the Fun of It." *New York Times*, November 26, 1976.

Schwartz, David. "A Pinewood Dialogue with Mike Nichols." Transcript of an event at the Museum of the Moving Image, March 19, 1990, http://www.movingimagesource.us/files/dialogues/2/18025_programs_transcript_pdf_203.pdf.

Weinraub, Bernard. "Mike Nichols Plans a Career Finale." *New York Times*, March 15, 1993.

May, Elaine. "Still in Fine Feather" (May interviews Nichols). *Los Angeles Times*, March 3, 1996, https://www.latimes.com/archives/la-xpm-1996-03-03-ca-42630-story.html.

May, Elaine. "An Interview with Walter Matthau." *New Yorker*, November 25, 1996.

Nichols, Mike. "Foreword: Talking with Mike Nichols," in May, Elaine. *The Birdcage: The Shooting Script*, New York: New Market Press, 1997, vii–xvii.

Rose, Charlie. "Mike Nichols." *Charlie Rose*, April 28, 1998; April 26, 2005; October 19, 2011.

Lahr, John. "Mike Nichols: Making It Real." *New Yorker*, February 21, 2000.

Gross, Terry. "Director Mike Nichols." *Fresh Air*, March 21, 2001. Excerpted: "*Fresh Air* Remembers Film and Broadway Director Mike Nichols." *Fresh Air*, November 21, 2014.

Marks, Peter. "Mike Nichols, Honors *Graduate*." *Washington Post*, December 7, 2003.

McGuigan, Cathleen. "War, Peace & Mike Nichols." *Newsweek*, December 17, 2007.

Kashner, Sam. "Here's to You, Mr. Nichols: The Making of *The Graduate*." *Vanity Fair*, February 25, 2008.

Green, Jesse. "The Evolution of Mike Nichols and His Revival of *Death of a Salesman*." *New York*, March 4, 2012.

D'Alessandro, Anthony. "Elaine May Brings Down the House at Writers Guild Awards West." *Deadline.com*, February 13, 2016, https://deadline.com/2016/02/elaine-may-woody-allen-wga-awards-laurel-award-1201702416/.

Brody, Richard. "Elaine May Talks About *Ishtar*," *New Yorker*, web-only content, April 1, 2016, https://www
.newyorker.com/culture/richard-brody-elaine-may-talks-about-ishtar.

Carter, Ash, and Sam Kashner. *Life Isn't Everything: Mike Nichols as Remembered by 150 of His Closest Friends.*
New York: Henry Holt, 2019.

Video and Audio Interviews

"Mike Nichols and Elaine May Discuss Their Acting Careers" (Nichols and May interviewed by Studs Terkel,
radio station WFMT, Chicago, May 29, 1958). Digitized: Studs Terkel Radio Archive. https://studsterkel
.wfmt.com/programs/mike-nichols-and-elaine-may-discuss-their-acting-careers.

Mike Nichols & Jason Reitman Talk "Carnal Knowledge" in 2011. Film at Lincoln Center YouTube channel, 2014.
https://youtu.be/ETRo-IcfsgQ.

Times Talks: A Conversation with Mike Nichols (Nichols interviewed by Douglas McGrath, May 7, 2012).
TimesTalks YouTube channel, 2016. https://youtu.be/IrDXX32A2gY.

Becoming Mike Nichols: A Portrait of an Artist (Nichols interviewed by Jack O'Brien, 2014; directed by
Douglas McGrath). HBO, 2016.

"Mike Nichols" (*American Masters* series) (includes interview with Nichols by Julian Schlossberg, undated;
directed by Elaine May). PBS, 2016.

Audio Commentary Tracks

Nichols, Mike, and Steven Soderbergh. "Audio commentary." *Catch-22*, DVD. Directed by Mike Nichols.
Hollywood, CA: Paramount Home Entertainment, 2001.

Nichols, Mike, and Steven Soderbergh. "Audio commentary." *Who's Afraid of Virginia Woolf?*, DVD, Blu-ray
disc. Directed by Mike Nichols. DVD: Burbank, CA: Warner Home Video, 2006. Blu-ray disc: Burbank, CA:
Warner Archive Collection, 2016.

Nichols, Mike, and Steven Soderbergh. "Audio commentary." *The Graduate*, DVD, Blu-ray disc. Directed by
Mike Nichols. Fortieth anniversary DVD: Beverly Hills, CA: MGM DVD, distributed by Twentieth Century
Fox Home Entertainment, 2007. Special ed. Blu-ray disc: [Irvington, NY]: Criterion Collection, 2016.

Index

About the Editor

Robert E. Kapsis is professor emeritus of sociology and film studies at Queens College and the Graduate Center of the City University of New York. He is author of *Hitchcock: The Making of a Reputation*, published by the University of Chicago Press; editor of *Woody Allen: Interviews, Revised and Updated*; *Jonathan Demme: Interviews*; *Charles Burnett: Interviews*; and *Conversations with Steve Martin*; and coeditor of *Clint Eastwood: Interviews, Revised and Updated*, published by University Press of Mississippi.

Printed in the United States
By Bookmasters